The Church
in the Power of the Spirit

Jürgen Moltmann

The Church
in the Power of
the Spirit

A Contribution to Messianic Ecclesiology

SCM PRESS LTD

Translated by Margaret Kohl
from the German
Kirche in der Kraft des Geistes
Chr. Kaiser Verlag, Munich, 1975

334 01941 9
First published in English 1977
by SCM Press Ltd
58 Bloomsbury Street, London
Translation © SCM Press Ltd 1977
Printed in Great Britain by
Western Printing Services Ltd
Bristol

To the World Council of Churches,
its General Secretary,
the Reverend Philip Potter,
and oppressed Christians throughout the world

CONTENTS

PREFACE

This book is intended to help the church to find its bearings. The swift change of external circumstances, the revolutionary progress in science and technology, and a simultaneously growing threat through social, military and ecological conflicts have disseminated a feeling of general insecurity among many people in our society. It is not for nothing that today everyone feels uncertain and insecure. The word 'crisis' is on every lip, whether it be the oil crisis or the crisis of the spirit. Instability, both inward and outward, is growing. Our political, economic, ethical and religious systems are more vulnerable than many people thought. Consequently the longing for security in all spheres of life is growing as well. The churches are no exception to this general feeling of uncertainty. Church members are asking critical questions about the sense of church services, and sceptical ones about the sense of liturgical reforms. Clergy, church leaders and church assemblies are all discussing the crises they see, and their own crises as well. The call for greater security and for religious stability can be heard here too.

Every crisis means finding new bearings. The fundamental questions have to be answered afresh: Where do you come from? Where are you going? Who are you? For every crisis calls the traditional and familiar answers in question. But because of this every crisis also brings with it its own unique opportunities of supplying a new, personal answer which will stand up to life – an answer a man can live and die with. Anyone who only talks about a 'crisis' without recognizing this implicit opportunity is talking because he is afraid and without hope. Anyone who only wants to have new opportunities without accepting the crisis of previous answers is living in an illusion. The church would have no hope if it were merely to share the general insecurity, or even to deepen it into an ominous expectation of the end of the world. The church would have no tradition were it merely to hasten after new opportunities. In the crisis of its tradition and in the opportunities afforded by its hope, the church will take its bearings from its foundation, its future and the charge given to it.

When its traditions are imperilled by insecurity, the church is thrown back to its roots. It will take its bearings even more emphatically than before from Jesus, his history, his presence and his future. As 'the church of Jesus Christ' it is fundamentally dependent on him, and on him alone. What the church is and wherein it exists is and exists from him, whatever securities or insecurities present themselves from time to time. We shall continually be discussing the relationship between *Christ and the church* (and shall be considering this in detail in chapter III). This orientation is in the forefront for the church which calls itself by his name.

When the future prospects of the church are dark, when its relationship to Israel, to the religions of the world, and to the political, economic and cultural policies of society are in dispute, then it will no less radically project itself towards the future it is certain of, because it is the future of Christ, who has called the church to life: the kingdom of God. In chapter IV, therefore, we shall be going into the relationship between *the church and the kingdom of God* in detail. Because hope means the power of life, and life is lived in open relationships, the kingdom of God ought not to be described in abstract terms. It must be seen concretely, in all the living relationships in which Christianity is involved. The future of the church is only described through the medium of a church of hope for other people and with other people.

Because of its foundation in Christ and its existence for the future of the kingdom of God, the church is what it truly is and what it can do, in the *presence and power of the Holy Spirit*. The Spirit renews the church in fellowship with Christ. The Spirit fills the church with the powers of the new creation, its liberty and its peace. In chapters V and VI, therefore, we shall give an account of the church's powers, potentialities and forms of life in the movement of God, of the Spirit which descends on all flesh.

This book was preceded by some lectures on ecclesiology given in Bonn in 1966 and in Tübingen in 1968 and 1972. Since 1968 several impressions of an unauthorized transcript of these lectures have been in circulation. Some of my listeners found this doctrine of the church too conservative; for others it was too progressive. In revising and completing these lectures for publication I hope to make it plain to both groups that it is possible to deal conservatively with the progressive elements in the Christian tradition, and that it is necessary to deal progressively with its conservative forms, if one wants to do justice to the dynamics of the Christian message. I have tried to discover the primal springs of the earliest perceptions of the Christian faith and the early forms of the Christian fellowship, in order to grasp the things in them that point us towards the future.

The contents of this book do not derive from the study, or from the lecture rooms of Tübingen University. Readers will rightly ask: What church is he actually talking about? Apart from the fact that for five years I was pastor in the country parish of Wasserhorst, near Bremen, lecture tours and ecumenical conferences during the past ten years have taken me to churches in other countries and other situations. The experiences of Christians in Korea, their missionary zeal and their suffering in political resistance; the charismatic experiences of the independent churches in Kenya and Ghana, their prayers and their exuberant dances; the work of Christian communes in the slums of Manila and the villages of the campesinos in Latin America, their life among their people and their persecution by the police – all these things impressed me more vividly than I probably realized myself. They have at least shown me the limitations of the church in Germany. I will not pretend to my readers abroad that I am not writing in the Federal German Republic, and on the basis of life in the established Protestant church to which I belong. But this point of departure does not, for all that, determine the book's content. One's own situation is only one of many. And some of Christianity's situations are truly very different. To carry on theology in an ecumenical context does not mean being abstract; it means starting, as far as possible, from the church's differing experiences and conveying them in a fruitful way. In the following theological discussions, therefore, I have tried to keep in mind both the established and the free churches, the national and the missionary churches, the local churches and the ecumenical movement, ecclesiastical institutions and the free Christian communities. My aim in doing this was not simply to add up all the different forms of Christian fellowship; my concern was the faith and authenticity of the one church of Christ.

Theological insight and the practical experiences I have mentioned would suggest that the book's practical intention might be formulated as follows: to point away from the pastoral church, that looks after the people, to the people's own communal church among the people. I do not believe that there is any other way in which the church can proclaim the gospel responsibly, theologically speaking, or can celebrate the Lord's supper, baptize with the sign of the new beginning, and live in the friendship of Jesus. There is no other way for the church to exercise its office, its charge and its ministry, in the congregation, with the congregation and through the congregation. Missionary churches, confessing churches and 'churches under the cross' are fellowship churches, or inescapably become so. They do not stray into social isolation but become a living hope in the midst of the people. The crisis of the national and established churches in 'Christian' countries of long standing which has so often been described – the churches' loss of function, the apathy of their members and their slowness to move – is a chance to build up the fellowship church and to realize the principle of the congregation, the community. The dangers of social adaptation and of the social ghetto are avoided when the church acquires and asserts its liberty of action. For this liberty it needs a fellowship which is more binding than other things. The experiences of the churches in other countries have confirmed me in my theological conviction that this is the church's proper form.

Finally, I must say a word about the relationship between this book about 'the church in the power of the Spirit' and my earlier books *Theology of Hope* (1964; ET 1965) and *The Crucified God* (1972; ET 1974). It looks as if I have now arrived theologically at Pentecost and the sending of the Spirit, having started from Easter and the foundation of the Christian hope and travelled by way of Good Friday and the exploration of God's suffering. But this would probably be to think too closely in terms of the pattern of the church's year. The lectures which form the basis for these three books were not given in that order. Consequently the books dovetail into one another and their subject-matter overlaps. It is true, however, that I was impelled theologically from the one book to the other and had to shift my perspectives, the better to understand the wealth of God's liberating dealings with the world. That is why I shifted the emphasis from 'the resurrection of the crucified Jesus' in *Theology of Hope* to 'the cross of the risen Christ' in

The Crucified God. Both perspectives would be incomplete if 'the sending of the Spirit', its messianic history and the charismatic power of its church were not added. To that extent this book about 'the church in the power of the Spirit' is intended to complement the earlier books.

I should like to express my thanks to Dr Michael Welker and Dr Konrad Stock for continual theological discussion about the book's subject-matter, for the criticism with which they accompanied me while I was writing, and for their reading of the proofs.

Tübingen
Pentecost 1975

JÜRGEN MOLTMANN

I

THE DIMENSIONS OF A DOCTRINE
OF THE CHURCH TODAY

At every period the church has a duty to be clear about its commission, its situation and its goal. But what is to determine its guiding lines? The theological doctrine of the church takes the church at its word.

The church is the people of God and will give an account of itself at all times to the God who has called it into being, liberated it and gathered it. It is therefore before the divine forum that it will reflect upon its life and the forms that life takes, what it says and what it does not say, what it does and what it neglects to do.

But the church is at the same time under obligation to men (Rom.1.14). Consequently it will at all times render an account to men about the commission implicit in its faith and the way it is fulfilling that commission. It will reflect on its life and the expression of its life in the forum of the world.

In the community of the incarnate God and the exalted man Jesus Christ there can be no division here. The church will always have to present itself both in the forum of God and in the forum of the world. For it stands for God to the world, and it stands for the world before God. It confronts the world in critical liberty and is bound to give it the authentic revelation of the new life. At the same time it stands before God in fellowship and solidarity with all men and is bound to send up to him out of the depths the common cry for life and liberty.

The church is on the move in free solidarity and critical fellowship, together with the world, people and peoples, nations and societies. It is called the wayfaring people of God. Because of that it will present itself and its relationship to the people and the peoples, to Israel and to the nations, in the forum of the future of

God and the world. It will comprehend the meaning of its commission in the light of its hope and it will interpret the sufferings of the time in the light of the coming kingdom. It will comprehend the meaning of its divine commission in world history and at the same time will understand the world in the context of God's history.

The theological doctrine of the church will observe these three dimensions – before God, before men and before the future – when it depicts the living nature of the church. For the church of Christ is an 'open' church. It is open for God, open for men and open for the future of both God and men. The church atrophies when it surrenders any one of these opennesses and closes itself up against God, men or the future.

In peaceful times the church could affirm itself by demonstrating the unbroken and unaltered continuance of its tradition and traditions. People appealed to these things, trusting in the permanent element in time's changes, and in what is repeatable in the accidents of history. In times of unrest this is no longer convincing. For the swift revolution in social conditions always spreads to the whole visible form of the church as well. Today we are living in a time of transition whose future we can as yet hardly perceive. Many people are painfully conscious that what was valid once no longer holds good. But what is going to be and what is capable of enduring we do not know. This causes an unrest which also affects Christianity and the church all over the world. Today tensions and conflicts between conservatives and the people who imagine they are conservative, progressives and the people who think they are conservative, and progressives and the people who suppose they are progressive, set their stamp on the sufferings of the church – and for many people, suffering over the church. At a time like this the church is challenged to think radically about its origins, to lay hold decisively on its charge, and to return to Christ's future from its now flawed and dying form. In a situation like this the theological doctrine of the church cannot simply be expressed in abstract terms about the church's timeless nature. It will have to provide points of departure for reforming the church, for giving it a more authentic form.

It is true that there are churches which particularly stress the permanent and repeatable elements in their traditions at times when everything is in a state of flux. Not every church is a 'Reformation' church in the sense that it expresses its vitality through continual reforms. But when 'traditional' and 'Reformation' churches think together about the one authentic Christian tradition, then they can discover the element of movement in what is permanent, and what continues to have essential validity in the reforms. The tradition to which the church appeals, and which it proclaims whenever it calls itself Christ's church and speaks in Christ's name, is the tradition of the messianic liberation and eschatological renewal of the world. It is impossible to rest on this tradition. It is a tradition that changes men and from which they are born again. It is like the following wind that drives us to new shores. Anyone who enters into this messianic tradition accepts the adventure of the Spirit, the experience of liberation, the call to repentance, and common work for the coming kingdom. Tradition and reformation, what abides and what changes, faithfulness and the fresh start are not antitheses in the history of the Spirit. For the Spirit leads to the fellowship of Christ and consummates the messianic kingdom.

From this it becomes finally clear that it can by no means be merely the unrest of our time which causes the unrest of the church. Nor can it merely be the present revolutionary situation which makes it essential for the church and its teaching to find new bearings. Of course the church must take changes in society into account in its language, its services and the forms of its life and organization. It has to accept these changed times. How else could it fulfil its charge before God, men and the future? But basically its 'unrest' is implicit in itself, in the crucified Christ to whom it appeals and in the Spirit which is its driving power. The unrest of the times points it to this inner unrest of its own. The social and cultural upheavals of the present draw its attention to that great upheaval which it itself describes as 'new creation', as the 'new people of God', when it testifies to the world concerning the future of 'the new heaven and the new earth'. What is required today is not adroit adaptation to changed social conditions, but the inner renewal of the church by the spirit of Christ, the power of the coming kingdom. The theological doctrine of the church will consequently allow itself to be guided by the inner unrest which is agitating the church. This inner unrest must be discernible when we talk theologically about 'the church of Jesus Christ', 'the church of the kingdom of God', and 'the church in the presence and power of the Holy Spirit'.

1. *The Church of Jesus Christ*

It used to be accepted without dispute that the doctrine of the church was bound to be a theological one, which in dogmatics had to be treated after christology and before eschatology. This is no longer a matter of course, for the paths leading to a theory of the church and its practice differ widely.

We can start from experience and describe the church phenomenologically. Then we obtain a picture of the church in the framework of the culture in which it lives. We can investigate the church sociologically, thus acquiring a picture of its organization in the framework of a given social system. We can depict the church historically, and gain insight into its historical movements and the way it has changed. We can examine it in the light of the history of religions, comparing it with other religions.

A theory of the church, in whatever way it is acquired, can also be determined by different spheres of interest. It can be drawn up in aid of the church's self-understanding; or to ward off heresy; or in order to compare one church with another; or as a defence against attacks from outside; or as a criticism of the church's present condition. Finally, a theory of the church can be claimed by different 'subjects'. Whose picture of the church does it represent and who is to profit by it? Is it the picture of pastor, priest and theologian? Or is it the notion held by laymen, whether outsiders or insiders? Is it a theory about church action drawn up for the church's leaders, or a theory about the needs of the people who are at the receiving end of that action? It is understandable that different 'subjects' inside or outside the church should have different pictures of the church, which can be conceptually depicted in different theories *about* the church. It is also understandable that the different theories about the church should reflect different pictures of the church and different interests within it. Every theory of the church must therefore raise the question, and allow it to be raised: whom is it intended to benefit, and for whom and in whose interest is it designed?

Whatever the church is or ought to be in other respects, the theological concept of the church must take the church and its own claim seriously, testing it against the one to whom it appeals. The theological doctrine of the church talks about the church of Christ. It therefore seeks to discern the subject of the church as clearly as possible and to give effect to it in the church's life and form. If the church does everything in the name of the triune God, then theological doctrine will see the church in the trinitarian history of God's dealings with the world. In this way it does not only serve the theological justification of the church's actions; it also serves the theological criticism of those actions.

But Christ is his church's foundation, its power and its hope. As the Reformed confessional writings show, that is the reason why the Reformation subjected all human rules and statutes in religion and the church to the yardstick of the gospel of Christ. The Confessing Church, therefore (as Thesis 1 of the Barmen Theological Declaration of 1934 makes clear), condemned all state claims to dominance over the church that are designed to reduce the church to dependence.[1] It is only where Christ alone rules, and the church listens to his voice only, that the church arrives at its truth and becomes free and a liberating power in the world. The theological concept of the church belongs to this specific tradition of the church's liberation through the lordship of Christ, and it knows that it is committed to that tradition. It does not talk about the church in the ideal sense; so it cannot be interpreted as one dimension of the church among others (the religious one perhaps). Acknowledgment of the sole lordship of Christ in his church makes it impossible to recognize any other 'sources of the proclamation apart from or in addition to this sole Word of God'. It cannot admit that there are any 'sectors of our lives in which we belong, not to Jesus Christ, but to other masters.' It must condemn the doctrine 'that it could be permissible for the church to leave the form of her message and her order to her own convenience or the fluctuation of the philosophical and political convictions in force at any given time'.[2] What the Confessing Church declared with these words, in opposing the state's claim to lordship, must also be said today in opposing the claim to domination asserted by unjust and inhuman social systems; and it must be said through the theological conception of the church. The theological conception of Christ's church is therefore always at the same time a political and social concept of the church. The lordship of Christ is the church's sole, and hence all-embracing, determining factor. It can neither be shared nor restricted. That is why Christianity's obedience to this liberating lordship is all-embracing and undivided. It too cannot be limited, either by the church or by the state. A consistent theological doctrine of the church is by its very nature an eminently political and social doctrine of the church as well. It will link up the theological interpretation of the church (*doctrina de ecclesia*) with the church's politics (*politia ecclesiastica*), so that the conflicts become evident and the need to alter the church's politics in the light of the lordship of Christ can no longer be ignored.

If, for the church of Christ, Christ is the 'subject' of the church, then in the doctrine of the church christology will become the dominant theme of ecclesiology. Every statement about the church will be a statement about Christ. Every statement about Christ also implies a statement about the church; yet the statement about Christ is not exhausted by the statement about the church because it also goes further, being directed towards the messianic kingdom which the church serves. The theological doctrine of the church can therefore by no means represent the theologians' view of the church, although it often enough gives the impression of doing just that, because of its language, mode of expression and interest. Like every theory about the church, the theological doctrine is claimed by different subjects and different interests, whether they be conscious or unconscious. But it is the task of theology to give effect to 'Christ's interest' in his church, while remaining self-critical and also critical towards other interests. It is in the interest of everyone who calls on the name of Christ to subordinate his own particular interests to 'Christ's interest' and hence, as Paul says, to 'live no longer for themselves but for him who for their sake died and was raised' (II Cor. 5.15); and consequently the theological concept of the church serves Christianity as a whole and not only the theologians in the church. In this respect every Christian is a theologian. The theological interpretation of the church does not divide; it is a bond that holds everything together in the all-embracing interest of Christ which is common to all. The experience that 'doctrine divides but service unites' is not a contradiction, for 'Christ's interest' applies to both doctrine and service. It knows nothing of a division between theory and practice. In the traditions we have mentioned where the church has been freed through the word and spirit of Christ – in the Reformation, the Confessing Church and the persecuted 'churches under the cross' today – the unity between theology and the congregation, doctrine and practical resistance, clergy and laymen was and is impressively experienced. The theological concept of the church under the lordship of Christ grows out of experiences like this and aims at practice that is in accordance with them. Theology is one function of Christ's church. Or, to be more precise, it is one function of Christ with regard to his church. Since the church emerged from Europe's 'Christian society' in the nineteenth century, this first statement has been endorsed by many theologians: 'theology is a function of the church'.[3] This statement rightly brings theology into the church's fellowship and commission; but the second statement must be stressed equally, if we are to express the freedom of theology towards the church in its existing form. When theology reflects the historical form of the church in the framework of Christ's 'interests' and lordship, then it is interpreting itself first of all as a function of Christ's lordship, and only secondarily as a function of his church. If this were not so, theologians could easily become 'functionaries' of the church in the form in which it exists at any given time. Theology is a 'Christian' and a 'spiritual' affair, and it is only as such that it is one of the church's tasks. Fundamentally there is no distinction here, but differences emerge often enough empirically. Just because theology is one function of the church of *Christ*, it belongs critically – like faith – in the fellowship of the *church* as it actually exists. If theology were to lose its freedom to criticize, it would turn into the ideology of the church in its existing form. If it were to lose the fellowship of the church, it would stop being Christian theology and turn into a kind of science of religion. As Christian theology, theology has to remind the church of the lordship of Christ and has to insist that the church's form be an authentic one. As the Christian church, the church must remind theology of God's people and insist on a theology which has relevance for that people.

2. *The Missionary Church*

Today one of the strongest impulses towards the renewal of the theological concept of the church comes from the theology of mission.

Conditions are being reversed and relationships are taking on a reciprocal character. It is no longer only the 'younger churches' in the non-Christian countries which are learning from the older churches in the Christian ones. The more the protective circle

shielding Christianity in the Christian countries is secularized, and
the more it disintegrates, the more the churches in these countries
too are forced to remember the missionary initiative and their own
particular missionary charge. They cannot continue to see themselves as the agents of European or American Christianity. They
have to discover their missionary calling in their own country,
using it to make the special form of the church in their own civilizations apparent. That is basically speaking the challenge of the
modern 'separation between church and state' in the political
constitutions of contemporary Europe. If there is no longer a
'state church', then the church has to mould its history by itself.
If the 'national' or 'established' church no longer exists as a living
reality, then 'the people of God' must present itself to the people in
a form of its own. The more the Christian West disintegrates
culturally and geographically, the more the church will find its
self-understanding in the context of the whole world. It cannot
merely conceive itself in the framework of European history any
longer. World history is now the frame in which it has to present
itself and its charge; and this presentation can only be a missionary
one.

Up to now missions have largely been Western missions –
one thinks of people in Europe sending out missionaries to Africa
and Asia. But the Mexico City Conference in 1963 talked about
'mission in six continents', so as no longer to exclude Europe, the
home of the traditional missionary bodies. The Bangkok Conference
in 1973 announced the end of the unilateral 'Western mission' and
the beginning of multilateral 'world mission'. Yet up to now the
European churches have found it hard to discover Europe as a
missionary field or to see themselves as missionary churches. The
historical recollection of the way the Protestant missionary movements began can help to break down these inhibitions.

The Protestant church in Europe started out on its missionary
task at precisely the moment when the *corpus christianum* and the
established church confined to a single denomination were
decaying. When in the seventeenth century Cardinal Bellarmine
reproached the Protestant churches with not being true churches
at all because they were not missionary churches, well-known
theologians of orthodox early Protestantism were still able to
reply: 'Long ago we were indeed told: "Go ye into all the world";
but now: "Remain in the place where God hath placed thee." '[4]

The early Protestant interpretation of the gospel took its bearings from the event of the justification of the sinner, but not, as Paul did, from the event of the calling of Jews and Gentiles. Consequently it rejected any missionary duty.

> Since there was at that time no proclamation of the Word outside the church, the call is no doubt seen as something that has already happened, something accomplished by the apostles, from which we still profit today; it is no longer a divine action in the present which we experience too.[5]

Since, according to this view, call and mission are something that have happened once and for all, then the church today calls no longer; it instructs and teaches Christians and baptizes the children of Christians. In this way it remains within the confines of 'Christian society', which continually reproduces itself through infant baptism.

It was not until the era of the Enlightenment and the beginning of world-wide trade that pietism and the missionary movement burst the narrow bounds of this Protestant understanding of the church. Pietism discovered 'the heart' and infiltrated into the different established churches as well as the class divisions of society. Personal faith made denominations and classes relative. The missionary movements which came into being at the same time discovered 'the world' as the horizon of the Christian charge, breaking through the frontiers of the Christian countries.

> The new development was that, as the dream of the Christian West faded, the world was accepted as the horizon. The new development was that Christianity was regrouped for its service in this world and that a beginning was made with what we so glibly call today 'the missionary structure of the congregation'.[6]

The *new* development was that the layman seized the chance of his call to apostleship as the modern world freed itself from clerical domination and came of age. On the threshold of modern times we find that Christianity's new answer to the altered situation in the world was: (i) a missionary church; (ii) the will to ecumenical fellowship between the divided churches; (iii) the discovery of the universality of the kingdom of God; and (iv) the lay apostleship. As the *corpus christianum* was secularized through these answers, the church became 'secular', that is, world-open and world-wide. As culture was stripped of clericalism, free communities of mature

Christians came into being, together with the lay apostleship. As faith was transferred to the private sphere and the modes of belief in society multiplied, ecumenical movements arose. It is important to see the start of missionary activity in this historical context. It is not merely a Christian answer to the discovery of unknown continents; it is also an answer to the changed situation in Europe itself. Consequently it has significance not merely for the spread of the Christian faith in Africa and Asia; it is also of eminent significance for the reshaping of the churches in Europe.

The theological interpretation of the church today must absorb these germs of a missionary church in the decay of the *corpus christianum*. What we have to learn from them is not that the church 'has' a mission, but the very reverse: that the mission of Christ creates its own church. Mission does not come from the church; it is from mission and in the light of mission that the church has to be understood. The preaching of the gospel does not merely serve to instruct Christians and strengthen their faith; it always serves to call non-Christians at the same time. The whole congregation has 'spiritual' and charismatic gifts, not merely its 'spiritual' pastors. The whole congregation and every individual in it belong with all their powers and potentialities to the mission of God's kingdom. In the *corpus christianum* the different tasks of the community were distributed between state, society, family and church. The church could confine itself to its specifically religious mandate. As the *corpus christianum* decays, the congregation will again recollect the wealth of its own charismata and thrust forward to the total testimony of salvation which leaves no sphere of life without hope, from faith to politics, and from politics to economics.

To grasp the missionary church theologically in a world-wide context means understanding it in the context of the *missio dei*. *Mission* comprehends the whole of the church, not only parts of it, let alone the members it has sent out. To proclaim the gospel of the dawning kingdom is the first and most important element in the mission of Jesus, the mission of the Spirit, and the mission of the church; but it is not the only one. Mission embraces all activities that serve to liberate man from his slavery in the presence of the coming God, slavery which extends from economic necessity to Godforsakenness. Evangelization is mission, but mission is not merely evangelization. In the missionary church the widow who does charitable works belongs to the same mission as the bishop who leads the church, or the preacher of the gospel. The church's endowment with the spirit of liberty and the powers of liberation knows distinctions, but not divisions. The all-embracing messianic mission of the whole church corresponds to Christ's messianic mission and to the charismatic sending of the Spirit 'which shall be poured out on all flesh'. If the church sees itself to be sent in the same framework as the Father's sending of the Son and the Holy Spirit, then it also sees itself in the framework of God's history with the world and discovers its place and function within this history. Modern Catholic and Protestant missionary theology is therefore right when it talks about the *missio dei*, a movement from God in which the church has its origin and arrives at its own movement, but which goes beyond the church, finding its goal in the consummation of all creation in God.[7] It follows from this that the church understands its world-wide mission in the trinitarian history of God's dealings with the world. With all its activities and suffering, it is an element in the history of the kingdom of God. The real point is not to spread the church but to spread the kingdom. The goal is not the glorification of the church but the glorification of the Father through the Son in the Holy Spirit. The missionary concept of the church leads to a church that is open to the world in the divine mission, because it leads to a trinitarian interpretation of the church in the history of God's dealings with the world.

3. *The Ecumenical Church*

The ecumenical movement has created new realities just as much as the missionary movement, and the theological concept of the church today has to absorb these. In the ecumenical context Christianity loses its provincial character. The parochial barriers begin to crumble whenever a church recognizes itself in the other churches in the world and sees itself as being a member of the one church of Christ. The ecumenical rapprochement of the divided churches began in the eighteenth and nineteenth centuries, but it needed the bitter experiences of two European world wars before the churches' eyes were opened to their imprisonment in national states, separate cultures and social ideologies. Closely bound up as they were with 'king and country', they could not even escape from the wartime propaganda of their own particular nations. 'The triune God had turned into an Olympus of tribal gods engaged in feuds with one another.'[8] The ecumenical movement seeks the visible unity of Christ's church. It serves to liberate the churches from their ties with the middle-class and political religions of their societies; and in this way it also serves to give the churches renewed life as Christ's church. There will be no unification of the divided churches without an inner renewal, and there will be no renewal without liberation. The inner reason for the ecumenical movement is to be found in Christ's plea 'that they may all be one' (John 17.21). The external reason is to be found in the catastrophic world situation, in which Christianity can only document the peace of God to the world through ecumenical fellowship within itself.[9]

Once the churches have entered the ecumenical movement, the doctrine of the church can no longer be the slave of the self-understanding of our own particular denomination, and its difference from all the others. Traditional controversial theology, with its 'doctrinal distinctions', will then give way to a theology of co-operation founded on common ground. This does not lead to the mixing up of the different churches or to theological indifference. But the question of the 'true church' moves into the foreground. Just as we seek for the true church in the shape of our own denomination, so we will seek it in the forms of other churches as well; for the true church is one and indivisible.

The way to the ecumenical concept of the church began with the attempt known as *comparative ecclesiology*.[10] The denominations learnt to know one another in the hope 'that a better understanding of diverging views about faith and church order would lead to a deepening of the desire for reunification and to corresponding official resolutions on the part of the denominations themselves'. The first result was a kind of 'negative consensus'. People discovered that the traditional doctrinal distinctions should not really be seen as dividing the churches from one another, for none of them had to be formulated exclusively; all of them could be expressed in an inclusive sense as well. They did not have to be employed as a means of excommunication; they could also be used to build up community. The different traditions as such remained, but they took on a different significance and status, even in the first ecumenical conversations. They were no longer found to provide a reason for separation, although (apart from the brief basic formula of the World Council of Churches) it was not yet possible to define the common ground in positive terms. It was only in Lund in 1952 that a step was taken away from comparative ecclesiology in the direction of *christological ecclesiology*:

> We have seen clearly that we can make no real advance towards unity if we only compare our several conceptions of the nature of the Church and the traditions in which they are embodied. But once again it has been proved true that as we seek to draw closer to Christ we come closer to one another. We need, therefore, to penetrate behind our divisions to a deeper and richer understanding of the mystery of the God-given union of Christ with his Church. We need increasingly to realize that the separate histories of our Churches find their full meaning only if seen in the perspective of God's dealings with his *whole* people.[11]

Since then the 'Commission on Faith and Order' is at all its conferences engaged in pressing forwards, through all the various traditions, to the tradition which is called by the name of Christ. On the way from the river to the source, from the churches to Christ, the churches are transcending their own forms and traditions. In their christological concentration they are discovering themselves, together with the others, as the one church of Christ. At the same time they are discovering that they are being drawn together into Christ's messianic mission and are becoming the church of the coming kingdom of God. In the ecumenical encounter the christological concentration has led to recognition of the universality of the eschatological hope. That is why anticipatory eschatology is equally stressed. Since the conference at Uppsala in 1968 the expressions promise, hope, mission and anticipation stamp the ecumenical declarations: 'We ask you, trusting in God's renewing power, to join in these anticipations of God's Kingdom, showing now something of the newness which Christ will complete.'[12] The Second Vatican Council talked in similar terms in the Constitution on the Church § 48:

> The final age of the world has already come upon us (cf. I Cor. 10.11). The renovation of the world has been irrevocably decreed and in this age is already anticipated in some real way.[13]

A christologically founded and eschatologically directed doctrine of the church is evidently able to overcome the initial 'negative consensus' of comparative ecclesiology which we have mentioned, and to bring about a consensus that is positive. Finally, it must be noted that the ecumenical movement has for a long time made people aware of the so-called 'non-theological factors' in the divisions between the churches. From the Edinburgh Conference of 1937 onwards the phrase 'non-theological factors' was applied to the economic, political and cultural conflicts which have played a particular role in most of the church's schisms. Because the expression is not a particularly illuminating one, it was dropped. Political and economic social criticism of the form of the church and the divisions between the churches and ideological criticism of the church's theology took its place. Once we become conscious of the churches' imprisonment in particular structures and political constellations, then, if the church is to be helped to find its freedom, there is need of *an ecclesiology which is critical of ideology*, an ecclesiology which reflects the true setting of the churches in the life of the various societies and states. Just as Luther proceeded from the 'unfree will' in order to find the freedom of faith, and from the church's 'Babylonian captivity' in order to discover the true church, so a critical doctrine of the church will start from the church's lack of freedom in societies and nations, in order to seek the church in the freedom of Christ. This is the justification for a theological adoption of Marxist analysis and ideological criticism in the ecumenical context. But it will be limited by 'Christ's interest' in his church and will therefore be also critically levelled against attempts to bring the churches in the socialist countries into line.

The path of the ecumenical movement is, relatively speaking, clear enough: it is already leading from anathema to dialogue. In practical matters it has led further, from dialogue to co-operation. It will lead from co-operation between divided churches to toleration and the arguing-out of differences within the one church. The way leads from co-operation to council. Even if the idea of an ecumenical all-Christian council and the hope that Christianity will speak with one voice at such a council must still be called utopian, yet that Utopia is already shedding its light on the present wherever the divided churches are beginning to live in council with one another. To live in council means consulting with other churches in questions affecting one's own church, and intervening in the questions of other churches. Living in council is not a life without conflicts, but it is a life which endures the conflicts in itself and tries to solve them. Up to now conflicts were often got out of the way by separating the disputing parties. But that is no solution. Solutions can only really be found for conflicts when one keeps the fellowship going, or picks it up again. If the ecumenical movement leads to life in council between the divided churches in their different places, then it does not make things easier for the churches. It undoubtedly brings difficulties in its wake. For it is then impossible to say that the controversy about papal infallibility is 'an internal problem for Catholics' or that the dispute about infant baptism is 'an internal problem for Protestants'. If the whole church is present in every individual church, then they all participate in problems of this kind. The ecumenical concept of the church leads to an inclusive interpretation of the one church of Christ which will become a critical and liberating force in history in the hope of the coming kingdom of God.

4. *The Political Church*

Historically, the church has always had a political dimension. Whether it likes it or not, it represents a political factor. It is hence only a question of how it presents itself as a political factor. As we saw in § 1, from the history of the Reformation, the Confessing Church and the 'churches under the cross', the acknowledgment of the sole lordship of Christ plunges the church into political conflict. A logical and consistent Christian discipleship always has logical political consequences. As we saw in § 2, a missionary church cannot be apolitical. If all the congregation's activities are part of the service of the messianic mission, the political sphere cannot be excluded. Witness to salvation belongs in all life's dimensions. The ecumenical concept of the church also comes up against the liberation of the church from its political imprisonment, as we saw in § 3. The expression 'political church' therefore does not mean a politicizing of the church. On the contrary, it means a Christianization of the church's politics according to 'the yardstick and plumbline of Christ', as Zwingli put it.

The church against world horizons does not only mean 'mission in six continents'; nor is it confined to the ecumenical unification of scattered and divided churches. The church against world horizons also means: the church's existence against the background of the world's increasing interdependence and its growing tension, the struggle for world domination and the fight against exploitation and oppression.

Modern *political theology* has pointed to the fact that 'the world' today can no longer be understood merely as cosmos, or only as 'worldliness' in the personal sense; the word now quite specifically and practically means 'a societal reality viewed in its historical becoming'.[14] Christianity lives in this social process. But *how* does it live, and *what* does it opt for in that process? Since the time of the political and social revolutions in Europe, the Protestant and Catholic churches have consistently made a conservative choice, presenting themselves in the social process as the power of order against enlightenment, emancipation and revolution. Since the French Revolution, a multiplicity of political ecclesiologies have grown up in both the Protestant and the Catholic camps, all of which, anti-revolutionary, anti-rationalist and anti-democratic as they were, wanted to hold in check 'the apocalyptic beast from the abyss' and mobilized the church for this purpose.[15] In the age of the restoration in Europe, the churches, consciously or unconsciously, made that basic conservative choice which determines their public statements even today. It is the intention of modern political theology to make people conscious of this basic conservative choice made by the European churches, and to put an end to it, so giving back to the church its political liberty. The church 'is an institution within [this world], having a critical liberating task in regard to it'.[16] It is only when the church's fixation on that basic choice in world politics is ended that Christianity can hopefully discover the political sphere as the place where responsibility for faith and life is accepted; and it is only then that it can decide freely, and for freedom, without that particular prejudice. Modern political theology, unlike its earlier equivalent, is not an ideology of political religions, to which the church has often enough surrendered. It is the critical ending of these unholy alliances made by the church.[17]

The theology of revolution which comes to us from Latin America demands from Christianity the new fundamental choice for socialism in the world-wide class struggle to liberate the oppressed and exploited people.[18] But the supporters of this decision did not simply take it over from one particular party in the present conflict. Generally speaking, the theology of revolution understands 'revolution' as the outward correspondence of man's inner repentance – that is to say, along the lines of *regeneratio, reformatio* and *renovatio mundi*. The theology of revolution has always interpreted the concept of revolution theologically, understanding it in the light of Christianity's messianic traditions. Consequently it has also laid bare repressed recollections of the biblical traditions and developed a political interpretation of scripture.[19] Reading the Bible with the eyes of the poor is a different thing from reading it with the eyes of the man with a full belly. If it is read in the light of the experiences and hopes of the oppressed, the Bible's revolutionary themes – promise, exodus, resurrection and Spirit – come alive. The way in which the history of Israel and the history of Christ blend with that of the hungry and oppressed is quite different from the way in which they have often been linked with the history of the mighty and rich. However the theology of revolution may be criticized, it has made it patently clear that the political responsibility of Christianity in the present conflicts must definitely take specific form in the people, with the people and for the liberation of the people.[20] In addition, it has set the word 'revolution' in the context of man's rebirth and the new creation of the world – the context to which it has always belonged in the history of the European revolutions.[21] It has at last led to the practical political interpretation of the Bible in the field of experience shared by the hungry and oppressed.

The new *theology of liberation* picks up insights from political theology and the theology of revolution, but takes them a stage further with the appropriate concept of liberation.[22] 'Liberation' is an 'open concept' which permeates and embraces the different dimensions of suffering. It runs from the economic abolition of the exploitation which results from the rule of particular classes, or the political vanquishing of oppression and dictatorship and the cultural elimination of racialism, down to faith's experience of liberation from the compulsion of sin and the eschatological hope of liberation from the power of death.[23] The chains which liberation has to strike off differ in every situation. But the freedom that is sought can only be a single and a common freedom. It is the freedom for fellowship with God, man and nature. The open concept of liberation is thus more comprehensive than the limited concept of political liberation or the fixed concept of revolution. Liberation includes economics and religion, the present and the future, experience and hope, because it is the concept of a commencing but incomplete process. Working for liberation means taking sides with the oppressed and humiliated. But these efforts are directed equally to the free and human future of the oppressor. The theology of liberation involves itself in a realistic analysis of the situation of unfreedom, but it also presses towards the projected goal of its defeat. Potentially this theology can overcome both the particularist thinking which divides and dominates mankind, and the narrow-minded and fanatical thinking which appears in every conflict.

The theological outlines which I have only briefly indicated here are to be seen as first attempts and tentative experiments on the road to a politically responsible church of Christ. Criticism of them cannot drop back into the illusion of a 'non-political church'; it must enquire about still closer political correspondences to the lordship of Christ, to the messianic mission and to the church's existence in a world-wide context. Its ties with ideologies, groups, nations, classes, races and particular interests damage the church's claim to authenticity in the world. The politically responsible concept of the church, on the other hand, leads to the church that suffers and fights within the people and with peoples, and to an interpretation of this people's church in the framework of the divine history of liberation, whose goal is the new creation in peace and righteousness.

All the different chapters of a doctrine of the church today will take account of at least these four dimensions of the church – the church of Christ, the missionary church, the ecumenical church and the political church. By so doing it picks up the church's experiences in our own century, experiences which did not always determine the doctrine of the church earlier, or not to the same degree. Every doctrine of the church starts from experiences in the church and with the church in the world. By enumerating our experiences in this first chapter, we have also marked out our specific place in history.

II

THE CHURCH IN HISTORY

By this heading I do not mean the history of the church in the past as we can survey it today; what is meant is the interpretation of the church in a history which encroaches upon it. The church cannot understand itself simply from itself alone. It can only truly comprehend its mission and its meaning, its roles and its functions in relation to others. The one relationship which everyone comes across at first hand is the relation between his experience of the church to which he belongs and the *credo ecclesiam* which he confesses in that church. The relationship which reaches out further is the relation between the church and the history of Christ from which it comes, in which it lives and for whose fulfilment it hopes whenever it calls on Christ's name. Another relation is the church's relationship to the historical situation in the world, the situation in which it is set and which it takes into account in attempting to interpret 'the signs of the times'. But we must see the all-comprehending reference in the church's relationship to the trinitarian history of God's dealings with the world. It is only in this last, universal context that it can grasp the meaning of its particular existence, without asserting itself in a particularist sense or dissolving in pseudo-universalism.

The church's first word is not 'church' but Christ. The church's final word is not 'church' but the glory of the Father and the Son in the Spirit of liberty. Because of this the church, as Ambrose said, is like the moon, which has no light of its own or for itself. If it is the true church, the light that is reflected on its face is the light of Christ, which reflects the glory of God, and it shines on the face of the church for the people who are seeking their way to freedom in the darkness.

Consequently no ecclesiology can stand on its own feet. The doctrine of the church must, as it were, evolve of itself from christology and eschatology, that is, from insight into the trinitarian history of God's dealings with the world. This means that the question 'What is the church?' cannot be answered by a definition which pegs out the limits dividing the phenomenon 'church' from other phenomena, determining it by a process of demarcation. We therefore ask about the relations in which what deserves to be called the church comes about and is to be expected. The advantage of this *relational ecclesiology* is that it leads to an understanding of the living nature of the church. Its disadvantage is that it does not answer the question about the idea, the nature or the concept of the church with a ready-made definition. We shall put up with this disadvantage here for reasons which will emerge in the course of our discussion.

1. *The Church and the Difference between Faith and Experience*

Most books about the church see the basic problem of ecclesiology as being the difference between faith and experience. 'Everything which we call the church is only available to us in a historical and social form; yet it is not totally absorbed by that form. The church is the object of faith, an article of the creed.'[1] How can the church see itself as at once 'an eschatological power' and 'an empirical and historical power'?[2] What can we make of the 'paradox' that the churches 'participate, on the one hand, in the ambiguities of life in general and of the religious life in particular and, on the other hand, in the unambiguous life of the Spiritual Community'?[3] How is the 'basis of the church' related to the church itself?[4] How can we talk simultaneously about the 'essence of the church' and 'the form of the church'?[5]

The problem is simple and pressing enough: in the Apostles' Creed the churches believe and confess 'one holy Catholic church' – churches which are visibly divided, scattered and disunited; churches which everywhere look human, all too human, and certainly not holy; churches which are not universal either, but exist in the world in highly individual ways. This tension between the faith of the church and our experience of the church is not just perceived today for the first time. It has existed from the very beginning, even at the very time when the church was formulating the church's creed. The church never existed in a historically demonstrable ideal form, a form in which faith and experience coincided. But this discrepancy constantly kept the hunger for correspondence between the two alive.

For ecclesiology this suggests two points of departure. It can start 'from above', unfolding the doctrine of the church as the object of faith in the framework of the confession of the triune God in the third article of the creed, which declares belief in 'the Holy Ghost, the forgiveness of sins, the resurrection of the body and the life everlasting'. It can then move 'downwards', drawing conclusions from the church's faith for its experience and practice. On the other hand it can work in the reverse direction, beginning 'from below'; it can describe the church as one empirical object among others, and then direct its thinking upwards in order to enquire into the theological significance of this object. That is to say: it can start from the church's essence and then proceed to an enquiry into the actual form of that essence; or it can start from the church's actual form, and then go on to enquire into its essence. Of course this division between the methods used by the various ecclesiologies is a simplified abstraction. But there is a real practical problem of how to link up and reconcile the theological doctrines of the church with empirical enquiries – 'How stable is the church?'[6] 'Religious system and socialization',[7] and so forth. No theological ecclesiology can ignore the fact that the creed speaks not only about a heavenly church but also about the church down the road. And no empirical ecclesiology can avoid seeing that the church down the road is – since it is the place of faith – also the object of faith. Creed and experience are related to the same object and they cannot, for all the tension between them, be distributed between different objects. It is true that faith talks about the church in a different perspective and relation from empiricism. Faith confesses the church in the framework of the overriding confession of the triune God. Empiricism perceives the church in its social and psychological functions. But even this distribution into different facets and relations does not resolve the tension when the facets reveal contradictions.

(i) Paradoxical Identity?

A first solution of this problem can be sought with the help of *the notion of paradoxical identity*.[8] The church is 'at the same time' the object of faith and the object of empiricism. It is 'at the same time' an eschatological and a historical power. By way of this paradoxical 'at the same time' it partakes of the paradox of Christ's proclamation, which preaches the historical cross of Christ as being at the same time an eschatological saving event. Its paradoxical 'at the same time' corresponds to Christian existence, which is at once eschatological and historical.[9] For the church too eschatology and history come together at the 'instant' when the 'eschatological instant' is grasped in faith.[10] In this figure of paradoxical identity the church's eschatological yet historical existence is understood in the framework of the Lutheran doctrine of justification. 'The paradox that Christian existence is at the same time an eschatological unworldly being and an historical being is analogous with the Lutheran statement *simul iustus, simul peccator*.'[11] For an understanding of the tension between faith and experience of the church, the conclusion to be reached from this would be that the church is 'one', and at the same time many, separated and divided; that it is 'holy', and at the same time unrighteous; that it is universal, and at the same time particularist. If we take the Lutheran doctrine of justification seriously in its application to ecclesiology, it does not, however, follow that this paradoxical identity can be applied to every form of the church's earthly condition.[12] Faith in the holiness of the church can no more be a justification of its unholy condition than the justification of sinners means a justification of sin. On the contrary, it is the sharpest attack on anything that believes that it can exist by its own strength, because it frees us from this delusion. If man as a sinner is justified and sanctified, he is freed from his self-justification and released from the fetters of 'the powers of this world'. What the forgiveness of sins just does not do is to justify his continuing sins; it cuts him off from them. The *remissio peccatorum* liberates men from the power of the past and therefore opens up the new future of righteous and eternal life. If the event of justification is transferred to the event of the church, then the statements about the church's unity, holiness and catholicity are not analytical judgments about its present condition and characteristics; they are synthetic judgments about what it will be and where it will be preserved in God's acts. If we understand the church as it has become and the church as it will be in the light of the justifying acts of God, it is not enough to point to the Lutheran phrase *simul iustus et peccator*; and the interpretation of the phrase as paradoxical identity becomes one-sided. For the Lutheran *simul* is incomplete without the further definition of the simultaneous non-simultaneity: *peccator in re – iustus in spe*.[13] The present simultaneity of the just man and the sinner is accordingly the simultaneity of the transient world of sin and the coming world of righteousness. If we take this definition of the Lutheran doctrine of justification into consideration, then the paradoxical 'at the same time' becomes the actual dialectical process of the righteousness of God which succeeds against the transience of sin, a process which only finds its end in the 'resurrection of the body' and the new creation. The notion of paradoxical identity is in this way suspended in the comprehensive mental figure of the dialectical process. The 'at the same time' of the righteous man and the sinner is joined with the growing struggle of the spirit against the flesh. The contradiction is not paradoxically perpetuated but is grasped as a tension which presses towards its own resolution in the new creation, where righteousness dwells. Consequently the 'at the same time' of the eschatological and empirical church, in the sense of the event of justification, leads directly to the actual process of struggle for the truth of the church in the sense of its sanctification. This does not mean that the 'at the same time' and the 'in one another' of the church (as at once an empirical and historical power and also an eschatological one) is replaced by 'an eternal dialectic between the two, kept going by a statement raised to a principle: that *ecclesia est semper reformanda*'.[14] The 'paradoxical identity' cannot be replaced by an 'eternal dialectic', which basically speaking only states the same thing on another level. Both formulae would nullify the conflict which reaches into the eschaton of the kingdom and in which the church is set as both the place and the object of faith. Through the justification of the sinner the church is at the same time *congregatio sanctorum* and *congregatio peccatorum*. But through this event it also becomes the field of conflict between spirit and flesh, righteousness and sin, and presses, in intention, beyond its historical forms towards redemption, by virtue of its hope. However, in so extending the application of the Lutheran doctrine of justification to ecclesiology we must bear in mind that the conflict is caused by the event of the justification of the sinner and his liberation from the power of sin. It therefore reaches in its profounder depths beyond the contradiction between faith and empirical experience, for even the state of being a sinner is not one and the same as the empirical being of man, and consequently not one and the same as the empirical and historical form of the church either. Its scope reaches beyond historically possible resolutions of the contradiction between faith and experience – reaches into the eschatological hope, and brings the possible correspondences between the church as it is believed and the church as it is experienced into the dynamics of the provisional. For the creative righteousness of God corresponds ultimately only to a new creation, and not to a new church already in existence.

(ii) The Anticipation of Hope?

A second solution of the problem can be looked for by way of the *notion of anticipation*. Basically speaking, this picks up the ancient doctrine of sanctification, which has justification as its premise and existence in this world as its condition. Here the church is 'at the same time' the object of hope and the object of experience. Through the messianic history of Christ a promise and a trend has been implanted in the church which it continually both realizes and compromises, testifies to and betrays through the form it assumes in history and society. But because, through the remembering actualization of Christ's presence, it relates this promise to itself, it is driven out beyond every historical form. It lives from the surplus of promise over its own realizations of the promise. It lives from the 'added value' of salvation, which is not exhausted by its historical form. The church cannot accept itself for what it is, either out of resignation or out of complacency, as long as this promise of Christ is unfulfilled. With his proclamation and through his embodiment of the kingdom of God, Christ made the church at the same time possible and impossible. He made it possible to the extent that the people of God gathers together in proximity to the kingdom of God. He made it impossible because this people presses on beyond itself to this all-fulfilling kingdom. Under the impression of the remembrance and the hope of Christ's promise, the church will therefore see itself as a mobile and temporary phenomenon in history, which tries in every age to live up to the promise of Christ in accordance with the needs of the situation.

Here the contradiction between the church's faith and its experience is understood in the light of the relationship between hope and reality. Hope is realized in history, but it also transcends its own incarnations. In this way the future element of the church's hope brings the actual fact of its experience into the process of becoming. The church is essentially experienced as an open and imperfect institution because it 'has the function of a *transition* to something else, to the kingdom of God'.[15] The theological aspect of 'the church of hope' expands the empirical aspect from 'the church as datum' to 'the church in the process of history'. The experience of the church as it has come into being is linked with the practice of the church that is in the process of becoming. The 'wealth of past experience' is made available for the future as 'the wealth of untried possibilities'.[16] In so far as that happens, the church's hope for the kingdom of God opens up perspectives for the hoped-for church of the future, and out of the hoped-for future church guiding lines for present church action emerge in their turn. 'The church according to its possibilities' is realized in the historically 'possible church'.[17] The church in the possibility of God is lain hold of in the possibilities and powers of the Holy Spirit.[18]

In the relationship between hope and experience the 'nature of the church' is conceived *teleologically* as the inner force that drives it. 'The Spiritual Community is the inner *telos* of the churches and as such it is the source of everything which makes them churches.'[19] 'The novelty of the presence of the kingdom of God is . . . its future: its unhistorical and non-objective futurity, which has to be continually and extremely dialectically won under the conditions of the social and religious present.'[20] Its *unity* in the face of its divisions is then an anticipatory judgment of hope, which fetches its future into its present. Its *holiness* in the face of its community of sinners then anticipates its future in the same way that the acknowledgment of its *catholicity* in the face of its particularity is an expression of its hope. Thus the church is conceived in terms of transition (*transitus*) and of conversion (*metanoia*) from sin to holiness, from division to unity and from particularity to universality. The church's hope and experience are conveyed in the concept of anticipation.

But this view already presupposes the freedom of the church, which is created by grace. If we were to ignore that we should also be overlooking the church's lack of social and cultural freedom too. The church would then fall victim to an illusory belief in progress such as we find in neo-Protestantism and its notions about the church in the history of the kingdom of God. Only by virtue of its remembrance of the one who was crucified can the church live in the presence of the one who is risen – that is to say, can live realistically in hope. The church only follows the promise of Christ and the trend of the Spirit when it accepts its own cross. 'It only becomes the *congregatio sanctorum* by accepting its existence as *communio peccatorum*. It only remains the church of the risen Christ by taking on itself the destiny of the Christ who was crucified.'[21] The teleological relationship between the church's hope and experience only remains eschatological in the tension of history opened up through Christ's crucifixion and resurrection.

(iii) Sacramental Identification?

A third solution of the problem can be sought with the help of *sacramental thinking*. Here the whole church is orientated towards the sacramental representation of the history of Christ and the eschatological future in, with and beneath the word, the bread and the wine. Sacramental thinking links together the remembrance of Christ with the hope of glory in the present tokens of liberating and uniting grace. The eschatological and the present, the particular and the universal, the heavenly and the earthly come together symbolically in the gospel and in the eucharist. Sacramental thinking is always applied in a more or less elaborate way to the interpretation of the believed and experienced church where there is talk about the being of the one *in* the other. This does not only mean the simultaneity of the believed and experienced church in paradoxical identity. Nor does it only mean the dialectical process of hope and experience of the church. Both ways of thinking are grounded and expanded through the sacramental statement about the existence of the one in the other.[22]

Paul Tillich links this sacramental thinking with the Lutheran paradox 'in spite of':

> The churches are holy because of the holiness of their foundation, the New Being, which is present in them. . . . The churches are holy, but they are so in terms of an 'in spite of' or as a paradox. . . . The churches are united because of the unity of their foundation. . . . The unity of the church is real in each of them in spite of the fact that all of them are separated from each other. . . . As was the case with respect to holiness and unity, we must also say of the churches' universality that it is present in their particularity.[23]

In the same way Hans Küng talks about the 'essence' of the church and its 'form'. 'Essence and form *cannot be separated*. . . . Essence and form *are not identical*.' Between difference and identity lies the sacramental idea of the coinherence of the one in the other.[24] 'The real essence of the real Church is expressed in historical form.'[25] If we want to understand the essential nature of the church, then we must always pay heed to its changeable, historical form. If we want to understand its changeable, historical form, we must pay heed to its essential nature. If the 'essence' of the church is connected with the coming lordship of God which Jesus proclaimed, then in this respect neither an identification nor a dissociation between the church and the divine lordship are possible.[26]

> Thus the promises and powers of the coming reign of God are already evident and effective, through Christ, in the Church, which so partakes in a hidden manner in the dawning reign of God.[27]

But then Küng dissociates once more, saying in closing: 'It is not the bringer or the bearer of the reign of God which is to come and is at the same time already present, but its voice, its announcer, its *herald*.'[28] If the church is thus 'not a preliminary stage, but an *anticipatory sign* of the definitive reign of God', then the real presence and coinherence of this future in the form and presence of the church seems once more to be called in question.

The difference between the form and the nature of the church, as well as between the church and the kingdom of God, always forces itself upon us when we look from the present into the eschatological future. But if, reversing the process, we look from the eschatological future which, in the history of Christ, has 'already begun' in the present existence of the church, then we recognize the essential nature already existing in the form, and the coming lordship of God as already present in the historical church.

The point of departure for both points of view must, however, be a definite event. This definite event which 'makes the church the church' is the sacramental event. We mean by this the preaching of the Word of God in the human word, the presence of the coming Christ in bread and wine, and the coming of the Spirit in baptism. To such an extent the church is what it is in the light of this event.

Because this sacramental happening cannot be 'created' and cannot be calculated, the solution of the problem of faith and experience, hope and reality, the nature and the form of the church, has to be looked for in *pneumatology*. That through which we perceive the history and promise of Christ, that through which we become aware of the coming rule of God in word and sacrament and church, and through which we enter into the fellowship of the history of the triune God – this perception, this awareness and this fellowship must itself be termed God, the Holy Spirit.[29] It is only in the history of the Spirit, which unites us with the history of Christ and is itself the history of the new creation, that all the definitions that have been given of faith and experience, paradox and dialectic, nature and form acquire their theological function and lose their partial character.

'The church in history' cannot be sufficiently comprehended in the momentary impression of the present tensions between faith and experience, hope and reality, nature and form. These tensions must be reflected in the wider context of the history of Christ's dealings with the world; for that is where they come from, and that is where they lead.

2. *The Church in the History of the Holy Spirit*

The question about the meaning of the history of Christ has always been of central concern for theology. Christian theology begins with it and comes back to it again and again. *Why* did Christ come and *what* is the purpose of his coming? *Why* did Christ die on the cross? *Why* was he raised from the dead, and *why* did he appear to the disciples in the splendour of the divine glory?

From early times theological interpretation approached the history of Christ with this teleological question, in an attempt to grasp its meaning. It was moved to do so by the messianic character of Jesus' mission and history itself. For the incompletion and the open-ended character of this history of Christ, pointing beyond itself, actually suggests the question. It is above all the 'double conclusion' of Jesus' life (M. Kähler) – out of messianic life into a Godforsaken death, and out of this death into eschatological life – which inevitably raises the question *why*.[30] The historical prophecy of Jesus must hence be assimilated into an eschatology of the history of Jesus Christ. And here the eschatological interpretation of his history must correspond to his historical embodiment of the eschatology. Hope must return to remembrance if it is not to lose its real foundation. That is why an orientation towards the history of Christ itself is constitutive for the unfolding of its eschatology. The teleological interpretation cannot be an arbitrary one. It can only bring to light what has already been plotted out. Conversely, the history of Christ cannot be properly understood other than in the light of its eschatology. This historical 'phenomenon' cannot in any case be grasped apart from the future for which it has significance.[31]

(i) The Meaning of the History of Christ

We find the teleological interpretation of the history of Christ in the 'theological final clauses' of the New Testament.[32] We find it in the whole Christian tradition wherever christology has been developed in conjunction with soteriology. Every statement about Christ's incarnation, mission, passion, death and resurrection corresponds to a soteriological statement expressing the intention, goal and meaning of this history of Christ.[33] We find it especially in Reformation theology, which leads over from the question of the *substantia historiae Christi* to the question of the *finis historiae Christi*.[34] The mere *notitia* of the history of Christ is not enough for faith. Only when we lay hold on the *promissio* which speaks to us out of that history, because it is inherent in it and because history is its experienceable sign, do we arrive at its application (*usus*) and an understanding of its meaning for us. The promise of the forgiveness of sins, which justifying faith lays hold of, is itself 'the testament' – the will which comes into force through Jesus' death and in the execution of which the crucified Jesus lives.[35] By discovering the promise as the meaning of the history of Christ, the Reformation also understood the history of Christ as the foundation of this promise. The promissory interpretation of the history of Christ corresponded to the christological foundation of the promise. That is why Melanchthon pressed forward from the christological perception of Christ's natures and incarnation to the perception of his benefits, of course without wanting at the same time to resolve the person of Christ into Christ's functions.[36] That is why the Heidelberg Catechism in interpreting the Apostles' Creed always asks about the uses and aids arising from the theological affirmations of faith.[37] We take the eschatological point of departure in understanding the history of Christ by asking the meaning of that history. The promise, the use and the aim are all included in the modern word 'meaning'.[38] What we have called 'the interest of Christ' and the 'trend' of his history are also inherent in it.

If we follow the theological final clauses in the New Testament, we first of all come up against the theology with which Paul interprets the credal statements which he takes over from the primitive church. One can say of them that 'the teleological principle has penetrated to the very heart of the Christian message and Christian theology'.[39] Paul understands the history of Christ as a saving event 'for us'. 'ὑπὲρ ἡμῶν is a brief, pregnant formula describing the whole saving event.'[40] We cannot go into Paul's theology in detail here,[41] but some important teleological determinations can be distinguished on the basis of the history of Christ, when it is understood as open and inclusive, on the basis of the 'for us'.

Since, as we know, the righteousness of God stands in the forefront for Paul, it can be said first of all that for him the justification of sinners is *the meaning of the history of Christ*. Christ 'was put to death for our trespasses and raised for our justification' (Rom. 4.25). The meaning of his giving of himself to death on the cross is the liberation of the sinner from the burden of sin by virtue of reconciliation; and his liberation from the power of sin by virtue of substitution. The meaning of his resurrection from the dead is our new life in righteousness. Christ is 'for our sake made to be sin, so that in him we might become the righteousness of God' (II Cor. 5.21). 'Christ redeemed us from the curse of the law, having become a curse for us' (Gal. 3.13). 'For your sake he became poor, so that by his poverty you might become rich' (II Cor. 8.9). Paul again and again linked faith in Christ with the *telos* of justification (Gal. 2.16; Rom. 4.16; 9.11; cf. also Eph. 2.9). Here the forgiveness of sins and the reconciliation of sinners through God first of all interprets Christ's self-giving in his suffering and death on the cross; whereas his resurrection from the dead and his exaltation as *kyrios* finds its present meaning in the opening up of new righteousness, new obedience and new fellowship. The two sides of the traditional doctrine of justification here correspond to the two statements made by christology. The meaning of Christ's death is the *remissio peccatorum*. The meaning of his resurrection is the *acceptatio personae ad vitam aeternam*.[42] The two sides of the conversion (repentance) also correspond to the double aspect of christology: In the *mortificatio sui* the crucified one is made present; in the *vivificatio in spiritu* the risen one reigns. The two can no more be divided from one another than the crucified Jesus can be divided from the risen Christ, or the risen Christ from the crucified Jesus. But if with Paul we understand justification and Christian existence in repentance as being the meaning of the history of Christ, then there is here no paradoxical identity and no eternal dialectic. Just as the raising of Christ represents a 'surplus' over the event on the cross and can only qualify it as a redemptive event because of that, so in the same way there is a surplus of grace in the justification of the sinner ('much more': Rom. 5.10). Its meaning is not totally absorbed by the forgiveness of sins but, through the operation of forgiveness, leads to new life and the new creation. That is why, in the Christian life of repentance too, the joy of the new life has a rapture greater than the pain at the dying of the old one.[43]

If we follow the theological final clauses further, we are led beyond the event of the justification of sinners. The meaning of the history of Christ reveals itself to the godless in their justification and acceptance first of all; but it is not totally absorbed by men's arrival at justifying faith.[44] On the foundation of justification, without which there is no new beginning for the unrighteous, and on the basis of liberation, without which there is no new life for those in bondage, the meaning of the history of Christ is then unfolded in the new obedience (Rom. 6.8ff.), in the new fellowship (Rom. 12.3ff.) and in the manifestation of the Spirit in the charismatic powers of the new creation (I Cor. 12.7ff.).[45]

'To this end Christ died and lived again, that he might be Lord both of the dead and of the living' (Rom. 14.9). If, therefore, the justification of sinners is the meaning of the history of Christ, then the meaning of the justification of sinners is the liberating lordship of Christ over the dead and the living, i.e., the new creation in him. If we ask about the christological conclusion that follows from the final clauses in Paul, we look beyond 'our justification', beyond the new obedience and the new fellowship, and through these things to the lordship of Christ over past, present and future.

If we go on to enquire into the meaning of the lordship of Christ, we come up against the eschatology of the history of Christ developed in I Cor. 15: 'For he must reign until he has put all his enemies under his feet. The last enemy to be destroyed is death ... When all things are subjected to him, then the Son himself will also

be subjected to him who put all things under him, that God may be
everything to every one' (I Cor. 15.25–28). If the goal of the
crucifixion and raising of Christ is his rule over everything, then
the goal of his rule is the complete rule of God in which God himself is 'everything to every one' (AV: 'all in all'). Even the rule of
Christ is provisional and limited.

> The only goal it serves is to give way to the sole leadership of God.
> Christ is God's representative over against a world which is not yet
> fully subject to God, although its eschatological subordination is in
> train since Easter and its end is in sight. . . . The *regnum Christi* is
> distinguished precisely by this very state of affairs: death has no more
> dominion over him, but it has over us. It (the *regnum*) is therefore
> defined by the two poles, his Resurrection and ours, and must be
> described materially as the realm of the power of the Resurrection in a
> world which has fallen a prey to death, and thus to the other cosmic
> powers.[46]

The teleological question about the purpose of the history of
Christ therefore leads, as it were, beyond every purpose that can be
comprehended in any present and particular sense. It leads into
universal eschatology. In the light of the all-embracing and
fulfilling eschatological purpose, the other purposes are then
included in the dynamics of the provisional. We might put it
negatively and, like Käsemann, call it 'eschatological reserve'.[47]
Or we could talk positively about an anticipatory mode of thought.
For the person involved, however, justification is something final,
so that he can say in comprehensive terms: 'Where there is forgiveness of sins there is also life and salvation.'[48] But in view of the
abundance of the promises of the history of Christ and its eschatological meaning, he will be placed in the dynamics of the provisional,
or what German calls the *Vor-läufige* – what runs ahead; so that he
is bound to say in the words of the Easter hymn:

> Christ is risen, Christ the first-fruits
> Of the holy harvest field,
> Which will all its full abundance
> At his second coming yield.[49]

Paul's 'theological final clauses' really point to the victory of
the lordship of God. This lordship of God over everything is at
the same time conceived of as his *indwelling* in everything. His
rule corresponds to his *glorification* through the new creation,
which is new in the very fact of this joy. The theological final

clauses, through which the meaning of the history of Christ is grasped and which are in the first place soteriologically determined, therefore really amount to doxological final clauses. This means, conversely, that this doxology is already beginning in the saving event itself, in justification, sanctification, new fellowship and the powers of the Spirit. Where God rules he is glorified; where he justifies he achieves what is his due; where he brings a sinner to repentance and frees the oppressed he finds joy. Soteriology and doxology are therefore intertwined from the very beginning, and hence are intertwined in the end as well. Consequently, for Paul too the ultimate purpose of the history of Christ is the universal glorification of God the Father through the Son in the Holy Spirit (Phil. 2.10; Rom. 11.33; I Cor. 15.28). In the eschatological thanksgiving of the new creation the destiny of all created being is fulfilled.[50]

(ii) In the Power of the Holy Spirit

The church as the community of justified sinners, the fellowship of those liberated by Christ, who experience salvation and live in thanksgiving, is on the way to fulfilling the meaning of the history of Christ. With its eyes fixed on Christ, it lives in the Holy Spirit and thus is itself the beginning and earnest of the future of the new creation. It proclaims Christ alone; but the fact that it proclaims him is already the advent of the future of God in the word. It believes Christ alone; but the fact that it believes is already the sign of hope. In its liberation it follows Christ alone; but this is already the bodily anticipation of the redemption of the body. In the Lord's supper it remembers and makes present the death of Christ, which leads to life; but the fact that this happens is a foretaste of the peace to come. It only confesses Jesus, the crucified, as Lord; but the kingdom of God is anticipated in this confession. This relationship between what happens and the fact that it happens can only be understood pneumatologically. The community and fellowship of Christ which is the church comes about 'in the Holy Spirit'. The Spirit is this fellowship. Faith perceives God in Christ and this perception is itself the power of the Spirit. As the historical community of Christ, therefore, the church is the eschatological creation of the Spirit. 'In this sense history passes into eschatology and eschatology into history.'[51] This transition is called the work of the Holy Spirit.

The teleological interpretation of the history of Christ coincides with the pneumatological interpretation of the fulfilment of that history's meaning. The believer's freedom from sin and from the godless powers of our worldly era is therefore also called 'the power of the Holy Spirit'.[52] The new life is 'life in the Spirit' and the new obedience takes the form of 'walking by the Spirit'.[53] The new fellowship is itself 'the manifestation of the Spirit' and of the powers of the new creation. Eschatologically, therefore, the Spirit can be termed 'the power of futurity',[54] for it is 'the eschatological gift', the beginning (Rom. 8.23) and the earnest or guarantee (II Cor. 1.22; 5.5) of the future. Pneumatologically, eschatology is the work of the Holy Spirit. For through the Spirit the believer is determined by the divine future. The powers of the Spirit are the powers of life, which determine the present, extending their influence forward from the future of the new life.[55] The fruit of the Spirit is the advance payment in joy of future blessedness, in spite of the experience of suffering; it is the advance payment in love, in spite of the experience of disappointment and hate. Consequently the whole eschatology of the history of Christ which is expounded in the theological final clauses can also be described as the history of the Spirit, a result of the workings and indwellings of the Spirit through which the future that is hoped for enters into history.

When we talk about the history of the Spirit in this sense, we do not mean the idealistic spiritual history of human subjectivity; we mean the dialectical process of interactions which is opened up and urged on by the future of the thing that is entirely new. The history of the creative Spirit embraces human history and natural history, and to that extent is to be understood in dialectical-materialist terms as 'the movement', 'the urge', 'the spirit of life', 'the tension' and 'the torment' which – as Marx said with Jacob Böhme – is matter's pre-eminent characteristic.

If we dispense with salvation-history terminology[56] and cease to pigeon-hole the teleological fulfilment of the meaning of Christ's history in terms of salvation history, then with John we can call the sending of the Holy Spirit as such the 'eschatology of the history of Christ'.[57] In the farewell discourses he is called the Paraclete, whom Jesus promises to his followers, whose coming he makes possible through his departure and pleads for in his act of self-giving. He is called 'the Spirit of truth' or 'the Holy Spirit'. He is the witness of Christ, who leads to knowledge of the truth. He is

one with the Son and the Father. He glorifies the Father through
the Son in those who belong to him. He is the giver of the eternal
life of God to the world which has fallen victim to death. So when
we say 'Pentecost is the *telos*, the highest goal of revelation in
Christ', it is true as far as the gift of the Spirit is concerned; but if
we are considering the fulfilment of the meaning of the history of
Christ we also have to talk about the 'history of the Spirit'. For 'it
is at the same time the beginning of the new time, the time of the
direct and lasting presence of revelation in history.'[58]

In its present tensions between faith and experience, hope and
reality, the church will have to understand itself as part of this
history of the creative Spirit. The church is the concrete form in
which men experience the history of Christ. In the longer-range
history of the Spirit the church is a way and a transition to the
kingdom of God. It lives in the experience and practice of the
Spirit from the eschatological anticipation of the kingdom. As the
fellowship of Christ it is hope lived in fellowship. The experiences
and powers of the Spirit mediate the presence of the history of
Christ and the future of the new creation. What is called 'the
church' is this mediation. As the church of Christ it is the church of
the Holy Spirit. As the fellowship of believers it is creative hope in
the world.

If we understand the church and that which makes it the church
in the overriding movements and coherences of the history of the
Spirit, then we must subject two ecclesiologies, the Lutheran and
the Orthodox, to a critical evaluation.

Reformed theology tends to focus the history of Christ on the
justification of the sinner and hence, in the third article of the
Apostles' Creed, to make 'the forgiveness of sins' the pivot on
which understanding of the church depends. The church is
essentially the community of those who are justified by faith
through grace. The *articulus iustificationis* counts as the *articulus
stantis et cadentis ecclesiae*.[59] It is true here (and it is a truth that we
must emphatically hold on to) that the sinner does not find the true
God in any other way than through the forgiveness of sins; and that
God does not achieve true man in any other way than through the
forgiveness of sinners. Anything else would be an illusion about
the reality of godless, unrighteous, unfree and inhuman man. For
that reason an appropriate ecclesiology of the true church cannot
meet us with dreams of the ideal church but only, essentially

speaking, with the doctrine of justification. At the same time, it
would be wrong to stop short at this concentration on the justification of the unrighteous and to overlook the purposes of the
history of Christ which move through justification and reach out
beyond it. For through justification the unjust man is led into the
history of the Spirit, so that he becomes obedient in hope and the
practice of divine righteousness. Man's history in its relation to the
history of Christ begins with the forgiveness of sins and his being
freed for a new life. There can be no other beginning for the unrighteous, the unfree and the hopeless. But the beginning does not
lead immediately to the end. Liberation leads to liberated life.
Justification leads to the new creation. Rightly understood, therefore, the *articulus stantis et cadentis ecclesiae* is a way of access to the
other articles about the Holy Spirit and his creation: the resurrection of the dead, eternal life, the kingdom of God and the glorification of God through the consummation of creation. It leads to
Zwingli's 'narrow confines of the cross', and through those very
confines into the new world of resurrection and eternal life. If it
does not, then it has not been properly understood.

The ecclesiology of the Orthodox churches, on the other hand,
has stressed the history of the Spirit, his continuing presence since
Pentecost, the breadth of the Spirit's gifts, the abundance of his
energies and his glorification of the Father with the Son, a glorification which we can already experience and celebrate with him in
the liturgy.[60] Orthodoxy has understood the revelation of the
Spirit in a trinitarian sense and resists the 'christomonism' of the
Western churches, especially the Protestant ones. Orthodoxy
understands the history of Jesus itself pneumatologically. His
incarnation, his mission, his anointing and his resurrection are the
works of the Holy Spirit. The Holy Spirit is the divine subject of
the history of Jesus. For that reason the Son of God is also present
in and through the Spirit in his church, and beyond it is at work in
creation. Pneumatological christology leads to a charismatic
ecclesiology. What is true here, and what we must emphatically
hold on to, is that faith's experience of the history of Christ and the
consummation of his history is the work of the Holy Spirit. To this
extent the *articulus de Spiritu Sancto* is the *articulus stantis et
cadentis ecclesiae*. But this perception of the breadth and fullness of
the Holy Spirit would become unrealistic if it were not continually
to begin with the work of the Holy Spirit in the forgiveness of sins

and the acceptance of forsaken man. The true perception that the messianic history of Christ from his incarnation to his exaltation is the work of the eschatological Spirit must not pass by Christ's death on the cross, through which the Father, in the Spirit of self-giving, has become the Father of forsaken men and women.[61] The transfiguration of Christ in the Spirit of glory must not be allowed to cast so dazzling a light that our eyes are blinded to his death in abandonment by God. Pneumatic christology is only realistic when it is developed into the trinitarian theology of the cross. Consequently charismatic ecclesiology too is only realistic when it makes the Spirit manifest in the conditions of the world that were without him.

Reformed theology cannot get along without Orthodox theology's perception of the breadth of the Holy Spirit and the abundance of the Spirit's gifts; just as Orthodox theology is seemingly thrown back on the Reformed perception of the depths of the cross of Christ and the realistic justification of the unrighteous. We will therefore try to overcome the 'christomonism' Orthodoxy deplores, as well as the dangers of 'pneumatomonism' by presenting the church in the comprehensive sphere of the trinitarian history of God's dealings with the world.

3. *The Church under the Spell of 'the Signs of the Times'*

As long as reality as a whole was primarily understood as a cosmos which, ordered by eternal laws and filled with divine significance, reflected the central order of all things, the political community found its justification in the correspondence of its laws to natural law; while the church saw itself as the guardian of the revealed meaning of the whole. Just as the cosmos is the space, wrung from chaos, in which all being lives, so church and state are the forces of order against chaos in human history. In its alliance with worldly authority, the church ceases to pray like early Christianity, 'Let thy kingdom come and this world pass away.' It now prays that the end may be put off, because it sees itself as the power which staves off 'the end'.[62]

Even if the churches in the modern world have lost their earlier character as the public, moral and political forces of order, yet the services they perform in baptism, teaching, marriage ceremonies, pastoral work and the burial of the dead are primarily claimed in

'Christian countries' at the key points and emotional crises of life. Psychologically and in the story of the individual life, the church goes on acting as a stabilizing factor against inner chaos and uncertainty.

Since the French Revolution, however, European thinking has come to accept the interpretation of reality as a whole as *history*.[63] A cosmological orientation gave way to new bearings drawn from the movements of time and from history. The present was understood in the framework of its future and its origin, and reality in the framework of its destructive and constructive potentialities. The widest framework for an understanding of the present in the light of its history was sought for in universal historical schemes. In this way the future as the field of hopes and fears took on a hitherto unknown role for the conferring of significance to historical experience and practice. This modern understanding of reality as history in the context of its potential future has been described often enough. The theologies of hope, evolution and process have taken it up and made it theologically fruitful. In this connection we must ask about the orientation of the church in the modern experience of reality as history. An orientation towards the eternal laws of the cosmos and the timeless natural laws is just as impossible as dependence on the other forces of order and authority in society. Since, with the French Revolution, 'revolution' *per se* has come to be understood as 'the distinctive mark of our era of world history' (F. J. Stahl) the church's orientation towards world history has become general; for 'history' is only a softer word for revolution, and historical experience is simply the experience of crisis. The church therefore has continually taken its bearings from 'the signs of the times'.

(i) The Signs of the Times

Theology under the spell of the 'signs of the times'[64] is today enjoying its heyday, and indeed growing in importance, in both the Protestant and the Catholic churches. It is therefore necessary for us to investigate the real meaning of the expression. It is derived from the biblical experience of history and from the language of the Bible; but it propagated itself by way of the apocalyptic traditions, and continually cropped up in Christian history whenever world history was going through periods and moods of crisis.[65] The modern expression 'the signs of the times' is in this way a form of the apocalyptic theme of 'the signs of the end'. The question about the signs of the times even today means that people do not merely order history, split it up into periods and trace its events, in order to discover what the present *kairos* demands. Instead time is put to the question – asked for portents that might point to its apprehended or hoped-for end. With the question about the signs of the times, history is interpreted with an eye to its coming end. Historical experiences take place in this context of expectation, accompanied and interpreted by fear and hope.

When the Old Testament talks about God's '*signs and wonders*', the writers are always thinking about the way in which Israel was led out of Egypt, the particular circumstances which surrounded the people up to the passage through the Red Sea, and in which Israel's God showed that he was mighty and that the people were his chosen people.[66] The talk about God's 'signs and wonders' is rooted in the Deuteronomistic view of history. The extraordinary circumstances which are meant point back to God and are, moreover, of such a kind that they proclaim some cataclysmic event to be imminent.[67] Old Testament prophecy of the coming acts of God in judgment and salvation is also accompanied by corresponding signs and symbolic acts. It was only the apocalyptic writings which then went on to talk about the portents of the coming end of the world, interpreting the events of world history and cosmic changes accordingly. Here we find the common idea that the dawning of the end will be preceded by terrible cosmic changes which cannot be ignored and which announce to the well-informed what is at hand.[68]

In the New Testament we find in Matthew and Luke the cryptic saying about the '*sign of Jonah*', which probably means the sign that is Jonah himself 'in the singularity of his historical manifestation'[69] – Jonah's call, his commission and his fate. That is God's 'sign'. The application of 'the sign of Jonah' to Jesus probably belongs to the context of '*the sign of the Son of man*'. This is 'of such a kind that present earthly-human existence reaches its ineluctable end therein. It proclaims this end unconditionally, and this is its true significance.'[70] Both signs have apocalyptic functions, revealing the future. In Matthew what is meant is 'that the *parousia* will not come directly, but will announce itself first. It may be that in the background is the certainty that the last act of history will begin with a final opportunity for conversion and faith.'[71]

Further, the demand for 'signs and wonders' addressed to Jesus is a question about the signs of the messianic era, as well as a request for a legitimation of his mission. Because signs and wonders will accompany the Messiah as the promised prophet, the question was put to his apostles as well. Here it is important to see that the author of the Acts of the Apostles was thinking back to the event of the exodus. The new Mosaic era of eschatological redemption is recognized among Christ's apostles from the signs and wonders which were to be expected of it. The signs and wonders 'which now take place afresh as they once did at the exodus with its miraculous accompanying phenomena, are a pledge of the certainty of eschatological occurrence'.[72] For Paul too (II Cor. 12.12) the 'signs of an apostle' are something visible, which make an apostle recognizable as such. 'The signs and miracles of the age of redemption which have been done by him "identify" him as an apostle of Christ.'[73]

In the tradition of the exodus story and in the hope of the new exodus of the end-time, 'signs and wonders' are the visible heraldings of the salvation which frees men and redeems the world. But parallel to this we also have the sequel of the apocalyptic tradition, according to which the terrors of history and the dissolution of cosmic and human order are portents, signs pointing forward to the terrible end. So in the Little Apocalypse of Mark (Mark 13.4ff.) the question: 'When will this be, and what will be the sign when these things are all to be accomplished?' is answered by the words:

> Take heed that no one leads you astray. Many will come in my name, saying, 'I am he!' and they will lead many astray. And when you hear of wars and rumours, do not be alarmed; this must take place, but the end is not yet. For nation will rise against nation, and kingdom against kingdom; there will be earthquakes in various places, there will be famines; this is but the beginning of the sufferings. But take heed to yourselves; for they will deliver you up to councils; and you will be beaten in synagogues; and you will stand before governors and kings for my sake, to bear testimony before them. And the gospel must first be preached to all nations.

According to these biblical traditions, the expression 'the signs of the times' is ambiguous. When it is combined with the mention of 'signs and wonders', positive pointers to the coming redemption are meant. In the apocalyptic tradition 'the signs of the end' mean the negative portents of the dreadful end of the world. The exodus tradition is applied to the interpretation of the messianic history of Jesus and the apostles; the apocalyptic tradition is applied to the end-time interpretation of world history and cosmic events. It is an open question whether the modern 'theology of the signs of the times' is talking about the signs and wonders of the coming exodus into freedom or whether it means the negative signs of threatening catastrophe. That is part of the reason for its increasing prominence and for its helplessness.

The modern orientation of the church towards 'the signs of the times' really follows both biblical traditions, arriving at diametrically opposite notions, depending on whether the present is read in accordance with the apocalyptic timetable or in remembrance of the exodus tradition. But while modern thinking has arrived at an independent position, thanks to its emancipation from the established forces of order and authority in state, society and church, the beleaguered and abandoned church has been taking its bearings primarily from the apocalyptic interpretation of the signs of the times.

(ii) The Apocalyptic Orientation towards the 'Signs of the End'

Let us briefly consider the development of the church's apocalyptic angle on the world in modern times.[74] It was this that led to the church's basically conservative decision against 'the revolution'. 'All revolutions are contrary to the kingdom of God', announced the revivalist theologian Gottfried Menken at the beginning of the nineteenth century, and had a lasting effect on conservative Protestant theologians in the age of revolution.[75] August Vilmar[76] (whose influence has made itself felt to this century, in some quarters of the Confessing Church and in today's evangelical confessional movement in Germany) considered in 1831 that 'revolution' was 'the monster from the abyss'.

> Here the evil Spirit of negation and destruction has, as far as it is able, demolished and shattered the divine order and equality of law, which is founded solely on the equality of our need for redemption; and in place of this divine equality has set up an equality which is not human but beastly.

Vilmar again and again interprets 'the revolution' apocalyptically as 'the abomination of desolation', and its results – democracy, rationalism, liberalism and secularism – as signs of the end. The Antichrist rears his head, for his followers know 'no God, no prince, no powers that be, no order, no laws. All this is a hindrance to them, and hence they strive with all their might to destroy Christianity.' In 1848, the year of the civil war in Germany, he wrote:

> If there is a republic, then the end is near, in so far as the great divorce will take place; for if I am not much mistaken, the republic is not merely fortuitously godless; it is so essentially. If king and empire come again, then the phases will supervene much more slowly.

Friedrich Julius Stahl interpreted the signs of revolution with the same apocalyptic forebodings and assigned to the church the role of saviour of the last days. 'Only the church can heal the nations from the sickness of revolution.'[77] The revolution is the sign that the world is entering 'the apocalyptic era' and has to prepare for 'the final struggle'. It is true that right through history there has always been insurrection, the expulsion of dynasties and the overthrow of constitutions; but with the principle of popular sovereignty, the French Revolution introduced permanent and 'absolute revolution'. Its nature is 'pure and clear-cut emphasis on the principle of evil'. For that reason it is useless to want to overcome the revolution with political measures. 'Revolution is not ended through a constitutional document.' 'Nor is revolution ended through mechanical power.' There is 'only one power that can end revolution. That is Christianity.'[78]

For Vilmar the apocalyptic interpretation of the revolution meant logically that the divorce between believers and unbelievers was imminent. The godless and anti-Christian revolution will bring forth its own contrary in power and independence, namely the church.

> When all existing worldly things are overthrown, she rises staunchly, with new power; it was she who, when the Roman empire crumbled into ruin, created a new life, and for this new life, new orders; and it will be she again who – even if this time in a different form (and, we confidently hope, a more perfect one) – will found and create a new order of things, a new order whose goal – a goal indeed invisible to worldly eyes – is none other than to prepare his people and his place for the Christ who will come again in his glory.[79]

The church's anti-revolutionary experience is simply the experience of the eschatological struggle between Christ and Antichrist. The church of the last days will become visible. And when 'the abomination of desolation' gains ground and everything tends towards the 'last divorce', then at the end 'the spiritual office alone . . . still has a divine mandate and authority' to prepare the way for 'the Christ who is coming again in his glory'.[80]

> For that reason still more violent struggles will doubtless kindle round this doctrine [i.e., of the church] and far sharper divisions appear than in the case of other doctrines, not only because this doctrine cannot be understood at all unless we stand fast in those other doctrines, but also because this doctrine has to deal with our standing together, with our fellowship; and the conflict can therefore have no issue other than that of divorce; consequently the issue of this struggle will coincide with the appearance of the Antichrist.[81]

Abraham Kuyper interpreted the storm signals of revolution and 'modernism' in a very similar way. For him the essence of revolution was the watchword 'ni Dieu ni maître' – i.e., the sovereignty of the people and emancipation from all divine and state authority. And he decreed: 'The principle of revolution remains anti-Christian and has since that time gone on eating its way like a cancer, in order to crumble away and undermine everything that was a matter of certainty for our Christian consciousness.'[82] Two ideologies are struggling together in a fight to the death: modernism wants to build up a world out of natural man, and to build this man out of nature; and on the other side everyone who kneels in reverence before Christ as the Son of God wants to preserve the Christian heritage for the world, in order to lead it, by virtue of this heritage, towards a still higher development. The anti-revolutionary principle is living Christianity and its purest revelation is Calvinism. Just as Vilmar preached Lutheranism, so Kuyper preaches Calvinism as 'the only defence that is able to stand its ground for the Protestant nations against the modernism that is penetrating them and flooding over them'.[83] Both support an apocalyptic sectarianism.

> Calvinism, more and better than any other view, offers a defence of principle – and hence a defence that is impregnable – against the Spirit of the Age, which desires to rob us of our Christianity. . . . [For] in the Calvinist heritage . . . man bows his knee before God, but raises his head proudly towards his fellow men; but here, where men adhere to the standpoint of popular sovereignty, they clench their fists arrogantly towards God, meanwhile crawling as men before their fellow men, covering up this self-abasement through the fiction of a . . . *contrat social*.[84]

Abraham Kuyper founded the 'Anti-revolutionary People's Party' in Holland, and was for years its general secretary.

In these conservative traditions of the nineteenth and twentieth century the old view of the church as the power of order against chaos really still prevails; but the grounds given for this view are now no longer cosmological; they are apocalyptic. 'The signs of the times' take the place of the cosmic order. If revolution is the anti-Christian sign of the last days, then the hour of final separation has arrived and the church is entering the anti-revolutionary struggle as the visible and pure community of the returning Christ. The discovery of ecclesiology on the basis of this type of experience of the church becomes the preliminary step to the discovery of eschatology on the basis of the impending experiences of the final apocalyptic struggle. Here we find an apocalyptic position and role being assigned to the church, while at the same time the church is finally turned into a political force, as the power of counter-revolution.

(iii) The Messianic Orientation towards the 'Signs and Wonders' of the Spirit

Messianic ecclesiology developed at the same time and with the help of the same phenomena, but its interpretation was a diametrically opposite one. It too was founded on an interpretation of the revolutionary 'signs of the times', in their bearing on the end of history. But here the French Revolution was greeted like a messianic event. 'The revolutionary desire to realize the kingdom of God is the propulsive point of all progressive education and the beginning of modern history,' declared Friedrich Schlegel.[85]

> Now I maintain that, even without the spirit of the seer, one can prophesy to the human race, according to the aspects and portents of our own days, the achievement of this purpose, and thereby at the same time the further advance of the same towards still better things; for such an advance can no longer become entirely regressive. A phenomenon of this kind *can never again be forgotten*, because it has disclosed a predisposition and capacity for improvement in human nature,

said Immanuel Kant, and interpreted the French Revolution with concepts borrowed from Thomist sacramental terminology: It is 'a historical sign (*signum rememorativum, demonstrativum, prognosticon*)' because it shows a 'tendency of the human race as a whole'.[86] The fact that his understanding of the 'historical sign' is in the direction of 'signs and wonders', but not in the direction of the apocalyptic portents of the end, is shown, not only by the sacramental terminology he is drawing upon, but also by his interpretation of the Enlightenment through the symbol of the exodus as 'emergence from a self-imposed minority' to the freedom of adulthood and a free use of the understanding; and by his millenarian interpretation of the present as a time of transition from belief in the church to a pure belief in reason. In this again the transition takes place to the continual approximation to the church of an invisible kingdom of God on earth, which unites all men for all time.[87]

We must also consider the history of that Protestant tradition which saw Christianity as 'the religion of freedom', human rights as the realization of the kingdom of God, and popular sovereignty as the coming of age of free citizens; and here we may take Richard Rothe as an example.[88] For Rothe the revolutionary struggles for freedom are not the abomination of desolation; in his view the Enlightenment's free use of the understanding was not atheism, neither was Christianity's estrangement from the church a sign of its downfall. For him these things are rather 'the signs and wonders' of the liberating Spirit.

> If we want to find our bearings in the present state of Christianity, then the prerequisite is a recognition that the ecclesiastical stage in Christianity's historical development is a thing of the past, and that the Christian spirit has already entered its moral, i.e., its political period. If the church is the essential form of Christianity's existence, then – and this we must honestly admit – it is nowadays in a lamentable condition; and this state of affairs did not begin yesterday either. . . . But Christianity in its inmost being will go beyond the church; it desires as its organism nothing less than the whole organism of human life in general, that is to say, the state. Its purpose is essentially to secularize itself ever more completely, that is, to put off the ecclesiastical forms which it was forced to assume on its entry into the world, and to put on the general forms of human existence: that is to say, the moral form of life *per se*.[89]

For by secularizing itself Christianity gives moral form to society. By proceeding from particular ecclesiastical forms of existence to general political ones, it humanizes politics. The church's approach to the kingdom of God takes place in this transition from the ecclesiastical to the moral, from hierarchy to universal Christianity, from religion to life, and from faith to political responsibility. God ultimately desires the state, the perfected state, the moral kingdom of God on earth, because he wants people who have arrived at full maturity. Once this is achieved the church will have become superfluous, since it was a transitional institution, designed for the education of men. Its goal has been reached, for it is there not for its own sake or for its own expansion but for the sake of the kingdom of God. The 'signs and wonders' of the history of the Spirit which Rothe saw in Enlightenment, science, independent morality, the democratic interpretation of the state, as well as a growing sense of freedom, made him conclude that the period of transition had come. 'The pious church-goer belongs to the past.'[90] All that remains now is the Christian as citizen in the perfected kingdom of morality and culture. As a result of the world-wide historical illumination of the notion of morality, today 'the Christian spirit', which is 'the exalted Christ himself', is in the course of giving up its religious and ecclesiastical formations, taking on instead the general forms of morality and politics. Of course Rothe did not believe that the present political situation was already a state of perfection; but in principle Christianity had arrived at the new level in which it was a matter of a continual approach to that perfection. The 'moral state' which he envisaged as the final purpose of the divine history, and the freedom which he saw as the goal of the history of the Spirit, were utopias; but they were utopias designed to regulate morality and the mature Christian's free use of the understanding. He did not want to dissolve the church in any existing nation or state; but he wanted to raise the existing churches and nations into 'the moral state' which can only be one, and hence can only be a single and universal world-state.

Rothe also developed an expressly political theology on the basis of his interpretation of the signs of the times. But he did not politicize the particular churches on the basis of dogmatic premises; instead he wanted to make universal Christendom, in its coming of age, conscious of its ethical and political task in world history. It is not the clerical office which enjoys the ultimate divine mandate behind all worldly orders (as in Vilmar), but the layman; for the layman is part of the movement of the 'Christian spirit', which has entered into its 'political age'. The only task now left for the cleric is the 'skilful conduct of an . . . orderly retreat'.[91] Because Christianity has left its ecclesiastical for its ethical age, it has thereby also entered its universal historical era. Rothe's progress from the church to Christianity has as its premise the interpretation of 'the signs of the times' as signs and wonders of the history of the Spirit.[92]

Did Rothe make the virtue of political Christianity out of the church's necessity, just as, conversely, Vilmar and the apocalyptic writers made an ecclesiastical virtue out of the revolutionary necessity of the world? What do 'the signs of the times' say, and in the light of what expectation of the future ought they to be interpreted? The problem is just as relevant today as it was in the nineteenth century. At that time it was the French Revolution which gave European history its revolutionary keynote, whether it was interpreted positively or negatively. Today it is the protest against the North Atlantic centres of power, the anti-colonialist and anti-imperialist struggles for freedom carried on by the oppressed nations, and the ever wider class conflicts which give those revolutionary keynotes a world-wide connotation. The signs have become more numerous, but they are still the signs of the same facts. The interpretations of the signs of the times through which the church tries to find its bearings in history have hardly become any more numerous. They still follow the two basic patterns of messianism or apocalyptic. The liberation of African and Asian peoples is welcomed by some people as 'a sign and wonder' in the history of the Spirit. Others view it with apprehension as the revolt of terrorists and the portent of the end of the world. Accordingly the opposition between the anti-revolutionary conservative choice and the revolutionary progressive choice among Christians all over the world is simply being intensified. Apocalyptic terrorism on the one hand and messianic enthusiasm on the other are threatening to lead to a split in the churches through opposing political ecclesiologies. There can be no doubt that both of them, with their obsession with the end-time, are eminently political.

(iv) Christ as 'the Sign of Hope' is also the Sign of Crisis

Ecclesiology based on 'the signs of the times' remains without any theological criterion. It is true that the particular eschatological expectations provide different categories of interpretation, but the impression remains that the picture of the times takes its colouring from what are fundamentally non-theological factors, that is to say, from unspoken political interests. *Dialectical theology* has hence turned away from this form of pious or impious inspection of the entrails of history, seeing in the person and history of Jesus Christ the one and only 'sign of the times' which has any relevance for faith.

> *Signs of the time* there are indeed; but not such as those after which apocalyptic fantasy peers. For 'God's Reign comes not so that it can be calculated; and none can say, "Lo here or there!" For lo, God's Reign is (all at once) in your midst!' (Luke 17.21). . . . The people, it is true, are blind to the true signs of the time; they can well enough interpret the signs of the heavens (clouds and wind) and know when it is going to rain or be hot – why can they not discern the signs of the present? . . . But what are the signs of the time? He himself! *His presence, his deeds, his message!*[93]

This christological concentration by the church on the one sign with which it began is necessary if the church is to get away from the time-conditioned pessimism or optimism which determine the speculations of disaster or salvation history. It is unavoidable, if the political interests which tacitly dominate those depictions of our times and our morality are to be submitted to the interest of Christ.

As the church of Christ, the church lives in the 'today' of Christ's messianic mission and presence (Luke 4.18ff.). All considerations about the times of world history and the hour when history will end must take their bearings from this. An allegedly higher wisdom based on a theology of history cannot take the place of the Christian proclamation. The proclamation of salvation – 'in season and out of season', we are told – must not be replaced by speculations about a secret divine plan of salvation which we are supposed to read from the course of history. In that case the morning papers would be the Bible. But the restricted christology of 'the signs of the times' and the concentration of the eschatology of world history on the eschatological proclamation are themselves bound to lead to questions about history. For what is preached and maintained is one thing – but the consciousness of the time in which it is preached and maintained is another. It is impossible to overlook the fact that the proclamation of salvation is simultaneously a revelation of disaster, simply because salvation is only proclaimed and not yet consummated. It cannot be forgotten that the universal call to the decision of faith, by virtue of this decision, itself brings about the separation between believers and non-believers. Rightly though the church sees itself as the people and the vanguard of the universal kingdom of freedom, it is equally important for it to realize that through its particularity it acts like leaven to produce discord. Neither world history nor eschatology provide any explanation for this double effect of the proclamation of faith and of the church, which could help the church to hold aloof from its charge in order to withdraw into the ghetto of 'the little flock'. But neither can christology provide any explanation through which the church could disregard the shadows of unbelief, of division and of discord which accompany it, in order to adapt itself to the progress of society.

It is in its very character as the saving leaven that the church is also the opposite; and it is in its character as proclamation of the righteousness of God that the gospel also reveals the world under the divine wrath. Just because it proclaims that salvation is near it provokes crises. Where belief comes into being, unbelief awakes. Where people lay hold of salvation, temptation comes. It is wrong to wallow in this dark, gloomy side of Christianity's mission and expansion, let alone to seek to bring on the coming of the end with 'apocalyptic pleasure' over crises and downfalls. For the declared intention of the gospel is not to provoke disbelief, separation and conflict, but to awaken faith, fellowship and peace. Disbelief, separation and conflict are not a call for apocalyptic declarations which serve the self-justification of believers; they are a call solely for ceaseless and still more vigorous witness to the justifying and liberating gospel. On the other hand, however, joy in the gospel does not mean that we should not take the disbelief, the separation and the conflict seriously.

If we follow the christological concentration of the 'signs of the times' and if we start from the evangelical mission of the church, then the point at issue is in the first place the 'signs and wonders' which accompany the messianic exodus in the history of the Spirit. To discover them in the historical context of the proclamation and the spread of the gospel that leads to freedom, means perceiving Christ in the history of the Spirit. Only afterwards and in addition, and therefore to a secondary degree, can 'the signs of the end' then be perceived as well – the signs of the growing crisis in world history. 'Where there is danger, the salutary also grows', said Hölderlin hopefully. Ernst Bloch realistically expressed the reverse side of this hope: 'Where the salutary is near, the danger grows.'[94] The 'signs and wonders' take place in the liberating history of the Spirit of Christ. But the Spirit also provokes – as well as these signs and wonders and on their behalf – the signs of crisis and danger. World history is not led towards its fulfilment in a continuous series of advances through the proclamation of Christ's victory and through the experiences of liberation in the Spirit; on the contrary, history becomes increasingly fraught with crisis. Just because Christ is 'the sign of the times', crises arise round him. These are not the portents of total crisis; they are always merely signs of particular and specific conflicts. For it is not world crisis that leads to Christ's parousia; it is Christ's parousia that brings this world with its crises to an end. Historical and personal crises are not signs of the last judgment, for they are always historical opportunities at the same time. Hence the signs that we have spoken about are not to be understood as signs of the end, but as what they are: signs of history.

4. *The Church in the Trinitarian History of God*

In the final paragraphs of this chapter our aim will be to explore the church's mission and its meaning, existence and functions in the comprehensive framework of the history of God's dealings with the world. This is as necessary as it is difficult. It is necessary, because no single life can comprehend itself without comprehending itself in the framework of the whole in which it acquires its significance. Every theology of history remains at the mercy of arbitrarily determined 'signs of the times' as long as it fails to grasp history itself in a trinitarian sense. It is difficult, because such an enterprise is all too easily exposed to the reproach of being remote from specific events, from experience and practice, and falls under suspicion of being a speculation with empty concepts.

Still, 'perceptions without concepts are blind', said Kant. The intuition or perception of the church in its field of tension between faith and experience, in its relationship to the history of Christ and to the history of the world, remains in our case blind as long as it does not press forward to the concept of the history of God's dealings with the world. But Kant also said: 'Concepts without intuition are empty.' The concept of the history of God's dealings with the world remains in our case 'empty' as long as it is not related to the intuition or perception of the church in the history of Christ and, further, in the history of the world.

In what follows we shall try to grasp the single event, the special experience and the particular practice in the context and in the movements of the history of God. That cannot be called 'abstract'. To be abstract rather means isolating the single event from its history, the special experience from the context of life to which it belongs, and the particular action from its period. We isolate objects in order to know them, by separating them from their contexts, subjecting them to a single viewpoint and excluding all other aspects. This is the way we arrive at definitions and clear judgments. True, some people believe that they are thinking 'in quite concrete terms' when they talk about 'the historical Jesus' instead of about the history of Jesus' relation with God, as this is expressed in the title 'Son of God'; or when they talk about getting rid of a class-stratified society, instead of about the future of history as it is described through the symbol of hope, 'the kingdom of God'. In actual fact this 'quite concrete' way of thinking is highly abstract, for it detaches one aspect from all the wealth of life's interrelations and particularizes it. The intuitions, experiences and actions which are isolated from the total cohesion to which they belong then become sporadic, blind and meaningless. Abstract, isolating thinking must hence be set aside again by integrating thinking and must be guided into life. This integrating thinking – or speculative thinking, as it used to be called – has nothing to do with remoteness from practice or poverty of experience. It attempts to understand the event in its history, experience as part of the whole of life, and action in time; and in this way it tries to understand the meaning of what is individual too.

Without an understanding of the particular church in the framework of the universal history of God's dealings with the world, ecclesiology remains abstract and the church's self-understanding blind. This will lead almost unavoidably to the danger that the church will lend a universal claim to quite limited tasks, and will support interests conditioned by a particular period with the solemnity of the absolute.

Particularist thinking is isolated, selective and really culpably self-satisfied thinking, which nevertheless – centred absolutely and relentlessly on its selected area – comes up with the claim of being complete, of being able to do all that is necessary on its own, if necessary by force.[95]

On the other hand, side by side with this goes the suicidal tendency to dissipate our own particularity, which cannot be universal, in another social particularity of history. These two dangers can only be avoided if we understand our own inescapable particularity in its significance for the whole. We avoid neither the false claim nor the false despair if we stop short at the question: does the salvation of the world come through the church? It is only when we reverse the question that we can move a step further: does the church come through the salvation of the world?

If a single and special phenomenon like the church wants to understand itself in the history of God's dealings with the world, then it has to conceive itself in the movement of this history, for it is itself standing in the midst of that movement, not above it and not at its end. But how is any definite statement possible in respect of a history conceived in terms of movement? Can the knowledge which in this history is always incomplete commit itself to a concept? Knowledge is faced with the task of understanding events which are themselves caught up in movement; and thus of understanding itself in such events as knowledge kept in movement by the still moving event. When we here call the total context in which the church ought to understand itself 'the history of God's dealings with the world', this means in the first place the living quality of God's relationship to the world, which can only be understood properly through the knowledge which that relationship moves and enlivens. If we talk about 'the trinitarian history of God', this then means the livingness of God which has moved out of itself, which cannot be fixed by any definition, but can only be understood through participating and engaged knowledge. This circumstance is theologically expressed in the phrase that enlivened, involved and engaged knowledge of the living God comes about 'in the Holy Spirit'. The movement of the trinitarian history of God's dealings with the world includes the movement of knowledge of that history. It is not possible for this knowledge to fix the history of God to a single point. Knowledge of God in the movement of the history of God, and in its being moved through the history of God, is like the flight of a bird and has no fixed abode.[96] It contains no Archimedean fulcrum from which one could move the world, for the world has been brought into movement, together with all

its fixed standpoints. For that reason the church can only understand its own position or abode in participation in the movement
of the history of God's dealings with the world, and therefore as
one element in this movement. Its attempts to understand itself
are attempts at understanding the movement of the trinitarian
history of God's dealings with the world; and its attempts to understand this movement are attempts at understanding itself.

(i) The Sending of the Son and the Spirit by the Father
   The determining outlook of seeing oneself in the movement of
the world through the history of God, starts from the perception
of the history of Christ and from the experience of the Spirit in
the light of its sending.
   The history of Christ is interpreted in the light of its origin. The
gospels relate the history of Jesus as the history of the Messiah
sent from God into the world for the purpose of salvation and
anointed with the Spirit of the new creation. They present the
history of Jesus in the light of his sending, his mission. For Mark,
Jesus' messianic commission begins when the Spirit is conferred
on him in baptism (1.9ff.). For Matthew (1.18ff.) and Luke
(1.26ff.) it begins earlier with his conception through the Holy
Spirit. For John (1.11ff.) the sending of Jesus begins before the
foundation of the world in the eternity of the Father. In the
history of tradition, therefore, the view taken of the history of
Jesus in the light of his mission is increasingly transcendent and
comprehensive. Linguistically 'sending' – πέμπειν – means
primarily the sending or mission as such, the fact of sending and
being sent; whereas 'sending forth' – ἐξαποστέλλειν – stresses a
'specific and unique' aspect of sending.[97] John stresses the fact of
the sending of the one sent by God into the world for its salvation, whereas Paul emphasizes the sending forth of the Son 'when
the time had fully come' (Gal. 4.4–6). In both cases the word
'sending' is intended to comprehend the perception of the
whole appearance, history and meaning of Christ in the light of
God.
   If the messianic history of Jesus is understood in the light of his
mission, then theological reflection must ask about the origin of
and reason for this mission, in order to understand the particular
appearance of Jesus in the context shown.[98] Is the mission of
Jesus a chance historical event or does it find its foundation in

God himself? If its foundation is in God himself, does it then correspond to God, or does God only appear in this manner, a manner which perhaps does not correspond to him at all? If we push our question further back like this, then we cannot find anything in God which is antecedent to the sending of Jesus and in which this sending was not included. As God appears in history as the sending Father and the sent Son, so he must earlier have been in himself. The relation of the one who sends to the one sent as it appears in the history of Jesus thus includes in itself an order of origin within the Trinity, and must be understood as that order's historical correspondence. Otherwise there would be no certainty that in the messianic mission of Jesus we have to do with God himself. The relations between the discernible and visible history of Jesus and the God whom he called 'my Father' correspond to the relation of the Son to the Father in eternity. The *missio ad extra* reveals the *missio ad intra*. The *missio ad intra* is the foundation for the *missio ad extra*. Thus theological reflection moves inevitably from the contemplation of the sending of Jesus from the Father to God himself. 'These movements or *processiones* in the Trinity are the deepest ground for the sendings or *missiones* of the Son and the Holy Spirit.'[99] From the Trinity of the sending of Jesus we can reason back to the Trinity in the origin, in God himself, so that – conversely – we may understand the history of Jesus as the revelation of the living nature of God.[100]

The experience of the Spirit is to be found in the experiences of the history of Christ which men have in their own history. It is the experience of faith in which the mission of Christ and the trend of his history exerts its influence in men and women. It is the experience of fellowship with Christ and through him with the one who sent him. It is, in faith and in fellowship, the experience of creative freedom for the renewal of life. This history of Christ in the Spirit is also interpreted in the light of its origin, so that it is understood as the history of God's dealings with the world. The experiences of the Holy Spirit are comprehended in the light of the sending of the Spirit. That is why Paul puts the sending of the Spirit parallel to the sending of the Son: 'When the time had fully come, God sent forth his Son. . . . Because you are sons, God has sent the Spirit of his Son' (Gal. 4.4, 6).

John too traces back the experiences of the Spirit to his sending by the Father and the Son (14.26; 15.26 and frequently elsewhere). The history of the Spirit as a whole is understood in the light of its origin. That is why here too theological reflection must enquire about *the origin of this sending of the Spirit*. The same reasons which led from the concept of the history of Christ in the light of his sending to the eternal generation of the Son by the Father within the Trinity, lead here from the experience of the Spirit in the light of his divine sending to his eternal procession within the Trinity, from the Father, or from the Father and the Son.[101] If this were not so experience of the Spirit could not be termed experience of God; and fellowship with Jesus, the Son, and his Father could not be understood as fellowship with God. But this is just what has to be said if the experience of Jesus and of the one who sent him takes place in the Holy Spirit. 'In what takes place between the man Jesus and us when we may become and be Christians, God Himself lives.'[102] The one who liberates men and leads them into the messianic fellowship of Jesus is God the Holy Spirit, because he is the Spirit of the love of God, Father and Son 'in himself first'.

The inference about the eternal generation of the Son by the Father drawn from the contemplation of the history of Jesus in the light of his sending and the inference about the eternal procession of the Spirit in God himself, drawn from the experience of the Spirit in the light of his sending, are theologically necessary if we are to grasp the history of Jesus and the experience of the Spirit in the totality of the divine history. Here the inference from the historical relations of the Trinity to the relations in its eternal origin has two functions. On the one hand it makes it clear that in the sending of the Son and in the sending of the Spirit men have to do with God himself; that God corresponds to himself in this history of his dealings with men. On the other hand, however, it presents the divine secret as being from the very beginning, and in its very origins, an open secret.

This second aspect deserves particular attention: the Trinity in the origin is the foundation of the Trinity in the sending, and hence the Trinity in the sending reveals the Trinity in the origin as being from eternity an open Trinity. It is open for its own sending. It is 'open' in order that it may 'make itself open' – may manifest itself – in the coming of the Spirit.[103] It is open for men and for all creation. The life of God within the Trinity cannot be conceived of as a closed circle – the symbol of perfection and self-sufficiency. A Christian doctrine of the Trinity which is bound to the history of Christ and the history of the Spirit must conceive the Trinity as the Trinity of the sending and seeking love of God which is open from its very origin. The triune God is the God who is open to man, open to the world and open to time.

In the sending of the Son and the Spirit the Trinity does not only manifest what it is in itself; it also opens itself for history and experience of history. We cannot speak of the love of God as being open to the world and time in the way that we can of the creature, which has to be open to the world and time out of 'deficiency of being', but we can do so on the basis of the divine fullness of being and superabundance of life which desires to communicate itself. If we therefore talk about a 'history of the Trinity',[104] we do not mean a history of deficiency and death; we mean the history of the self-communicating livingness of God which overcomes death. This history of the Trinity opens up through the sending of the Son and the sending of the Spirit. But just because of that, the inference drawn from the contemplation of the history of Christ and the experience of the Spirit in the light of their sending does not yet embrace the whole trinitarian history of God's dealings with the world. The origin of this history is comprehended, but not yet its future.

(ii) The Origin and Future of the History of Christ

If we come back once again to the contemplation of the history of Christ, we discover that this history can be viewed from two sides: from its origin and from its future.[105] If our enquiry is directed towards the past, then this history is understood in the light of the sending and mission of Christ. If we think forwards, then it is seen from the point of view of its goal. Its origin stands in the light of his messianic mission. Its future stands in the light of his resurrection from the dead. Both perspectives belong to a full understanding of the history of Christ. It must be comprehended in the light of his sending and in the light of his glorification, in the light of his origin and in the light of his future, and in such a way that both angles are continually related to one another.

The same thing is true of the experience of the Holy Spirit. In it the meaning of the history of Christ is revealed to men through faith, new obedience and new fellowship. But in so far as this takes place, men are also set in the powers and movements of the new creation. Understood in the light of his sending, the Spirit links up with the history of Christ. Understood from the angle of his goal, he brings about the new creation. The Holy Spirit is hence both the manifesting and the newly creating power. Both perspectives belong together to the understanding of the history of the Spirit. It too must be understood both in the light of its origin and at the same time in the light of its future.

As far as an understanding of the history of Christ and the Spirit in the history of God's dealings with the world is concerned, it follows that the perspectives of this history in the light of the sending of the Son and the Spirit must be complemented by its perspectives in the light of the glorification of the Son and the Spirit. The full implications of the history of Christ and the Spirit cannot be understood in any other way. In the light of the sending of Jesus and against the background of the order of origin within the Trinity, tradition has always stressed the incarnation, the baptism, the ministry, the passion and Christ's giving of himself to death on the cross; and has stressed them in that order. His sending was consummated in his self-giving and his incarnation was consummated in his death. The eschatological statements about the history of Christ, his transfiguration, resurrection and exaltation and the consummation of the lordship of God, retreated into the background. There was a one-sided interest in Christ's origin and, casting back from his history, theologians asked about the ground of that history in time and eternity. If we now enquire eschatologically about Christ's future, the purpose of his mission and the meaning of his history, then we are not criticizing the previous doctrines about the origin within the Trinity and the trinitarian sending; we are simply taking them further, in accordance with the double understanding of the history of Christ 'in the light of his sending' and 'in the light of his resurrection'. We are then looking to the trinitarian glorification and the eschatological unity of God. Starting with the origin of the history of Christ and of the Spirit from God, we come to the eschatological goal of the history of Christ in the completion of God's history with the world.

(iii) The Glorifying of the Father and the Son through the Spirit
When we consider the history of Christ in the light of its future,

the concept of glory is at the centre of attention.[106] In both the Old and the New Testaments *doxa* means the divine power and glory, the divine unfolding of splendour and beauty. *Doxa* is the term used both for the godhead of the Father and for the godhead of Christ. Christ was raised from the dead by the glory of the Father (Rom. 6.4). He was taken up into the glory of the Father (I Tim. 3.16). For the glory of God the Father he was exalted after he had humbled himself to death on the cross and was made *kyrios* over all things (Phil. 2.11). Whereas for Old Testament prophecy 'the glory of God' was the quintessence of the promised divine future and the hoped-for liberation of creation – 'the whole earth is full of his glory' (Isa. 6.3; cf. 40.5) – the raising of Jesus through the glory, into the glory and for the sake of the glory of the Father means that he was raised into this promised and hoped-for divine future. For that reason the eschatological statements about the coming, liberating glory of God can be proleptically transferred to Christ. If he is raised into the coming glory of the Father, then this future is already present in him, and in him the glory has already entered into the misery of this present time. That is why in this world of sin and death the crucified 'lord of glory' stands for the coming 'God of glory' (I Cor. 2.8; Acts 7.2). In the lordship of the one who was crucified the coming rule of God has taken on historical form. That is why the glory of the Father has appeared in the glorifying of Christ. The radiance of the divine glory is reflected in the face of Christ and through him illuminates the hearts of men, as the light shone out of darkness on the first day of creation (II Cor. 4.6).

The eschatological statements about the glory of Christ concern his eschatological existence after the resurrection. The application of the word *doxa* to the earthly Jesus is considerably restricted. In Luke the angels' hymn of praise at his lowly birth (Luke 2.9) and also his transfiguration on the mountain (9.28ff.) point to his future and can be termed an anticipation of his glorification. Only John talks about the glory of the earthly Jesus, about the glorifying of the Father in the suffering of the Son and the glorifying of the Son in his death on the cross; and he does so because he describes the whole life of Jesus from a viewpoint focused on the exalted one.

In the eschatological interpretation of the history of Christ, which sees it in the light of its future, this history is understood as the beginning of God's glorification. The Son glorifies the Father through his obedience. The Father glorifies the Son through his resurrection and exaltation.

When we consider the history of the Spirit in the light of its future, glorification is also at the centre. Fellowship with Christ in the Spirit is the fellowship of Christ's sufferings and the fellowship of his death. But in being this it is also at the same time the fellowship of his resurrection through newness of life and participation through hope in his life in glory (Rom. 6; Phil. 3). The mission of Christ achieves its purpose when men and creation are united with God. In this union God is glorified through men and in it they partake of the glory of God himself. That is why Christ is called 'the hope of glory' (Col. 1.27) and why we expect that he 'will glorify our lowly body to be like his glorious body' (Phil. 3.21). The power which glorifies men in the glory of God is the Holy Spirit. That is why he is called the first fruits and guarantee (AV 'earnest') of glory (Rom. 8.23; II Cor. 5.5). He glorifies Christ in believers and unites them with him. Through union with Christ in the Holy Spirit the coming glory already becomes efficacious in the present life. That is why the hope of the assailed glory of the present fellowship of Christ is directed towards the unchallenged glory of the coming fellowship with God. The Spirit glorifies the Father and the Son by freeing men for fellowship with them, filling men in their freedom with joy and thanksgiving. The glorifying of the Son and the Father through the Spirit sets men on the road towards the glory for which they themselves are destined.

In the movements of glorification the experience of the Spirit is understood in the light of its future, as the first fruits and advance payment of the perfected glory of man in God's glorification in him: the Spirit glorifies the Son and the Father in creation. Together with the Son he glorifies the Father. This trinitarian history of glorification points beyond itself to the goal of the trinitarian history of God's dealings with the world. Here the thinking which directs its questions back to the origin is out of place; what belongs here is the eschatological thinking that hurries eagerly ahead towards the goal and towards the consummation. For this points the trinitarian history of glorifications towards the glorified Trinity at the end. But this will only glorify itself in the liberated and new creation. The glory of God is only completed (Rom.

11.36) when the 'creation at the beginning' is consummated by the 'new creation at the end' and when the whole redeemed existence joyfully raises the hymn of eternal thanksgiving: 'To him be the *doxa* for ever and ever' (Rev. 1.6). Wherever on the way to this goal the gospel is preached to the poor, sins are forgiven, the sick are healed, the oppressed are freed and outcasts are accepted, God is glorified and creation is in part perfected.

The eschatological meaning of the messianic mission of Christ and the Spirit lies in the glorifying of God and the liberation of the world, in the sense that God is glorified through the liberation and healing of creation, and that he does not desire to be glorified without his liberated creation.

If we compare the two directions in which the history of Christ and the Spirit can be understood in the history of God's dealings with the world, we find correspondences, additions and one irreversible direction. The Trinity in the sending is, from its eternal origin, open to the world and to men. For with this the history of God's seeking love is begun. The Trinity in the glorification is, from its eschatological goal, open for the gathering and uniting of men and the whole creation with God and in God. In it the history of the gathering love of God is completed. Through the sending of the Son and the Spirit the history of the Trinity is opened for the history of the gathering, uniting and glorifying of the world in God and of God in the world. The opening and the completion correspond to one another in the openness of the triune God. 'The relationship of the divine persons to one another is so wide that it has room for the whole world' (Adrienne von Speyr). At the end God has won his creation in its renewing consummation for his dwelling place. He comes to his glory in the joy of redeemed creation.

(iv) The 'Union' of God

When we speak about the sending and the glorification, we are talking in a highly concentrated way about the triune God. The Holy Spirit glorifies Christ in the world and the world in Christ to the glory of the Father. By effecting this he unites creation with the Son and the Father, as he unites the Son himself with the Father. As the force that glorifies, the Holy Spirit is also the power of unification.

In historical reflection, we work from the sending of the Son

and the Spirit back to the Trinity and arrive at the divine unity –
either by going back to the Father as 'source of the Godhead' or
by proceeding to the one divine nature behind the three persons.
In this scheme, the unity of God is viewed as that which is ontologically the foundation of the sendings of Son and Spirit (or
even as the foundation of the Trinity itself).[107] In the eschatological anticipation of history, however, the unity of God contains
within itself the whole union of creation with God and in God.
Eschatologically, the unity of God is therefore linked with the
salvation of creation, just as his glory is linked with his glorification through everything that lives and rejoices. Just as his glory is
presented to him from creation through the Spirit, so his unity
through the union of creation is also brought to him through the
Spirit. In the eschatological considerations of historical thinking,
the idea of the unity of God has a high soteriological content.
For that reason it would be better to talk in this respect about the
'union' of God.

Unusual though this phrase may sound to the West's way of
thinking about origins, there are none the less models for it in Old
Testament and Jewish thought. Franz Rosenzweig interprets the
Shema Israel as follows: 'To acknowledge God's unity – the Jew
calls it uniting God. For this unity is, in that it becomes; it is a
Becoming Unity. And this Becoming is laid on the soul of man and
in his hands.' Rosenzweig relates this 'divine union' in prayer to
that 'cutting off of God from himself' which is suggested in the
mystical doctrine of the Shekina:

> God himself cuts himself off from himself, he gives himself away to
> his people, he suffers with their sufferings, he goes with them into the
> misery of the foreign land, he wanders with their wanderings . . . God
> himself, in that he 'sells himself' to Israel – and what should be more
> natural for 'God our Father'! – and suffers its fate with it, makes him-
> self in need of redemption. In this way, in this suffering, the relation-
> ship between God and the remnant points beyond itself.[108]

Is not what is here, according to Rosenzweig, entrusted to Israel,
in an analogous way entrusted by Christian thinking to the Holy
Spirit, who through believers 'unites' God by glorifying him?
Does not God's separation from himself in order to suffer with his
people correspond on another level to the separation of God the
Father from his Son in the cross, in order that he might suffer
with the Godforsakenness of the godless and so vicariously abolish

it? How much more could the glorifying of the Son and the Father in the Spirit of liberation and of fellowship then be understood as the 'union' of the triune God! The unity of the triune God is the goal of the uniting of man and creation with the Father and the Son in the Spirit. The history of the kingdom of God on earth is nothing other than the history of the uniting of what is separated and the freeing of what is broken, in this being the history of the glorification of God. If the unity of God were described in the doctrine of the Trinity by *koinonia* instead of by *una natura*, this idea would not seem so unusual.

(v) The 'Experience' of God

Between the Trinity in its origins before time and the eschatological glorifying and unifying of God lies the whole history of God's dealings with the world. By opening himself for this history and entering into it in his seeking love through the sending of Christ and the Spirit, God also experiences this history of the world in its breadth and depth. We must drop the philosophical axioms about the nature of God. God is *not unchangeable*, if to be unchangeable means that he could not in the freedom of his love open himself to the changeable history of his creation. God is *not incapable of suffering* if this means that in the freedom of his love he would not be receptive to suffering over the contradiction of man and the self-destruction of his creation. God is *not invulnerable* if this means that he could not open himself to the pain of the cross. God is *not perfect* if this means that he did not in the craving of his love want his creation to be necessary to his perfection.

The history of the Son and of the Spirit therefore brings about, even for God himself within the Trinity, an experience, something 'new'.[109] After the Son's exaltation the relationship between the Father and the Son is no longer absolutely the same as before. The Father has become 'another' through the Son's self-giving, and the Son too has become 'another' through his experience of suffering in the world. Through his love for the Son, who experiences the sin of the world in his death on the cross, God experiences something which belongs essentially to the redemption of the world: he experiences pain. In the night when the Son dies on the cross, God himself experiences abandonment in the form of this death and this rejection. We must add that this is a new experience for God, for which he has laid himself open and prepared himself from eternity in his seeking love. God experiences the cross, but this also means that he has absorbed this death into eternal life, that he suffers it in order to give the forsaken world his life. Because of that he does not want to be glorified in any other way than through the glorification of the one who was crucified, 'the Lamb who was slain' (Rev. 5.12; 7.14; 12.10ff.). In becoming the 'eternal seal and stamp' of the lordship of God, the one who was crucified also becomes the eternal seal of God's glorification and of the eschatological trinity.

What applies to the experience of God in the history of the Son also applies in its own way to the experience of God in the history of the Spirit. God does not desire glory without his glorification through man and creation in the Spirit. God does not desire to find rest without the new creation of man and the world through the Spirit. God does not desire to be united with himself without the uniting of all things with him. It is in this context that the vision in Revelation belongs in which 'Salvation (*soteria*) is come to (RSV 'belongs to) our God and to the Lamb' (Rev. 7.10; 12.10; 19.1). The 'salvation' which God receives in the end is offered to him through glorification, through thanksgiving and the pleasure of the new creation in redeemed existence. The world-embracing pneumatology which we find in Revelation corresponds to the no less comprehensive christology of Paul, according to which the Son only completes his obedience to the Father when everything is put under his feet, when all dominion, authority and power, and finally death itself, have been destroyed, and when he gives the lordship entrusted to him to his Father, 'that God may be all in all' (RSV 'may be everything to every one'). The transference of lordship from the Son to the Father at the end-time is both the completion of the history of the liberation of the world and a happening within the Trinity. Analogously, the glorification of God in the Spirit at the end-time is also an event which perfects the world and at the same time a happening within the Trinity. God comes to his glory in that creation becomes free. Creation is perfected in that its unclouded joy glorifies God. 'Salvation' comprehends God and creation in the unity of doxology and soteriology.

The divine experience of history also has two sides to it. If we trace the thought of the sending of the Son consistently to the end, we are bound to talk about God's vulnerability, suffering and pain, in view of Christ's passion, his death on the cross and his descent into hell. God experiences suffering, death and hell. This is the way he experiences history.

If we think in the direction of the glorification, then – in view of the resurrection, exaltation and perfection of Christ, and remembering the history of the Spirit – we must talk about God's joy (as already in Isa. 62.4–5; Zeph. 3.17), God's happiness and felicity (I Tim. 1.11; 6.15; Luke 15.7; Matt. 25.21; John 15.11; 16.20; Rom. 14.17; 15.13).[110] This is the way God creates history.

God experiences history in order to effect history. He goes out of himself in order to gather into himself. He is vulnerable, takes suffering and death on himself in order to heal, to liberate and to confer new life. The history of God's suffering in the passion of the Son and the sighings of the Spirit serves the history of God's joy in the Spirit and his completed felicity at the end. That is the ultimate goal of God's history of suffering in the world. But once the joy of union is complete the history of suffering does not become obsolete and a thing of the past. As suffering that has been endured, and which has brought about liberation, eternal life and union, it remains the ground of eternal joy in the salvation of God and his new creation.

(vi) The Participation of the Church in the History of God

In the movements of the trinitarian history of God's dealings with the world the church finds and discovers itself, in all the relationships which comprehend its life. It finds itself on the path traced by this history of God's dealings with the world, and it discovers itself as one element in the movements of the divine sending, gathering together and experience. It is not the church that has a mission of salvation to fulfil to the world; it is the mission of the Son and the Spirit through the Father that includes the church, creating a church as it goes on its way. It is not the church that administers the Spirit as the Spirit of preaching, the Spirit of the sacraments, the Spirit of the ministry or the Spirit of tradition. The Spirit 'administers' the church with the events of word and faith, sacrament and grace, offices and traditions. If the church understands itself, with all its tasks and powers, in the Spirit and against the horizon of the Spirit's history, then it also understands its particularity as one element in the power of the Spirit and has no need to maintain its special power and its special charges with absolute and self-destructive claims. It then has no need to look sideways in suspicion or jealousy at the saving efficacies of the Spirit outside the church; instead it can recognize them thankfully as signs that the Spirit is greater than the church and that God's purpose of salvation reaches beyond the church.

The church participates in Christ's messianic mission and in the creative mission of the Spirit. We cannot therefore say *what* the church is in all circumstances and what it comprises in itself. But we can tell *where* the church happens. The phrase 'The church is present where . . .', used in article VII of the Augsburg Confession and in article III of the Barmen Declaration, is a correct one, but it cannot be restricted merely to 'true proclamation' and 'a right administration of the sacraments'. Both are included, yet we shall have to say more comprehensively: the church is present wherever 'the manifestation of the Spirit' (I Cor. 12.7) takes place.

The church participates in the glorifying of God in creation's liberation. Wherever this takes place through the workings of the Spirit, there is the church. The true church is the song of thanksgiving of those who have been liberated.

The church participates in the uniting of men with one another, in the uniting of society with nature and in the uniting of creation with God. Wherever unions like this take place, however fragmentary and fragile they may be, there is the church. The true church is the fellowship of love.

Love participates in the history of God's suffering. Wherever men take up their cross and in their self-giving are made like the one who was crucified, wherever the sighings of the Spirit are heard in the cry for freedom, there is the church. The true church is 'the church under the cross'.

But in suffering and under the cross the church also participates in the history of the divine joy. It rejoices over every conversion and every liberation, because it is itself the fellowship of the converted and the liberated. Wherever the joy of God can be heard, there is the church. The true church is joy in the Spirit.

Thus the whole being of the church is marked by participation in the history of God's dealings with the world.[111] The Apostles' Creed expresses this truth by integrating the *credo ecclesiam* in the *credo in deum triunum*. And no ecclesiology should sink below this level.

III

THE CHURCH OF JESUS CHRIST

'Without Christ, no church.' This simple sentence expresses an incontrovertible fact. There is only a church if and as long as Jesus of Nazareth is believed and acknowledged as the Christ of God. But the sentence also raises the question of the reciprocal relationship between knowledge of Christ and acknowledgment of the church. The way one thinks about Christ is also the way one thinks about the church. What one believes about him and expects from him also gives interest in the church its stamp. The doctrine of the church, therefore, where it concerns the foundation of the church and the conditions in which it exists, is indissolubly connected with the doctrine of Jesus, the Christ of God. The name the church gives itself – the church of Jesus Christ – requires us to see Christ as the subject of his church and to bring the church's life into alignment with him. Thus ecclesiology can only be developed from christology, as its consequence and in correspondence with it.

But on the other hand the history of the Christian faith since its beginnings in the New Testament shows that the titles given to Christ, in which the churches express their faith and their hope, are historically conditioned, vary from time to time and change in substance. Like them, the self-understanding of the church is also historically conditioned, varies from time to time and changes in substance. The image of Christ and the image of the church also always reflect 'the spirit of the age', the political and economic circumstances, and the cultural and social conditions, in which the churches are living.

In intention faith's consciousness is directed towards the 'object' of faith, but functionally it is conditioned by the situation.

We must distinguish between the two if we are to uncover the tensions which arise for the Christian faith from this fact. In intention all the variable christological titles in history are related to that one fixed point which is summed up in the name of *Jesus* and the unique history of this person. All the christological titles, from 'Messiah', 'Son of man' and *'kyrios'* to *'Logos'*, 'example' and 'representative', are seeking to say who this Jesus is and what he means. Their truth must therefore be tested against Jesus himself and his history, and it is here that their meaning has to be understood. In intention the statements about the church – 'the body of Christ', 'the house of God', 'God's people', 'the communion of saints', etc. – are also directed towards the person of Jesus and his history, by way of the christological titles on which they depend. Their content can only be criticized or find legitimation from this point. But functionally the church's titles, like the titles of Christ, belong to their particular period. The church belongs to the field of tension between the history of Christ and its own contemporary history, and is itself this field of tension. If it wanted to understand itself merely out of its knowledge of the history of Christ, it would be 'orthodox' in the sense that it would be taking the picture of Christ and the church held in past times in an absolute sense and would be forgetting the picture's historical conditioning. If it wanted to understand itself merely from the history of its own time, it would become the religious reflection of present conditions and movements and ought, if it were honest, to strike the name of Christ out of its title. If it accepts the tensions at the point of intersection between the history of Christ as it is realized in the present, and contemporary history, then it becomes alienated from its environment. It will then, through the present realization of Christ, be alienated from its environment in Christ's way. The fixation of its past form through the repetition of ancient rites, symbols and formulae always leads the church into the wrong sort of non-contemporaneity with the present. It is only the present realization of the person, the mission, the cross and the future of Christ himself that brings the church into its necessary and hopeful non-contemporaneity with the present. The consciousness which is directed towards Christ will then alter the subjective conditions of its consciousness and the specific form of its existence in society. It will then, at least partly, see through the plausible complex of society, the classes, races and generations in which it has settled down, as being a complex of alienation and will get beyond the blindness of its own professional establishment.

Christ's strange nature alienates contemporaries, and even the devout who have settled down in contemporary society. But the strangeness of Christ cannot be a matter of historical remoteness. That could be endured and overcome, as it is in analogous traditions. It must be a matter of the strangeness of his mission, his cross and his promise; for in no other way could the church's alienation from its environment (an alienation which he brings about) be legitimated, nor would it be a hopeful alienation. It is only when the church is alienated from its environment in Christ's way, that it can perceive and show in an alienated world that the kingdom of God which Christ has promised is our home. It is this conflict which is at issue whenever the church in its contemporary environment dares to appeal to Christ and is prepared to hear his voice and no other. It will then be drawn into his mission: the messianic liberation of those who are imprisoned in its present day. It will then be drawn into his destiny of passion and bear its cross. It will then return to his future and answer for its hope.

1. *Jesus and the Church*

If the church does not see itself as 'the church of society', or as the 'German', or 'white', or 'male' church (even though it can often enough really be described as these things in terms of its actual situation), but calls itself instead 'the church of Christ', then it will also have to make Christ its starting point in its own self-understanding. But in what relationship does the church stand to Christ and – according to its faith – what is the relationship of Christ to the church? The answers that are given differ considerably. Christ's priority over the church finds clearest expression in Question 54 of the Heidelberg Catechism. There the question: 'What dost thou believe about the holy, catholic, Christian church?' is given a surprisingly indirect answer:

> That out of the whole human race the Son of God gathers, protects and upholds a community of the elect destined for eternal life, through His Spirit and Word, in the unity of faith, from the beginning of the world unto its end; and that I am a living member of the same and will eternally remain so.

The question about the being of the church is here answered by a confession of faith in Christ and what he does. The ecclesiological question is given a christological answer. The being of the church is described through the activities of Christ, who 'chooses, gathers, protects and upholds'.[1] The church has its true being in the work of Christ. That excludes an independent ontology of the church and permits merely the account of the history of Christ's acts. He works through 'Spirit and Word' (the mention of the Spirit before the Word is surprising in a Reformation catechism but is correct in view of the breadth of the Spirit and the abundance of the Spirit's gifts).[2] The activity of God's Son is universal. It extends in space to 'the whole human race' and in time to all generations 'from the beginning of the world to the end'.[3] However the pre-Christian workings of the Son of God were conceived of by the authors Ursin and Olevianus, what is meant is the spatial and temporal lack of restriction. The 'Son of God' is neither a lord of the church nor a cultic hero; he is the Christ of the one God for the whole human race. His choosing, gathering and protective activity creates the church, not as an institution for salvation or a cultic group, but as a brotherhood to which the individual can profess loyalty as a 'living member'. Ultimately, the election, gathering and preservation of the church are not an end in themselves but serve 'eternal life', as the final goal of Christ's activity, and of the church created out of that activity, is called. This outlook is reflected in the individual's assurance of 'remaining for ever' in this fellowship. It is the assurance of hope found in persevering to the end.[4]

What is missing in this declaration in the catechism is the positive world-wide aspect of Christ's mission and the mission of the church.[5] The whole human race only seems to be material for the election and gathering of the community of the saved, as if mankind were there for the church and not the church for mankind. We also miss the call to service for the world and, finally, the vision of hope for the new heaven and the new earth. The fact that the Johannine eschatology of 'eternal life' was chosen suggests that we have here the misunderstanding of an unworldly hope. The answer to the question about the church, with its acknowledgment of the activity of Christ (which is in this form so curiously inadequate, even though it is justifiable in content) deserves to be adhered to.

But in modern times other formulas for an understanding of the relationship between the church and Christ have suggested themselves, because the christological presuppositions of the Heidelberg Catechism have become questionable.

(i) Was Jesus *the founder*, or rather *the foundation*, *of the Christian religion?* This statement was made by historicism and liberal theology in the age of the Enlightenment. People started from the history of Christianity and asked about its 'founder' because Christianity (unlike many other religions) harks back to a central figure. Jesus of Nazareth, who taught, suffered and died under the Roman empire, must somehow have founded Christianity, rather as Romulus and Remus founded Rome, or Plato was the foundation of Platonism or Aquinas of Thomism. To this way of thinking, the 'founder' lays the foundation stone without leaving behind any binding regulations about what should be built on top of it, and how. One can continue to build on this foundation, or one can deviate from it. With the help of this idea, the church can certainly appeal to Jesus of Nazareth as its founder, but it need not allow itself to be disturbed in its historical development by remembrance of him. Everything that we find disconcerting about his mission, his fate and his hope can be reduced to its historical context and thus made innocuous.

(ii) Was Jesus *the founder of the church as an institution?* This model goes beyond the earlier 'founder' idea.[6] If the church sees itself as an institution established by Jesus, and the Christian religion as a religion devised by a particular individual, then it was called into life by a legal act. At the same time it was given an unalterable testamentary definition. This is fixed by the founder's intention and determines the form of the institution's administration. The church then does not derive from the free 'coming together of individuals who have been born again'. It lives according to the intention of its founder, who has preceded it, established it and determined its form. In using this model the student of the history of religions has sought to designate those religions which in addition to the deity pay attention to their founder – as has happened with Mohammed, with Moses and perhaps also with Buddha. But in the case of Christianity the picture is inadequate. It is true that by its very definition it reckons with the continuingly effective will of the founder of Christianity, but also with his irrevocable death. Apart from the fact that historically Jesus did not act as the founder of a religion and did not 'establish' any church, even in the literal sense – according to this picture only his intention as founder would survive his death. Interpreted as an institution set up by Jesus of Nazareth, the church would live from the last will and testament of a dead founder, but it would not live in his presence, or for his future. Its feasts – Christmas, Good Friday, Easter – would then be the 'founder's days' of an institution. This would certainly take account of the difference between the present and valid intention of the founder and its temporally conditioned execution, but not of the alienation which emanates from his death on the cross, nor the hope which kindles at his resurrection. Both models see the church's relationship to Jesus only in the context of influence emanating from a historical person. They indicate Jesus' historical precedence over the church, but not a qualitative difference.

(iii) Was Jesus the '*author of faith*' and the origin of the proclamation? The relationship between Jesus and the church can be depicted in a similar way when the specific character of the church is stressed. We then find continuity in the kerygma. Expressed as a christological statement, this means:

> Jesus is the Word. All the activity of Jesus is centred in the Word.[7] . . . That is why John always represents Jesus as saying almost nothing except that he is speaking the Word of God. For John, from beginning to end, Jesus is not meant to be the 'historical Jesus'; he is the 'Word', the Word of the Christian proclamation.[8]

Expressed as an ecclesiological statement this means:

> Therefore nothing needs to be taught about Jesus except 'that', nothing except *that* in his historical life the event had its beginning and the event continues in the preaching of the community.[9]

If then Christian proclamation and the history that communicates it coincide and are one and the same thing, then christology and ecclesiology can no longer be qualitatively distinguished, for the two meet in the doctrine of the kerygma. The name of Jesus then denotes the origin, the beginning or the establishment of the church's proclamation. This is no different if one replaces the kerygma by faith.[10] Jesus' faith then becomes the historical beginning and fruitful prototype of the Christian's faith. The continuing history of faith actually begins with the faith which Jesus calls to life. Christology and ecclesiology then coincide in the doctrine of faith. The ground of faith and the genesis of faith are here so closely intertwined that it is hard to make a logical distinction between them.[11]

In the case of the 'foundation' model, the history of Christ's work provides the continuity of christology and ecclesiology. In the 'founder' model it lies in the continuing action of Christ's will. But in the model which sees Christ as the origin of faith and proclamation, the difference between Christ and the church is abolished in the kerygma or in faith.

(iv) *Is the church 'the other Christ'?* This formula of the *Christus prolongatus* links up logically with the last one we have described.

> As Bellarmine acutely and subtly observes, the name 'Body of Christ, means more than that Christ is the Head of His mystical Body; it means also that He so upholds the Church and so, after a certain manner, lives in the Church that she may be said to be another Christ (*altera Christi persona*).

So we are told in the *Mystici Corporis* of 1943.[12] The difference is still preserved in the *quasi*, but stress lies on the identification. The idea that follows from 'the body of Christ' image of the church, that Christ can only be called the *totus Christus* together with the church, goes back to Augustine.[13] Heinrich Schlier has adopted it in his commentaries: because there is no head without a body, Christ must in the fullest sense be understood as a unity of head and body.[14] The church is the body of Christ. The body and the head together are Christ. Christ is therefore only Christ in the full sense together with the church. He adds that through the growth of the church the universe grows towards Christ, so that through the growth of his body Christ ultimately becomes the head of the universe and the ἀνακεφαλαίωσις τῶν πάντων is fulfilled. Here too the qualitative difference between Christ and the church seems to be dissipated. The Protestant inclination to resolve ecclesiology in christology corresponds to the opposite inclination on the Catholic side. But if one really thinks at all in terms of the image of the head and the body, then one must keep in mind the irreversible descent from the head to the body: the head rules the body, not the body the head. If it were otherwise the image would break down of its own accord. On the other hand the difference between the growth of the church and Christ's parousia must be preserved. The ἀνακεφαλαίωσις can only be hoped for from Christ's parousia; it cannot be brought about as the result of a process of ecclesiastical growth or through the development of cosmic maturity.[15]

This model of the church as *Christus prolongatus* proceeds from the incarnation of the Logos in Jesus of Nazareth and understands the church as the continuation of that incarnation. But it is then very difficult to capture the necessary difference between the incarnation of the Logos and Christ's indwelling in his church through the Spirit. Either the incarnation must be reduced to an indwelling of the Spirit in Jesus, which is then continued in the Spirit's indwelling in the church; or the indwelling of the Spirit must be understood as the continued incarnation of the Logos. In both cases the otherness of Christ, his mission, his death and his future for the church are all shut out. Out of the critical and liberating relationship of Christ to the church an affirmative, continuing or 'organic' relationship arises between the head and the body. This blurs Christ's freedom with regard to his church. Finally, in these ideas pneumatology and christology slide into one another and merge to such an extent that their difference and solidarity within the Trinity is no longer visible. The particular work of the Spirit is subordinated to the work of Christ.

(v) *Christ as the eschatological person.* The old dogmatic ecclesiology started from Christ as God's representative to the world and distinguished between the hypostatic union of Godhead and manhood in him, and the union in grace of the divine fellowship of the church through him. He is 'the only son'; believers are through grace the adopted sons of God. Fellowship with the qualitatively different Christ was conceived of as the work of the Spirit. Modern outlines of ecclesiology incline to assume a merely quantitative, historical difference. The 'work of the exalted Christ' is replaced by the continuing, demonstrable history of the work of the man of Nazareth. God's representative towards mankind is replaced by man's representative towards God. In this way modern christology and ecclesiology 'from below' come close in structure to the idea of the extended incarnation, which brings christology and ecclesiology into an organic connection with one another.[16] It is in this respect immaterial in what sense we talk about 'the historical Jesus' as the founder of the church; or whether we talk about the preaching and believing Jesus as the beginning and origin of the history of the proclamation and of faith; or whether we talk about a prolongation of the incarnation in the church. The relationship between Christ and the church is seen in a different light when we approach it from the end instead of the beginning. In the light of his giving of himself to death on the cross and his resurrection from the dead to be exalted as *Kyrios*, the differences between christology and ecclesiology, and the things they have in common, come out more clearly. As New Testament research has shown, all the christological titles are in essence founded on what happened at the first Easter. Through his resurrection from the dead Jesus was enthroned as *Kyrios*, the Christ of God. The resurrection establishes Jesus' 'eschatological position'.[17] In him the God who is to come, with his lordship and his glory, is already present. The risen Christ represents in this transitory era of the world the God who is to come. He therefore represents the coming freedom and salvation of creation at the same time. The one who is risen is hence not a historical, private person, nor is he merely the 'head' person of his body, the church. In the light of the resurrection and exaltation, the dying of Jesus is therefore retrospectively interpreted as the dying of this eschatological person. This takes place when his passion is understood and preached as representative suffering and his death as a self-giving 'for us' and 'for the world'. Just as he is raised in advance of all other men, as 'the first fruits of those who have fallen asleep', and can therefore be named comprehensively 'the leader of life', so he was exclusively given over to death, forsaken by God, in order to free the forsaken and to save the lost. His death took place exclusively 'once and for all', and is hence unrepeatably *his* sacrifice for the salvation of men. His resurrection shows that he goes ahead of mortal men and therefore also shows his precedence over his own followers. In the light of his crucifixion and resurrection it is impossible simply to talk about the divine person of Christ; one must speak more precisely about his eschatological person. He is not only the representative of the 'wholly other' God; he is also the representative of the coming God who makes everything else 'other'. In the light of his crucifixion and resurrection it is impossible simply to talk about 'the historical person' of Jesus, if we mean by that a private person with a considerable effect in history. We must grasp his appearance in the open eschatological forum, as the representative of that future history in which God is God and man comes to his glory. The crucified and risen Christ represents this future of history in his person and in his whole suffering and activity.

This New Testament declaration is lost if we only start from the presence of the church and enquire back to its founder, beginning, origin or head. In the light of the eschatological person of Christ, the church does not live from the past; it exists as a factor of present liberation, between remembrance of his history and hope of his kingdom. Its remembrance of Jesus, his mission, his self-giving and his resurrection is past made present and can be termed 'remembrance in the mode of hope'. Its hope of his parousia is future made present and can be termed 'hope in the mode of remembrance'.[18] If the eschatological orientation is lost, then remembrance decays into a powerless historical recollection of a founder at the beginning of things. The church can then itself take the place of hope, setting itself up as the prolongation of his former incarnation, and the aim of its growth as being his parousia. If, on the other hand, the christological remembrance is lost, then the church is filled by other hopes, visions and aims, taken over from non-Christian movements, or Pentecost pushes out Easter, and new experiences of the Spirit push out Christ. And then the criterion for choosing between the spirits disappears. It is only when the church comprehends itself in its present exist-ence as the present realization of the remembrance and hope of Christ, that it perceives Christ's 'otherness' and the openness of his future. Its main problem is not the relationship between time and eternity, or between the present and the origin; it is the rela-tionship between history and eschatology. It is alive as long as it combines with remembrance of Christ hope in the coming God, and as long as it can link with the present existence of his mission and his self-giving the liberation of men for their true future. Then, as the community of the cross it consists of the fellowship of the kingdom – and not of church members; and as the community of the exodus – and not as a religious institution – it spreads the feast without end.

The present significance of the eschatological person of Christ for the world and his church was developed in the doctrine of Christ's threefold office (*munus triplex*).[19] We shall take up this doctrine as a regulative principle, so as to understand the church's existence and its tasks in the light of its participation in the messi-anic mission, the representative self-giving and the liberating lordship of Christ.

2. *The Messianic Mission of Jesus and the Community of the Exodus*

The synoptic gospels depict the whole appearance and history of Jesus in the light of his messianic mission. They put his messianic mission under the aspect of his proclamation. His proclamation brings the gospel to the poor and calls men to repentance. His preaching is therefore 'evangelization' and he himself is 'the evangelist' of the end-time. Luke 4.18f. sums up his mission with words taken from Isaiah 61.1f.: 'The Spirit of the Lord God is upon me, because he has anointed me to preach good news to the poor. He has sent me to proclaim release to the captives and recovering of sight to the blind, to set at liberty those who are oppressed, to proclaim the acceptable year of the Lord.' Picking up Isaiah 35.5ff. and Isaiah 61.1ff., Matthew makes Jesus answer John the Baptist's question with: 'The blind receive their sight and the lame walk, lepers are cleansed and the deaf hear, and the dead are raised up, and the poor have good news preached to them. And blessed is he who takes no offence at me' (Matt. 11.5f.). According to Matthew 10.7–8 the disciples are sent to the lost sheep of the house of Israel with the same mission: 'Preach as you go, saying, "The kingdom of heaven is at hand." Heal the sick, raise the dead, cleanse lepers, cast out demons. You received without pay, give without pay.' The messianic mission of Jesus embraces his whole activity and has an all-embracing meaning for his disciples as well. The word εὐαγγελίζειν has a sharply demarcated meaning in the context of this activity. The proclamation of Jesus and the disciples is mission, but his mission and theirs is not merely the proclamation. Healing the sick, liberating the captives, and the hunger for righteousness belong to the mission and go together with the preaching of the gospel to the poor.

(i) *The Herald of Joy*

What do εὐαγγελίζειν and εὐαγγέλιον mean in the framework of the all-embracing messianic mission?

The equivalent Hebrew expressions in the Old Testament mean: to proclaim a message of joy, to bring a message of victory, or to announce victory.[20] Anyone who proclaims joy or victory sees himself as a messenger of good news (II Sam. 4.10) and is viewed as such by other people (II Sam. 18.26). In the religious sense the victory of God over the enemies of the people is proclaimed cultically (Pss. 68.12; 40.10). The man who has been saved from some desperate situation proclaims before the congregation the joyful message of 'the mighty acts of God'. As is well known, Deutero-Isaiah and the tradition influenced by him is of great importance for the understanding of the New Testament concept. For he prophesies 'a new exodus' to the people in exile, and with it the coming eschatological victory of God, his final enthronement and the dawn of a new and everlasting era of salvation. Isaiah 52.7 gives us the classic passage: 'How beautiful upon the mountains are the feet of him . . . who publishes peace, who brings good tidings of good, who publishes salvation, who says to Zion, "Your God reigns." ' What the writer has in mind are the heralds who hurry ahead of the people returning home to Zion from Babylon, and who announce to the people waiting in Jerusalem the return of Yahweh from his exile. In that these messengers are proclaiming the royal rule of God, the new era of God's nearness is beginning after the time of exile and alienation. Salvation, running ahead of itself, appears in the gospel.[21] It comes into force through the announcement of Israel's restoration, of God's coming, and the eschatological era. The gospel is not a statement about some remote future; it is the dawn of that future in the Word. The Word is understood as creative power, like the Word of creation at the beginning. It effects what it says. In the Word the future of the royal rule of God becomes present. The gospel is already understood in the eschatological, universal sense in Deutero-Isaiah and in Psalm 96. 'Yahweh is king' means salvation for the world of the nations, beyond the restoration of the people of God: 'Tell of his salvation from day to day. Declare his glory among the nations, his marvellous works among all the peoples! . . . Say among the nations, "Yahweh reigns!" ' (Ps. 96.2ff.).

Isaiah 61.1 personifies the gospel as *the* messianic prophet who comes in the spirit of the Lord, creating liberty, salvation and peace through his word. The gospel announces the lordship of Yahweh, which will be without limits and without an end. Anthropologically it is bound up with the saving words of righteousness, fellowship and peace. It is addressed to the prisoners, the wretched, the poor, the people forsaken by God and the hopeless, even though in Isaiah 52 the liberation of the captives of Israel seems to stand in the forefront.[22]

The message that God has seized the power over his enslaved people is the call to the new exodus: 'Awake, awake, put on your strength, O Zion. . . . Shake yourself from the dust, arise, O captive Jerusalem; loose the bonds from your neck, O captive daughter of Zion' (52.1f.). That is why the section ends with the words: 'For you shall not go out in haste, and you shall not go in flight, for the Lord will go before you, and the God of Israel will be your rear guard' (52.11f.). The new exodus into freedom surpasses the old one through its festive character. Here the message of the coming God and his rule is at the same time and from the very beginning the call to freedom. Conversely the call to freedom is founded on, and made possible by, the approaching rule of God, already present in the gospel. In the proximity of the rule of God, what was till then impossible becomes possible. The fetters are no longer binding. They can be thrown away. Weakness is no longer unnerving. Men can lay hold of his strength. Dust is no longer degrading. It can be shaken off. In the proximity of the rule of God, that is to say, 'petrified conditions begin to dance'.[23] Hope becomes realistic because reality is full of every potentiality. Even though liberation of the captives is made possible through the message 'God is king', yet it is equally the act of men who 'free themselves', who repent and go forth. The message about the coming rule of God does not reduce man's freedom; it makes it possible and empowers it. The modern alternative, according to which either there is a God, in which case man cannot be free, or man is free, but then there cannot be a God, is not valid here. Here the modern conclusion whereby faith goes with slavery and liberation with atheism is false. Here it is solely the nearness of the coming God which frees the enslaved and empowers them for their own freedom. For that reason the initial form of God's coming rule is the gathering and exodus of the people from slavery. There is no contradiction between the hoped-for rule of God and the experience and practice of the liberated people.

(ii) The Gospel for the Poor

The synoptic writers, in the tradition of Deutero-Isaiah, evidently present Jesus as 'the One who brings the good news of the expected last time'.[24] His proclamation and ministry are completely under the sign of the gospel. He preaches the gospel of the kingdom to the poor and calls captives into the liberty of the coming kingdom. The focal point of his message is that God is drawing near and will set the people free. In that sense, the exodus of the last time begins with Jesus. It begins with the broken, the captives and the blind, as Luke says, or, in Matthew's words, with the blind, the lame, the lepers, the deaf and the dead. Both writers sum up the people who are primarily affected under the expression 'the poor'.[25] The 'poverty' meant extends from economic, social and physical poverty to psychological, moral and religious poverty. The poor are all those who have to endure acts of violence and injustice without being able to defend themselves. The poor are all who have to exist physically and spiritually on the fringe of death, who have nothing to live for and to whom life has nothing to offer. The poor are all who are at the mercy of others, and who live with empty and open hands. Poverty therefore means both dependency and openness. We ought not to confine 'poverty' in religious terms to the general dependence of men on God. But it cannot be interpreted in a merely economic or physical sense either. It is an expression which describes the enslavement and dehumanization of man in more than one dimension. The opposite of the poor in the Old Testament is the man of violence who oppresses the poor, forces them into poverty and enriches himself at their expense. 'Riches' are equally multi-dimensional and extend from economic exploitation, by way of social supremacy, to the complacency of the people who look after themselves in every sector of life, ignore the rights of others and do not want to have to say thank-you to anyone for anything. What is meant is an attitude, and the thing it depends on. What is meant are possessions and the violence through which they are acquired and maintained. 'The rich' are all the people who live with tightly clenched hands. They are neither dependent on others nor open for others. The rich will only be helped when they recognize their own poverty and enter the fellowship of the poor, especially the poor whom they have made poor through violence. If the gospel of the coming kingdom, like the first beatitude, is directed to 'the poor', then it can only be heard as a message of joy in the revelation of our own poverty and in fellowship with the poor. The abasement which is meant by humility is not a private virtue but the social entry into solidarity with the humble and the humbled. It is precisely as the partisan 'gospel to the poor' that the kingdom of God brings freedom to all men, for its brings rich and poor, healthy and sick, the powerful and the helpless for the first time into that fellowship of poverty in which it is possible to talk without distinction about 'all men'. In a divided, unjust and violent world, the partisan gospel reveals the true universality of the coming rule of God and the indivisible liberty.

In the gospel of Jesus the specific form of the coming rule of God is the fellowship of the blind who are to see, the prisoners who are to be freed, the poor who are to be happy, and the sick who are to be healed.[26] With them the exodus of the whole people begins. They already praise and thank God here and now in the fellowship of the wretched.

(iii) Conversion to the Future

The other context in which the gospel stands in the history of Jesus is *conversion*, the fresh start.[27] Mark's summing up of Jesus' mission is: 'The time is fulfilled, and the kingdom of God is at hand; repent, and believe in the gospel' (1.14). According to this the promised messianic era has dawned with Jesus' coming. In his person and in his ministry the God who was far off has come near. The phrase 'the kingdom of God is at hand' is only a paraphrase of the prophet's cry: 'God is king'. It is therefore time for men to make a fresh start and to free themselves, and this they can do. The gospel itself is the mediation between the coming kingdom of God and the person who is turning to freedom. In it the coming kingdom is present through the Word and in this way is powerful in the present wherever men and women entrust themselves to it. The future of God set in the present Word is therefore at the same time the call to a new start. The imminence of the kingdom, as it is preached and believed, makes men free to repent, free to turn away from their godless way of life and their Godforsaken circumstances (Rom. 13.12ff.). The turning away from this world of oppression, death and evil to the future of life, righteousness and freedom is in itself the anticipation of the kingdom of God under the conditions of this world and this society. Here the new start includes both persons and the relationships and conditions in which these persons live. Conversion includes soul and body, the individual as well as his community, his own way of life as well as the system in which he lives. Conversion is in tendency as universal as the kingdom of God, in whose imminence it is both made possible and demanded. For that reason there is no room here for a narrowing down to the individual *or* the collective, the religious *or* the political sphere. But for that reason too conversion is the concrete form of the people of God, which gathers together for the kingdom of God and lays hold on its freedom in the kingdom's imminence. Just as the fellowship of the sick who will be healed, the blind who will see and the poor who have heard the gospel is the preliminary form of the church in the messianic mission of Jesus, so the fellowship of discipleship which exists among the converted is the other provisional form of the church of the Messiah. The fellowship of the poor, about whom the messianic history of Jesus tells, and the fellowship of the converted, which it also describes, are proto-forms of the church of Christ – not in the sense that they have been superseded, but in the sense that they give their stamp to the church's basic forms. The church loses its fellowship with the messianic mission of Jesus if it is not 'the people of the beatitudes' and does not consist of the poor, the mourners, the meek, those who hunger for righteousness, the pure in heart and the persecuted.[28]

(iv) From the Proclamation of Jesus to the Preaching of Christ

The special thing about Jesus' gospel is that he proclaims the dawn of the messianic age 'today', in his own present and his own hour. Consequently his word, in which the rule of God and the liberation of men become effective for the present, is bound up with his person and his imprint. 'Blessed is he who takes no offence at me' follows the quotation from Deutero-Isaiah in Matthew 11.6. Jesus' proclamation of the gospel and his person cannot be separated from one another in the way that religious, philosophical and moral doctrines can be detached from the people who have postulated them. The authority of his messianic announcement of the time, and with it the truth of his proclamation, depend on his person and are not transferable. That is why Rudolf Bultmann rightly stressed that Jesus' whole existence, as far as we can know it, is completely merged in his proclamation.[29] But when he goes on to draw the conclusion that Jesus is 'the Word', then the converse which Julius Schniewind stressed, that the Word is Jesus, must be taken seriously too.[30] The gospel and its claim (the nearness of God and the liberation of men) are so closely bound up with Jesus' earthly appearance that his human nature ('a carpenter's son from Nazareth') and his vulnerability ('the Son of man must suffer many things') become a scandal for those who have dreamed of the Messiah in divine splendour and worldly glory. A poor man as liberator of the poor, a vulnerable man as saviour of the helpless – that seems like a contradiction in terms. It is either blasphemy or a complete reversal of the concept of God. The crucifixion of Jesus as a blasphemer and rebel, as history testifies to it, and his resurrection from the dead, attested by the Easter faith, are the answers to his contradiction between Jesus' messianic claim and his unmessianic appearance. In the light of Easter we must therefore say in retrospect that the gospel of Jesus, because it is indissolubly bound up with his person, also enters into his history, hence taking on the features of his passion and death on the cross. The gospel of the coming kingdom and of present liberation is incarnate in the suffering of Jesus and finally assumes the form of the one who was crucified. On the basis of the identification of his message with his person Jesus can be called 'the incarnation of the promise' of the kingdom.[31] That is why Jesus' proclamation of the kingdom of God can only, after his death and in the light of his resurrection, be continued as the proclamation of Jesus the Christ of God, the crucified and risen liberator of men. There is hence no fundamental difference between the proclamation of Jesus and the proclamation of the church. Through his history itself, Jesus' gospel about the kingdom of God became the church's gospel about Jesus, the Christ of God. On the other hand this cannot lead to a narrowing down of Jesus' preaching of the kingdom, for the church's proclamation of Christ is in essence the gospel of the kingdom, and the word of the cross essentially contains the call to start anew towards freedom. The gospel of the crucified and risen liberator leads to a universality – 'to the Jew first and also to the Greek' (Rom. 1.16) – which goes beyond the limits of the earthly history of Jesus, even if this Pauline universality, which directs the gospel to all men in their deprivation of the divine splendour (Rom. 3.23, NEB), is already implicit in the first of Jesus' beatitudes. The gospel of Christ as 'the word of the cross' even reaches into the depths of the Godforsakenness of the godless, filling them with a sense of God's nearness and of their liberation, which was begun in the forgiveness of sins conferred by the earthly Jesus.

(v) *The Messianic World Mission*

The messianic mission of Jesus is only fulfilled in his death and is put into full force through his resurrection. Through his history it becomes the church's gospel for the world. Through his death and resurrection the church participates in his mission, becoming the messianic church of the coming kingdom and man's liberation. In so far as the church participates in his mission, it is drawn into his fate and will experience 'the power of his resurrection' in 'the fellowship of his sufferings' (AV). The prophetic mission brings it into conflict with the society in which it lives, and evokes conflicts between the powers of the past and the forces of the future, between oppression and liberation.

If the proclamation of Christ is the legitimate way of preaching the gospel of the coming kingdom and the present liberation of men in the light of Christ's cross and resurrection, then this proclamation ought to be seen against the horizon of messianic world mission. This gospel makes the coming rule of God a present reality in the Word and through the Word. With this it seeks to open the world, sealed up within itself as it is, for the coming of God. Where the kingdom is at hand, the people gather together for the kingdom and free themselves from the power of slavery. Where the future of God in Christ is at hand, men are converted and move towards him. The church of Christ is hence simultaneously the people of the kingdom. It is not 'the not-world'; it is the world which is now already turning anew to the future of God because it follows the call of freedom. It understands its movement as the new *eschatological exodus*. The church of Christ can therefore be characterized as the 'exodus church'.[32] This does not mean the 'emigration of the church' from society into the ghetto; it means the exact opposite: the departure from exile and ghetto into freedom.[33]

The exodus of the people of Israel from Egypt and also the new exodus from Babylon which the prophets proclaim were, and were supposed to be, movements out of a land of captivity into the land of freedom, away from Egypt or Babylon into the land of Israel and to Zion. The exodus of the last days in whose movement the church finds itself, is in the first place universal, and sees itself as the beginning of liberation of the whole of enslaved creation for its consummation in glory. In the second place it is to be understood historically, as an eschatological movement away from the past and out of death, towards the future and into life. What is meant is therefore emigration from 'the world that is passing away' to 'the future world', and out of slavery to freedom in every land on earth. The symbols of 'Egypt' and 'Babylon', the long 'wanderings in the wilderness', 'Jerusalem' and 'the city of God' are hence interpreted historically and eschatologically by the Christian hope.

In this framework the exodus church can interpret itself as corresponding to the rule of God and as the beginning of the liberation of man and creation. The fellowship it forms is incarnate hope if, as Paul says, it abolishes mankind's aggressive divisions and fatal separations, and if it can be said of it that here 'there is neither Jew nor Greek, there is neither slave nor free, there is neither male nor female; for you are all one in Christ Jesus' (Gal. 3.28). The way the passage continues shows the hope in which the church lives: 'And if you are Christ's, then you are Abraham's offspring, heirs according to the promise' – that is to say, heirs of the kingdom. This community is the present form of the messianic liberation. It is the present form of conversion and the new beginning. It is the exodus of the people out of captivity, poverty and inhumanity into the freedom, the glory and the righteousness of God's new man.

By proclaiming the history of Jesus as the history of the liberator and by relating the history of its relationship with him as the history of the universal eschatological exodus, the church carries the gospel into the world, infecting men with the germ of hope and liberation.[34] Because of that this gospel cannot be 'the word of the church'; on the contrary, the church understands itself as 'the church of the Word'. It is the vehicle of the gospel of freedom, not a schoolmaster for the nations. It is not the church that has the gospel; it is the gospel that creates for itself a people of the exodus, which is the true church of Christ. Insight into the messianic dimension of the gospel will crystallize in the practical recognition of the missionary dimension of the gospel. As a call to freedom the gospel is an event of missionary calling. Its aim is not to spread the Christian religion or to implant the church; it is to liberate the people for the exodus in the name of the coming kingdom. The future which the mediator proclaims and into which he waits to lead his people is: 'No longer shall each man teach his neighbour and each his brother, saying, "Know the Lord", for they shall all

know me, from the least of them to the greatest, says the Lord'
(Jer. 31.34; cf. Rev. 21.3). It is precisely for the sake of this
future of the immediate presence of God experienced by liberated
and glorified man that the missionary movement must take the
messianic Word to the ends of the earth and to the end of the
world's history of suffering, continually pressing for the transformation of mediation through the Word into the power of the
Spirit.

Under the influence of the messianic mission of the earthly
Jesus, the poor were blessed, the sick healed and prisoners freed.
Men were called to repentance and a new start into freedom. These
proto-forms of the church become explicit in the post-Easter
community, in which Jesus' mission begins to fulfil itself through
the gospel. It is the community of the liberated, the community
of those who are making a new beginning, the community of
those who hope. Their fellowship serves to spread the call of
freedom in the world and, as new fellowship, should itself be the
social form of hope. Fundamentally, all Christians share in the
prophetic ministry of Christ and are witnesses of the gospel.

3. *The Passion of Jesus and 'the Community of the Cross'*

At the centre of the New Testament stands the proclamation of
salvation through the suffering and death of Christ. What makes
the gospel a pure message of joy and an unequivocal call to freedom is Jesus' offering of himself, his vicarious suffering and death,
in abandonment by God. His cross indeed seems paradoxical compared with the *doxa* which men strive for when they deify themselves and humiliate God and their neighbours. But it corresponds
in the deepest sense to the glory of the one who became man, the
God who humbled himself and whose love reached to the point of
suffering death. Consequently it also reveals the unlimited freedom
of the person who is accepted, loved and therefore united with God.
According to the prophetic and messianic ministry of Jesus, his
giving of himself to death on the cross for the life of creation can
be called his priestly ministry. But just as his messianic mission
surpasses the remembrance of the prophets of Israel and goes
further than the hopeful picture of the messianic prophet, so his
sacrifice on the cross also goes beyond all priestly prototypes and
copies. Whatever is termed 'the priestly ministry' in the church

must take its bearings from the one who was crucified; the crucified one cannot, conversely, take his bearings from the church's priestly ministry. Fellowship with Jesus' self-offering therefore points beyond the church's particular priestly ministry and affects the existence of the whole church and every individual Christian in the world. But the meaning of Jesus' self-offering even goes beyond this fellowship, for in principle and tendency it comprehends the reconciliation and liberation of the world (II Cor. 5.19; Rom. 11.32).

It is undoubtedly superficial to ask about the moment when the church was born, for all datings fall short and therefore restrict the church's mission and the movement of God in which it finds its meaning. But if we all the same want to ask about its origin, we are led from Pentecost and the 'outpouring of the Spirit' to Easter and the visions in which the apostles experienced their calling. But Easter points unequivocally to the cross. In the framework of this question, therefore, it is correct to see the origin of the church in the crucified Jesus. 'Having established the Church in His blood, he fortified it on the day of Pentecost with special power from on high.'[35] 'It begins in the wounded side of Christ on Calvary, goes through the "tempering" of the Pentecostal fires, and comes onward like a burning flood.'[36] When devotion sees the church springing from 'the heart of Jesus', then it is meditating on the cross, for there 'his heart' is revealed in his sacrifice of himself 'for many'. On the cross there takes place what Luther so vividly calls 'the merry exchange', as he draws on the bridal imagery of medieval mysticism, in which Christ and the soul become one body, Christ makes the soul's sin and suffering his own, conferring on her in her poverty his own righteousness, his freedom and his divinity.[37] Here man's sufferings become Christ's history, and Christ's freedom becomes man's history. As the community of Christ the church understands itself as the church out of the cross, and the church in solidarity with the men and women who are living in the shadow of the cross. We will therefore try to put the theologumenon *de nativitate ecclesiae ex corde Jesu in cruce* at the centre of ecclesiology and to gauge its consequences.[38]

In the history of the passion we can see three dimensions in which Christ's suffering and death take on significance. For a church which sees itself as the church under the cross, it is important to perceive all three of these dimensions.[39]

(i) Liberation from the Compulsion of Sin

On the basis of his messianic proclamation of the kingdom to the poor and of grace for sinners, Jesus was declared a blasphemer and was condemned as one in accordance with his people's understanding of the law. Anyone who preached God's law as the law of grace for the unrighteous and those without rights, anyone who – when he was only a carpenter's son – set himself above the authority of Moses, was bound to come into conflict with the established law and its custodians. And he was bound to be the loser in this conflict, humanly speaking. The fact that Jesus, as the suffering Son of man, demonstrated the power of God as prevenient love to the powerless and the outcasts, made him vulnerable. The conflict which finally killed him was etched into his life from the very beginning. His story began in a stable and ended on the gallows. But in the light of his resurrection and the Easter faith, his death on the cross is not a story ending in disappointment; it is the completion of his mission and his obedience. As an outcast he brought the gospel to outcasts through his death. Through his self-sacrifice he brought God to those who had been sacrificed. Through his death under a curse he brought liberating grace to those who were cursed according to the law. In the light of Easter his end on the cross is therefore his real beginning.

His earthly life ended with the open question of whether he was right to direct the gospel to the lost in God's name, or whether he was breaking the law of the holy God. Is he 'truly the Son of God' (Mark 15.39) or is he one who is to be 'reckoned with transgressors' (Luke 22.37)? Just as his helplessness on the cross confirmed his 'godlessness' in respect of the gods in whose name he was executed, so his resurrection from the dead justifies him for all who believe in him. The trial of Jesus, which ended in the earthly sense with his death, must therefore be reopened in the light of the resurrection faith. In his trial, in which the church has to appear as witness, the real question at issue is the question of the divine righteousness.

If the 'lawless' and 'godless' man of Nazareth was rightly condemned, then in this world the law applies in its most legalistic sense, as the law of reciprocity – the requiting of like by like, in both the good sense and the bad. On its fringes justice may be tempered with mercy, but there can be no merciful justice as such, repaying evil with good, letting enemies be loved and creating justice for the unjust. This understanding of the law is not identical with the Old Testament's understanding of the *torah*. It must rather be understood as what governs the world, the foundation of the systems of life with which people try to defend themselves politically and psychologically against chaos, evil and death, and yet by so doing disseminate chaos, evil and death as the same time. We might describe this law archaically and psychologically, and in the general religious sense, as *Ananke*. If Christianity takes its understanding of itself from the cross of Christ, then it lives from the experience of the new righteousness proclaimed by Jesus (Rom. 1.17) and revealed to the godless in his death. The new righteousness of God is manifested in the 'godless' death of the Son of God, and with it the outcasts are accepted, the unrighteous are made righteous and justice is secured for those without rights. That is the new divine righteousness revealed in the gospel.[40]

Those who are caught up in this live from 'the forgiveness of sins' through 'the blood of Christ'. They have been born again to new life and new righteousness through Christ's surrender of himself to death on the cross. The theological expressions which are used to describe being born again to the righteousness of God, by means of the forgiveness of sins through the blood of Christ, are as radical as they are because they seek to bring out the scandal of the qualitative difference from the system of life imposed by the law which rules the destiny of this world. Anyone who lives in the righteousness of Christ through the experience of the forgiveness of sins is 'dead' to the legal systems of life in this world. Anyone who lives from and for the righteousness of Christ will, like Jesus, be 'reckoned with transgressors'; for he no longer believes and follows the protective gods of those legal systems of life. He no longer accepts the inescapability of that law and its consequences. Since he has been forgiven, he will forgive. Since he has received good for evil, he will repay evil with good. Since, even when he was the enemy of God, God loved him, he will love his enemies. Because this life of the new righteousness cannot be restricted to the private sphere, but in the trend of its being presses towards the new creation or the new order of all things, it is bound to operate as rebellion amid the legal systems of life. For here things are experienced and done which are impossible and inadmissible according to the law which humanity in its misery has taken up.

Between the church and that world whose character is described as 'law, sin and death', stands the cross of Christ. It is not too high-flown – it is in line with faith and experience – when Paul maintains that the world is crucified to him and that he is crucified to the world (Gal. 6.14).

Anyone who follows the 'godless' Son of God because he is beginning to live from his self-giving, sees that no one becomes righteous through the law. For him the legal systems of life are vicious circles, made up of unrighteousness, the law which tries to control that unrighteousness, and the death to which the law leads, because it has been pressed into service by unrighteousness (Rom. 7.10ff.). He cannot try to improve the previous systems of life on the basis of the law, but will spread the new righteousness of the gospel in their midst, the new righteousness which serves the new creation of all things. He can no longer adapt himself to the pattern of this world, but will change and renew his aspiration, seeking after the living will of God towards new creation (Rom. 12.2). The birth of the church out of the cross of Christ leads the church to take its stand beneath the cross, if it remains consistent, in opposition to the systems of life governed by *nomos* and *ananke* and assailed by these systems of life, their laws and their gods. 'Forgiveness of sins' through 'the blood of Christ' has dangerous results in experience and practice. But it holds within itself liberation for new creative righteousness.[41]

(ii) Liberation from the Idols of Power

Jesus did not suffer the penalty for blasphemy, which was stoning. He was crucified for political reasons by the Roman occupying power, for inciting unrest and for rebellion. At that time crucifixion was the Roman punishment for runaway slaves and rebels against the *pax romana*. That is to say, it was a punishment designed to protect the slave-owning society and the *imperium*. Pilate undoubtedly misunderstood Jesus himself and his mission, for he was no zealot leader in the holy war to free Israel from Rome; nor was he a second Spartacus. But since Pilate had to see to it that there was peace and order in the occupied country, he was bound to misinterpret the trouble-maker from Nazareth as a political trouble-maker, and to have him executed in the name of the *lex romana*. It was therefore not a chance misunderstanding. As a crucifixion by the Romans, the death of Christ has an

irrevocably political dimension. In the passion stories of the New
Testament, the scene in which Jesus appears before Pilate is
adorned with typical features which have theological overtones.[42]
The representative of God and the gospel appears before the
representative of the Roman state and the holder of political
power. Even Jesus' declaration that 'his kingdom is not of this
world' does not solve the conflict that is inherent in this confrontation, for in the first place 'this world' does not mean the earth
but the 'age of this world' which will pass away, and secondly the
kingdom that Jesus is talking about is 'in this world' through
Jesus himself. The statement speaks of the origin and the foundation of the kingdom which Jesus proclaims and represents; but
it does not mention its place. It is neither in heaven nor is it
'purely religious', so it cannot be called 'non-political' for the one
reason or for the other. It is, as we are bound to say in this context, 'Jesus in person', and it becomes political through the confrontation with Pilate and through Jesus' crucifixion.

On one level, in this political dimension Pilate with his judgment represents the Roman imperium and with it Roman law and
the Roman Caesar. This means that he is not merely representing
a policy, but a political religion as well.[43] There can be no talk
here about a demarcation between religion and politics. That was
only brought about in Christendom in modern times, after pro-
longed struggles between emperor and pope. If what Pilate is
representing towards Jesus is religious politics or a political religion, then there is inherent in the trial of Jesus the conflict between his messianic message and his self-giving on the one hand,
and the religious and political reality on the other. This alternative
could be called 'either Christ or Caesar'.[44] For the church which
appeals to the crucified Jesus, it is an alternative which is highly
relevant in its continual conflict with the political and bourgeois
religions of the societies in which it exists. The idolization of
political power and the religious legitimation of economic, social
and political conditions of rule are compulsions which no people
and no society and hardly any political movement escapes. The
idolatry of power, the fetishism of money and 'things', as well as
political messianism are as modern as they are archaic. They go
on living as long as the heart of man is 'a manufactory for idols' (in
Calvin's phrase), because fear makes him aggressive and in need of
legitimation. Even the churches are not free of this. But inasmuch

as the Christian faith is born out of the death of Jesus, 'the rebel', the political religion of its society is 'crucified' to it, and it is 'crucified' to the political religion of society. Between faith and political idolatry stands the remembrance of the crucified Jesus. That remembrance allows the believer to see 'the nation's most treasured values' as idols. In the sphere of political religion he will support the iconoclasm of the cross. He will be considered 'godless' in the sense of the idolized nation, class or race. In so far as the church of Christ as a whole is born 'from the wound in Christ's side', it will also as a whole, through its existence and way of life, be a ferment to break down political idolatry. It will press for the desacralization of political power and the democratization of political rule. As a critical ferment to break down economic fetishism it will spread freedom in solidarity. It was dangerous for Christians in the Roman empire to appeal to a God who had been crucified for political reasons. The martyrs who refused to participate in the cult of the emperor took the consequences of their confession of faith and so spread liberty. Churches which forget the martyrs who were 'political' in this sense are in danger of adapting themselves to the political religion of the society to which they belong.

On the other level of this 'political dimension', through his public mocking, torture, rejection and crucifixion 'outside the gate' (Heb. 13.12), Jesus enters the company of the despised, the tortured, the rejected and the murdered. His public execution together with two 'robbers' (they were probably zealots) can be interpreted as a sign of his solidarity with these lost people. When he says to the dying man beside him, who recognizes him for what he is, 'Today you will be with me in paradise', it shows that in the act of dying he brings the liberating rule of God into the situation of deepest abandonment. According to Luke his mission begins with the 'today' in Nazareth. 'Today this scripture has been fulfilled in your hearing.' And it is completed on earth in the paradise opened 'today' for the one who has been crucified with him. 'He who gives help to the lost is lost himself', writes Brecht.[45] But for Jesus it is the other way round: the one who gives himself up for lost in this way, helps the lost. It is not a question here of assent to the motives which had made them fight and for which they were being executed. Jesus' crucifixion together with two Jewish freedom fighters cannot be interpreted as his blessing on their struggle. But what this public scene on Calvary does do is to reveal the unconditional fellowship of the Son of man with tortured and executed men and women whoever they are. This scene too has typical features with theological implications. It can be viewed as the counterpart to Jesus' encounter with Pilate.

The Easter faith sees the one who was crucified in the light of the divine glory. The disciples recognize the risen Christ from the marks of the nails. What does that mean for the 'political dimension' of the cross? It means that for believers the divine glory is revealed on the face of the crucified Jesus; it no longer belongs to the crowns of kings or the fame of a nation or any other earthly authorities. 'The worldly dishonour, the cross, is transfigured; what according to the common idea is lowest, what the State characterises as degrading, is transformed into what is highest.'[46] 'When the cross has been raised to a banner and to a banner whose positive tenor is the kingdom of God', then there is inherent in it a 'revaluation of all public values', as Nietzsche acutely reproached Christianity – a revaluation which is as dangerous as it is liberating, and a revolutionary tendency. It is true that the Christianity of the major church soon allied itself with the Roman empire, after the Emperor Constantine claimed to have triumphed 'in the sign of the cross'. The fact that according to the history of Christ's passion the kingdom of God is present, not in the Roman empire but in the person reviled for his name, was pushed aside. The crucifixion of the Son of God was laid at the door of the Jews rather than the Romans by the church of the empire, and the Jews were therefore suppressed, as the laws of the emperors Theodosius and Justinian show. But wherever remembrance of the crucifixion of Christ revived in the church, it produced estrangement from the religious legitimation of the political authorities and solidarity with the people whom they were humiliating and persecuting.

As the community of the crucified Jesus the church is drawn into his self-surrender, into his solidarity with the lost, and into his public suffering. His suffering is in this respect not exclusive but inclusive and leads to compassion.[47]

That is shown in the public form of the church, as Paul sees it:

> For consider your call, brethren; not many of you were wise according to worldly standards, not many were powerful, not many were of noble birth; but God chose what is foolish in the world to shame the

wise, God chose what is weak in the world to shame the strong, God chose what is low and despised in the world, even things that are not, to bring to nothing things that are, so that no human being might boast in the presence of God . . . as it is written, 'Let him who boasts, boast of the Lord' (I Cor. 1.26–31).

Like the exaltation of the one who was crucified, the calling of the lowly in the world has a critical significance for the great. Like the glorification of the one who was dishonoured on the cross, the election of the despised has as its result the rejection of the proud. That is a double predestination in the dialectical process of the history of man's calling.[48] Only its goal is universal: 'That no human being might boast but all boast of the Lord.' In order that 'all flesh shall see the glory of the Lord *together*' (Isa. 40.5), the mountains are made low and the valleys are lifted up.[49] In this respect the calling and gathering within the church of those who are foolish, helpless, contemptible and unworthy in the sight of the world has significance for salvation history, a meaning which every church must face that appeals to Christ. The church has 'the form of a slave'.[50] It is 'God's plebs'. It must in this sense be the church *of* the people (ὄχλος). The aristocratic attitude of wanting to be 'a church *for* the people' is denied it. 'Christ belongs to all those who have a humble attitude and not to those who set themselves above the flock.'[51] 'The life of Jesus' is only manifested through the church if its form is like 'the death of Jesus'.[52] This cross-like form of the church cannot be achieved through a mysticism withdrawn from the world. It was for Paul a 'bodily' (II Cor. 4.10) and a public form, which came into being through the apostle's temptations, the contempt he experienced and the persecutions he endured. For Christianity too it will be a bodily and public likeness, for it comes into being in public apostleship and in public intervention on behalf of the lost and the despised. We might call it a worldly, bodily and hence also a political Christ-mysticism. How else should the life of Jesus, the life of the one who is risen, be manifest 'in our mortal flesh'?

(iii) *Liberation from Godforsakenness*

Jesus died on the cross not merely as a condemned blasphemer and as an executed rebel, but also as one forsaken by God.[53] To the God whom he called 'my Father' and whose kingdom he had proclaimed to the poor, he cried: 'My God, why hast thou

forsaken me?' (Mark 15.34). That is the innermost, in the true
sense of the word the theological dimension of his death. It is also
the special and unique thing which distinguishes his death on the
cross from the many others in the history of mankind's suffering.
In this respect what killed him was not only his people's interpretation of the law and Rome's power politics, but his God and
Father; for the pain in his torment must have been this abandonment by God. With it a misery descends on the crucified Jesus
which is in truth the misery within the misery of all abandoned
men and women, though recognition of this fact is so unbearable
that it is repressed. It is a pain which, indeed, makes itself felt in
many forms of experienced abandonment, but it is not completely
revealed and realized. We should note that in Rom. 1–3 Paul used
the word παραδίδωμι – to deliver up, to surrender, to hand over –
to describe the divine abandonment of all godless men who cling
to idols, boast of themselves and desire to become righteous through
the works of the law. They have abandoned the living God, and
so God has abandoned them and 'handed them over' to their self-
chosen path, which leads to death. This 'handing over', which
shows itself as it were in 'God's silence' at man's self-glorification
and in his 'permitting' the murderous and suicidal consequences
which stem from it, is for Paul 'the manifestation of God's wrath'.
In his abandonment by God the Son of God takes upon himself
both the fate of the man who has been handed over and 'the
wrath of God'. In the light of his message about the impending
kingdom of God, this abandonment on the cross is the end of
Jesus' mission. But in the light of his resurrection we have to say
with Paul that through his forsakenness Jesus has brought God to
the Godforsaken. The Father did not 'spare his own Son' but
'gave him up for us all' (Rom. 8.31ff.), in order through him to be
the Father of the forsaken, the God of the godless and the refuge
of those without hope. The full depth of his forsakenness on the
cross only becomes recognizable in the light of his exaltation. His
agonizing abandonment by God is revealed as his self-giving for
those 'given away' by the God whom he calls 'my Father'. It is at
the same time and in this way recognizable as his self-surrender
for the redemption of the lost (Gal. 2.20). The whole history of
his passion stands under the sign of this self-surrender, which is
on the one hand to be seen as abandonment by God and on the
other as the consummation of God's love.

Christ's surrender of himself to a Godforsaken death reveals the secret of the cross and with it the secret of God himself. It is the open secret of the Trinity.[54] The Father gives up his beloved Son to the darkness of Godforsakenness. 'For our sake he made him to be sin' (II Cor. 5.21). 'He became a curse for us' (Gal. 3.13). There is no remoteness from God which the Son in his forsakenness did not suffer, or into which his self-giving did not reach. The doctrine of Christ's descent into hell seeks to make it clear that his self-giving reaches and opens every hell. The Father gives up his own Son, the Son of his eternal love, in order to receive those who have been given up and so that he may be there for them. The Son is given over to this death and this hell so that he may become the lord of the dead and the living. That is why the Father suffers with his Son in his passion. The Son dies in abandonment, suffering the death of sin, curse, wrath and hell. But the Father suffers the death of the Son in the unending pain of love. In his pain he participates in the Son's death. The Son is given over to the power of this death, a power contrary to God. In his abandonment by the Father he experiences the fate of the godless and takes it upon himself for them. But as he is surrendered by the Father, so he surrenders himself as well in his limitless love. Thus, even though Jesus' dying cry reveals his total abandonment by the Father, he is at the same time entirely one with the Father, and the Father with him, in this event of self-surrender, which sunders the two so far from one another that heaven and hell are included in its grasp, and all men can live in it. As the Gethsemane story aims to show, Christ's giving of himself to death on the cross unites the Son with the Father at the very point where the separation and mutual abandonment is at its deepest. The Son offers himself through the Spirit (Heb. 9.14). The power which leads him into abandonment by the Father is the power which at the same time unites him with the Father.

The event of Christ's giving of himself to death for the life of creation is continually summed up in the New Testament in terms of an event of God's love: 'God so loved the world that he gave his only Son, that whoever believes in him should not perish but have eternal life' (John 3.16). In the Son's cross God takes this death on himself in order to give those who are lost his own eternal life. The first epistle of John fuses together the event of the cross and God himself even more tersely: 'God *is* love.' What happens in the

Son's self-offering on the cross is the revelation of the nature of God himself. In this happening God is revealed as the trinitarian God, and in the event between the surrendering Father and the forsaken Son, God becomes so 'vast' in the Spirit of self-offering that there is room and life for the whole world, the living and the dead. The trinitarian history of the self-offering of the Son on the cross therefore reveals in summary form 'God for us' – for us, the godless; 'God with us' – with us, the Godforsaken (Rom. 8.31ff.). And from this follows the double assurance: 'Nothing will be able to separate us from the love of God' and 'Will he not also give us all things with him?' (Rom. 8.38f. and 8.32).

In this theological dimension of Jesus' passion it is completely clear for the first time why the church of Christ lives, believes and hopes from the sacrifice on the cross. It is the fellowship of the godless who have found fellowship with God through Jesus' abandonment by God. It is the fellowship of the sinners who through the one who for them was made sin have arrived at righteousness. It is the fellowship of the accursed, who were blessed through the accursed death of Jesus as their representative and who become a blessing. And because the Father is reconciled to 'the world' through the death of the Son, its new life must also serve the reconciliation of the world. In so far as, with the epistle to the Hebrews, we can term Christ's sacrifice on the cross a priestly ministry, its consequence is the priesthood of all believers. They are all 'ambassadors of reconciliation' in Christ's stead. They live in fellowship with God by virtue of Christ's giving of himself for them. Because of this their life is also destined for self-giving – they are destined to love, to be representatives and to intercede. That does not divide them from mankind or raise them above others. What is true of Christ in this respect – that he 'had to be made like his brethren in every respect, so that he might become a merciful and faithful high priest in the service of God', and that it is only through his experience of suffering and temptation that he can help those who suffer and are tempted (Heb. 2.17f.) – applies in its corresponding degree to them too. The priestly ministry of the representative can only spring from *sym-pathy*, from 'suffering with' (cf. also Heb. 4.15). The fellowship called into life by Christ's self-surrender serves to reconcile the world through solidarity with the suffering of the people and through participation in the representative work of Christ in the Spirit. The

Christian 'being-there-for-others' cannot be detached from 'being-with-others' in solidarity; and being-with-others cannot be separated from 'being-for-others'. Consequently there can really be no fundamental division between the general priesthood of all believers and the particular priestly ministry.[55] The whole church lives from Christ's self-giving and in self-giving for the reconciliation of the world. It is a question for the whole fellowship whether the deepest suffering of the forsaken world is experienced and finds expression in it, together with the present realization of Christ's self-giving; whether in that fellowship the lonely find the healing fellowship of Christ and the Godforsaken find the brethren of Christ, who show them the Father of the forsaken in the spirit of acceptance. It is a question for the whole fellowship how it realizes the 'priestly ministry', about which Dietrich Bonhoeffer said that 'participation in the sufferings of God in secular life' makes the Christian.[56] Fundamentally speaking all Christians participate in Christ's priestly ministry and are witnesses of his intercession and sacrifice in the lives they live.

The church is called to life through the gospel of Christ's self-giving. Hence it is fundamentally born out of the cross of Christ. At its centre is 'the word of the cross' and the eucharist with which the death of Christ is proclaimed. It is from the cross of Christ that there develops the fellowship of the godless with God. What makes the church the church is reconciliation 'in the blood of Christ' and its own self-giving for the reconciliation of the world.

The church of Christ is therefore at the same time the church under the cross. The fellowship of Christ is experienced wherever Christians take their cross on themselves. This fellowship is experienced in common resistance to idolatry and inhumanity, in common suffering over oppression and persecution. It is in this participation in the passion of Christ and in the passion of the people that the 'life' of Christ and his liberty becomes visible in the church. Christian fellowship proves itself in temptation and resistance.

Finally, fellowship with the crucified Jesus is practised where Christians in solidarity enter the brotherhood of those who, in their society, are visibly living in the shadow of the cross: the poor, the handicapped, the people society has rejected, the prisoners and the persecuted. Fellowship with the crucified one cannot be lived in any other way than in fellowship with the least of the brethren of the Son of man (Matt. 25.40).

4. *The Lordship of Jesus and the Brotherhood of the Kingdom*

All the New Testament proclamations about the person of Jesus and all the narratives relating his history are set against the horizon of Easter.[57] The appearances of the crucified Jesus in the splendour of divine glory call into being the confession of faith in 'Christ the Lord'. Christian faith is the acknowledgment of the lordship of Christ through public testimony, through new fellowship and through lived life. Christian existence is new life in Christ's sphere of influence. Confession and life in the lordship of Christ are founded on faith in his resurrection from the dead through God the Father. Conversely, this faith in the resurrection is only alive in acknowledgment of the present lordship of Christ (Rom. 10.9f.). Without new life, without the ability to love and the courage of hope in the lordship of Christ, faith in the resurrection would decay into belief in particular facts, without any consequences. Without faith in the resurrection, new life in the lordship of Christ would cease to be a radical alternative to human forms of sovereignty and – adapting itself religiously, morally or politically – would lose its power to overcome the world. Where there is certainty that death has lost its power there is an alternative to those power structures that are built up on the threat of death. The removal of death's power brings to light a life which overcomes the systems of domination and oppression and demonstrates freedom in fellowship. Faith in the resurrection and a life of liberty in the lordship of Christ therefore belong indissolubly together and mutually interpret one another.[58]

(i) *Christ's Resurrection and Exaltation*

The specific starting point for the titles with which the early Christian congregations acknowledged and lived the lordship of Christ is the Easter event.[59] It has a double significance.

In so far as Easter is understood as Jesus' resurrection 'from the dead', it means – in the framework of the general expectation of the resurrection 'of the dead' – the anticipation and beginning of the general resurrection.[60] Easter is not an isolated miracle confined to Jesus alone. It is the hidden beginning of the open new creation of all things (Rom. 8.11). In the midst of the history of death, the future of the new creation and the glory of God has already dawned in this one person. The earthly Jesus used to proclaim: 'The kingdom of God is at hand'; so now after Easter the church understands the age in which it lives as the presence of the God who was to come: 'The day is at hand' (Rom. 13.12); 'The end of all things is at hand' (I Peter 4.7). As the church now understands it, with Jesus' resurrection from the dead the power of death and all the domination built up on the threat of death have already been overthrown and their end is already in sight. For these people liberty under the sovereignty of God is already present, in so far as it already determines their lives.

But if it is in the first place only the crucified Jesus who has been snatched from death and raised to new life, whereas all other men are still subject to this destiny, then this one person takes on a particular significance for all the others. In the New Testament this significance is expounded through the formulae of adoption and enthronement: through his resurrection from the dead Jesus was adopted as God's son for others, and was appointed *Kyrios* for the world. As the Son of God he represents the God who is to come in this godless world. As Lord he spreads the rule of God in a world which is still subject to violence and death. As Christ he brings freedom to a world that is enslaved. Easter therefore means, together with his resurrection, Jesus' exaltation to be Lord of the kingdom of God and his coming to power in the Spirit of freedom. The churches which acknowledge Jesus as Lord recognize in him the representative of the coming, all-redeeming kingdom. They live in the power of his Spirit and no longer recognize any other masters.

(ii) God's Redeeming Kingdom

In order to understand the point at issue about the coming kingdom of God which Jesus proclaimed and to which, according to the testimony of the resurrection faith, he was appointed to rule, we must consider the wider context of the history of the biblical tradition.

(a) Here the kingdom of God does not mean God's rule over the world in general through creation and providence, but the ultimately liberating, all-redeeming and therefore eschatological kingship of God over his creation.[61] It differs from providence because it makes an end of the history of violence, suffering and death and brings about a new creation of all things. It differs from the creation at the beginning through the fact that God himself, with his eternal life and glory, will dwell in this creation and be 'all in all'.

(b) This redeeming and renewing kingdom of God is *universal*. It embraces heaven and earth. Therefore hope for this kingdom leads us to speak not only of a new earth, but of a new heaven as well. The eschatological kingdom of God means: 'Behold I make *all* things new' (Rev. 21.1–5). It is not a 'purely religious kingdom'[62] which could be realized through the power of a new religion. Nor does it merely hold sway over man's personal relationship to God, which could be represented in the private religion of the heart. It is not a moral authority, confined to a changed way of life on the part of men. It is not even kingship only over the living, from which the dead would be excluded (as they are in the Old Testament). Like God himself, it is universal and without limitation. That is why Matthew makes the risen Christ say: '*All* authority in heaven and on earth has been given to me. Go therefore and make disciples of *all* nations . . .' (28.18f.). That is why Paul sees Christ as 'the Lord both of the dead and of the living' (Rom. 14.9). The eschatological reign of God, whom Jesus as *Kyrios* represents and whose power he exercises, cannot therefore be limited. It bursts the bonds of a divided world. It embraces the religious life as well as the political one, the private as well as the social, the living as well as the dead.

(c) The proclamation of the nearness of God's kingdom and the preaching of Jesus as Lord therefore raise the theological and political question: who has the right to rule over the world?[63] This question takes us far back into the biblical traditions. According to the creation stories 'man' was created as the image of God in order to rule over creation (Gen. 1.27f.). As God's image 'man' is God's earthly representative, deputy and vice-gerent.[64] Corresponding to the creator of all things, he is to rule over creation. Hence the way in which man is expected to rule over the world is neither arbitrary nor unlimited. It takes its dimensions and limitations from the way in which man corresponds to the Creator, who loves his creation and has pleasure in it. It is only this correspondence which legitimates man's rule over the world. The fact that he rules over the world does not make man like God or equal to him.

According to Old Testament tradition, the fact that 'man' is destined to be the image of God and to rule over the world is also to be understood as a promise of an ideal 'man' who has not yet appeared. For that very reason this designation can be perverted by the man who is no true man at all, but man's negation.

According to Daniel's great historical vision (ch. 7), world history is marked by the usurpation of 'man's' rule over the world by a series of 'bestial' rulers.[65] Out of the sea of chaos rise, one after another, 'the lion with eagle's wings' (a symbol of the Babylonian empire), 'the voracious bear' (a symbol of the empire of the Medes) and the winged leopard (a symbol of the Persian empire). Then comes the iron empire of an indescribably terrible monster which crushes all the other empires. In this image the universal rule entrusted to 'man' is seized for themselves by usurpers in beast-like form. As the symbols of their rule show, in their kingdoms bestial conditions prevail, not human ones. With these political perversions of the universal rule of 'man', says Daniel, wickedness and sin will be brought to their peak. The future of these kingdoms is the downfall of mankind. But then, according to Daniel, one like the 'Son of man' comes with the clouds of heaven. He is given dominion and glory. All peoples will serve him. His kingdom will be an everlasting one (7.13ff.). This 'son of man' probably means 'man' or 'mankind'. He is a representative person. He does not arise out of chaos but comes from God. The promise made at creation that man should be the image of God and should rule over the world finds fulfilment in the human 'kingdom of the Son of man'. Through his coming the usurpers' struggle for world domination is ended.

When in the New Testament Jesus is understood as being the Son of man, and when 'all power is given him in heaven and on earth', this statement of faith belongs to this context in the history of tradition: the struggle for world dominion is decided in favour of those who recognize in Jesus the Son of man. If they live in the sphere of his humanity, they leave behind the compulsions of the bestial kingdoms of the world and cease to obey them. The promise made to humanity at creation finds fulfilment in the human kingdom of the Son of man. As representative of the coming, redeeming rule of God, Jesus is also the representative of the true human existence that is to come. For that reason he is also called 'the image of God' (Rom. 8.29; I Cor. 15.49; Phil. 3.21; II Cor.

3.18; II Cor. 4.4; Col. 1.15), the one whom believers are made like to, so that they may become 'men'.[66] That is why they are promised that they will 'rule' with Christ. Man's likeness to God and his dominion over the world are fulfilled through Christ, in Christ and with Christ. That is the purpose for which he is sent into the inhuman world and raised from a violent death and called '*the new man*'.

The acknowledgment of Jesus as lord is (*a*) to be understood eschatologically, (*b*) to be recognized in its universality, (*c*) to be set in the context of the theological and political question of world domination and (*d*) to be grasped as the fulfilment of the promise made to man at his creation.

(iii) 'The Revaluation of Values'

What is special and revolutionary about the Christian faith in Jesus, the Lord of the world, is not his deification and glorification by the church, which adorned him with many of the theological and political titles of worldly rulers. The statement that Jesus is now by virtue of his resurrection 'Lord' is open to misunderstanding, and so is talk about the 'kingly rule of Jesus Christ'. For in this way he could be understood – in analogy to earthly rulers – as these rulers' heavenly overlord. But a personal cult of this kind is not intended. The real statement is really the reverse: 'The Lord is Jesus.' It is only through this reversal of emphasis that this image of the ruler is related to the person and history of Jesus and thus radically transformed. For early Christianity to use titles of rule and lordship in order to term Jesus the true Lord and ruler of the world – the Jesus who was mocked because of his helplessness and murdered on the cross by the world's rulers – involves about the most radical reversal of the ideal of rule that can be conceived: the Lord as a servant of all; the ruler of the world as a friend of tax-collectors and sinners; the judge of the world as a poor outcast.[67] That is the 'revaluation of all values' with which Nietzsche reproached Christianity. The phrase 'Jesus – the Lord' is in danger of relating Jesus to the usual picture of lordship, which is derived from the experience of and longing for power. The phrase 'the Lord is *Jesus*', on the other hand, models the ruler's title on the man from Nazareth, the crucified Son of man on Golgotha, and gives it a completely new impress. As the gospels show, the history of Jesus is the history of service for freedom. The 'lord of the world' washes his disciples' feet like a house slave (John 13.1–16). The Son of man does not rule through acts of violence and oppression but through self-surrender for the purpose of liberation.

> You know that those who are supposed to rule over the Gentiles lord it over them, and their great men exercise authority over them. But it shall not be so among you; but whoever would be great among you must be your servant, and whoever would be first among you must be slave of all. For the Son of man also came not to be served but to serve, and to give his life as a ransom for many (Mark 10.42–45).

True dominion does not consist of enslaving others but in becoming a servant of others; not in the exercise of power, but in the exercise of love; not in being served but in freely serving; not in sacrificing the subjugated but in self-sacrifice.

But even service can make people dependent and be a concealed form of the love of domination. In Christendom titles like *servus servorum* and 'the first servant of the state' were claimed by spiritual and secular potentates. It is therefore important to grasp that acknowledgment of Jesus as Lord leads not to domination through service but to service for freedom. Here a switch-over from service to domination, or from work to possession, is not possible, nor is the surreptitious dominance achieved through 'service' and the making oneself indispensable. What is meant is selfless service, which is solely out for the human rights and dignity of the other. Christ's surrender of his life, his freedom and his divinity 'as a ransom for many' is intended as a sacrifice for the liberty, dignity and happiness of others, without the desire to make them dependent and grateful. We could link Matthew 28.18 and Philippians 2.5ff. by saying that the one to whom 'all authority was given in heaven and on earth' 'emptied himself even unto death on a cross'. It is only in this way that he exercises the authority given to him. The one who is risen is the one who was crucified, and the Lord is the slave. He is slave to the task of liberating all for their true humanity, their likeness to God and their rule over the world which corresponds to God's own rule. He is the Son of God who humbles himself for their true exaltation to God's glory.

The dialectic of lordship and servitude in society is many-faceted. There is dominion through the enslavement of others. But there is also domination through service, and through taking on the

burdens of others. Domination can be gained through direct sub-
jugation. But it can also be acquired indirectly through service. If
'the Lord's' name is Jesus, and if lordship is read out of the story
of his passion, then neither the one nor the other is meant. What
is meant is rather freedom in the fellowship of created being, built
up on brotherhood, the freedom which was intended by him and
will be attained as the culmination of his 'rule', according to Paul's
vision of hope. That is why in I Cor. 15.24 hope for the abolition
of 'every rule and every authority and power' is linked with the
expectation of the consummation of the lordship of Christ in the
universal rule of God. On earth his abolition of all earthly power
in the eternal presence of God can be interpreted as anarchy.
Human subordination and super-ordination, and a system of
justice enforced by power, is to be replaced by the brotherhood of
all men with the Son of God in the atmosphere of the all-pervasive
glory of the Father.[68] Then, as the indwelling of the divine glory
in all being brings protection against futility, chaos and wickedness, earthly protective measures and human repressions become
superfluous and void. Then freedom is fulfilled in the sphere of a
new creation free of all dominion. If this dominion-free brotherhood is the final goal of the history of Jesus, then the universal
rule ascribed to him means liberation from both lordship and
servitude – liberation for messianic life. In this 'crooked generation' the hoped-for conquest of the structure of lordship and
servitude is achieved in no other way than through the social and
political form of a voluntary self-surrender on behalf of the liberation of those who are oppressed at any given time.

(iv) Liberated Church – a Church of Liberation

The church exists if, and to the extent to which, men are
obedient to the rule of the Servant of God and receive their
liberation from his self-giving. Participation in the liberating rule
of Christ through a new way of life presupposes that men have
experienced and believe in this liberation through the lordship of
Christ in themselves. Before the practical question comes the
question of experience; and before the question of the new obedience comes the question of faith. Only the person who through
Christ has been snatched from the powers of this world wins the
freedom and the strength to make these powers powerless. That is
the meaning of the early creeds, which talk about a redemption

from the power of the devil through the sacrifice of Christ, so that believers become Christ's property. In other words, the church reaches as far as the rule of Christ reaches, and it is made up of the poor who are called blessed, the sick, now healed, freed prisoners, and justified sinners. Its new freedom is freedom in the spirit of the new creation of the world. It does not act out of freedoms or alternatives which are already implicit in a social system, and are conceded to the church; it proceeds from the freedom and the qualitative difference from 'the form of this world' which has been revealed to all things through the spirit of the new creation. If we are not to fall a victim to confusion, it is important to remember constantly that the lordship of Christ is the lordship of the risen one. As the conquest of death, it is directed towards the conquest of the domination of death and all deadly tyrannies.

The church is the fellowship of those who owe their new life and hope to the activity of the risen Christ. The use of its new freedom in this world ought to correspond to the rule of Christ and to reflect this physically and politically. Every human community corresponds to its environment and reflects it.[69] The church is no exception. In its concrete form it corresponds to its social environment and reflects the conditions which govern the society in which it lives. Most of these are not in dispute but are considered 'self-evident'. Most people find them self-evident because, as they say, 'there is no other way of doing things'. This is the point at which the churches begin to be criticized by those who are oppressed by the normative power of what actually exists and in which they have no share. This is where the churches begin to be criticized by those who arrive at a self-understanding which is not 'self-evident'. They criticize the church for betraying its Lord to the existing system of domination and oppression, because it reflects and corresponds to this system instead of to Christ. Whether this criticism 'from outside' is justified in any given case or not, it at all events brings the church up against criticism 'from within'. How far and in what way does its common life and its use of freedom correspond to the liberty of the one who has called and liberated it? Where and in what way must its correspondence to the liberating lordship of Christ contradict the systems which rule its environment? Christ and society are reflected in the life of the church, as well as in the life of every Christian. The different claims of the two sides lead to conflicts in every specific case. In these conflicts the question which of the two has the greatest claim to obedience has to be answered in practical terms. It has already been decided by faith. The requirements and the beatitudes of the Sermon on the Mount speak unambiguously for following Christ, setting love in opposition to a loveless world.

The church must first of all reflect and represent the lordship of Christ in itself. It cannot adopt its social order from the way in which the society in which it lives is run, or allow its social order to be determined by that; for it has to correspond to its Lord and to represent new life for society. It cannot be a racial church, which permits racial separation and discrimination within its own fellowship. It cannot be a class church, which sanctions from above a separation or conflict of classes in its own fellowship. It cannot be a male church, tolerating patriarchal forms of rule within itself. It cannot be a national church, which bolsters up national arrogance by its own limitations and ideas. For the church, as it seeks to conform to the liberating rule of Christ, the watchword must be: 'Here there is neither Jew nor Greek, there is neither slave nor free, there is neither male nor female; for you are all one in Christ Jesus' (Gal. 3.28; cf. also Rom. 10.12 and I Cor. 12.13). In the church of Christ the religious, economic and sexual privileges that obtain in the world around lose their force. But if they lose their force and their validity, then another power holds sway – the power of the Spirit. Then other values obtain, the values of acceptance of the other. The church is not a 'holy autocracy';[70] it is the fellowship of believers who follow the one Lord and have been laid hold of by the one Spirit. It is in principle the community of equals, equipped with equal rights and equal dignity. All have the gift of the Spirit. If, in thinking of Christ's self-surrender, we talk about 'the priesthood of all believers', then in thinking of Christ's lordship we must speak of 'the sovereignty of all believers'. In this sense the church cannot be anything other than the council of believers or the synod – the common way – of the liberated. The social realization of these ideas is a continual problem and a continual opportunity.

We start from the idea that before God every man is a person in an identical way, and that as a person he has received grace, rights and dignity from God. Then the church is a fellowship of persons, which as such transcends society's power struggles and conflicts about the role to be played by different groups.[71] But where is this personal dimension 'before God' actually visible? It cannot be interpreted in an ideal sense, for in the church it becomes visible through the fellowship in the Word and the fellowship of the Lord's Supper. In this fellowship divine law prevails. Consequently no divisions of race, class or anything else can be tolerated here, not even if state and society demand them. But if these divisions are not permissible at the central point of the congregation gathered for worship, they are not permissible in the congregation's public and everyday life either. The common life comprehends the whole of life. To split the congregation into a vertical dimension 'before God' and a horizontal dimension 'in the world', so that contradictory laws are set up, is both wrong and practically impossible. Important though the idea of personal fellowship in the church is, it cannot be separated from an alteration in our way of life.

Recently people have started from the idea that the church of Christ must present itself as a 'derestricted area' amid the restrictions imposed by society. Schleiermacher meant by this a fellowship without an ulterior purpose; modern writers mean communication without repression.[72] A 'liberated zone' of this kind in society would certainly fulfil that unfulfilled promise of the French revolution – 'fraternity'. The problem is only that this 'fraternity' cannot exist without 'liberty' and 'equality'. The idea becomes illusory when it overlooks these presuppositions for unrestricted communication, or simply assumes that they exist. In a society without 'liberty' and 'equality', fraternity cannot be presented all by itself. This is true even of the Christian fellowship itself, so that even there brotherhood is achieved not through the idea of freedom from restriction but in the first instance only through the removal of the privileges enjoyed by one person beyond another, and by one group beyond another. In its new application, the removal of privileges already possessed or acquired cannot be for its own sake but only 'for others'; it must therefore be directed towards the equal distribution of power and responsibility to all who are endowed with the Spirit. The idea of the 'derestricted area' is no more, but also no less, than the specific idea of a goal which ought to be realized as far as possible. In reality power structures and divisions in society penetrate the church as well. There is no point in passing over these realities by way of ideal notions about personal fellowship, partnership or a 'derestricted area'. If faith's ideas and love's hopes are to be realized, we must begin at the bottom, starting with the raising of the downtrodden, the liberation of the oppressed and the right of those who have been silenced to speak out. The ideas of personal fellowship, of partnership and of unrestricted communication cannot be used to stifle the cry for freedom and the call to freedom. It is therefore realistic to begin in the church of Christ by freeing the poor, the unimportant, women and victims of racial discrimination, freeing them for their human rights in order to make room for that joyful experience of the partnership and fellowship which can be shared in a 'derestricted area'.[73] The goal of emancipation in the church is not the reversal of earthly rule as such, important though the experience of their rights, and even their power, is for the powerless; the goal is the 'new man', who no longer acts within the system of lordship or servitude, and hence cannot be the slave of any master or the master of any slave. The church finds the yardstick for new humanity in the lordship of the humiliated Son of man, and the possibilities of it in the experience of the Spirit. In the conflicts between the claims of Christ and the claims of society it will discover its historic opportunities.

Basically, all Christians participate in the kingly service of the Son of man and are witnesses of his liberating rule in their ecclesiastical life, as well as in their social one. The kingdom of all believers sets its stamp on the life of Christ's church, both inward and outward. With the raising of the crucified Jesus the church becomes manifest. In the spirit of the risen Jesus it experiences the reversal of the idea of lordship. In the fellowship of the Son of man it experiences the fulfilment of the promise of 'man'. Liberation for fellowship is experienced in the church, and fellowship for the liberation of the world is practised through it – if, and in so far as, the church follows the one whom it acknowledges not only as 'its' lord but as 'the Lord'.

5. *The Glory of Jesus and the 'Feast without End'*

Our understanding of the meaning of the risen Christ remains one-sided if we see this meaning only in his exaltation as *Lord*. The new life in his spirit does not merely reside in the overcoming of domination and bondage through service for liberation to true humanity. In the Western church a one-sided stress on the lordship of Christ has led to an ethicization of the freedom of faith in new obedience. This ethicization has often enough led to a new legality in which Christ was conceived of as the new law-giver, and in which faith took its public form from this legality's demands. This is why it is important for us to perceive the aesthetic side of the resurrection as well.[74]

(i) The Transfiguration of Christ

The aesthetic significance of Christ's resurrection lies in his transfiguration. The word transfiguration means both Christ's spiritual irradiation, and the metamorphosis from the form of the slave into the form of glorified man (Phil. 3.21). In this twofold sense the risen Christ is both the irradiated Son of man and the crucified Jesus, transformed into divine beauty. He is not only exalted to be lord of the coming kingdom of God, but as such is also transfigured into 'the Lord of glory' (I Cor. 2.8). By virtue of his conquest of death he already lives, the new fulfilled humanity, in the Spirit. As the exalted, transfigured and transformed man of God he works on downtrodden, barely human and mortal man not only through his liberating power and new demands, but through his perfection and his beauty as well. Consequently the new life under his influence cannot be understood merely as new obedience, as a reversal of life's direction and as an endeavour to change the world until it visibly becomes God's creation. It is also, and with equal emphasis, celebrated as the feast of freedom, as joy in exist-ence and as the ecstasy of bliss. These aesthetic categories of the resurrection are part of the new life in faith; without them the imitation of Christ and the new obedience would become a joyless legalistic task. Easter begins with a feast, for Easter is a feast and that makes the life touched by Easter a festal life. 'The risen Christ makes of man's life a continual festival,' declared Athana-sius; and Roger Schutz has rightly picked up this idea, making it the centre of the Council of Youth at Taizé in 1973.[75] Jesus him-self compared the approaching kingdom of God with a marriage feast. How much more will Christianity see his resurrection into this divine lordship as an eternal joy and an unfading bliss!

(ii) The Feast of Freedom

Easter is the feast of freedom, when the risen Christ sits at table with his disciples. Originally, Easter epiphanies and celebrations of the Lord's supper probably belonged together. In the Lord's supper the risen Christ, as the leader of life against death, takes his own followers into his indestructible life, letting them partake of it. That is why the eucharist is full of remembrance of his death on the cross and full of hope for his coming, and is, in the unity of remembrance and hope, a demonstration of present joy in grace. Before the liberation experienced in faith is translated into new obedience, it is celebrated in festal ecstasy. There is no other way of realizing the extravagance of grace towards the misery of sin. There is no other way of measuring the breadth of the new life compared with the narrowness of death. In the Christian tradition the freedom manifested in the appearances of the risen Christ was first of all apprehended in aesthetic categories, and was celebrated through the feast.

With Easter the laughter of the redeemed, the dance of the liberated and the creative play of fantasy begins. According to Hippolytus the risen Christ is the 'leader of the mystic round-dance' and the church is the bride who dances with him.[76] From ancient times the Easter hymns have celebrated the victory of life; they laugh at death, mock hell and drive out the demons of the fear of sin. The earliest of all the Easter hymns, I Cor. 15.55–57, makes this clear:

> Death is swallowed up in victory.
> O death, where is thy victory?
> O death, where is thy sting?
> The sting of death is sin,
> and the power of sin is the law.
> But thanks be to God, who gives us the victory
> through our Lord Jesus Christ.

In Paul Gerhardt's Easter hymn the sight of Christ's resurrection is 'ein rechtes Freudenspiel' – a proper game of joy. And consequently sin and death and hell, the world and its tribulation, have all lost their power over him. 'Misfortune is my fortune and night to me is day', he ends. But the same ideas recur in all the great Easter hymns. English-speaking readers will remember Wesley among many others:

> Lives again our glorious King;
> Where, O death, is now thy sting?

Once he died, our souls to save;
Where thy victory, O grave?

What is expressed in this way in song and laughter, in the play and dance of joy, corresponds to the liberation experienced in the presence of the risen Christ. The exuberance of freedom is depicted and anticipated in the exuberance of ecstasy. The feast of freedom is itself the festal liberation of life. For a particular time, in a particular space, through a particular community, the laws and compulsions of 'this world' become invalid. The laws, purposes and compulsions of everyday life no longer apply. An alternative emerges and is presented in festal terms. This feast always means first of all that a community is freed from every compulsion and arrives at the spontaneous expression of its feelings, spontaneous ideas and spontaneous bodily movements. The liberating feast of the resurrection cannot be without euphoria. But it is not simply rousing a passing euphoria when it seizes men in the heart of their oppression and, with the freedom they celebrate, wakes their hunger for freedom; when it meets men in their suppressed feelings of loneliness and through the fellowship they celebrate wakes their cry for the other person. Then the liberating feast radiates into everyday life a remembrance which cannot be forgotten again in the daily round. It works as an antitype to normal standardized life and lets us seek for possible ways of changing it. The liberating feast builds up a tension towards life in this world which can only be resolved through conscious suffering over its lack of freedom and through conscious intervention for more freedom and more open fellowship.

If the feast of freedom is itself celebrated as a liberating feast then it takes on the character of anticipation. It is anticipated in song, in laughter, in play and in dance – not yet in everyday life, but potentially there too. For the feast of freedom does not play with unreal possibilities but with the actual potentialities of the future of Christ in the creative Spirit. Its purpose is not to compensate present lack of freedom through a merely dreamed-of freedom, so that one can better come to terms with lack of liberty later; it is rather to break the spell of life's immutability and encourage men and women to find true liberation and new fellowship. It is true that the liberating feast is in the same danger as all feasts: namely of being pressed socially into the functions of lightening the burdens of daily oppression, offering a safety valve for pent-up pressures, and providing compensation for daily failure. But as the feast of freedom of the risen Christ, the transfigured and transformed Son of man, it will have to defend itself against this misuse. As an anticipation of what the redeemed life will be in the future it demonstrates the alternatives offered by the creative Spirit. The spell of destiny and the feeling of personal helplessness are lifted where the possibilities and powers of the creative Spirit are experienced in the feast. The helpless discover their power as they are seized by this Spirit. Those who have adapted themselves discover their own personalities as they begin to sing, talk and move within the feast. They discover that they are something and can do something. They 'come out of their shells' in a way that surprises themselves. We do not have to think here immediately in terms of speaking with tongues or healing the sick at the liberating feast, though phenomena of this kind certainly ought not to be excluded from the outset. But the Pentecostal churches and the independent churches in Africa have discovered that worship can be experienced and organized as a liberating feast.[77] Their experiences can teach churches with fixed liturgies to be open-minded towards the spontaneous. According to the epistle to the Ephesians (1.19; 3.19; 4.13ff.) the church of Christ counted as the place of the overflowing fullness of the Spirit's powers. This fullness of the Spirit ought not to be smothered by established and regimented forms of worship. The understanding, in the spirit of Easter, of worship as a liberating feast ought rather to abolish the traditional quenching of the Spirit.

The liberating feast finds its foundation, but also its limits, in the risen Christ himself. Remembrance of the crucified Jesus forbids us to see and use this feast of his resurrection as a flight from earthly conditions of suffering. Hope for the coming of the risen one and the transformation of our mortal bodies (Phil. 3.21) forbids us to confine ourselves to a lament over suffering and earthly misery, and keeps us from simply attacking its causes without rejoicing in its future transformation. In the liberating feast we discover that the resurrection hope is realistic and that reality is hopeful. Joy in the resurrection of Christ therefore actually leads to solidarity with the groaning creation. It turns dumb suffering into articulate pain. It does not separate us from the wicked world. Joy in present freedom remains together with pain over lack of freedom and even with grief over each of our dead. But it also links pain and grief with hope for the redemption of the world. The ecstasy of the liberating feast constantly produces new attitudes of resistance to the unfree life to which men are subjected. Even if the festal experience of freedom cannot be completely translated into movements of liberation, and so for this reason seems purposeless to some people, it none the less remains meaningful in itself; for it points enduringly to the resurrection as the great alternative to this world of death, stimulating the limited alternatives to death's dominion, keeping us alive and making us take our bearings from the victory of life. The freedom of the resurrection and the victory over death which are ecstatically celebrated in the liberating feast rise above this 'body of death'. They are still 'the Lord's song in a foreign land'. The certainty of triumph celebrated in the Easter hymns will continue to rise above the bounds of our human life, because it cannot remain content with any other victory. It works on the possibilities of the creative Spirit in the world of death in a twofold way: it produces attitudes both of resistance and of consolation. Without resistance, consolation in suffering can decline into a mere injunction to patience. But without consolation in suffering, resistance to suffering can lead to suffering being repressed, pushed aside so that in the end it actually increases. In this double function of resistance and consolation the liberating feast becomes a 'messianic intermezzo' (A. A. van Ruler) on the risen Christ's way to the new creation of the world.

(iii) Life – a 'Feast without End'

In the way which we have just been discussing, Jesus' earthly life can be termed *a festal life*. It was not the life of a ruler, nor was it the life of an unwilling slave. Luke (4.19) linked the kingdom of God which Jesus proclaimed with the remembrance of the Israelite 'year of release' (Lev. 25) and with the prophetic hope for its messianic equivalent (Isa. 61.1–2). The coming kingdom of God is hence understood as the time of liberation and as the opportunity for true human fellowship. The kingdom of God which Jesus embodies in his life has a correspondingly festal character. How much more, therefore, are we bound to interpret the life of the risen, transfigured and transformed Christ as a festal life! It is life without death, time without transience, and participation in the glory of God without hindrance.

The participation of believers in the life of the risen Christ through their hope, their new obedience and their festal ecstasy makes their own life a feast in a similar way. These expressions only seem illusory if we forget that the risen 'Lord of glory' is the humiliated servant, the crucified Son of man. When the lord of the feast is the crucified Son of man, then the unfestive, dark side of life – defeat, guilt, fear and death – all belong to his feast of freedom. Then everything really does 'work for good' (Rom. 8.28, RSV marg.). Nothing excludes us from the feast, not even 'my sins' (Augustine). To gaze on the risen one makes life a feast, but it is only the gaze on the one who was crucified and who descended into hell that makes 'the whole of life' a feast, and a perpetual feast, a feast which even death does not terminate, so that it is indeed a 'feast without end'.

The *liberating feast* and *life as a feast without end* complement one another. Neither of them can remain in the truth of Christ without the other. Essentially, ordinary days and holidays are merged here into a single 'reasonable service' (Rom. 12.1, AV) – that is to say, they are fused into joy in freedon. Fundamentally all Christians partake of the transfiguration of Jesus in the Spirit of freedom. The general participation in the liberating feast of the risen one, with the powers and potentialities of every individual, is the mark of the assembly of Christ. The feast without end puts its stamp on the personal life, on intervention for the liberation of the oppressed, the sad and the apathetic, and on the struggle for a happier world. In view of the transfiguration of Christ and the transfiguration of the world anticipated in it, Dostoevsky's remarkable saying that 'beauty will save the world' proves to be true.[78] He meant by this redeeming beauty the bodily form of grace. And he described this loveliness of lived freedom in the prostitute Sonia, who had pity on the unhappy murderer Raskolnikov. The glory of God on the face of the rejected Son of man frees us for this freedom. The risen Christ works through his lordship and through his glory. These two aspects cannot be divided from one another.

6. *In the Friendship of Jesus*

The titles through which the church defines what Jesus means are usually called his titles of office. Whether Jesus is understood and acknowledged as prophet, priest or king, these titles always express his divine dignity towards men and his saving task on their behalf. The christological titles describe his uniqueness and set up a certain distance between him and the church. In devotion, this distance finds expression in the worship and adoration of Christ, and in obedience to him. In the garb of his titles of honour he appears with divine authority. Even if – in the light of his passion and his death on the cross – his exaltation is perceived in his lowliness, his wealth in his poverty and his power in his helplessness, he still stands at God's side and suffers and dies for men at God's behest. But the fellowship which Jesus brings men, and the fellowship of people with one another to which he calls, would be described in one-sided terms if another 'title' were not added, a title to describe the inner relationship between the divine and the human fellowship: the name of friend.

(*i*) *The Concept of Friendship*

Friendship is an unpretentious relationship, for 'friend' is not an official term, nor a title of honour, nor a function. It is a personal designation. Friendship unites affection with respect.[79] There is no need to bow before a friend. We can look him in the eye. We neither look up to him nor look down on him. In friendship we experience ourselves for what we are, respected and accepted in our own freedom. Through friendship we respect and accept other people as people and as individual personalities. Friendship combines affection with loyalty. One can rely on a friend. As a friend one is a person for other people to rely on. A friend remains a friend even in disaster, even in guilt. Between friends the determining factor is not an ideal, a purpose or a law, but simply promise, loyalty to one another and openness. Finally, friendship is a human relationship which springs from freedom, exists in mutual freedom and preserves that freedom. Friendship is 'the concrete concept of freedom'.[80] We help our friend without any reward or return, for friendship's sake. We trust our friend and entrust ourselves to him. We need friends in order to communicate the joy of our own life and in order to enjoy our own happiness. Common joy creates friendship. Sympathy only follows from this, so that it can be said that true friendship proves itself in sorrow. Friendship lives without any compulsion or force, but it is something permanent. That is why friendship conquers enmity, for permanence counts more than the moment, and one cannot be an 'enemy' for ever. Force and violence spoil human relationships. Friendliness makes them live and keeps them alive. That is why ultimately friendship is stronger than enmity. The world will belong to enduring friendliness.

When, in the field of human relationships, the parent-child relation comes to an end, when the master-servant connection is abolished and when the privileges based on sexual position are removed, then what is truly human emerges and remains; and that is friendship. The new man, the true man, the free man is the friend. Existence *for* others within the regulation and functioning of the social order is necessary. But it is only legitimated as long as the necessity continues to exist. On the other hand existence *with* others, in unexacting friendliness, is free from necessity and compulsion. It preserves freedom because it unites receptivity with permanence. Friendship is the reasonable passion for truly human fellowship; it is a mutual affection cemented by loyalty. The more people begin to live with one another as friends, the more privileges and claims to domination become superfluous. The more people trust one another the less they need to control one another. The positive meaning of a classless society free of domination, without repression and without privileges, lies in friendship. Without the power of friendship and without the goal of a friendly world there is no human hope for the class struggles and struggles for dominance.

(ii) Jesus the Friend

Jesus is only called 'friend' in two passages in the New Testament. 'The Son of man has come eating and drinking; and you say, "Behold, a glutton and a drunkard, a friend of tax collectors and sinners!"' (Luke 7.34). These words are to be found in the discourse about John the Baptist.[81] John neither ate bread nor drank wine, and was thought eccentric. Jesus accepted sinners, ate and drank with them, and was thought to disregard the law. This is the way the people described the obvious differences between Jesus and John the Baptist. The inner reason for Jesus' friendship with 'tax collectors and sinners' was to be found in the joy of the messianic feast which he celebrated with them. It was not sympathy, it was overflowing joy in the kingdom of God, a joy that sought to share and to welcome, that drew him to people who were outcasts in the eyes of the law. The dawn of the kingdom is celebrated in the messianic feast, often described as a marriage feast. The regard which Jesus showed for the unregarded and despised when he ate and drank with them was determined by the law of grace. Jesus laid claim to this law by forgiving sins and by living in fellowship with tax-collectors and sinners.

This law of grace is nothing other than the righteousness of the kingdom of God. When the people call Jesus a 'friend of tax-collectors and sinners', they are meaning to compromise him, for they identify men with their sins and talk about 'sinners'. They identify men with their job of collecting taxes, and call them 'tax-collectors'. They identify men with their disease and call them 'lepers'. Here they are expressing the law which pins men down to what they do. But as the Son of man, Jesus becomes the friend of the sinful and the sick. By forgiving them their sins he gives them respect as people and becomes their friend. By eating together with them in celebration of the messianic feast he brings them the fellowship of God. When the people denounce Jesus by calling him 'the friend of tax-collectors and sinners', they are expressing a profound truth from Jesus' own point of view. As a friend, Jesus offers the unlovable the friendship of God. As the Son of man he shows them their true and real humanity, through which they are liberated from their unrighteousness. A liberating fellowship with the unrighteous like this always has something compromising about it outwardly.

According to John 15.13f., Jesus declares himself the friend of his disciples and calls them into the new life of friendship.[82] 'Greater love has no man than this, that a man lay down his life for his friends. You are my friends if you do what I command you.' Here the sacrifice of a man's own life for his friends is the highest form of love. Whereas love in general can be interpreted as 'existence for the other, pure and simple', friendship leads to actually risking one's life to protect a friend. When John makes friendship the motive for Christ's suffering and death, then he means by this love as clear-sighted faithfulness and conscious self-devotion for the salvation of others. Through the death of their friend the disciples become his friends for ever. On their side they remain in the circle of his friendship when they keep his commandments and become friends of one another. According to John too Jesus' friendship with the disciples springs from joy: 'These things I have spoken to you, that my joy may be in you, and that

your joy may be full' (15.11). That is the divine joy, the joy of
eternal life, the overflowing joy that confers fellowship and gives
joy to others. He has come, he suffers and dies for them out of the
divine joy, not out of condescension, and for the joy of those who
are his, not out of sympathy. That is why the disciples are called
'friends' and not 'servants' (15.15). The relationship of servants
to God, the Lord, comes to an end. Through the friendship of
Jesus the disciples become the free friends of God. In his fellowship they no longer experience God as Lord, and not merely as
Father either; they experience him as a friend, in his innermost
being. It is true that there is no equality in the divine friendship
revealed through Jesus' friendship. But it is a relationship of
mutual friendship none the less. If God is experienced as a friend,
then men become the friends of God. Friendship becomes the
bond of their fellowship.

(iii) *The Divine Friendship*

According to Luke and John, friendship with God comes pre-
eminently to expression in the prayer of the free man. A man may
feel himself to be God's servant in obedience to the commandments. He may see himself as the child of God through faith in
the gospel. But in prayer he talks to God as to his friend. The
parable which follows on the Lord's Prayer in Luke (11.5ff.) talks
about a quite everyday request for bread made to a friend. Although the time is inconvenient, he still fulfils the request for
friendship's sake, and because he cannot refuse his friend's urgent
appeal. When a man prays in the name of Jesus, he prays to God
as to a friend and is insistent for friendship's sake. In John too
Jesus' friendship leads to certainty in prayer: 'so that whatever you
ask the Father in my name, he may give it to you' (15.16). The
prayer offered in the assurance that prayer will be heard therefore
becomes the expression of life lived in friendship with God. God
can be talked to. He listens to his friend. Thanks to this friendship
there is room in the almighty liberty of God for the created liberty
of man. In this friendship there is the opportunity for man to have
an effect upon and with God's sole effectiveness.

> The grace of God to sinful man is that He encounters him as the
> hearing God; that He calls him not merely to the humility of a servant
> and the thankfulness of a child but to the intimacy and boldness of a
> friend . . . [83]

Apart from obedience and faith, this prayer is therefore the highest stage of human liberty. In it man as the friend of God participates in his lordship. By bringing the sighs and groans of the world's misery to God, he claims God's friendship for those who sigh and groan. God shows his friendship by listening to man. By doing so he gives man an irreplaceable dignity, respects him in his freedom and responds to him. Prayer and the hearing of prayer are the marks of man's friendship with God and God's friendship with man. The relationship expressed in prayer is one of mutual freedom and respect. It would be thinking like a servant to assume an obligation for prayer to be heard. It would be thinking like a child if the one who prayed did not respect God's freedom. God's friend prays out of freedom and trusts to the friendship of the free God.

(iv) Open Friendship

The concept of Jesus' friendship sums up everything that can be said about fellowship by the titles of office we have used up to now: As the messianic harbinger of joy, Jesus brings the gospel of the kingdom to the poor and becomes the friend of tax-collectors and sinners. As the high priest he offers himself 'for many', and consummates his love by dying as a friend for a friend. As the exalted Lord he liberates men from their bondage and makes them friends for others. As the one who is glorified he intercedes with the Father for the world. In his name friendship with God through prayer and the hearing of prayer comes into being.

Thus, theologically, the many-faceted work of Christ, which in the doctrine of Christ's threefold office was presented in terms of sovereignty and function, can be taken to its highest point in his friendship. The joy which Christ communicates and the freedom which he brings as prophet, priest and king find better expression in the concept of friendship than in those ancient titles. For in his divine function as prophet, priest and king, Christ lives and acts as a friend and creates friendship.

Of course the expression 'friendship' is just as much misunderstood today as the ancient titles of office. It must therefore be clearly defined and differentiated. Friendship was the quintessence of the Greek doctrine of society.[84] It is the principle of companionship. Because righteousness without concord remains sterile, friendship fulfils the meaning of righteousness and is itself the most righteous of all. But for Plato and Aristotle the reciprocal character of friendship is connected with the equality of the partners. It is true that wise men and heroes are called 'the friends of God', but it is not really possible to talk about friendship with Zeus. It is true that a free man can be friends with a slave, but only in so far as he sees him as a man and not as a slave at all. Because of the principle of equality and rank, the Greek ideal of friendship tended to conceive of it in exclusive terms. Jesus breaks through this closed circle of friendship, reaching out alike to God, the disciples, and the tax-collectors and sinners. In the Christian tradition the name of friend was often exclusively applied to the circle of the devout, the saved, or to the mystics, who sought by this means to distinguish themselves from the ordinary brethren.[85] According to this interpretation, Jesus' friends would be the group of people who see themselves as his disciples in a particular way. Through this exclusive use, which shows the powerful influence of Greek thinking, Jesus' open and public friendship for the unrighteous and the despised is lost. But in fact Christian friendship cannot be lived in the inner circle of one's equals but only in open affection and public respect for other people.

In Old High German 'friend' and 'enemy' were still public concepts based on alliances of protection and aid. Friendship was forged through alliances and publicly proved through loyalty. The modern division between public and private life has led to the concepts being differently distributed. The enemy has remained a public and political concept, whereas friendship has moved into the private sphere, there acquiring a purely inward significance. The friend has become the personal friend, the 'bosom' friend; friendship has become individualized and emotionalized. Inner agreement, natural affection, mutual goodwill and free choice have now become the determining factors in friendship. In the modern world it has consequently become necessary to give moral stability to the feeling of friendship through the ideas of respect, virtue, loyalty and reliability. Because the individual becomes lonely when the private sphere is separated from the public one, he needs friends. But they do not break through the loneliness in any essential way. The friendship of heart or soul becomes 'the loneliness of two people'. Goethe called the man happy who shut himself off from the world without rancour, enjoying the society of a bosom friend:

Selig, wer sich vor der Welt ohne Haß verschließt,
einen Freund am Busen hält und mit dem genießt...

This modern intimacy and transference of friendship to the private
sphere is quite foreign to Jesus' friendship with his disciples and
with people who were publicly known as tax-collectors and
sinners. In order to live in his friendship today, Christians must
remove friendship from the private sector, so that it may again
acquire the character of public protection and public respect.

The friendship of Jesus cannot be lived and its friendliness cannot be disseminated when friendship is limited to people who are
like ourselves and when it is narrowed down to private life. The
messianic feast which Jesus celebrates with his own and with the
despised and unregarded is not merely 'the marriage of the soul
with God'; it is also 'the festival of the earth'.[86] Because it is the
core on which his open friendship is based, a total concept of
friendship will have to be developed which includes the soul and
the body, the people who are like ourselves and the people who are
different. When we compare the ancient and the modern concept
of friendship it becomes clear that Christians must show the
friendship of Jesus in openness for others, and totally. In his
Spirit they will become the friends of others. They will spread
friendliness through a sane passion for humanity and the freedom
of man. The Quakers, who call themselves 'the Society of
Friends', have shown this in exemplary fashion through their
open social work in the slums and their struggle for the abolition
of slavery.[87]

Open and total friendship that goes out to meet the other is the
spirit of the kingdom in which God comes to man and man to man.
From Ambrose to Augustine, and from Augustine to Thomas
Aquinas, Christian love was continually given the name of friend-
ship. Love is the friendship of man with God and all his creatures.
In this inclusive sense friendship really is the most righteous of all.
Open friendship prepares the ground for a friendly world.

7. *The Place of the Church in the Presence of Christ*

The question *what* the church is, is not the same as the question
where it is. To give an account of the church's nature and purpose
is not to answer the question about the place where it has to give
an account of its nature and its purpose. It is true that traditionally

this question of where the true church is to be found is often answered by a pointer to the signs of the true church, and by a catalogue, whether extensive or brief, of its essential characteristics. But if the question is seriously directed towards the church's truth, then the question is not fundamentally about this or that characteristic at all; the question is about the one who leads the church into its truth and makes it what it ought to be. If the church is, according to its own claim, 'the church of Jesus Christ', then it is Christ who leads the church into its truth. In this case the true church is to be found where Christ is present. We sever the question of the true church from the doctrine about its visible characteristics and answer it by pointing to the happening which makes the church the church and leads it into its truth. This happens with the phrase, 'the church is to be found *where. . . .*' It indicates that the church is a happening which is not totally absorbed by its definition. The concept of the church ought rather to point to the event which makes it a living church, compared with its concept. We cannot start from the concept of the church in order to discover the happening of Christ's presence; we have to start from the event of Christ's presence in order to find the church. In this sense we start from the proposition: *ubi Christus – ibi ecclesia.*[88]

But if the church finds the place of its truth and its true constitution in the presence of Christ, the difficult question arises: where, then, is Christ present? The simple answer is: Christ, as the crucified and risen one, is only there where he promised to be present – but there he truly is present. In the Old Testament Yahweh was experienced, not as heavenly substance but as a divinely historical person, and the promise of his presence was believed in his name: 'I am who I am' – 'I will be who I will be' – 'I will be there' (Ex. 3.14).[89] In the same way, in the New Testament Jesus is not remembered as a dead man belonging to the past, nor is he defined as a heavenly authority; he is believed as the subject of his own presence. It is also true of the one who has been exalted to God that 'I am who I am' – 'I will be there'.[90] Christ is therefore present where he has expressly given the assurance of his presence. And here we must distinguish between the promises of his presence in something other than himself, and the promise of his presence through himself, between the identifications according to which he is to be expected in something else, and his own identity, according to which he himself is to be expected.

If we enquire about the promises of his presence in this way, we find three different groups of assurances in the New Testament:

(*a*) By virtue of his identifying assurance, Christ is present in the apostolate, in the sacraments, and in the fellowship of the brethren.

(*b*) By virtue of his identifying assurance, Christ is present in 'the least of the brethren'.

(*c*) By virtue of his assurance, Christ is present as his own self in his parousia.

If the thesis *ubi Christus, ibi ecclesia* is correct, then the church in its existence and method of activity will unite in itself and mediate to others these three modes of his promised presence. It will find the place of its truth in this field. If it omits any one of these promises of Christ's presence, its truth will be obscured.

(*i*) Christ's Presence in the Apostolate

Here the word apostolate is used to sum up the medium of the proclamation through word and sacrament, as well as the persons and community of the proclaimers. Here Christ's identifying promise runs: 'He who hears you, hears me.' 'As the Father has sent me, even so I send you. If you forgive the sins of any, they are forgiven; if you retain the sins of any, they are retained. Receive the Holy Spirit' (John 20.21–3). In Matthew 28.18ff. the missionary charge to the disciples is linked with the promise: 'and lo, I am with you always, to the close of the age'. Paul knows that he is an 'ambassador for Christ' and beseeches the Corinthians 'on behalf of Christ' to be reconciled to God (II Cor. 5.20).

Here the exalted Christ promises his presence to the church in the church's apostolate. It takes up his missionary charge, participating in it as Christ's representative. That is why the exalted Lord is also to be present in the church's testimony through the Spirit. He identifies himself with the apostolic word and joins the human word of his witnesses with the eschatological word. He unites the powerlessness of his witnesses with his own fullness of power in the assurance of the Spirit. This gives the human word its authority, without doing away with its human character. The word of Christ is present *in* the apostolic word and *as* the apostolic word. But the converse is not true: the apostolic word is not identical with the word of Christ. Formally, there is here an *indirect and limited identity* by virtue of the unilateral *identification*. The apostolic word takes its certainty from Christ's promise, not from itself. The equation: 'He who hears you, hears me' is set up by Christ and hence is not reversible.

This indirect identity by virtue of the promise does not merely cover the apostolic proclamation; it applies to the apostolic existence as well. In the movement of the apostolate the person of the apostle takes on the form of Christ's destiny.[91] He does not merely bear Christ on his lips in the word of the gospel. He also 'carries in the body the death of Jesus, so that the life of Jesus may also be manifested in his body' (II Cor. 4.10). Here Christ's substitution is reflected: 'So death is at work in us, but life in you' (II Cor. 4.12). The 'beseeching on behalf of Christ' in the ministry of reconciliation also corresponds to Christ's intercession (II Cor. 5.20).[92] The promised presence of Christ is the presence of the one who was crucified. For that reason the apostolate has the bodily and social dimension of the passion, and the power of the resurrection.

A corresponding promise of Christ's presence is to be found in the Lord's Supper (I Cor. 11.23ff.). The thanksgiving and the breaking of bread is described in the words 'This is my body which is broken for you'. And the thanksgiving and the drinking from the cup is described as 'This is the new covenant in my blood'. The whole eucharist is given the meaning: 'For as often as you eat this bread and drink this cup, you proclaim the Lord's death until he comes' (I Cor. 11.26). We are bound to understand this as an identification of Christ's presence with bread and wine and the whole eucharist, by virtue of the promise. The feast of his presence is surrounded by the remembrance of his death and the expectation of his coming.

Baptism contains a corresponding promise of Christ's presence (Rom. 6). People are baptized into his death so that they may walk in new life, just as Christ has been raised. They become of like form with him in his presence, by virtue of his promise.

Finally, a corresponding identification of Christ is to be found in the fellowship of believers itself: 'Where two or three are gathered in my name, there am I in the midst of them' (Matt. 18.20).

To sum up, according to the view of the New Testament churches, the exalted one is present where he desires to be present. He desires to be present where he promises his presence according to his own assurance: in the apostolate, in baptism, in the Lord's supper, and in the fellowship of the brethren. This is a Real Presence in the Spirit through identification, and an identification on the basis of promise. This leads to the proposition: where the apostolate, baptism, the Lord's supper and brotherly fellowship take place in Christ's presence, there is the church.

Article VII of the Augsburg Confession therefore uses the phrase *in qua* when discussing the place of the church: 'Est autem ecclesia congregatio sanctorum, *in qua* evangelium pure docetur et recte administrantur sacramenta.' The German version expounds the right use of the sacraments with the provision 'laut des Evangelii' – according to the gospel. This means the institutionary promises (propter ordinationem et mandatum Christi). The Barmen Declaration has clung to this form of words in article III: 'The Christian church is the community of brethren *in which* Jesus Christ acts as Lord in the present, in word and sacrament, through the Holy Spirit.' Here the brotherly fellowship is stressed on the one hand, and the present actions of Christ through the Spirit on the other. The logic of the *in qua*, or *in which*, is not entirely clear, and its interpretation is therefore a matter of dispute. Does the *congregatio sanctorum* precede what happens in it through word and sacrament, or does it proceed from it? Is 'the community of brethren' the premise for the place in which Christ as Lord is present and acts in word and sacrament through the Spirit, or does this place only come into being out of Christ's activity? Here we are assuming a truly mutual relationship, which is factually constituted through the present actions of Christ. The risen Christ makes himself present in the Spirit through word, sacrament *and* brotherly fellowship. The church exists in its truth as the church of Christ where it stands at the place of these manifestations of Christ's presence, and where it itself becomes this place.

In the realization of Christ's presence *per identificationem* with the apostolate, baptism, the Lord's supper and fellowship, his presence, his parousia, announces itself. That is why the church constituted through his presence in word and sacrament lives 'in expectation of his appearance' (Barmen III). This means that Christ arrives at his identity in the world by way of his identifications with something else, and that conversely his parousia is anticipated in the realization of his presence through word, sacrament and fellowship.

(ii) Christ's Presence in the Poor

Another group of similar promises of Christ's presence is found in the picture painted in Matthew 25.31-46 of Jesus as the Son of man in his function as Judge of the world. The Judge of the world gathers men and women before his throne on the right hand and the left. To those on the right he says: 'I was hungry and you gave me food, I was thirsty and you gave me drink. I was a stranger and you welcomed me, I was naked and you clothed me, I was sick and you visited me, I was in prison and you came to me.' Then the people he is addressing will ask wonderingly: 'Lord, when did we see thee hungry or thirsty?' And the Judge will answer: 'As you did it to one of the least of these my brethren, you did it to me.' The judgment pronounced on the people on his left is a corresponding one: 'I was hungry and you gave me no food.' When they ask in surprise, 'Lord, when did we see thee hungry or thirsty?' they are given the answer: 'As you did it not to one of the least of these, you did it not to me.' According to this story the coming judge is already hidden in the world – now, in the present – in the least of his brethren – the hungry, the thirsty, the strangers, the naked, the sick and the imprisoned. Whatever we do to them we are doing to him. Because, according to this story, the Son of man, who is also the world's Judge, calls all men to their account, judging them according to what they have done to him in his hidden presence in the poor, 'the least of the brethren' cannot only mean poor and persecuted Christians.[93] That would also be contradicted by the people's ignorance about what they were doing. Just as the last judgment is universal, so is the Judge's anticipatory identification with the hungry, thirsty, naked, imprisoned and sick wherever and whoever they are. If this identification is perceptible anywhere, it is in the path of suffering of the one who told the story: the way to Golgotha trodden by the hungry, thirsty, naked prisoner, the Son of man from Nazareth.

The way in which the identification between the Judge of the world and the least of men is formulated is remarkably closely parallel to the identification of Christ with the community of believers. Whereas there we are told: 'Whoever hears you hears me', here we read: 'Whoever visits you visits me.' In both cases there is an identification, by virtue of which the one is present in the other. But in the case of the apostolate there is an identification with the active *mission*; whereas in the least of the brethren, it is an identification with the suffering *expectation*. In the apostolate the exalted Lord speaks. Ought it not to be the crucified one who speaks in the least of the brethren? Does not the church of Christ then stand between Christ's missionary charge – 'Whoever hears you hears me' – and the expectation of Christ – 'Whoever visits them visits me'? Can the church exist in the truth and presence of Christ if it does not link this mission and this expectation together and, acting in the presence of the exalted one, seek the fellowship of the crucified one in the poor? Up to now the ecclesiological significance of Matthew 25.31ff. has hardly been perceived. But if the thesis *ubi Christus, ibi ecclesia* is to be considered a valid one, then this story with its promise of the presence of the Judge of the world is part of the doctrine of the church and the place where it is to be found.

The giving drink to the thirsty and food to the hungry, the sheltering of strangers and visiting of prisoners has often been treated ethically, with somewhat colourless talk about 'love of our neighbour'. But on the basis of what we have just said about the identification of the Judge with the least of the brethren, we really have to talk here about 'love of Christ'. It is not only the case that a man becomes 'a Christ like Christ' to the other by opening himself to him in love, as Luther said.[94] It is also true that the other, the one who is overlooked, the Lazarus before Dives' door, becomes one like Christ, a saviour and judge. The Christian programmes of neighbourly love, works of charity, care for the poor and development aid, often cover up this sting in the story, because they think that the hungry, thirsty, naked and imprisoned Christ would be helped with a little trouble. But it is not only love that is demanded. It is in the first place faith, the faith, namely, that the least of the brethren are waiting in Christ's stead for the deeds of the just man. It is not that the wretched are the object of Christian love or the fulfilment of a moral duty; they are the latent presence of the coming Saviour and Judge in the world, the touchstone which determines salvation and damnation. The hidden presence of the coming Christ in the poor therefore belongs to ecclesiology first of all, and only after that to ethics.

On the other hand Rudolf Bultmann has called Matthew 25.31–46 'the most striking account of the "transformations undergone by God"'.[95] This expression, taken from Ernst Barlach, is meant, according to Bultmann, to describe the 'unity of Creator and creature in the sense that the present moment is only a mutable fragment of eternity'. 'God encounters us in the here and now, as the Unconditioned in the conditional, the Transcendent in the transitory present, the other-worldly in the this-worldly.' That is why we have to hold ourselves open for encounters with God in the world and in time. True faith is 'readiness for the eternal to encounter us in the present, in the changing situations of our lives'. 'This readiness can be questioning or it can be completely unconscious. God can encounter us overwhelmingly where we least expect it.' The great picture of the last judgment which Jesus draws contains, according to Bultmann, 'the two closely linked doctrines of the "transformations" of God and of the presence of the eternal in time'. It is right to make Matthew 25 part of the doctrine of God, because the point at issue is the Judge of the world who is present in concealed form in the poor; but it none the less appears questionable to take this story as an illustration of the doctrine of the 'transformations of God' and the potential presence of eternity in time. Does this not make this discourse about concrete reality into a general truth about what is universally possible? For this is not simply a question of the changing situations of our lives, but of specific encounters with the hungry, thirsty, sick, naked and imprisoned – that is to say, the encounters on which neither divine nor human splendour is shed, according to our general view of things; encounters which everyone who wants to live, and to live well, is bound to avoid and flee from. Nor is it simply a question of possible transformations of the presence of God in time; it is a matter of the identification of the coming Judge of the world with those who are oppressed in the present – an identification which challenges the righteous to act. Finally, the story does not seem to talk about the paradox of 'the presence of eternity in time', but rather about the presence of the coming Judge hidden in the poor.

If we introduce Matthew 25 into ecclesiology, then an unheard-of tension arises for the church, which finds its truth in the presence of Christ. Where is the true church? In the fellowship manifest in word and sacrament, or in the latent brotherhood of the Judge hidden in the poor? Can the two coincide? If we take the promises of Christ's presence seriously, we must talk about a brotherhood of believers and a brotherhood of the least of his brethren with Christ. 'He who hears you hears me' – 'He who visits them, visits me.' The two have seldom been successfully combined in the church's history. The Christian church in its manifest form has always appealed to the exalted Christ's promises of authority, interpreting itself as the body of the exalted Lord.[96] The apocalyptic Christ, the poor, hungry, forsaken Judge, has generally remained outside the door of church and society. The only people who have asked about him have been the Christian religions of the oppressed and Christian communities which were themselves pushed out of society and church as sects.[97] But if the church, in appealing to the exalted Christ's promises of authority, understands itself as his earthly presence, must it not also, and with equal emphasis, seek the presence of the world's humiliated Judge? Evidently there are two brotherhoods of Christ, the professed and professing brotherhood which is the community of the exalted one; and the unknown and disowned brotherhood of the least of men with the humiliated Christ. If the church appeals to the crucified and risen Christ, must it not represent this double brotherhood of Christ in itself, and be present with word and Spirit, sacrament, fellowship and all creative powers among the poor, the hungry and the captives? Then the church would not simply be a 'divinely human mystery' but the mystery of this double presence of Christ. Then the church with its mission would be present where Christ awaits it, amid the downtrodden, the sick and the captives. The apostolate says what the church is. The least of Christ's brethren say where the church belongs.

If Matthew 25 is applied to the teaching and practice of the church, then the conflict between a 'dogmatic' and an 'ethical' Christianity must be resolvable. Statements about the 'manifest' and the 'latent' church could also be understood in the sense of the double presence and brotherhood of Christ.[98] Admittedly one could not then simply talk about a 'Christianity outside the church' or about 'the workings of the Spirit outside the church'. For then the question is not how people or happenings outside the church respond to the church, but how the church responds to the presence of Christ in those who are 'outside', hungry, thirsty, sick, naked and imprisoned.[99] It is not a question of the integration of Christians outside the church into Christianity in its ecclesiastical form; it is a matter of the church's integration in Christ's promised presence: *ubi Christus, ibi ecclesia.*

Here too it must be noted that the hidden presence of the coming Judge in the least of the brethren means identification but not transformation or identity. The realization of his presence *per identificationem* with the least of men is the harbinger of the presence of the Judge in identity – that is to say, in his parousia. By way of his identification with the poor, Christ attains his identity in glory. Conversely, his parousia is anticipated in the fellowship of those whom he calls the least of his brethren.

(iii) Christ's Parousia

Finally, we find in the New Testament those promises of Christ's presence in glory and open appearance and manifestation. Parousia literally means *presence*, but in prophetic and apostolic usage it has taken on the sense of *future*. Luther translated the '*Parusie Christi*' by '*Zukunft Christi*' – Christ's future. Because of this the word 'future' became the equivalent of the Latin *adventus*, not the translation of *futurum*. Later it came to be rendered as 'Christ's second coming'. But there are objections to the word 'second', because through its use Christ's parousia seems to presuppose a period of absence.

> Primitive Christianity waits for the Jesus who has come already as the one who is to come. The hope of an imminent coming of the exalted Lord in Messianic glory is, however, so much to the fore that in the New Testament the terms are never used for the coming of Christ in the flesh, and παρουσία never has the sense of return.[100]

It is only since Justin that theology has counted several parousias of Christ; he came in the flesh – he comes in the Spirit – he will come in glory. That would be Christ's threefold parousia,[101] interpreted according to the three temporal modes. But is this not to weaken the significance of the Christian faith's eschatological orientation, to fit it into the general flux of time? The three temporal modes speak fundamentally not about a future, but only about the *futurum* of being. There is what was, what is and what will be. 'What is to come' is, it is true, close to what will be, but is not totally absorbed by that; it stands in relationship both to the future and to the present and past. For what is to come does not emerge out of the forces and trends of growth and decay but comes in liberation to meet what is becoming, what has become, and what has passed away. To this extent, what is to come also contains the end of growth and decay.

When they conceive of the coming of Christ in messianic glory, the New Testament writers are simultaneously thinking of the end of the world, or the end of all things (Matt. 24.3ff.; I Peter 4.7). Consequently Christ's coming parousia is expected in universal, all-embracing and openly manifest form. For the primitive church the 'end of the world' expected in his future was not merely the close of history but the key to an understanding of the history of Christ, the history of the Spirit, and the history of the world.[102] People remembered his history, experienced the Spirit and saw world history in the light of his future. For this experience of history his future took on priority in the interpretation of time, with respect to past, present and what can develop out of both.

Is this orientation of the future towards Christ's parousia factually necessary, or a dispensable piece of mythology belonging to that particular period? It proves itself to be necessary in the fact, not in the content of the idea, from the dynamism of the provisional in the remembrance and experience of history which it occasions. The character of promise in the history of Jesus, the eschatological character of his cross and resurrection from the dead, the hopeful character of faith and the unique nature of the experiences of the Spirit, which point beyond themselves, would be incomprehensible without this future orientation towards Christ's parousia and would hence ultimately themselves be null and void.

The messianic presence of Christ in glory cannot, it is true, be conceived of, because conceptions are formed out of experience, and we have not yet experienced this presence. The events of 'the end of the world' cannot be told either, because we can only tell of what is past. But his messianic future in glory and the end of the world in it can be expected and anticipated. They are expected in the hope which is kindled at the remembrance of Christ and which in its suffering over this world cries out for the new creation in righteousness. It is anticipated inasmuch as the present is brought into 'messianic abeyance',[103] or, better, into the dynamism of the provisional. The hope of the parousia brings the historical present of Word and faith into the dynamism of the 'not yet' which thrusts forward to what is ahead. The faith that points to the word of promise therefore presses on to the seeing face to face (I Cor. 13.12). Hence the Spirit is understood as earnest, advance payment and foretaste of the coming glory. The presence of Christ in baptism and the Lord's supper is hence believed as the hidden presence 'on the way' to his direct presence.

Christ's presence in word and sacrament points beyond itself (by virtue of its indwelling logic of identification) to his presence itself, to his identity in the world. The identification of Christ with the poor and his brotherhood with the very least belong, according to Matthew 25, within the framework of the coming judgment. The Judge who is to come actualizes his presence in the least of his brethren, realizing through the judgment what was done to them as something done to him. Without this orientation the least of the brethren lose their eschatological dignity as brethren of the universal judge. Without his anticipatory incarnation in them the universal Judge loses his present significance.

If we try to link Christ's presence in the apostolate and his presence in the least of the brethren with his presence in glory, then on the one hand the dynamism of the provisional in the apostolate and in the poor runs to meet his consummating and redeeming appearance in glory. On the other hand the one who is to come is then already present in an anticipatory sense in history in the Spirit and the word, and in the miserable and helpless. His future ends the world's history of suffering and completes the fragments and anticipations of his kingdom which are called the church. His parousia in messianic glory is universal, all-comprehending and openly manifest. Here it can only be convincingly upheld and testified to in its breadth and depth through a fellowship which hears both assurances simultaneously: 'He who hears you, hears me' – 'He who visits them, visits me'. If the church were to confine itself to the first (as it has always traditionally done) then it would not be able to expect the one who was crucified in the coming Lord. If we were only to direct our gaze towards the second, then the church would all too easily wait for the coming Lord as an apocalyptic angel of revenge on behalf of those who are oppressed on earth. The fellowship of Christ lives simultaneously in the presence of the exalted one and of the one who was humiliated. Because of that it expects from his appearance in glory the end of the history of suffering and the consummation of the history of liberation.

IV

THE CHURCH OF THE KINGDOM
OF GOD

1. *Hope in Relationships*

In the previous chapter we enquired into the foundation of the church in the person of Christ, in his threefold messianic ministry and in his promised presence. In this chapter we must now assess the breadth of the horizon of hope opened up through Christ for Christianity as it lives and suffers in history. No life can be understood from its own standpoint alone. As long as it lives, it exists in living relationships to other lives, and therefore in contexts of time and with perspectives of hope. It is these that constitute in the first place a living being's unique vitality, openness and capacity for communication. Accordingly the church's reflection on itself cannot be carried out merely through the exploration of its foundations and the motives that impel it. We must investigate with equal intensity the context of the time in which it displays its vitality, develops its relationships to other lives and unfolds its activities. Just because the church is given a christological foundation, its vitality must be developed eschatologically and 'in catholicity'. The two dimensions are necessarily related to one another: 'The more exclusively we acknowledge and confess Christ as our Lord, the more fully the wide range of his dominion will be disclosed to us', said Dietrich Bonhoeffer.[1] There cannot be any christological concentration unless we simultaneously go to its utmost limits. There can be no knowledge of the centre without the simultaneous knowledge of the furthest horizon for which this centre *is* the centre. 'Loss of the centre' is the dominant characteristic of a church that loses itself in time. 'Loss of the horizon' is the mark of a church that seeks to preserve itself into eternity. But centre and horizon will always be lost or won together.

In the following paragraphs our intention is not to develop in abstract visions the future for which the church is alive, but to discover the horizons of hope that lend meaning to the specific conditions of the church; or, to be more precise, of Christianity in the world. If the church is only interested in itself, it will only be able to see its own perfection on the horizon of its hope. But if it is interested in a different life – and as Christ's church it is bound to be so interested – then it enters into relationships with partners in history who are not the church and will never become the church. It has therefore to ask about the future of these relationships in which it is involved. In the following pages we shall be developing the concrete doctrine of hope for Christianity's relationships in the world – not an abstract doctrine and not an ecclesiastical or personal one either. Every relationship to another life involves the future of that life, and the future of the reciprocal relationship into which one life enters with another. When the church talks about hope, it is talking about *the future of Israel*, for it proceeded from Israel, and only together with Israel can its hope be fulfilled. When Christianity talks about hope, it is talking about *the future of the nations* – the whole of mankind – because it exists for the nations and its hope is given it for mankind's sake. When Christianity talks about hope, it is talking about *the future of the world*, mankind and nature, in whose history it is, in practical terms, involved. Living hope is always connected with relationships. Even where hope is understood purely personally, it is connected with man's relationship to himself and in this way with his relationship to God. Eschatology is always only specific as relational eschatology.

But if hope is specific in the relationships of one life to another, then it indicates a line, a tendency or a direction for these relationships: a temporal line, along which these relationships ought to be developed; a tendency which can be missed or followed in the relationships; a direction in which changes in fellowship become meaningful. The formulation of hope's horizon therefore affects both sides, their relationships to one another and the time in which the two appear in relationship to one another. Without this comprehensive framework of hope, the relationships remain without meaning. They do not continue to live but turn into contradictions, lead to deadly conflicts, and die.

Up to now we have indicated the comprehensive Christian horizon of life by the symbol 'the kingdom of God'. We have described the present effect of the imminent kingdom as being man's conversion and his liberation from the godless and inhuman relationships of this world. Now we are concerned with the positive meaning of this hope and its consequences for the liberation of life's relationships. Conversion, the new turn to the future which follows from the gospel of the kingdom, will prove itself in the new turn given to life's relationships in the direction of the other life. That is why 'the church of the kingdom of God' asks about Israel's hope, the hope of the world religions, the hope of human society, and the hope of nature. Christian eschatology is not merely eschatology for Christians; if it is to be the eschatology of the all-embracing kingdom, it must also be unfolded as the eschatology of Israel, of the religions, of human social systems and of nature.[2]

We have now taken for granted, as if it were a matter of course, that in the context of the kingdom the church has first of all to clarify its relationship of hope to Israel, and that its other relationships of hope – to the world religions, to the social systems and to the systems of nature – must follow on that, and follow from it. But this is by no means a matter of course in the Christian tradition; it is new. In saying this we are expressing the conviction (which still has to be proved) that the task of mission, and with it the relationship to the religions of the world, is founded, in fact and in time, on the church's relationship to Israel; that, further, the church's relationship to the state, and the political commitment of Christians, is determined by their understanding of the Old Testament and their relationship to Jewish messianism; and, finally, that the relationship to nature and our hope for this relationship is dependent on the acceptance or suppression of Israelite thinking. Israel is Christianity's original, enduring and final partner in history. If the church loses sight of its orientation to Israel, then its religious, political and earthly relationships will also be turned into pagan ones, indeed into post-Christian and anti-Christian ones. The church of Christ can only understand its historical consciousness of its own nature in accordance with the kingdom and messianically (that is, in specifically liberating terms) if it grasps its relationship to Israel, to the Old Testament, and to the divine future. And the same must be said of its relationships in the world to the state, society, technology and the natural environment. But for centuries the church has notoriously failed to do this. Its anti-Judaistic tendencies have paganized and corrupted it and have robbed it of the power of its hope. The crises to which these paganized and corrupted forms of Christianity have brought the world, economically, politically, culturally and ecologically, today require the church to turn back to its Israelite origin: to turn back to the Old Testament, which at the same time means turning to the messianic hope for the world. For Christianity, to turn back to its Israelite origin cannot mean anything other than the Christian release of Israelite messianism, so that Christians and Jews can turn to the world together, with the ardour of hope.

2. *The Church and Israel*

Questions about the relationship of the church to Israel and of Israel to the church have cropped up afresh in the twentieth century.[3] The reasons are obvious:

(a) 'After Auschwitz' the Christian church, which gives the name Christ to Jesus, the Jew, is bound to revolutionize its thinking. Through their anti-Judaism, sometimes beneath the surface, sometimes obvious, the Christian churches have been paganizing themselves for centuries. They turned into institutions belonging to the single religion of their respective countries and persecuted people of different beliefs as the enemies of both religion and the state. Just as before the time of Constantine Christians themselves were persecuted as 'atheists and enemies of the state', so Christianity, once it had become established as the state religion, persecuted Jews and dissenters as godless people for whom nothing was sacred, and as 'people with no allegiance at all', that is, irreligious destroyers of society.[4] The more the church frees itself today from this abuse of itself, the more clearly it will recognize Israel as its enduring origin, its partner in history, and its brother in hope.

(b) Through the triumphalism it maintained and practised for centuries, the church has set itself up as the kingdom of God on earth in absolute form.[5] But in setting itself up as absolute through this claim, it is bound to detach itself from the history of Israel, because it is unable to recognize any other representation of divine rule on earth, or to promise the world any other future than itself. This absolutism has divided the church from its origin and its future. Christian hate of the 'impenitent' Jews is ultimately based on Christians' self-hate of their own impossible claim, namely 'hatred of one's own imperfection, of one's own "not yet" ',[6] which constantly has to be repressed through this absolute assertion. The rediscovery of the relevance of the Old Testament, the new discovery of Christianity's own provisional nature in the framework of the still unfulfilled hope of the messianic kingdom, and the recognition of Israel in a partner-like relationship are the elementary presuppositions for a Christian abolition of ecclesiastical triumphalism.

(c) The founding of the state of Israel in 'the land of Israel', which was brought about by 'Auschwitz', has put the relationship of Christians to Jews on a new footing.[7] When Jews encounter Christians they are no longer merely 'the dispersion'; they have returned home. When they meet the church they are no longer merely the synagogue; they are also a nation. Judaism today lives both in the dispersion and in the land of its fathers. For the Jews, after two thousand years, this is a new situation which they have to grasp not merely practically but theologically as well. For the church, even more, it is a new situation which is fraught with difficulties for theological interpretation. Difficulties arise for the Jews in the question whether after the occupation of Jerusalem the temple should be rebuilt and the priestly sacrificial cult reintroduced, or whether this ought to be left to the Messiah who is to come. For Christians problems emerge when they consider what attitude they should take in the conflict between Israel and the Palestinians.

(i) Israel's Special Calling

The significance of the church's derivation from Israel was always a matter of dispute in Christian theology. It is true that we can simply say: 'Without Judaism, no Christianity.'[8] But is that a historical reminiscence or a theological judgment? In theology the question of origin was often put as follows: Does the divine history of Israel merge into church history in such a way that Israel, as 'the ancient people of God', has been superseded and rendered obsolete by 'the new people of God'? Or does Israel retain its own particular 'vocation for salvation', side by side with the church, down to the end of history?

The expression 'Old' and 'New' Testaments, which started with Marcion, seems to make the book of God's promises something out of date, which is eclipsed by the splendour of the new. We no longer need the light of the moon after the sun has risen. Yet the Christian church has always understood itself and its proclamation in the light of the Old Testament and has lived from the Old Testament, as well as the New, as if the Old Testament belonged to it too. It has never actually viewed the Old Testament as out of date and superseded. The adjective 'Old' is open to misunderstanding. Besides, must the church not read the Old Testament as the book of the promise of present-day Israel as well?

Israel has a 'call to salvation', independent of the church, which remains to the end. This thesis was maintained by 'salvation-historical' theology, which extends from the Reformation theologian Johannes Cocceius, by way of Pietism and the nineteenth-century Lutheran school at Erlangen, down to the present day.[9] It is based on two ideas:

(*a*) The messianic promises of the Old Testament are only in principle fulfilled through the appearance and history of Christ; and only provisionally and partially through the eschatological gift of the Spirit. Through Christ and in the Spirit, they are at the same time also given universal force. That is why Christianity too still waits and hopes for the fulfilment of these messianic promises. Just because Jesus is believed in as the promised Messiah, and his messianic rule is already experienced in the Spirit, the surplus of the still unfulfilled promises of the Old Testament must be transplanted into the soil of the New. The church is only moving towards their fulfilment. Consequently it has to see an expectant and hopeful Israel by its side as its partner in this history. It is only Christ's parousia that will bring the fulfilment of both the Christian and the Jewish hope – not the one without the other – that is to say, only in the fellowship of Christians and Jews.

(*b*) This salvation-historical thesis is closely connected with millenarianism, the hope that Christ will rule for a thousand years in history before the end.[10] But 'we shrug our shoulders over the chosen people and hence over millenarianism as well'.[11] From the time of Tyconius and Augustine onwards this thousand-year rule of Christ was continually interpreted as the era of the church following Christ's resurrection and ascension. But if the church understands itself as the messianic kingdom of Christ, then it cannot acknowledge Israel's separate existence alongside itself. Since in the millennium Christ and his followers are to 'rule' over his enemies, they must, according to this way of understanding themselves, view the unbelieving Jews as their enemies and suppress them. From the time of Eusebius of Caesarea the millennium was also interpreted as the Christian state, ruled by Christian emperors and 'apostolic majesties'.[12] But if the Christian state is the earthly representation of the kingdom of God on earth, if the *corpus christianum* is the visible body of this God, if 'the Christian West' or 'Christian civilization' is the moral and political form of the invisible kingdom of God, then dissidents must not only be put under the church's ban but must be subject to the imperial ban as well; and then, as a condition of baptism or of emancipation within this state, the Jews must surrender their hope of a Messiah.[13] For Jewish messianism points out to the Christian state its own unredeemed character, thus calling its Christian and religious legitimation in question. In the Reformed confessions this led to the rejection of the millenarian hope as *judaicae opiniones*.[14] It was only Reformed federal theology, pietist theology, and the Erlangen school which once again won theological recognition for millenarianism in a biblical or 'biblicist' way. Israel will only be converted to the Lord through the direct and special intervention of Christ before the end. So just as the mission to the Gentiles developed out of the Jews' rejection of Christ and the gospel, so the period of this mission is to come to an end when Israel is converted. Israel's conversion in the last days will be the external sign of the transition from messianic world mission to the messianic kingdom. Out of this the following divine plan of salvation for history emerges: the mission to the Gentiles has its springtime during Israel's obduracy; the conversion of Israel follows; then come the thousand years of Christ's messianic kingdom on earth. During the era of mission to the nations the church has to make compromises and alliances with Christian states. But at the end all its supports in the Christian nations and states will be taken from it. For the remnant of believing Christians there will be no other place of refuge than restored and converted Israel.[15] It is not Pepuza or Münster, not Rome or Geneva that will be the place of Christ's second coming; it is Jerusalem. It is there that his followers must gather. For though the first shall be last, they will not be forgotten. Through his crucifixion Christ has become the Saviour of the Gentiles. But in his parousia he will also manifest himself as Israel's Messiah. Whatever we think about this modern salvation–history apocalyptic, it has vanquished anti-Judaism by vanquishing ecclesiastical absolutism. Through it the church withstood the temptation to baptize Jews under compulsion with the assistance of social pressure, or to summon them to 'emancipation' in bourgeois society or a 'humanist state' of socialism. The future of Israel is not with Lenin but in Jerusalem.[16]

(ii) Israel like all Nations?

Paul Althaus and Rudolf Bultmann have discussed the theology of salvation history in its bearing on Judaism. Althaus would like to distinguish between eschatological realism and national realism in the Old Testament. 'The realism of the promise [points] beyond its fulfilment in the New Testament to total fulfilment.'[17] But Christianity breaks with national realism. Anyone who continues to maintain it as the hope of Israel is thinking 'Calvinistically'. From this it follows for Althaus that 'Israel has its particular . . . place in God's plan of salvation: the church is built on the foundation of the history of God's dealings with Israel. The church is based on Israel as the chosen people of God, but Israel also flows into the church. . . . Israel no longer has any special position or any special "vocation to salvation" in the church and for the church.'[18] For Christ is 'also the end of the Messiah'.[19] Because of this, since Christ's coming Israel has receded of itself into the ranks of the other peoples and is included in the missionary charge to 'all nations'. In a similar way Rudolf Bultmann was only able to view prophecy in Old Testament Jewish history as the history of shipwreck on the law.[20] To be called by God and yet to be imprisoned in secular history – it is this which brought Israel into that inner contradiction from which only the gospel freed the believer, by 'desecularizing' his existence.[21] In this way Israel's unique history becomes an example of the shipwreck of human existence under the law in general. If this idea is isolated and stressed by itself, the Old Testament can then be interpreted in terms of human history as a whole, and Judaism can easily be seen merely as the negative foil to the gospel and Christian existence. The history of the promise recedes behind the antithesis of 'law and gospel'. Israel is then, through the gospel of the justification of the sinner, demoted to the ranks of the nations and made 'profane'.[22] Its history loses its special quality, becoming a matter of indifference: all men, whether Jews or Gentiles, are sinners and fall short of the glory of God. The justifying gospel is therefore directed towards all men, Jews and Gentiles alike. No special existence in the history of salvation can be ascribed to Israel any longer, because the Christian faith is not interested in world history, but only in the individual history of the justified sinner. But in this stress on the universality of sin and grace (which is in itself correct), specific historical differences are levelled out, which is just what Paul did not do.[23] Although both 'Jews and Greeks' are 'under the power of sin' (Rom. 3.9) and God justifies 'the circumcised and the uncircumcised' through faith (Rom. 3.30), the gospel none the less takes its way historically 'first to the Jew and also to the Greek' (Rom. 1.16). Just because God 'has consigned all men to disobedience, that he may have mercy upon all' (Rom. 11.32), he remains faithful to his promises to Israel and has not cast off his people (Rom. 9.4f.; 11.2). That is why according to Paul Christ became a servant to the Jews 'to show God's truthfulness, in order to confirm the promises given to the patriarchs'. But the Gentiles 'glorify God for his mercy' (Rom. 15.9). The universality of sin and the gospel is by no means a leveller of the theological difference between Israel and the nations, but becomes historically specific in this remaining difference. The gospel is 'the end of the law' but the endorsement and fulfilment of the promise.

(iii) Jews and Gentiles

Historically, the church moved from being a community of Jewish Christians to being a community made up of Jews and Gentiles; and from there to becoming a community of Gentiles. The Pauline epistles reckon specifically with a community of Jews and Gentiles and this is their 'Sitz im Leben' – their situation in life. For the almost exclusively 'Gentile' Christian churches today they are consequently as difficult to understand as they were then for exclusively Jewish Christian congregations. This difference must be taken into account more emphatically than hitherto in Pauline interpretation. Does this historical path which the church took justify a purely Gentile Christian theology of the church and a corresponding remoulding of the New Testament? It is precisely this that Erik Peterson has asserted in a number of provocative theses.[24]

(a) It is a basic assumption of the church that the Jews, as the chosen people, did not become believers. It is part of the idea of the church that it is in essentials a Gentile church.

(*b*) It is a basic assumption of the church that the coming of Christ is not immediately imminent, i.e., that precise eschatological expectations are eliminated and are replaced by a 'doctrine of the Last Things'. This leads to a renunciation of Semitic forms of thinking and the Hellenization of Christianity. It involves the legitimate moralization of Jesus' eschatological sayings; e.g., 'Everyone who exalts himself will be humbled' becomes 'the virtue of humility'.

(*c*) It is a basic assumption of the church that the twelve apostles under the guidance of the Holy Spirit took the decision to go to the Gentiles.

If we look more closely, however, the situation in the first days of the church looks somewhat different:

(*a*) It is true that Jesus did not found a church, but he made a fellowship of his disciples possible. Through his fellowship with tax-collectors and sinners, he broke through 'Israel's fence', the law. That took place inside the nation, but in tendency it points outwards as well.

(*b*) The community of the disciples which gathered round the twelve apostles after Easter symbolizes the messianically renewed people of the twelve tribes. It therefore remained within the sphere of the law, which was to be fulfilled in the power of love, and in the sphere of the synagogue. It could be termed a revival movement within Israel itself. Mission to the Gentiles was rejected because the Gentiles were only supposed to come to Zion and to receive the divine law after Israel's renewal. This, indeed, did not exclude proselytes; but it did exclude an active mission to the nations.

(*c*) The transition from 'the Christian synagogue' to the *ecclesia* probably first came about in the circle of the seven gathered round Stephen.[25] It was they who discovered for the first time that Gentiles believed without first becoming Jews, that is, that the Spirit descended directly on Gentiles. It must have been in Antioch that the Christian community termed itself *ecclesia* for the first time (Gal. 1.14). The acceptance of this political self-designation (*ecclesia* originally meant the general assembly of the free citizens of the *polis*) contains an element that is critical of the law, and a rejection of the temple cult in Jerusalem.

(*d*) Finally, the mission to the Gentiles is by no means bound up with the surrender of imminent expectation and an exclusion of precise eschatological expectations, but is the reversal in practice of the Jewish order of hope. If now, during Israel's rejection of the gospel, Gentiles are already coming to faith in Jesus the Christ, then what is already happening is what, according to Jewish hope, should only happen after Israel's redemption at the end. In faith in Jesus the Christ, the Gentiles are now already praising the God of Israel as the God of all men. In this way 'the last' (namely the Gentiles) shall be 'the first' in the church even now, whereas 'the first' (namely the Jews) through their rejection will be 'the last'. The difference between the Jews and the Gentiles is not levelled down. But the order is reversed. Even if the church becomes a purely Gentile church, it is still a church for Israel and with Israel – not contrary to Israel or without her. In spite of Erik Petersen's view, I can find no reason why mission to the Gentiles and the praise of the Gentiles (i.e., the church) should not amount to 'precise eschatological expectations'. There can be no question of a moralization of Jesus' eschatological promises.

(*e*) If the world-wide mission to the Gentiles, i.e., the church, makes the reconciliation of the Gentiles 'the last thing but one' and the acceptance of Israel the very last, then the messianic expectation of a remote future turns into a present hope in action. The expected salvation of the Gentiles is already experienced now, and experienced in active mission. Expectation of the future becomes a present task. Seen against the background of the enduring Israelite origin of the church, the mission to the Gentiles and the church of the Gentiles are eschatological signs and wonders. As long as the structure of the order of salvation for 'Jews and Gentiles' is preserved, even in the temporal reversal into 'Gentiles and Jews', Christianity and Judaism remain bound to one another. It is only if they separate that 'the first' will disappear and 'the last' be all that is left. But

> Paul is completely convinced that Israel will be converted when the full number of Gentiles is won for Christ. He reverses the prophetic promise, according to which the Gentiles come and worship when Zion is redeemed from earthly humiliation in the endtime. The mission of the apostle is a colossal detour to the salvation of Israel, whereby the first become the last.[26]

The church itself *is* this mission of hope and its initial fulfilment through the faith of the Gentiles. Consequently the church itself is this detour to Israel's salvation. The inmost reason for the detour lies in Christ's self-surrender for the reconciliation of the world, but its external cause is Israel's rejection of the gospel. If the church understands its origin, its historical path and its future in this way, then the church itself is lived hope for Israel, and Israel is lived hope for the church. Through the Christian mission to the nations Israel's messianic hope is brought to the whole world. Through the redemption of the world Israel's future will be fulfilled. 'Without the redemption of all creation Israel will not be redeemed either.'[27] The reconciliation of the world with God through the gospel is the historical way to the world's redemption, and it is hence the historical way to Israel's redemption too. For 'if their rejection means the reconciliation of the world, what will their acceptance mean but life from the dead', declared Paul, the Jew, who for Christ's sake went to the Gentiles in order to save Israel (Rom. 11.15).

(iv) New Appraisals of Israel

In the long history of the Christian creeds right down to the present day, we hardly find a single mention of Israel, let alone a theological appraisal. It was only after the Second World War that the silence about Israel in the Christian creeds was broken. As far as I am aware, the Dutch Reformed Church came first with its Church Order of 1949 and the *Fundamenten en Perspektieven van Belijden* which are embodied in it.[28] Article 8 of the church order divides Christian witness into three parts, the conversation with Israel, the gospel's mission to the peoples of the non-Christian world and the Christianization (*kerstening*) of one's own nation. This distinction takes account of different situations: in the case of Israel there is the dialogue which Jews and Christians carry on about the Old Testament; to the peoples of the non-Christian world the gospel is proclaiming something new. That is why we talk about mission here. In a Christian or post-Christian world the Christian witness must consider the history of its own influence. That is why the word used here is *kerstening*. Article 17 of the *Fundamenten en Perspektieven van Belijden* says of Israel:

1. Since God cannot repent of his gifts of grace and his call, we believe that the people of Israel (through whose ministry God desired to bless all generations on earth) is not rejected and forsaken by him. It is indeed true that Israel, when it rejected its king, was for a time re-

jected by God, the light of salvation being directed towards the Gentiles. This divine judgment consists in the fact that Israel was surrendered to the way which it chose for itself: the way in which man uses the law for his self-justification, thus shutting himself away from the shaming and liberating preaching of the grace which is in Christ Jesus.

2. Thus Israel lives among the nations as the token and mirror of God's judgment. But both its continuance as a people, and also the bringing to faith of individuals belonging to it, are the earnest and pledge of Israel's ultimate re-acceptance. God still has a future for his ancient people. It remains the people of the promise and the people of the Messiah. Anyone who finds this a stumbling block is making a stumbling block of God's sovereign acts, to which he himself owes salvation. Anyone who impugns it is impugning God's goodwill and will not escape his judgment.

3. The church of Jesus Christ has not grown to its full stature, nor has the kingdom of God arrived at its full manifestation, until Israel has been brought back to its Messiah (when and how God alone knows), so that Israel and the world of the nations both learn to acknowledge the free grace of the one who has consigned all men to disobedience, that he may have mercy on them all.

In the Catholic church the Second Vatican Council brought about the turning point. In the 'Declaration on the Relationship of the Church to Non-Christian Religions' we read:[29]

As this sacred Synod searches into the mystery of the Church, it recalls the spiritual bond linking the people of the New Covenant with Abraham's stock.

For the Church of Christ acknowledges that, according to the mystery of God's saving design, the beginnings of her faith and her election are already found among the patriarchs, Moses, and the prophets. She professes that all who believe in Christ, Abraham's sons according to faith (cf. Gal. 3.7), are included in the same patriarch's call, and likewise that the salvation of the Church was mystically foreshadowed by the chosen people's exodus from the land of bondage.

The Church, therefore, cannot forget that she received the revelation of the Old Testament through the people with whom God in his inexpressible mercy deigned to establish the Ancient Covenant. Nor can she forget that she draws sustenance from the root of that good olive tree onto which have been grafted the wild olive branches of the Gentiles (cf. Rom. 11.17–24). Indeed, the Church believes that by His cross Christ, our Peace, reconciled Jew and Gentile, making them both one in Himself (cf. Eph. 2.14–16).

Also, the Church ever keeps in mind the words of the Apostle about his kinsmen, 'who have the adoption as sons, and the glory and the covenant and the legislation and the worship and the promises; who have the fathers, and from whom is Christ according to the flesh' (Rom. 9.4–5), the son of the Virgin Mary. The Church recalls too that from the Jewish people sprang the apostles, her foundation stones and pillars, as well as most of the early disciples who proclaimed Christ to the world.

As holy Scripture testifies, Jerusalem did not recognize the time of her visitation (cf. Luke 19.44), nor did the Jews in large number accept the gospel; indeed, not a few opposed the spreading of it (cf. Rom. 11.28). Nevertheless, according to the Apostle, the Jews still remain most dear to God because of their fathers, for He does not repent of the gifts He makes nor of the calls He issues (cf. Rom. 11.28–9). In company with the prophets and the same Apostle, the Church awaits that day, known to God alone, on which all peoples will address the Lord in a single voice and 'serve him with one accord' (Zeph. 3.9; cf. Isa. 66.23; Ps. 65.4; Rom. 11.11–32).

Since the spiritual patrimony common to Christians and Jews is thus so great, this sacred Synod wishes to foster and recommend that mutual understanding and respect which is the fruit above all of biblical and theological studies, and of brotherly dialogues.

True, authorities of the Jews and those who followed their lead pressed for the death of Christ (cf. John 19.6); still, what happened in His passion cannot be blamed upon all the Jews then living, without distinction, nor upon the Jews of today. Although the Church is the new people of God, the Jews should not be presented as repudiated or cursed by God, as if such views followed from the holy Scriptures. All should take pains, then, lest in catechetical instruction and in the preaching of God's Word they teach anything out of harmony with the truth of the gospel and the spirit of Christ.

If we compare these two texts, certain differences strike us:

(a) The Dutch confession recognizes Israel's special position for the church and for the world. It talks about dialogue, not about mission. The Second Vatican Council, on the other hand, still talks about Israel in the framework of the 'non-Christian religions' and the church's general relationship to them. It is only more recent Catholic declarations about Israel[30] that go beyond this view of Israel as one of the 'non-Christian religions'. But up to now neither the Vatican nor Geneva has drawn appropriate conclusions as far as organization is concerned. Israel is still allocated to the secretariats for relations with non-Christian religions.

(b) Common to both is the recognition of the abiding vocation of the people of Israel. The Reformed declaration concludes from this that Israel – according to Paul – is indeed for a time rejected and given over to its own devices as regards the use of the law, so that through this temporary rejection the light of salvation comes to the Gentiles; but that on the basis of Israel's enduring vocation, its reacceptance and redemption are to be hoped for. The Catholic declaration sees the connection with salvation-history in linear terms rather than in such dialectic ones. The people of the new covenant remain spiritually linked with the tribe of Abraham, because the salvation of the church is prefigured in the exodus; because Christ, according to the flesh, the apostles, and most of the first disciples were Jews; and because the church waits for the day in which all the nations – Israel included – will call on the Lord with a single voice. Here Israel seems after all only to be regarded as a preliminary step to the church, even if it is a preliminary step which is preserved in all the steps that follow and which therefore recurs at the end of the road. Here the difference between the catholicity of the church and the catholicity of the kingdom of God is not seen clearly enough.

(*c*) According to both declarations, the question remains open: in what does the positive fellowship between the church and Israel consist? Israel's enduring vocation 'to be a light to lighten the Gentiles' can be founded on the abiding faithfulness of God, who could not repent of his choice, his covenant and his promise. But does this faithfulness to Israel on God's part correspond to an empirical fact? Here Christians like to point to the bare fact of the existence and survival of Judaism in dispersion and persecution. But that is not enough. We must also recognize how the Jews have subjectively remained alive. As the French episcopal statement, already quoted, makes clear, the special calling of this people is 'the hallowing of the divine name' through which the life and prayer of the Jewish people becomes a blessing for all nations. If that is true, then the Lord's Prayer would suggest that the enduring hope of 'the coming of the kingdom' is also part of this people's special calling.[31] This messianic hope intensifies the experience of the world's unredeemed nature and destroys the positive illusions of the self-satisfied, as well as the negative illusions of the despairing. It then follows that obedience to the will of God according to the Torah – that is to say, living commitment to the service of righteousness – is also part of the special calling of the Jews.[32] Obedience to the Torah cannot be legalistically deprived of its legitimacy, for the Torah is the prefiguration and beginning of the divine rule on earth. If, then, we perceive and acknowledge in the Jews' particular calling the hallowing of the divine name, in hope for the kingdom and in the doing of God's will, we find a surprising consensus with the first three petitions of the Lord's prayer. But this consensus can only be heard in two voices. On the Jewish side it comes from the story of the exodus and covenant, and from the teachings of the Torah. On the Christian side it comes from the history of Christ and the Spirit, and from the teachings of the gospel.

(*d*) According to both declarations, another question remains open: in what are the differences between Jews and Gentiles to be seen? That is the question of *Christianity's special calling*. The church is not the organization that succeeds Israel in salvation history. It does not take Israel's place. So it cannot have any desire to push Israel out. But neither is the church a revival movement within Israel, merely hoping for the national restoration of Israel and the rebuilding of Zion, and working towards that. The redemption of Israel coincides with the redemption of all creation. There is no homecoming to Israel for the church before the world is redeemed. The church of the mission to the nations proceeded from the reconciliation of the world with God in the self-giving of Christ, and was prompted to its ministry for the salvation of the nations by Israel's rejection of the gospel. The special calling of Christianity, compared with Israel, consists in precisely this service of reconciliation between the Gentiles and God, which heralds the redemption of the world. It consists in the sending of hope into the world, so that the world may return to God's future and may become free through this conversion and new beginning. The church cannot therefore remain within 'the fence of Israel' if it is to prepare mankind for the dawn of the promised messianic era. Nor can it adhere to law and circumcision. Its special calling is to hallow the name of God in the world on the foundation of the gospel of Christ, to spread hope for the kingdom, and to fulfil the will of God in liberation for love.

(*e*) According to both declarations it is clear that Israel and the church have different callings, which cannot be resolved in history in favour of the one or the other of them. Where Israel remains true to its calling, it remains a thorn in the church's side. 'This existence of the Jew forces Christianity at all periods to face the idea that it is not arriving at its goal, not arriving at truth but is always – a wayfarer.'[33] Judaism impresses on Christianity the experience of the world's unredeemed nature. But where the church remains true to its calling, it remains a thorn in Israel's side too. It testifies to the presence of the reconciliation of the world with God, without which there is no well-founded hope of its redemption. Thus the church 'makes Israel jealous' in order to save it, as Paul said (Rom. 11.11, 14). And thus Israel makes the church jealous in order that it may hope.[34]

(v) 'The Land of Israel'

The present problem, and the one that is most difficult theologically, is 'the land of Israel' and the foundation of the state of Israel in that land.[35] Anyone who recognizes Israel theologically cannot fail to know that for Israel God, people and land are inseparable. Earlier it was usual to try to separate the Jewish idea of God from the Jewish people, in order to adopt the Old Testament's monotheism while despising the Jews; and similarly it is easy to acknowledge God and his people while despising the land and the state. But for Jewish and Christian theology the wars over the foundation and existence of the state of Israel have a double aspect. On the one hand the state is a sign of the end of the dispersion and the beginning of Israel's homecoming. For the first time for two thousand years the Jews can live not only in an alien land but in their homeland. For the first time Jewish life can be lived again *wholly*. On the other hand this brings with it a recognizable danger that Israel may become a nation like all the others – not only a blessing to the nations but also a curse to the people who have been driven out of Palestine.

If Franz Rosenzweig is right, and the redemption of Israel coincides with the redemption of all creation, then the founding of the state of Israel in the land is a foretoken, but an ambiguous one. It can give Israel's special calling the ground under its feet which it needs; but must not this ground be first sanctified through calling and through righteousness? In so far as Christians recognize that the God, the people and the land of Israel belong together, they can express, out of their own uncertainty, questions to which they themselves have no answer ready.

On the other hand, for Christianity the founding of the state of Israel cannot yet be the sign of the end of its own messianic mission to the world. It does not yet bring 'the era of the Gentiles' to an end. Conversely, the stagnation of the mission to the world cannot be taken as a sign that now Israel is going to repent. Paul links the redemption of Israel with 'the resurrection of the dead'. Franz Rosenzweig ties up the redemption of Israel with the transfer of the kingdom from the Son to the Father, that is, with the redemption of all creation. The church cannot therefore rest content with a lesser fulfilment of its hope. It cannot surrender its particular mission for any other future. The Jews too will not ultimately equate Zionism with messianism, but – looking beyond the land and Zion – will wait for the coming God and his redeeming kingdom.

3. *Christianity and the World Religions*

Having given an account of the special relationship of Christ's church to Israel, we must now (while constantly revising our bearings in the light of this relationship) investigate the relations of the Christian faith to the world religions. The church's abiding origin in Israel, its permanent orientation to Israel's hope, Christianity's resulting special vocation to prepare the way for the coming kingdom in history – all this will also give its stamp to the dialogue with the world religions.[36] The dialogue cannot be determined by arbitrary and predetermined attitudes, but only by attitudes and judgments which are based on Christianity's special promise and are directed towards the universal future of mankind in the kingdom of God. But just because of this we must note the changed world situation in which the world religions find themselves today and to which they are adapting themselves.

(i) *The New World Situation*

At one time every nation, every civilization and every religion on earth had its own history, its particular origin and its own future. History only existed in the plural form of all the different histories on earth. There was no world history – merely human histories in the world. Today nations, civilizations and religions unavoidably enter a 'single, common world'. The economic, military, political and social web of interdependencies and communications is growing visibly. With the increasing density of the interweaving, the present conflicts are becoming a general threat. Because this general threat can only be overcome by common efforts, there is a demand for new community. With this the quality of history is changing too; it is making a leap, as it were, into something new: the nations will continue to have their pasts and their traditions in the plural, but their future and their hope will now only exist in the singular. This means that the future of the nations is a *single* humanity. Either the nations will run aground on their divisions or they will survive in new community. Consequently survival in the future will no longer be by the unaltered prolongation of national, cultural and religious pasts: it is something new, because it can only be what is in common. It has to be what is in common if mankind is still to win through to a future. The phrase 'world religion' has hitherto been understood to cover the great supra-national 'higher' religions, Buddhism, Hinduism, Confucianism, Islam and Christianity. The only religions that will be able to present themselves and to maintain their ground as 'world religions' in the future will be the ones that accept the 'single world' that is coming into being and the common world history which can be created today for the first time. This is the new situation for the religions, Christianity included.[37]

Historically, mission and the spread of Christianity created certain particular centres: the Roman empire, Europe and America. As a result a Christianity came into being which was centred on Rome; later this was followed by a Christianity centred on Europe and America. For a long time the Christian nations and states of Europe and America were the bulwark of Christianity against other nations and states, and also against other religions. In modern times, hand in hand with North Atlantic colonialism and imperialism, Christianity then spread all over the world. The other religions were either viewed as enemies or as the superstitions from which Christianity (in conjunction with Western civilization) freed men and women. This period of 'Western mission', with its opportunities and its burdens, is irrevocably coming to an end. The era of 'world mission' is beginning.[38] But what does this mean? Christianity is more or less present in all nations. But it is frequently only present in its Western form. Indigenous forms must therefore develop, so that an authentic Indian, Chinese, Japanese, Indonesian, African and Latin American Christianity may grow up, with corresponding indigenous theologies. The centring on Europe will come to an end. It further means that indigenous Christianity will enter into dialogue, exchange and mutual co-operation with the respective indigenous religions. In this way, without the support of Christian peoples and states, Christians will enter into living relationship with people of other faiths. The dialogue between powerless Christian minorities and the prevailing religions will look very different from the dialogue carried on by powerful Christian majorities. It will be pursued without the temptation to apply force. That is a new situation for the Christianity which is scattered all over the world.

What task can Christianity have towards the other world religions? It is one goal of mission to awaken faith, to baptize, to found churches and to form a new life under the lordship of Christ. Geographically this mission proceeds to the ends of the earth. It proceeds numerically and tries to reach as many people as possible. It thinks in terms of quantity and evolves strategies for 'church growth'. We have no intention of disputing this or belittling it. But mission has another goal as well. It lies in the qualitative alteration of life's atmosphere – of trust, feeling, thinking and acting. We might call this missionary aim to 'infect' people, whatever their religion, with the spirit of hope, love and responsibility for the world. Up to now this qualitative mission has taken place by the way and unconsciously, as it were, in the wake of the 'quantitative' mission. In the new world situation in which all religions find themselves, and the new situation of Christianity in particular, the qualitative mission directed towards an alteration of the whole atmosphere of life should be pursued consciously and responsibly. It will not be able to diffuse *en passant* the atmosphere of the Christian West, nor will it desire to do so. For this is neither particularly 'Christian' nor very helpful; and it is not what is wanted. But it will have to direct its energies towards the climate which is essential if solutions are to be found to the most serious problems which face mankind today – famine, domination of one class by another, ideological imperialism, atomic wars, and the destruction of the environment.

Qualitative mission takes place in dialogue. If it is a serious dialogue about the most fundamental problems, then it does not lead to non-commital permanent conversations. In dialogue the religions change, Christianity included, just as in personal conversations the expressions, attitudes and views of the partners alter. The dialogue of world religions is a process into which we can only enter if we make ourselves vulnerable in openness, and if we come away from the dialogue changed. We do not lose our identity, but we acquire a new profile in the confrontation with our partner. The world religions will emerge from the dialogues with a new profile. It may be said that Christians hope that these profiles will be turned towards suffering men and women and their future, towards life and towards peace.

If Christianity is to adapt itself to this process of dialogue, openness and alteration, a series of prejudices about other religions will have to be demolished.

(ii) The Absolutism of the Church

The church's exclusive absolutism has made Christianity invulnerable, inalterable and aggressive. 'Outside the church no salvation' was the definition of the Council of Florence in 1442, appealing to Cyprian and Origen. What it meant was:

> The Holy Roman Church . . . firmly believes, acknowledges and proclaims that 'no one outside the Catholic Church, neither heathen nor Jew nor unbeliever, nor anyone separated from the unity, will partake of eternal life, but that he will rather fall victim to the everlasting fire prepared for the devil and his angels, if he does not adhere to it [i.e., the Holy Roman Church] before he dies'.[39]

Here Jews, unbelievers and schismatics are lumped together into a group destined for mass perdition. The Roman church is maintained as being the church of salvation. It was at that time the imperial church as well. The crusades, the Albigensian wars and the political persecutions of the groups mentioned were both the presupposition and the result of the declaration. It was not until five hundred years later that the Second Vatican Council amended the Catholic church's attitude. Now 'all men of good will can achieve salvation', including Jews, Moslems and Christians belonging to other denominations, at least in principle.[40] For the whole group comprising all men 'of good will' (who are no more closely defined than that) is pronounced capable of salvation. This certainly opens the frontiers of the visible church, defined by baptism and membership, and makes them more permeable; but the problem remains unsolved. A milder, opener, perhaps even 'more enlightened' absolutism takes the place of the old rigorous and violent one. But must the church not rethink its position even more radically? Outside Christ no salvation.[41] Christ has come and was sacrificed for the reconciliation of the whole world. No one is excluded. Outside the salvation that Christ brings to all men there is therefore no church. The visible church is, as Christ's church, the ministry of reconciliation exercised upon the world. Thus the church is to be seen, not as absolute, but in its relationship to the divine reconciler and to reconciled men and women, of whatever religion.

(iii) The Absolutism of Faith

The absolutism of faith with regard to the world religions also needs revision. Against the background of the modern criticism levelled at religion by Feuerbach, Marx, Freud and Nietzsche, the 'dialectical theologians' Karl Barth, Emil Brunner, Friedrich Gogarten and Rudolf Bultmann have emphatically shown that faith is not to be equated with religion. From the prophets and apostles onwards, the biblical faith itself has been conspicuously critical of religion. The enemies of faith are not lack of faith but superstition, idolatry, man's 'Godalmightiness' and self-righteousness. As the successor of the prophets, true faith acts iconoclastically against the idols and fetishes of timorous man. Following the crucified Christ, it acts irreligiously and 'atheistically' against the political religions and idols of countries and nations. Trust in the triune God strips away the aura of divinity from actualities that have been made into idols and makes life in the world in the framework of creation possible. Faith in 'the crucified God' robs power and fortune of the careless confidence from which they live and the superstitious fear which is the basis of their rule. Modern philosophical criticism of religion grew up from the religion of middle-class society. Feuerbach, Marx, Freud and Nietzsche understood relatively little about the world religions or the comparative study of religions. The criticism of religion levied by early dialectical theology had in view the relationship between faith and religion at a time when the bourgeois Christian world was declining. But it deepened the conflict of faith and religion theologically in such a way that man was presented with a general alternative: religion as the self-assertion of man, who feels himself lost – or faith as man's response to God's self-revelation? Its Christian criticism of religion was directed against the Christianity which had become 'religious' in this sense, not against the world religions. For that reason we cannot deduce the absolutism of Christianity over against the world religions from the theological difference between revelation and religion, faith and superstition. The relationship of Christianity to the other religions must be defined differently. The criticism of religion is directed on a quite different level to everyone, whether he be Christian, Jew, Moslem or Hindu. If we make a clear distinction here, we escape the absolutist misunderstanding of the Christian faith on the one hand, and avoid on the other the compulsion to set up a general concept of religion which levels down all religions, including Christianity.[42]

(iv) The Relativism of the Enlightenment

The absolutism of the church in Europe came to an end through the wars of religion and was replaced by the relativism of the Enlightenment and of humanism. People sought for the 'third way', the 'third era of the spirit'[43] in the conflict between Catholics and Protestants. The more unknown continents were discovered, and the more strange religions became known, the more intensively people also looked for a general human basis in this whole field, in order to understand the things that were strange and to find peace. The tolerance of modern states towards Catholics and Protestants developed into a general tolerance towards the world religions. This tolerance, which was essential for peace, could be sustained for different reasons. It could be *sceptical tolerance*. If different groups claim absolute truth for very different things, then it would seem obvious to dispute such claims in general, and to hold anyone that maintains them for a charlatan. Sceptical tolerance is shown in the story of 'the three impostors' (Moses, Jesus and Mohammed are meant), which probably originated in the tenth century in the border region between Arabs and Christians.[44] It has also been ascribed to the 'enlightened' Hohenstaufen emperor Frederick II. At all events this story acquired great influence during the period of the Enlightenment. But sceptical tolerance does not itself avoid the necessity of having to commit itself to the non-committal nature of all claims to truth. Lessing took up the story of the three impostors in his parable of the ring; but here *productive tolerance* replaces its sceptical counterpart:

> So let each man hold his ring
> To be the true one – even so
> Let each man press on uncorrupted
> After his love, free from all prejudice.

Lessing's productive tolerance did not criticize the different subjective modes of faith for their certainty, but he did criticize their dealings with one another. He wanted to see the dialogue of the world religions in history as a noble contest, in which every religion displays its best, without disparaging the others. For him history as a noble contest between the religions had as its goal the revelation of truth at the end of history. Because of that he relativized the religions in the light of this future, seeing them all side by side as forerunners of the future truth, which they only think they already possess. In the present he was able to discover the hidden future truth only in the ethos of humanity. The truth itself is 'undemonstrable'. It is only 'demonstrated' here and now through humanity. That is why Nathan says to the Sultan Saladin, after the parable of the ring, 'Ah, if I had but found one more among you for whom it sufficed to be a man!'[45] For productive tolerance, every religion is a means of educating humanity and a transitional stage to pure morality. Lessing lived in a period of abolutist assertions of truth. 'Possession makes a man quiet, indolent and proud', he remarks critically. His pointer to the hidden nature of truth seemed to mobilize man's best powers. If truth is 'undemonstrable', then continual striving after truth, even with the admitted risk of error, stands higher than its possession. Today, on the contrary, the hiddenness of truth does not seem to release any striving towards truth at all. The change from productive to sceptical tolerance dominates the secular age. The proposition that 'everyone should find salvation after his own fashion' had a meaning as long as people actually wanted salvation, and as long as one or another fashion of finding it presented itself. The relativity of 'the religions' which Lessing maintained in the face of the future manifestation of truth, and its relativity in view of humanity's present ethos, are perverted into their opposites when they turn into relativism. For religious, historical and moral relativism either has no basis at all, or it is based on another absolutism. Even today, if we would like to channel the world religions towards the essential peace of the world or the necessary classless society, so as to relativize their differences, we do not escape the mutual play of relativism and absolutism. For who has the right, or who is in a position, to set up the conditions and the goal which are to determine the ethos of the religions and their functions? Whose picture of humanity is to prevail and whose image of the goal is to dominate humanity's future? In most cases religious relativism seems simply to be a cloak for a new absolutism, even if it does not already behave absolutely itself. The truth of relativism and the tolerance founded on it is no doubt to be sought in relationality. A life and a religion are relative in that they behave relationally and enter into living relationships to other life and other religions. In living relationship 'everything' is not of equal consequence, and therefore of no consequence at all. The one is of extreme significance for the other. It is only out of the growing web of living relationships that something new can come into being for a wider community. Absolutism and relativism are really twins, because both view 'everything' from a higher, non-historical watch-tower. In the open history of potentiality one can only move specifically from one relationship to other relationships in the hope that living relations will enable us to gain 'everything' and to combat the threat of 'nothingness'.

(v) Nature and Supernature

At this point we may briefly consider the traditional theological models for the relationship between Christianity and the world religions. They start from Christianity in order to define the relationship according to Christian concepts; that is to say, they still belong to the period of Christian absolutism. 'Nature and supernature' was one model. According to this the other religions belong to the realm of nature, the natural knowledge of God and reverence for him. But the Christian church lives from and represents a mystery which is known as 'supernatural'. It must therefore present itself as the supernatural truth of natural truths, or as the fullness of truth behind the elements of truth in the other religions. It is true that grace does not destroy nature, but rather completes it. But just for that very reason the church must take up the other religions and perfect them in itself. Wherever the church is implanted, therefore, it will take over all the elements which according to its supernatural wisdom, it holds to be 'good, true and beautiful', and will heighten them, correct them and so perfect them. We can find examples in the Christianization of Greek, Roman, Germanic and Latin-American religion. There was also a historical interpretation of the same model, according to which all the heathen religions are historically interim religions. Only Christianity can term itself 'the absolute religion' because it lives from the absolute self-manifestation of God and the eschatological presence of the Spirit. It contains within itself the completion of the history of divine Being and it represents the end of the history of religion. This model too allows for the integration of everything which is 'good, true and beautiful' in the provisional religions, measured by the yardstick of the absolute self-manifestation of God. It is also syncretistically open to the aspects of truth in other religions. But it is precisely because of its syncretistic openness that the Christian religion is to excel all others, so proving itself 'the absolute religion'.[46]

(vi) The Critical Catalyst

If Christianity renounces its exclusive claim in relation to the other religions, and if it does not assume an inclusive claim either, then the formula of the critical catalyst suggests itself as a new model for its post-absolutist era.[47] A catalyst causes elements to combine simply through its presence. The simple presence of Christians in environments determined by other religions provokes effects of this kind, provided that Christians live, think and act differently. This can be called the indirect infection of other religions with Christian ideas, values and principles. If it is true that the Indian religions think 'unhistorically', then their world picture is altered by the experience of reality as history which Christians present to them. This is already taking place through the historical investigation of Hinduism and Buddhism, through the introduction of, and stress on, the future tense in the Indian languages, and, finally, through the different relationship Christians have to time. If it is true that Islam produces a fatalistic attitude, then the encounter with Christianity brings about the discovery that the world can be changed and that people have a responsibility for changing it. If it is true that many religions have their faces so turned away from the world that they disseminate social indifference, then the presence of Christians makes them recognize social responsibility and the activities appropriate to it. But these indirect catalystic influences of Christianity on other religions are never unequivocal; they are always ambiguous, especially when they are linked with the spread of Western science and technology. Science and technology, capitalism or socialism, cannot be viewed as an indirect 'Christianization' of other religions. But these effects are there and must be noted. We must become conscious of them today so that the catalystic influences of the Christian faith can be less ambiguous than they have been, and are not confused with the influence of the West, merely under Christian auspices.

The models we have discussed are still not based on dialogue since they proceed from the Christian monologue, not from the dialogue itself. They all formulate the Christian position before the entry into dialogue. They do not formulate it in the context of dialogue. Consequently they still do not show any profile of Christianity in the context of dialogue. Christianity's vocation must be presented as clearly as possible, but it must be a presentation in relationship, and must not precede that relationship.

(vii) Profile in the Context of Dialogue

The life in dialogue of the world religions is in its first modest and hesitant beginnings. It is therefore more important to formulate the first steps than to fix the comprehensive goals. Bilateral dialogues between Christians and Jews, Christians and Moslems, Christians and Buddhists, Buddhists and Hindus, Moslems and animists, etc., can lead to multilateral dialogues; and multilateral dialogues can be the genesis of the tension-fraught universal community of religions for a universal society, though no one yet knows what it will look like.

We have talked about a qualitative mission, aimed at creating a climate for life in fellowship; and we have called its method dialogue. Out of bitter experience, the expression 'mission' has come to be taken as a threat by many people. Christians can only talk about their particular mission if they take note of and respect the different missions of other religions. They can only enter usefully into dialogue with them if they do not merely want to communicate something, but to receive something as well. Fruitful dialogue involves clear knowledge about the identity of one's own faith on the one hand; but on the other it requires a feeling of one's own incompleteness and a real sense of need for fellowship with the other. This is the only way in which real interest in another religion comes into being, a 'creative need for the other'.[48] The dialogue itself changes the atmosphere in which the religions formerly existed, separated from or even actively hostile to each other, and creates the conditions for fellowship in which mutual participation, exchange and cross-fertilization become possible.

The first experiences of dialogue of this kind led to a catalogue of the insights which other religions can pass on to Christianity.[49] The uniqueness of Islam's call 'Let God be God', its total recognition of the divine lordship over the whole of life, and its criticism of idolatry, both ancient and modern, must impress Christians and call them to self-examination. The meditative power of Buddhism, its insight into the self and man's inner freedom brings back to light repressed mystical elements in the Christian faith, and can lead Christians to re-examine their modern activism. Perception of the complicated systems of balance which bind together the individual, his community, the natural environment, his ancestors and the gods does not permit the prejudicial adjective 'primitive' to be applied to the animist religions of Africa and Asia. They probably preserve ecological and genetic knowledge which has long since been lost to modern Christianity.

The three-cornered dialogue between Jews, Christians and Moslems can fall back on common historical presuppositions and many existing parallels. The dialogue with Buddhists will first of all concentrate on the general human problem of suffering. Conversations with the popular religions can, in the first place, revolve round 'the feast'. There are starting points enough, once interest has been awakened. But we shall only be able to discover what they are through dialogue. Here the level of the dialogue will first have to be found in each individual relationship. It is not possible to determine this level from the Christian side by means of theological scholarship; for 'theology' is a Christian speciality and peculiarity, and theology as a discipline has only existed in Christianity since the Middle Ages. Other religions have other forms of expression, and so will wish to choose their own level of dialogue, e.g., the cult, meditation, or other areas of religious practice. For this reason Christians cannot determine in advance that the relationship is to be one of dialogue on an intellectual level. But, like every other religion, Christianity must none the less be clear about what it hopes for when it enters into living relationships and into dialogue with others. And here the dialogue cannot be the means to an unspoken end; how far the dialogue itself is hope is something that must be clarified.

'Dialogue strives to bring to expression the love which alone makes truth creative.'[50] For Christianity dialogue and the relationships to other religions are not a means to an end; they are meaningful in themselves as an expression of its life in love. For it lives in the presence of a God who is love and who desires love. It lives in a God who can suffer and who in the power of his love desires to suffer in order to redeem. In their dialogue with people of a different faith, Christians cannot therefore testify through their behaviour to an unalterable, apathetic and aggressive God. By giving love and showing interest in others, they also become receptive to the other and vulnerable through what is alien to them. They can bear the otherness of the others without becoming insecure and hardening their hearts. The right thing is not to carry on the dialogue according to superficial rules of communication, but to enter into it out of the depths of the understanding of God.[51] In that way we testify to God's openness to men in our openness to other people and other things. In that way we show God's passion through our living interest in the other. In that way we manifest God's vulnerability in the vulnerability of our love and our readiness for change. To isolate oneself and to seek to dominate even in mission are probably always signs of incapacity to suffer. The God who wins power in the world through the helplessness of his Son, who liberates through his self-giving, and whose strength is mighty in weakness can only be testified to in dialogue and in the wounds and transformations which dialogue brings with it.

It was said to be one of the highlights of the ecumenical dialogue when a Shiite Moslem, with his tradition of the sovereign God, felt the lack of God's self-surrender to man, the God who suffers and sacrifices himself.[52] This must not be overvalued, or stressed as a missionary success, but it can be interpreted as an indication that human suffering is the central problem in most religions. Is it solved when the Buddhist tries to extinguish the 'desire' of life as the ground of suffering? Is it solved if the animist sees it as a disturbance in the cosmic balance and tries to put the disturbance right through sacrifice? Is it solved when the Moslem accepts his destiny in total self-surrender to God? Is it solved if the Christian accepts suffering in the love of God and transforms it by virtue of his hope? Dialogue is not merely a way of discussing suffering; it is also a way of practising our attitudes to suffering on one another.

This complex of dialogue, vulnerability and the question of suffering leads to the step beyond inter-religious dialogue, to the human situation today. The fellowship in dialogue of the religions would be misunderstood if it went under the slogan: religions of the world unite against growing irreligious secularism or antireligious Communism! On the contrary, inter-religious dialogue must be expanded by dialogue with the ideologies of the contemporary world. Together with them, it must ultimately be related to the people who are living, suffering and dying in the world today.

When we consider the indigenization of the Christian churches and Christian theology in any given society, this orientation also raises the question of the place of their presence in the social structure. In societies which are divided up into castes and classes, it matters very much whether the Christian churches and theology make themselves at home in the ruling castes or classes, in the lower castes or classes, or among the casteless and classless. Historically, too, it made a difference whether Christianity spread through the conversion and baptism of kings, or through the conversion and liberation of the poor. It is true that today national and social identity often overlap. But just because of that the national and cultural indigenization of Christianity is by no means sufficient. It must also come to be at home among the people; and what will be at home among them is whatever shares their necessities and works for their liberation.

This orientation towards the suffering of the present time also raises questions about the social position of the partners in the dialogue between world religions. Top-level discussions between privileged persons usually do very little to relieve the suffering of ordinary people. Dialogue is a sign of hope for these people if it is carried on in the interests of their life and liberation. In the interests of cultural indigenization, a truly Indian, Chinese, Japanese, Indonesian, Arabic and African Christianity must come into being. Moreover, in the dialogue with the world religions a Buddhist, Hindu, Moslem, animist, Confucian, Shintoist Christianity will come into being. There were Jewish reasons for believing Jesus to be the Christ. There were Greek reasons for believing in Jesus as the Logos. There were Germanic reasons for reverencing Jesus as the leader of souls. In their own period these reasons were not merely cultural; they were more religious in kind. Culture and religion cannot be separated. Consequently, today we shall also have to enquire into Hindu, Buddhist and Islamic reasons for faith in Jesus. This must not be condemned as syncretism. A Christianity coloured by different civilizations does not result in a cultural mixture; and a Christianity tinged with different religions does not simply produce a religious mixture. What is at issue is the charismatic quickening of different religious gifts, powers and potentialities for the kingdom of God and the liberation of men. The syncretism which dissolves Christian identity only comes about if people lose sight of this future, to which Christianity is called. Mere indigenization in another culture and religion looks back to what has come into existence and to what is actually present. The charismatic activation of cultural and religious forces in the interests of the messianic future looks forward. If it is Christianity's particular vocation to prepare the messianic era among the nations and to make ready the way for the coming redemption, then no culture must be pushed out and no religion extinguished. On the contrary, all of them can be charismatically absorbed and changed in the power of the Spirit. They will not be ecclesiasticized in the process, nor will they be Christianized either; but they will be given a messianic direction towards the kingdom. For this, people of other religions, and the other religions themselves, bring a wealth of potentialities and powers with them; and Christianity must not suppress these but must fill them with hope. Then the dialogue of world religions can also become a sign of hope for the people who have no definite religion or religious practice, but whose elemental cry is for liberation, life and redemption. For Christianity the dialogue with the world religions is part of the wider framework of the liberation of the whole creation for the coming kingdom. It belongs within the same context as the conversation with Israel and the political and social passion for a freer, juster and more habitable world. Christianity's dialogistic profile ought to be turned to the future of the liberating and redeeming kingdom in the potentialities and powers of the world religions. That is a profile which Christianity can only acquire in dialogue with others.

4. *Christianity in the Processes of the World's Life*

(i) *Necessary Differentiation*

Now that we have looked at the church's position with regard to Israel, and the position of Christianity in relation to the world religions, we must enquire into Christianity's position in the secular order. Here too we shall be concerned with institutions and processes which can neither be ecclesiasticized nor Christianized, but to which the church adapts itself and in which Christians adopt particular viewpoints. As the heading indicates, here we are giving a new name to the partners who are entering into living relationship. The word 'church' always suggests the official church, or the regular organization; but here responsibility clearly lies with responsible Christians in their secular professions. So at this point we shall talk about 'Christianity'.[53] On the other hand we shall not talk in the usual way about the secular order – family, economy, state and culture – because the conceptions of this 'secular order' are based on the model of the state of pre-modern times with its class distinctions; and also because the expression 'order' sounds too static. We are really concerned with h'storically mobile and interdependent areas of activity where it is important not to preserve a fore-given 'order' but to regulate ordering processes. We shall therefore talk about processes instead of orders, processes in whose conflicts and trends Christianity is involved, and has to be involved today, more consciously than ever before.[54] Earlier, people saw the secular order in the limited circumference of their own people, their own nation and their own society. The church's doctrine about the secular order had in mind those societies which could be termed the *'corpus christianum'*, or 'Christendom'. But in the age of the growing interdependence of all the peoples and societies on earth, limitation to one's own society or to 'Christendom' becomes more and more provincial. Wherever Christianity is involved in economic, political or cultural processes – and that means everywhere, practically speaking – it is involved in *world* processes. It has to recognize this interdependence and free itself from national and cultural narrow-mindedness. Christianity does not exist for its own sake; it exists for the sake of the coming kingdom. Christians look forward to this kingdom as the future of the whole of creation; and so they can only prepare for it together with other people. For Christianity's hope is not directed towards 'another' world, but towards the world as it is changed in the kingdom of God. Christian ideas about the goal of the world processes therefore do not simply belong to social ethics, either; they are a part of Christianity's comprehensive mission in history for the kingdom. The church does not understand itself if it does not understand its mission in this world process and its hope for this world process. Notwithstanding the ever-closer interrelations of the different elements, let us differentiate the world process according to three dimensions:

1. The economic process, which is acted out in economic

struggles and the exploitation of nature. Here the economic liberation of man and nature from man's exploitation is essential.

2. The political process, which is acted out in the struggle for power and the control of power. Here the need is for man's political liberation from man's repression.

3. The cultural process, which is acted out in the struggle for educational, racial and sexual privileges. Here the aim is man's cultural liberation from his alienation from other men.

Today the uneven and egoistical advances made in the different dimensions have brought the world to a global crisis in which mankind is driving itself and the natural basis of its life towards destruction. Progress is beginning to devour itself. That is why the image of the vicious circle suggests itself everywhere, in big and little things alike. Actions prompted by hope for mankind's survival and a meaningful and humane life must be gathered together into the appropriate counter-strategies if they are to achieve anything. Statements about the theology of economic, political and cultural liberation do not mean that we should split up theology into separate sections; they simply point to the necessary differentiation of theological reflection about specific action in the various dimensions, in the light of Christianity's special messianic mission and its all-embracing hope for the coming kingdom.

(ii) The Will to Live in the Face of Destruction

Our contemporary economic, political and cultural world crises are shaking people to the depths of their *will to live*. That is why what is demanded of Christianity is not merely ethical commitment to liberation from the vicious circles in which man is involved; the presence of its faith is of equal importance. These crises are not to be solved with the help of an improved morality alone, for the loss of courage is so widespread that many people are not doing what they could do, even though they know that they have to do it. In this crisis faith means the courage to be, the affirmation of life, loyalty to the earth.

> Only a vigorous will towards this world permits faith in the next to germinate, after life's crisis; the man who does not *will* simply does not believe. . . . That is the reason for the decay of religion – the decay which we cannot get to the root of. When circumstances are bearable people quite enjoy living. But the word 'enjoy' has no strength in it. The film ends, the picture on the television screen fades. Shall we see

it again? Shall we go on watching? Why? . . . For the rest, the glow of the mushroom cloud spreads through the air. The sword strikes. Lucky is the man for whom it has all ended already! So if we wanted to missionize we would have to strengthen the will for this world; fear is useless. But what arguments are there?[55]

In this situation of paralysing apathy and the creeping recession of the will to live, the Christian faith must show itself in courage for incarnation, in a passionate love of life, and in its ardent interest in existence, so that the feeble 'enjoyment' of life acquires the power to resist death, catastrophe and all the people who pursue them. We can break the spell of creeping acclimatization to the deterioration in the quality of life brought about by injustice, oppression and man-made catastrophes. The paralysing feeling of helplessness must be overcome if mankind is to go on promising itself a future.

The enthusiastic hopes which mobilized an earlier generation and set the industrial revolution on foot are decaying. Today the hopes which were invested in progress, growth and profit are turning into fatalism, suicidal despair and nostalgia. They have been deeply disappointed. Moreover they must be drawn out of the industrial revolution so that, newly formulated, they can be made capable of taming that revolution. It is for that that they must regain their true vitality. *The power of hope* is only manifested in the crisis of progress today if it leads to life even in the face of deadly crisis. In confrontation with the economic, political and ecological processes that are taking place, it must make people ready to act in time and to make the necessary sacrifices. There will be no survival for mankind without the rebirth of the power of hope, which in the face of the possibility of the world's death wills to live and prepares to live.[56]

Finally, the rediscovery of *the capacity for suffering* is part of the will to live and the power of hope. The industrial, political and cultural undertakings of modern times are splendid endeavours to overcome suffering, or at least to reduce it. But progress in the conquest of human suffering has taken place to a great extent at the cost of increased suffering for other people. If the mass of suffering is shifted, the people who have been relieved of it easily get the impression that the suffering has been conquered. But if a society only overcomes its hunger by letting other people go hungry in its stead, if it only overcomes its oppression by enslaving others, it is impossible to talk about the conquest of suffering. If it is true that the limits of growth are becoming recognizable on the horizon of an imminent and datable future – and of this there can be no doubt – then there are limits to the conquest of suffering as well.[57] The ideal of Western progress – to lead a life free from pain or suffering – is intolerable because it inflicts suffering and pain on others. We cannot just minimize this by talking about regrettable 'side effects'. This is the actual price that has to be paid. Consequently there can only be an equal and just distribution of the burden of suffering that cannot be overcome. The ideal of a life without suffering makes one group of people apathetic and brutal towards other groups, which are supposed to pay the price. The shifting of the cost on to other people is intolerable for both. Humanity only has a future if it looks to a *common* future. If humanity wants a common future, and if people are not to bring one another to suffering and death, then the people who are now capable of acting must rediscover the meaning of suffering. It is only the dignity of solidarity in suffering which makes people capable of fellowship. And here the capacity for suffering in the sense of receptivity for the other and a quick eye for what is new must be awakened too.

In this context Christianity in the world can be expected to overcome the fatal loss of courage with its *passion for living*. It can be expected to make life possible in face of the threat of death through the power of hope given by its faith. It can be expected to put a stop to the shifting of suffering on to others, through the capacity for suffering of its own love; and – contrary to the 'struggle for existence' – to build solidarity within the frontiers of existence.

The church is not in a position to put itself in the forefront of the imperfect, natural orders as a perfect society. Its own hierarchical constitution is a historically developed structure eminently determined by the times in which it grew up; as such it does not as yet reflect the kingdom of God. It cannot be the church's commission to form the world after its own image. Every direct intervention by the church in economics, politics and culture has up to now been subject to the suspicion that it was serving the church's own interests; and this suspicion is hard to destroy. For this reason the church ought not to claim any direct power in secular matters. The model of partnership, of mutual limitation

and complement, between the church and the secular order func-
tioned as long as there was a 'Christian world'. But since the
secular order has increasingly emancipated itself from the Christian
world, the limiting and complementing function of the church has
ceased to work. The church's faith certainly continues to claim the
right to liberate the secular order for its true secularity by keeping
it free from surrogate religious and ideological idolatries. But since
reason has long since acquired an independence of its own, alike
in the economic, political and cultural sphere, faith's claim generally only acts as a subsequent justification of what has been achieved
without it. The church's claim to free the secular order for its
secularity, and faith's claim to bring reason to its secular reason-
ableness is based on an indirect power of the church and of faith.
This claim too has become ineffectual today.

If we start from the situation of world-wide Christianity, and of
Christians in their secular professions and responsibilities, then
what is in question can neither be the ecclesiasticizing of the world
nor a helpless respect for the inherent laws of the secular spheres;
the aim can only be the perception of certain trends and lines of
Christian action. For Christians these trends are motivated by the
will to live, the power to hope and the capacity for suffering that
are part of their faith. They are directed towards the future of
creation in the kingdom of God and are actualized in the powers
of the Spirit and the potentialities of history. Coming from liberation through Christ, determined by the surplus of hope that over-
flows every historical present, they will as far as possible do whatever is vitally necessary if we are to resist the power of death as
well as the deadly powers.

(iii) Christianity in the Processes of Economic Life: Symbiosis

Economics originally meant domestic science.[58] In its Greek
origins, economics was a part of the politics of the city state, for
the larger household of a Greek citizen was his *polis*. That is the
reason why Aristotle treats economics as part of political philosophy. Down to modern times, economics was dealt with in the
framework of moral theology and moral philosophy. It was still a
part of politics. It was only when natural philosophy came to be
separated from moral philosophy, and the natural sciences from
ethics, at the end of the eighteenth century, that the autonomy of
the economic sciences grew up, an autonomy which is expressed

in the concept of 'pure economics'.[59] It corresponds to the middle-class division between society and state and the industrial division between work and family. Rapid industrial development and the economic expansion of the industrial countries has led to a situation today when economic categories are more comprehensive than political ones, and political institutions are less and less able to regulate the large-scale economic organizations, with their power and the conflicts they evoke. World markets have grown up which escape the control of governments and inter-governmental institutions.

Practically speaking, the only 'universal' in the contemporary world is money.[60] Although the rates of exchange fluctuate, the monetary system is a universal reality. It is the medium of economic communication. It makes community possible through buying and selling, because money itself is something like symbolized possibility. People do not merely 'speculate' with money; money itself is a speculative reality. Labour and goods stop being realities and turn into potentialities when they are re-calculated in terms of money. Money can then be transferred in different ways into the reality of goods and services. But money is speculative in another respect as well. As long as the economy was regulated by politics, coins bore the picture of the emperor (cf. Matt. 22.21). They represented the imperial sphere of influence. Even today coins and bank notes bear national emblems, for the political community is supposed to guarantee the value of money. US dollar notes are not only a claim to confidence in the nation; they are a claim to religious confidence as well, with their assertion: 'In God we trust.' Really, however, bourgeois industrial society has long since created a world in its own image through the world currency system and the world market. When currencies become universally convertible, they are no longer a *speculum* of a political ruler or an individual nation; they reflect this society which is, in trend, 'universal'. It is our own reflection which looks back at us from coins and bank notes, and enables us to enter into relationships and exchange with every other person. But these relationships by way of the potentialities of money cannot be called 'human' relationships. For through them the person only enters into communication as *homo oeconomicus*, as labour and as a purchaser. On this level all other human designations and relationships are of no significance, because they cannot be summed up in terms of money. At the same time, 'economic man', reduced to his capacities as producer and consumer, is the first 'universal man' visible today. 'Pure' economics are only pure because they are confined to this aspect of man and are related to a universe in which political, cultural, sexual, national and religious differences between people have no significance.[61]

But human reality is never 'purely economic' and even 'pure economics' are never pure. Human needs, claims and values always run ahead of the economy; they are incorporated in its systems and bound up with its progress. The economy belongs within the context of a social ethic, and lives from it. As long as this ethic is 'a matter of course' we need not pay any attention to it and can confine ourselves to 'pure economics'. But if it is called in question, then the economy has to consider its ethical and political context critically, just as, conversely, ethics and politics have to subject their economic basis to a critical examination. By ethics and accepted values we mean here a society's vital wishes, fundamental claims and ruling interests.[62] This still does not tell us anything about its moral qualities. These wishes, claims and interests have their situation in the life of society and regulate that life. They are not unalterable, but in their own period they count as 'absolute' in the sense that people have the impression that things could be no different. It is only when the fulfilment of these wishes, the satisfaction of these claims and the realization of these interests lead to crises and catastrophes that a 'revaluation of values' becomes possible and necessary.

What values have governed the rise of modern economics? If we compare modern economics with the economics of pre-modern societies we find that the most important distinction is the difference between growth, expansion and universality on the one hand, and equilibrium in limits on the other.[63] Earlier civilizations were by no means primitive; they were actually highly complicated systems of equilibrium in the relationship of man to man; of groups to nature; and of both to the gods. The modern world, on the other hand, is fundamentally out for growth, expansion and conquest, without inward moderation and without external scruple. For the modern world, non-expansion or 'nil growth' counts as stagnation. Here inflationary monetary policy can even make standstill look like progress or force it into a recession. The particular nature of modern economics presupposes in men and women an insatiable hunger for life which makes them strive beyond every state of affairs which they have already achieved. Man wants to live, but mere life does not content him. He wants an intensified, full and happy life. For him there is no such thing as life in a limited and constant dimension. There is always either more life, or less. Intensified life means being able to 'live it up', being able to realize to the full life's potentialities – which are thought to be unlimited – being able to overcome everything negative which is a drag on vitality, and to acquire the positive things that enhance it. This limitless hunger for life is coupled with the will to power and the interest in rule. Life is power and the will to power.

If one is a European one can see in this unrest the unique nature of human existence *per se*:

> At all events man in relation to the animal is . . . the eternal 'Faust', the *bestia cupidissima rerum novarum*, never content with the reality encompassing him, always hungry to break through the limits of his existence-as-it-is-now, always striving to transcend the reality that surrounds him.[64]

For an African, however, this can merely be seen as the modern European's Vasco da Gama mentality. The notion that the value of a person lies in the fulfilment of his claims and the increase of his power is a conviction which only grew up in the period of early capitalism, at the beginning of modern European times. It also led to a reinterpretation of the biblical teaching that man was made in the image of God; and this reinterpretation had disastrous consequences.[65] According to the biblical and Christian tradition it is only the fact that he is made in the image of God that justifies and upholds man's commission to rule over the earth. But since Francis Bacon and René Descartes this idea has been reversed: it is man's expanding rule over nature which makes him the image of God and leads him to be like God. The goal of man's lordship over the world through science, technology and economics is supposed to be the restoration of his position in paradise. Through this he is to become 'maître et possesseur de la nature'. This perversion of the Christian picture of man gave rise to the conviction that man must do everything he can with the world he dominates.[66] Lordship therefore implies a taking possession, and possession means using and exploiting for the purposes of one's own life.

The effects of this modern ethic on economics and ecology are sufficiently well known. The scientific subjection (objectification) of nature was followed by the technical demolition of the natural systems of life and their exploitation as 'raw material' for human industry. Rising consumption must be followed by rising production, just as, conversely, expanding production must be boosted by rising consumer demands. As a result, everywhere processes of growth have come into being which escape our control: growth of industrial production, growth of environmental destruction, growth of populations, growth of the need for raw materials and energy, growth of man's dependence on a flood of outward stimuli, and his inward instability. These different processes of growth goad one another on reciprocally. This results in an ever more comprehensive spiral, whose future today can be seen as no longer being life, more life and greater power, but the universal death of humanity and organic nature. Yet the ethos of the society which is perpetuating these growth spirals has not changed. The claims to life and power are as immoderate as ever they were, and accentuate the progress. Earlier, people were glad if they could satisfy life's elementary needs. But in the imperialist society needs do not stop short at the necessities of life. As needs are satisfied, demands are stepped up, so that demand and satisfaction accelerate one another. This race between demand and satisfaction is the inward motor that drives expansionist economy.

However 'the limits of growth' are described today, it is obvious that unlimited growth is impossible with limited resources, and that unrestricted demands cannot be fulfilled with restricted potentialities. If the immoderate acceleration of demand and satisfaction goes on, the race will force us into a global crisis which will put an end to all claims alike. If the idols of growth, expansion and exploitation remain a part of economics, then a global destruction can be seen ahead that will make all human economics alike impossible. The limitless growth of claims for more life, greater power and expanded rule has up to now been the inner fuel of 'progress'. We can now look ahead to the time when it will be the fuel of catastrophe as well.

In this catastrophic situation it becomes clear that economics is not 'pure economics'. It was never a mercantile science, without any values, for it always lived from the ethos on which society was based and from the demands, claims and interests of man and of society; and this was particularly true of its so-called 'pure' form. Consequently respect for 'inherent economic laws' and their 'factual compulsions' is out of place. Today people are aware of the reciprocal action of human demands and the economy, because the demands built into the economy up to now are driving us into conflicts and catastrophes. Today the interaction between demand and the economy which we knew in the past has become highly dangerous. The essential point is to end the race between demand and satisfaction (a race which cannot be won in any case), through a revaluation of values, so that we may seek for other satisfactions with changed desires. For 'economic man' is after all not merely a hypothetical picture set up by economic science; he is also the real person who acts according to the picture. Without society's capitalist ethos, and without the person who reduces himself, and allows himself to be reduced, to labour and purchasing power, pure economics, with its orientation towards the exploitation of 'manpower' and nature's raw materials, would not exist at all.

What line ought Christianity to take in economics, and what trend ought it to pursue with the means at its disposal? The Old Testament always recognized the earth as 'the Lord's property'. 'The earth is the Lord's and the fulness thereof, the world and those who dwell therein' (Ps. 24.1). Rabbinical exegesis used the word *oikonomos* at this point, and explained: 'God is the Lord of the house, because the whole world is his property, and Moses is his *oikonomos*.'[67] When in the New Testament Christ is acknowledged as the Lord of God's kingdom, it means nothing less than this. The 'house' of which Jesus is Lord and which is to be kept in order according to his will, is called *oikoumene*, the world, and 'those who dwell therein' are called *katoikountes*. In this sense economics cannot be excluded from the liberating lordship of Christ. In the all-embracing sense of salvation, Christian theology is economic theology as well – and, if you like, 'materialistic theology' too. This is not meant in a clerical sense, but every withdrawal of the presence and living testimony of Christians from any sphere of life would be the equivalent of a surrender of their hope. The change of life's direction towards the kingdom of God, through which people become Christians, is a comprehensive one; it includes turning away from the lethal tendencies inherent in our present economy and towards a life which overcomes death.

We can take it as our premise that for Christianity it is not the will to power and to domination over the earth that makes man the image of God, but that the very reverse is true: because man is made in the image of God, his rule over the earth has its bounds and its responsibilities. Christians who take this seriously will consequently break with those values and requirements which are the driving power behind our modern economy. They will choose the path that leads away from the ruthless satisfaction of demands, to community; away from the struggle for existence, to peace in existence; away from the will to supremacy, to solidarity with others and with nature. They will strive to break through the previous social and economic ethos and to introduce changes in people's economic and social behaviour. The catastrophe we can already see ahead of us can only be averted if people are no longer forced by their social system, and its public marks of approval and condemnation, to see one another as mutual competitors in the struggle for existence and the hunt for happiness, and if, instead, individuals, groups and nations move towards a symbiosis with one another. Ecological death can only be avoided if social and economic systems cease to be directed towards the exploitation of labour and the breaking up of natural systems with a view to their exploitation. There are always correspondences between the social relationships of people with one another and the relationship between the social system and the natural environment. For a long time the system of domination and suppression affected slaves and animals in the same way. Changes in the social relationship of people to one another will therefore also bring in their wake changes in the relationship between human societies and nature. Conversely, the change in man's relationship to nature from exploitation to co-operation, and from suppression to symbiosis, will bring radical alterations to the social structure in its train.

The most important element for the development of a society that deserves the name 'human' is *social justice*, not economic growth. Consequently it is no longer the ideal of *beate vivere* which can have ultimate validity, but only the ideal of *recte vivere*. The will towards private or group-orientated self-realization must give way to the will to build a just society and a contented existence. The desire for the mounting satisfaction of mounting wants was not always the centre of human intentions. It only grew up out of modern European imperialism. The hunger for justice and the longing for fellowship with one another can be much stronger. Among other peoples and cultures, and among many young people in the industrial societies, solidarity is higher up the list of values than the material enrichment of life through production and consumption. For it is solidarity and fellowship alone that make even suffering and the necessary curbing of natural desires bearable. If Christians in the world understand themselves as world-wide Christianity – and that means *ecumenical* Christianity – they will strive for this ethic of solidarity and a corresponding new economic orientation. That includes renunciation of further economic expansion in the wealthy countries for the sake of the economic development which is necessary in the hungry ones. 'Development aid' cannot exhaust itself in alms won from one's own development at the cost of people who are kept undeveloped; it must be directed towards an alteration of the economic structure in the interests of economic justice among men. We cannot consistently 'share and share alike' in private if we are not prepared at the same time to alter the economic structure in such a way that there will be 'equal shares' globally as well. In face of 'the limits of growth', the ecological crisis and the increasing shortage of raw materials and sources of energy, this means for Christianity in the rich industrial countries renunciation in favour of the development of the poorer ones. Such a renunciation of values will only be bearable if new values are acquired instead. The new values will have to be found in the wider community and in the symbiosis of people with people, nation with nation, and culture with culture. Today a frightened clinging to privileges that have been acquired in the past leads first to others' starvation, but then destroys ourselves. For these forms of satisfaction of our own demands through wealth and possessions divides man from man and society from society. The poverty of riches is always social isolation. That is not only true of people and classes in a society; it applies to whole societies as well. It also applies, incidentally, to the relationship between people and the natural systems of the environment and their own bodies. Domination that suppresses and exploits isolates, and leads through isolation to lack of relationship; and that means to death. In this sense the line which Christianity in the world ought to follow seems to come down to 'socialism' in the relationship of people with one another and 'socialism' in the relationship of humanity to nature.

Independence, in the sense of liberation from oppression by others, is a requirement of justice. But independence, in the sense of isolation from the human community, is neither possible nor just. We – human persons – need each other within communities. We – human communities – need each other within the community of humanity. We – humanity – need nature within the community of creation. We – the creation – need God, our Creator and re-Creator.

Humanity faces the urgent task of devising social mechanisms and political structures that encourage genuine interdependence, and which will replace mechanisms and structures that maintain domination and subservience.[68]

We would therefore call symbiosis our guiding line for economic action and for our support or resistance to economic trends. It is only the fellowship of men and women and of human societies, participating equally in responsibility and a just distribution of goods, which gives everyone, collectively and individually, a chance of survival. It is only fellowship in respect for the unique character and needs of the natural environmental system which gives humanity and nature a chance of survival. Such symbioses, in both limited and wider contexts, are to be seen as corresponding to and anticipating the kingdom of God in history. For it is only fellowship with the Creator in the coming kingdom that gives the coming together of men and women in the history of humanity and nature its transcendent and thus its stimulating meaning.

(iv) Christianity in the Processes of Political Life: Human Rights

By politics we mean here the *res publica* in the widest sense; that is to say, the public affairs which a community has to order. As a member of a community of this kind man is a political being. His participation in the public processes of decision, which affect the whole community, are an indispensable part of his life and the dignity of his person. A political association of people is an association for rule, which is able to enforce its decisions with the threat of physical compulsion. For that reason 'the monopolization of the legitimate use of physical force in the enforcement of its authority'[69] is generally conceded to the state and its institutions. If this covers the particular conditions and possibilities of political action, then the question of the legitimacy of political processes of decision and rule arises. Because every state is a relationship in which some of its members rule over others, this rule can only be legitimated if it is exercised for the benefit of those involved. Only the people affected can say whether this is the case or not. Political rule must therefore

be justified by the people, for the people and with the people. Man's
rule over other men is only possible on the foundation of equal
rights. This is the only basis on which it is possible to talk about
identity between rulers and ruled. When men are governed by
people like themselves, this must inevitably lead to democratic
forms of government. For 'democracy offers the opportunity to
realize the best possible association between the fact of political
rule and the idea of general co-operation, the greatest possible
justice and social security for all.'[70] The principle of popular
sovereignty demands self-government by the people, the participation of all in political processes of decision, the continual control
of government through the separation of powers, and limitation
of the period during which government is exercised. Only solidarity makes the people strong and overcomes that method of
inhumane government: divide and rule. Democracy is not an
ideal and not a state of affairs; it is the continual, open and incompletable process of the democratization of political objectives.[71]

Because popular sovereignty and the self-government of a
political community are really inconsistent with the assignment of
sovereign rights to men to rule over other men, they can only be
realized in the open process of the constant limitation and control
of the exercise of power. Where power is permanently established
and evades control, where sectors of life – the economy for
example – evade co-determination and democratic control, conflicts arise which can only be solved through further democratization, when rulers and ruled, administrators and administered,
employers and employees are to be addressed as 'people', in an
equal and identifiable sense. The democratizing process of politics
does not relieve people of responsibility and decision, but is
actually an imposition, the imposition of freedom and participation. It is an imposition which is nothing less than the imposition
of human existence, human rights, and human duty.

In the changing political situations of the communities in which
it has lived, Christianity has always had difficulty in finding a line
of its own to follow. Wholesale judgments suggest themselves all
too easily and these lead either to opportunistic adaptation or to
an escapist condemnation of political rule. The line of 'critical
solidarity', combining independence with participation in political
decisions, was and is hard to pursue in absolutist and totalitarian
states. Of course Christianity has always used the chance which

was offered in a number of countries to testify to its faith in social forms of love and to present publicly its hope of the kingdom of God. But because political constitutions and forms of government are themselves going through a process of alteration, Christianity must also encourage the forms of government which best serve human fellowship and human rights and dignity, and it must resist those forms which hinder or suppress these things. The political task of Christianity is not merely to live in an already existing political order, but actually to take part in forming it.[72]

The Christian church sees in the history of Christ the revelation of the divine justification of the sinner and the acceptance of the one who is forsaken by God. Because justification and acceptance are intended to reach all men, they also provide the reason for the uninfringeable dignity and the equal rights of all. God has a right to every person, the right of liberating grace. In this grace everyone has his liberty and his rights before God. But what he has before God he also has before men; so it must as far as possible be put into force in the political community. 'Man's domination over man' cannot be viewed as a matter of course. For according to the Christian understanding it would be the domination of God's image by God's image, of the pardoned by the pardoned, of the liberated by the liberated. The Christian hope has therefore limited the historically unavoidable domination of man over man by its expectation of the fulfilment of the brotherhood of Christ, anticipating from this, not only the abolition of death but also the abolition of every rule, authority and power (I Cor. 15.24–6). In this belief and hope Christianity has pursued a particular line in political history. The early church condemned the emperor cult, replacing it by intercession on the emperor's behalf, which set a limit to his power. In this way political rule was de-sacralized.[73] The Reformation relativized the political orders, making them necessary orders in this world which can serve the welfare of all, and ought to do so, but do not minister to salvation. By making this critical distinction between salvation and welfare, it secularized political rule, with its promises and legitimations. In the English-speaking world, Puritanism abolished the divine right of kings, replacing it by the political contract, the 'covenant' or constitution of free citizens.[74] The demand for freedom of religion and conscience was followed by demands for freedom of assembly, freedom of the press and civil liberties. Resistance to religious and political tyranny was followed by demands for the contract of rule and the social contract.[75] Christianity must stay on this path of the secularization, desacralization and democratization of political rule if it wants to remain true to its faith and its hope. Today's orientation towards human rights, and further work in that field, is a help here.

In their present form *human rights* had their genesis in the Mediterranean world – Greece, Israel, Rome, Christendom – and they took form in the course of the Christianization of Europe. Human rights are by definition rights which man as man has towards the state – man meaning every human being, without regard to his birth, race, religion, health or nationality. They are rights which have always been termed irrelinquishable, inalienable, inviolable or absolute. They are rights that are integral to man's being man. They are therefore also termed pre-political or supra-political rights. They are not at the state's disposal and the state is bound to respect them. They must consequently be introduced into national constitutions as fundamental and civil rights.[76]

The arguments for human rights are many and varied. They have been traced back to a primeval state of nature, when there was complete human freedom and equality; to the biblical idea of the Garden of Eden; to the law of reason; and so forth. The sources for the beginnings of formulated human rights are more numerous than is often supposed. It is not correct simply to call on English, American and French constitutional history. Even though the Mediterranean civilizations and modern bourgeois society have a particular share, almost all continents and cultures show beginnings of the development of human rights, and have made their own contributions. It is not an exclusively European idea.[77] For that reason Christianity can by its faith make its own contribution to the understanding of man's humanity and his rights as human being.

1. If God the Creator destined man to be his image on earth, then human dignity, freedom and responsibility precedes every society and every established system of rule. God's image on earth is not a king. It is man as such. Consequently man is not made for the state; the state is made for man. And political rule must be tested and legitimated against this fact.[78]

2. Ruler and ruled must *together* be identifiable as 'people'. A constitution which guarantees fundamental human rights as the

basic rights of its citizens will bind rulers and ruled together.

3. If they are to claim their human rights people must be freed from poverty, hunger, contempt and persecution. Without basic economic rights to life, work and social security, it is impossible to realize human rights in the political sphere.[79] The biblical traditions have proclaimed liberation from all inequalities of class and caste, as well as from the privileges of race, sex and health, and have looked forward to the time when 'the glory of the Lord shall be revealed, and all flesh shall see it *together*' (Isa. 40. 5). Monotheism led to the concept of a single humanity. Remembrance of Israel's exodus from slavery into freedom, and the expectation of a coming, universal exodus of the whole enslaved creation, led to a progressive and forward-looking understanding of human rights.

4. The traditions of hope in the Son of man are a constant reminder that human rights are irreconcilable with political orders in which hunger, persecution and deprivation of civil rights prevail. They demand that we first of all establish human rights among and for those who are oppressed and robbed of these rights. Human justice becomes concrete when it is specifically viewed as 'the rights of my neighbour'.[80]

5. If the rights of man are substantiated through their justification by God, and if human liberty finds its basis in the divine liberation, then human duties must be formulated as well as human rights. 'Freedom by itself does not yet constitute anything', said Mazzini. It is an important and indeed inalienable duty to formulate the rights of the individual over against the state, so as to limit and control the state's power and to force it to continual legitimation; but it is equally important on the other hand to formulate the fundamental obligations which man as a human being has towards other men, when he claims his human rights. One of these is the right and duty to resist illegitimate and illegal rule.[81] Another is to combine the rights which secure the freedom of the individual with the duty to liberate those to whom these rights are denied.

6. The Universal Declaration of Human Rights of 1948, which is part of the United Nations Charter, laid particular stress on individual human rights and the protective aspect of the state, because of the recent experience of dictatorships. Its further development will involve the formulation of the rights of humanity as a whole which society and state have to personify for the indi-

vidual. Man and mankind belong together. Does mankind have rights over individuals? Who represents mankind: individual nations or the individual person? When political rule is constitutionally bound to human rights and has to respect them in its own constitution as the basic rights of its citizens, then the particular manifestations of political rule must, on the other hand, be orientated towards mankind and its rights, its freedom and its fellowship. There is no other way in which the rights of the community over the individual person can be legitimated. But that means that individual nations and societies must legitimate their rule in the context of humanity, which is still divided now, but has to be united. They must see themselves as transitions on the way to a common organized humanity and must direct their policies towards world peace, without which mankind has no chance of survival. It has been rightly demanded that national foreign policies be changed into 'world-wide home policy'. Not 'What good does it do my own nation, my own class and race?' but 'What good does it do our common peace and the coming community of all mankind?' This is the question that must be asked in every political and economic decision. Solidarity in overcoming common economic and military world crises must take precedence over loyalty to one's own people, one's own class or race or nation. There can be no respect for human rights in one's own nation without the simultaneous alignment of the nation towards humanity.[82] Human rights are single and indivisible. They cannot be a privilege.

7. Finally, human rights are neither a possession nor an ideal. They are legal and political aids on the road to man's becoming man and the unification of mankind. They are to be apprehended as a process, which is unfinished and, historically speaking, unfinishable. They are effective to the degree in which people are prepared to realize them for others and themselves. The more people unite and enter into wider communities, the wider the discussion about human rights will be, and the more those rights will be deepened into economic rights and expanded by the rights of humanity over individuals, i.e., by human obligations.[83]

We can make human rights the guide-line for the political action and the political resistance of Christians, thanks both to their Christian foundation and to their orientation towards humanity as a whole. Without the enforcement of fundamental human rights to life, freedom and security, the lordship of man over man cannot be 'human'. Without the declaration and enforcement of economic human rights, little opportunity is left for political human rights. Without the orientation of particular national groupings towards world peace and the unification of mankind, there are no 'human' states. It is in these three directions that Christians will proceed in their political professions, and that ecumenical Christianity will avail itself of its universal political responsibility. In their national groupings and between these groupings they will follow these trends as far as they can and will resist countermovements. Human rights and the rights of humanity are to be viewed as answering to and anticipating the kingdom of the Son of man in the power struggles of history.

(v) *Christianity in the Processes of Cultural Life: Open Identity*

By culture we mean here the sphere of the self-representation of persons, groups and peoples in relation to one another and as a whole before the ground of their existence. Cultural self-representation is always bound up with the creation of economic bases for life and the political processes of bringing order into the community; but it is not totally absorbed by these things; it represents a human need of its own as well. The production and consumption of the necessities of life, political conflicts and associations, are also means by which people continually express themselves. They define a personality for themselves, give themselves a particular countenance, try not to 'lose face', justify their life, legitimate the form their life takes, seek for identity and the recognition of others. For what a person is is not fixed once and for all. 'The human element' is sought for in history but eludes us, it is hoped for but the hope is disappointed. Man is a 'questionable being' and hence a being who has constantly to put himself to the question. We can therefore find a reason for the protean forms of mankind's cultural history in man's constitutional amorphism, out of which he can and must perpetually give himself a new face.[84]

In place of a general anthropology of culture, I should like here to describe a few (though typical) culture-conflicts, which are examples of the way in which the cultural record of the Christian faith and the Christian community is being challenged today.

At the present day racialism is a world-wide problem. The economic and political interdependence of peoples of different races is increasing. People of different races have to live together in societies. This confronts mankind with the task of developing foundations on which people of different races can live together. It is understandable that such situations increase people's inner insecurity, because, and to the extent in which, their previous identity – legitimated in their own group and race – is now called in question. The person belonging to another race is felt to be a challenge and a threat to one's own identity. 'Like draws to like'; but those who are unlike nurse mutual mistrust and tend to draw away from one another.

> By racism we mean ethnocentric *pride* in one's own racial group and preference for the distinctive characteristics of that group; belief that these characteristics are fundamentally biological in nature and are thus transmitted to succeeding generations; strong negative feelings towards other groups who do not share these characteristics coupled with the thrust to discriminate against and exclude the outgroup from full participation in the life of the community.[85]

In racialism the characteristics of one's own race are identified with the characteristics of mankind *per se*; and people of other races are seen as 'lesser breeds'. In racialism the characteristics of one's own race are used for self-justification and to legitimate hegemony over other people. One's own identity is built up through pride in one's own particular race and through discrimination against other racial characteristics. Forms of racialism exist everywhere, in group egoism and the hatred of aliens. But racialism is especially dangerous where it is used to organize and defend economic, social and political systems of government which contradict the Universal Declaration of Human Rights. Then racialism is not simply a group phenomenon; it is a means of waging psychological war with the purpose of subjecting others. People of other races are not recognized as people in the fullest sense at all. They are degraded to 'second-class citizens'. The feelings of superiority enjoyed by the one race then evoke feelings of inferiority in the races that are downtrodden. In its specific form racialism always has two sides. It is an emotional mechanism for self-justification, and an ideological mechanism for the subjection of others. It can therefore only be overcome when people win through to a liberated, non-aggressive identity 'as people' – when, that is to say, they cease to identify 'being human' with membership of a particular race, and then they arrive at a 'redistribution of social, economic, political and cultural power from the powerful to the powerless'.[86]

Another cultural conflict is often described by the expression 'sexism'.[87] What is meant by this is masculine supremacy on the basis of imagined privileges and the subordination of woman to man. There are cultures which see the woman as the man's property over which he has sovereign rights, as he has over slaves, animals and land. The Hebrew and Christian traditions have often taught the subordination of woman as an order of creation and the result of the Fall: the woman was created 'second' and was 'the first' to fall a victim to sin; and this legitimated her double subordination. The man is to be the 'head' of the woman in creation and redemption. As a result the man counts more than the woman. With this legitimation and others like it, his claim to dominance in public life, in religion and in the family is justified. The 'man's world' and the 'woman's world' are both separated from and related to one another in such a way that masculine privileges are preserved. Masculine and feminine forms of behaviour are established, social roles are assigned and rights are codified which hinder the woman's free human development and hence, fundamentally speaking, the man's development as well. The man is decreed activity, intellect and responsibility; the woman passivity, feeling and obedience. The man's world is supposed to be public life, the woman's world home, children and the kitchen. We need not describe this pattern of behaviour any further here.[88] Male discrimination against the woman and his suppression or humiliation of her is evidently based on the phenomenon that social privileges are built up on natural sexual differences and that claims to rule are derived from biological distinctions which are not inherent in these things themselves. Masculine pride in the male sex, and the higher value given to 'masculine' characteristics than to 'feminine' ones, the claims and the social positions derived from the fact that certain things are declared to be 'men's business' – all these therefore originate in something different. In sexism male characteristics are used for self-justification and for the legitimation of privileges. But as long as 'being human' is primarily identified with 'being a man', the man does not arrive at human identity. As long as social roles and economic privileges are justified by sexual differences, it is impossible to talk about a 'human' society. As in racialism, sexism breeds feelings of superiority among men and feelings of inferiority among women; and this hinders the 'human' development of both. Sexism has two sides as well: it is as emotional mechanism of self-justification, and an ideological mechanism of subjection. It can therefore be overcome only when a 'human' sense of identity takes the place of the masculine sense of identity, which then no longer needs to justify itself on the basis of special sexual characteristics. On the other hand the woman must at the same time be put on an equal footing before the law and her free human development must be made economically possible. Here too the change in sense of identity must go together with the 'new distribution of power' if it is to be effective.

As a third cultural conflict we may mention the relationship between the healthy and the handicapped. In this relationship defence mechanisms both of psychology and also of social psychology come into play in our society, making the situation of the handicapped unendurable, and robbing them of their human dignity too. In the suffering of the handicapped we can distinguish between the disability and its social consequences and here the latter are often worse than the former. It is true that these social consequences would not exist without the handicap; but the handicap could well be there without the social results. We 'welcome' some people and only 'put up with' others. The fate of the mentally and physically handicapped can be termed the fate of being 'put up with'. The spontaneous reaction of the healthy person to his encounter with the handicapped can be described as follows:

> The non-handicapped person is thrown off his mental balance. The strange appearance of a malformed body does not fit into the stereotype which he has of a human counterpart. The unharmonious appearance . . . can lead to reactions of defence and disquiet. . . . He does not succeed in seeing his counterpart as a human being first of all; he only sees the handicap and generalizes it into covering the total personality.[89]

In a similar way, the world surrounding the handicapped person views him as a threat, an insecurity and disturbance of its sense of its own value; people develop defence reactions which are coupled with suppressed feelings of guilt. This produces in the handicapped themselves a 'leper syndrome',[90] a feeling of isolation, subservience and inferiority. If we pursue the reason for the 'fear syndrome' which the healthy develop in the face of the handicapped, we again come up against the sense of identity, which builds up the sense of one's own value out of the foregiven characteristics of health. If being human is identified with being healthy, then the sight of a handicapped person brings insecurity. In the mirror of his deformity we only see ourselves as we do not want to be. We do not see the handicapped *person*; we only see the handicap, because we do not want to see ourselves simply as a person, but only as a healthy person. That is why the encounter with the handicapped evokes fear and aggressiveness. With their first reactions the healthy present the real problem of the handicapped. The handicapped are only a problem for the healthy to a secondary degree. Unless the sense of identity of the healthy becomes a free human identity, we cannot arrive at a recognition of the handicapped as people, or at recognition of their human dignity and human rights. It is only when the healthy cease to present a problem for the handicapped that the practical problems of the handicapped can really be solved.

We have mentioned three cultural conflicts belonging to three different levels. At the centre of these conflicts in each case stands in different ways the fundamental question of the human identity of men and women. For every particularist and narrow-minded identification (the human being as a white man, the human being as a man, the human being as a non-handicapped, healthy person) leads in the form of racialism, sexism and the idol of health to the suppression, disparagement and pushing aside of other people, so that it is impossible for us to talk about 'human identity' at all.

Psychologically one can distinguish between a person's I-identity and his ego-identity.[91] The experience of the ego is marked by the fact that I experience myself as an object: as the body that I have, as the social position or power that I possess. Every ego-identity is based on the idea of *having*, whether it be membership of race or sex, or simply health. The identity of the 'I' on the other hand points to the category of *being*. The crises of identity which we have named come from making a person into a thing; and this happens where people equate their 'I' with race, sex or health. In this ego-identity the person remains uncertain, and consequently he has continually to defend his ego-identity against other people. For he only acquires it by having and holding fast to what other people do not have; i.e., he only acquires it through fear and aggression. 'In contrast, the person who experiences himself not as having but as being permits himself to be vulnerable.'[92] The relationship in a person between having oneself and being oneself can only continue to exist without fear and aggression as 'the act of leaving the prison of one's ego and achieving the freedom of openness and relatedness to the world'. For 'the basis for love, tenderness, compassion, interest, responsibility, and identity is precisely that of being versus having, and that means transcending the ego.'[93]

Theologically we must distinguish between the person's self-justification through having or achieving, and his justification through grace. The ego-identity described in psychological terms fulfils the theological definition of self-justification. But this goes beyond the diagnosis open to psychology. For theologically we must talk about the godless person's compulsion to justify himself and substantiate himself over against the ground of his existence, which he has abandoned. This follows from a deep-lying primal fear of nothingness and is joined with hate of one's own existence. Because of this it is never possible to substantiate oneself without depreciating the other. This fact finds expression in racialism, sexism and defensive reactions towards the handicapped, as well as in many other inhumane phenomena. This primal fear makes people constantly seek new 'possessions' to cling to; this fundamental insecurity makes them constantly cry out for new security; and it is only when this primal fear and insecurity is changed into primal trust that a person can find free self-acceptance and free acceptance of people who are different from himself.

Christian faith is faith in justification. That is to say, it is the confidence that man is already justified by God. As a result all attempts at self-justification are superfluous and contradict the life which has already been accepted by God. Human life has eternal value because it is loved and accepted by God. Consequently the whole of human reality is freed from exploitation in the interests of human feelings about the value of the self, and can be lived in its relative and fragie beauty. The being of man is justified; so having and not having are freed from their burden of ego-identity.

As faith in justification Christian faith will spread this human freedom from self-justification, contrary to what must be called the superstitious and idolatrous perversions of man through racialism, sexism and a mania about health. The freedom of the Christian faith in justification stands the test in the face of mainly white racialism and the living together of different races, in the face of sexism and the liberation of women, and in the face of the handicapped and the further handicap laid on them by the healthy.

The freedom of justifying faith is a personal reality, but it also has a *social* side. For if a person is justified and does not have to prove himself through racial, sexual or other prerogatives, he is free to recognize the other person in his human dignity and his human rights. It is true that the early Christian churches were also familiar with the subordination of slaves to masters and women to men. In this respect they reflect their time and are not a visible token of the gospel of Christ. But there too we have 'the breakthrough of Gal. 3.28',[94] according to which in Christ there is 'neither Jew nor Greek, there is neither slave nor free, there is neither male nor female', for all are 'one' and common 'heirs according to the promise'. What is being claimed here is not only equal validity, but also equal being in Christ; not only equality in faith before God, but also equality in the fellowship of Christ; not only equal pardon, but also equal rights. The first pair, 'Jew or Greek', touches on religious differences – the different position in salvation history, according to the Jewish-Christian view. The second pair, 'slave or free', means the economic and social difference. But the third pair, 'man or woman', goes back to the creation of mankind as 'man and woman' and reaches beyond the order of creation to a new order of these relationships. The intention of the declaration in Gal. 3.28 is that this conquest of differences and privileges is realized in the Christian fellowship by virtue of its hope that the promise of the inheritance of eternal life will be fulfilled (Gal. 3.29). The Christian fellowship in which the one accepts the other, just as he himself is accepted by Christ for the praise of God (Rom. 15.7), is the social form of justification by faith. It ought to be a fellowship of persons with I-identity, free from ego-identity; a fellowship of the justified, who no longer have to justify themselves on the basis of their own characteristics; and hence a fellowship of the unequal and different, held together by free and courteous recognition.

There is an old principle for the social existence of men and women. As Aristotle puts it, 'Like cleaves to like.' Friendship (*philia*) binds together people who are like-minded: freemen with freemen, slaves with slaves, rich with rich, poor with poor, the healthy with the healthy, the sick with the sick, etc. 'Like strives with like', 'like is only perceived by like' and 'like is recompensed by like'; these ideas seem to form a natural principle underlying society, knowledge and justice. But wherever people apply this principle it implies the compulsion towards self-justification and self-corroboration. People who are like us confirm our attitudes. People who are different from us make us insecure. Things which correspond to our own ideas reassure us. Things which are strange to us disturb us. If evil is repaid by evil, then our world is putting itself in order. If evil is repaid by good, then our balance is upset. That is why we naturally love the people who are like ourselves, and dismiss from our orbit the people who are alien and different. These attitudes, intellectual processes and judgments are called natural; but in the situation of insecure, fearful and aggressive man they are not natural at all. On the contrary, they are the foundation for the segregation of person from person, for the subjection of person by person, and for the handicap imposed on one person by another. If Christian faith breaks with the compulsion towards self-corroboration, the Christian fellowship will also have to break with the 'natural' principle of 'like cleaves to like'. For Christianity the basic principle of liberated humanity can only be the principle of the recognition of the other in his otherness, the recognition of the person who is different as a person. It is only this recognition which makes it possible for people who are different to live together – Jews and Greeks, masters and slaves, men and women; it is only this which makes it possible for them to be there for one another in fellowship, to share with one another and to fulfil man's common being in hope for the kingdom. That is why the Christian fellowship is a fundamentally open fellowship and not merely a community of fellow-believers.

In cultural conflicts Christianity will live the I-identity of faith, freed from the ego, and will demonstrate recognition of the other as a person in his dignity and his rights. In this dimension I-identity and the recognition of the other, and liberation for one another through justification can all be seen as corresponding to and anticipating the kingdom of God and its righteousness.

5. *The Kingdom of God in the Future and the Present*

We will end this chapter with some systematic reflections which may be a help for our understanding of the kingdom of God in the future and the present.[95]

(i) The Fulfilment of the Lordship of God

The eschatological fulfilment of the liberating lordship of God in history is termed the kingdom of God. The Greek word *basileia* can mean both the actual rule of God in the world, and the universal goal of that divine rule. It is one-sided if we merely see the lordship of God in his perfect kingdom, just as it is open to misunderstanding if we equate the kingdom of God with the actuality of his rule.[96] In his kingdom God's rule is undisputed and universal; no shadow falls upon it. In history God rules through the word of promise and the Spirit of freedom. Both are assailed and come up against contradiction, resistance and antagonism. In history, therefore, God rules in a disputed and hidden way. That is why his liberating rule in history points towards its own fulfilment in the coming kingdom, just as, conversely, the coming kingdom already casts its light on the conflicts of history. The liberating rule of God can thus be understood as the immanence of the eschatological kingdom, and the coming kingdom can be interpreted as the transcendence of the believed and experienced rule of God in the present. This understanding forbids us to banish the lordship of God to a future world totally unrelated to our earthly, historical life. But it also forbids us to identify the kingdom of God with conditions in history, whether they be already existing or desired.

If we view history, with its conditions and potentialities, as an open system, we are bound to understand the kingdom of God in the liberating rule of God as a transforming power immanent in that system, and the rule of God in the kingdom of God as a future transcending the system. Without the counterpart of the future of the kingdom, which transcends the present system, the transforming power immanent in the system loses its orientation. Without the transformation immanent in the system the future transcending the system would become a powerless dream. That is why in actual practice the obedience to the will of God which transforms the world is inseparable from prayer for the coming of the kingdom. The doxological anticipation of the beauty of the kingdom and active resistance to godless and inhuman relationships in history are related to one another and reinforce one another mutually.

(ii) The Anticipation of the Kingdom of God

If the coming kingdom is present in history as liberating rule, this liberating rule of God is manifest in his promises and in the proclamation of the gospel. The promises call people out of the environment in which they have settled down and put them on the path to the fulfilment of the promises. They free people from earthly slavery and call them to take the road to freedom. The gospel calls men and women out of the bondage of sin, law and death and puts them on the road to righteousness and the freedom of eternal life. Because this road is not yet the goal, it leads to tribulation, resistance, suffering and struggle. The path's goal only sheds its light on the path: redemption in tribulation, the victory of life in the struggle against the power of death, ultimate freedom in the resistance against servitude. The kingdom of God is present in faith and new obedience, in new fellowship and the powers of the Spirit. The presence of the Holy Spirit is to be understood as the earnest and beginning of the new creation of all things in the kingdom of God. God rules through word and faith, promise and hope, commandment and obedience, power and Spirit.

Since faith and obedience, new fellowship and liberating action are now to be understood as the reality of the Spirit and as the presence of the coming kingdom in history, the subjective and objective potentialities of history, in which these realities of the Spirit are realized, also belong to the present realization of the kingdom of God. The Spirit of God makes the impossible possible; he creates faith where there is nothing else to believe in; he creates love where there is nothing lovable; he creates hope where there is nothing to hope for. But, as the Pauline teaching about the charisma says, he also wakes sleeping, suppressed or otherwise imprisoned potentialities and activates them for the divine rule. The Spirit of God works in history as the creator of a new future and as the new creator of what is transient for this future. No reality or potentiality that was in creation at the beginning is suppressed by the Spirit. As the perfecting power of God he makes enslaved creation live and fills everything with the powers of the new creation. Consequently the subjective and objective potentialities of history, which are seized upon in faith and obedience, are also part of the history of the new creation of all things. It is not a matter of indifference or insignificance whether doors open and opportunities offer themselves, just as it is not a matter of indifference whether men go through the door and seize upon the objective possibilities in accordance with the liberating rule of God.

Finally, we shall then no longer be able to see co-operation between Christians and non-Christians in their endeavours to free the world from misery, violence and despair as purely fortuitous and without theological significance. They too are made possible and are brought about by the Holy Spirit, who purposes life and not death. His saving influence on people will not replace dialogue and co-operation, let alone make them unnecessary. As the world crisis threatens, however, Christians will recognize the Spirit's world-sustaining operations as being very close to his activity in redemption. Christian tradition has long taught the sharp division between the two modes of operation. Today their joint working must be recognized, so that co-operation with people of different religions and secular ideologies can be freely practised, without loss of identity on the part of Christians, and without any attempt at drawing a line of demarcation. The kingdom of God becomes present in history through the rule of God. The rule of God is manifested through word and faith, obedience and fellowship, in potentialities grasped, and in free co-operation for the life of the world.

(iii) Messianic Mediation

If the eschatological kingdom of God enters into history in the present, disputed and hidden rule of God, then – if we look in the opposite direction – this history of the rule of God is also to be understood eschatologically. History and eschatology cannot be metaphysically divided, as this world and the next, in the world and out of the world. Nor can the two merely be brought to paradoxical identity in the single point of the eschatological moment. Through his mission and his resurrection Jesus has brought the kingdom of God into history. As the eschatological future the kingdom has become the power that determines the present. This future has already begun. We can already live in the light of the 'new era' in the circumstances of the 'old' one. Since the eschatological becomes historical in this way, the historical also becomes eschatological. Hope becomes realistic and reality hopeful. We have given this the mediating name of 'messianic'. The lordship of Christ points beyond itself to the kingdom of God. Faith in the word hungers for the seeing face to face. The presence of the Spirit puts the new creation into force. Obedience in the body is directed towards the redemption of the body, and the signs and wonders of experienced liberation are understood as fore-tokens of the resurrection of the dead. The messianic life is in this sense not life in constant deferment, but life in anticipation. Just as the messianic era stands under the token of 'not yet', so it also stands under the sign of 'no longer' and therefore under the sign of 'already'. Life in the messianic era no longer stands under the law and in the midst of the compulsions of this transient world; it already stands in the sunrise of Christ's new day. Its freedom lies in its transcending of the present through the power of hope for what is to come, and the actual in the light of the potential. But this is also its pain: it has to seize the new against the resistance of the old, so that a new beginning cannot be made without an ending, and freedom cannot be realized without struggle. The dreams of hope lead to the pains of love.

(iv) Anticipation

The messianic concept represents a categorical mediation between the kingdom of God and history. It is Christian when, and to the extent in which, its mediations take their bearings from the history of Jesus and his mission. The first mediating category which must be mentioned in the messianic sphere is *anticipation*. An anticipation is not yet a fulfilment. But it is already the presence of the future in the conditions of history. It is a fragment of the coming whole. It is a payment made in advance of complete fulfilment and part-possession of what is still to come.

Epistemologically, Epicurus used the word *prolepsis* to describe the preliminary concepts and tentative images through which we adapt ourselves to experience and true ideas. Cicero translated the word *anticipatio*, meaning by it the *praenotio inchoatae intelligentiae*. According to Kant, every anticipation legitimated by the criticism of pure reason is valid *a priori* when it establishes the objects of possible experience according to their form, as the anticipation of perception. Husserl uses the term anticipation for the structure of knowledge itself which, through the perception of a single thing, perceives its outward horizon. Every individual experience is bound up with the perception of what is not yet present, but to which the manifest core of experience points. Consequently all knowledge comes about intentionally. Heidegger then based the hermeneutical structure of intentional, anticipatory knowledge ontologically on the structure of existence itself, which is ahead of itself in the existential 'anticipation of the whole of existence'. Finally, in all living beings which are to be addressed as 'open systems', one can term the anticipation of future behaviour a vital primary category. It is the mode of our self-modifying dealings with future possibilities.[97]

The mediatory character of anticipation emerges from the term's history. If it is applied to the relationship between history and eschatology it is a defence against both fervent enthusiasm – 'the kingdom of God is already present and we are already risen' – and tragic resignation – 'the world is unredeemed and everything is still ambivalent'.

(v) Resistance

Resistance to the power of closing oneself against the other, of corroborating oneself and repeating oneself is necessarily part of the mediating anticipation of what is to come. The withdrawn and introverted person – *homo incurvatus in se* – has no future and desires no alteration. He is twisted in on himself, in love with himself and imprisoned by himself. He can only desire the prolongation of his present in the future. The anticipation of what is to come is bound to break this resistance and to open the withdrawn person for experience of the future in the hope of what is to come. But this also makes him vulnerable and capable of being hurt. The closed and introverted society – *societas incurvatus in se* – has no future and wants no prolongation. It wants to corroborate itself, to perpetuate itself and to write its possession of the present into the future. The anticipation of what is to come will break this political resistance too and will change the closed, immunized society into an 'open' one, open for the experience of the future in the hope of what is to come. It opens society's institutions and society itself for others, but also makes it vulnerable and alterable. Without the price of this perilous openness to the world and time, there is no future, no freedom and no life for people or for human society. For what closes itself within itself is condemned to death and has a deadly effect on other life.

(vi) Representation

In the Christian understanding of the messianic mediation of what is to come, anticipation and resistance are bound up with representation and self-giving. If the anticipation *pars pro toto* represents a fragmentary taking possession of the coming whole, then the part anticipated stands in the present, not only *ahead of* the whole but at the same time *for* the whole. Anticipations are hence always a preliminary taking possession of what is to come for other people and other things. In this way they represent what is to come and not themselves. If this were not so, they would not be forms of hope but merely forms of self-fulfilment. Anticipations in both knowledge and life therefore always have a representative character for something else and for other people. Where liberty is anticipated in individual acts of liberation, these can only be legitimated as acts of liberation for others, not as the struggle for one's own privileges. It follows from this that individual anticipations of what is to come can only prove themselves as such through intervention and self-giving for the future of others. True hope is lived in the giving of oneself to the future of the hopeless. Anticipated liberty is practised in the liberation of the oppressed. Faith is manifested in love for those in need.

(vii) The Limits of the Possible

In terming anticipation, resistance, representation and self-giving the messianically mediating categories of eschatology and history, we must also recognize the limits of what is possible. According to Paul, the limit of messianic activity in history is death. We are already freed from the 'body of death' (Rom. 7) through justifying faith; and we walk in new obedience by virtue of newness of life (Rom. 6). But we are still living in the 'body of death' and are still waiting with eager longing, together with the whole of creation, for 'the redemption of our bodies' (Rom. 8). Otherwise the messianic action would no longer be action in history; it would already be free movement in the kingdom of God. As long as people are not redeemed from 'the body of death' they can only practise their freedom from the body of sin in our mortal life. As long as the dead are dead, freedom is fighting freedom, but not yet freedom in its own world, in the kingdom of God. The 'body of death' does not only mean physical death; it also means a deadly cohesion to which all life belongs. This cohesion has been broken in principle, but not yet in fact, through liberation from the power of sin. That is why new life in the spirit of freedom has a fragmentary form. This form cannot be identified with the general ambiguity of history and the ambivalence of all historical activity,[98] but is the particular ambiguity of historical experience and practice between life and death. If Christian anticipation is directed towards the resurrection and eternal life, then it will encourage everything in history which ministers to life, and strive against everything that disseminates death.

(viii) The Messianic People of the Coming Kingdom

The church, Christendom and Christianity understand their own existence and their tasks in history in a messianic sense. Their life is therefore determined by anticipation, resistance, self-giving and representation. Everything that they are and do cannot be legitimated through themselves but must continually be legitimized by the Messiah and the messianic future, so that through their profession of faith, their existence and their influence, people, religions and societies are opened up for the truth of what is to come and their powers are activated for life. The church in the power of the Spirit is not yet the kingdom of God, but it is its anticipation in history. Christianity is not yet the new creation, but it is the working of the Spirit of the new creation. Christianity is not yet the new mankind but it is its vanguard, in resistance to deadly introversion and in self-giving and representation for man's future. The provisional nature of its messianic character forces the church to self-transcendence over its social and historical limitations. Its historical finality gives it certainty in still uncertain history, and joy in the pains over its resistance. In provisional finality and in final provisionality the church, Christendom and Christianity witness to the kingdom of God as the goal of history in the midst of history. In this sense the church of Jesus Christ is *the people of the kingdom of God.*

V

THE CHURCH IN THE PRESENCE
OF THE HOLY SPIRIT

The church lives in the history which finds its substantiation in the resurrection of the crucified Christ and whose future is the all-embracing kingdom of freedom. The living remembrance of Christ directs the church's hope towards the kingdom, and living hope in the kingdom leads back to the inexhaustible remembrance of Christ. The present power of this remembrance and this hope is called 'the power of the Holy Spirit', for it is not of their own strength, reason and will that people believe in Jesus as the Christ and hope for the future as God's future. It is true that people believe and hope with all their strength, reason and will. But the certainty of faith and the assurance in hope is joined by the consciousness that in these we are already living in indestructible fellowship with God. It is not faith that makes Jesus the Christ; it is Jesus as the Christ who creates faith. It is not hope that makes the future into God's future; it is this future that wakens hope. Faith in Christ and hope for the kingdom are due to the presence of God in the Spirit. The church understands the tension between faith and hope as the history of the Spirit that makes all things new. Its fellowship with Christ is founded on the experience of the Spirit which manifests Christ, unites us with him and glorifies him in men. Its fellowship in the kingdom of God is founded on the power of the Spirit, which leads it into truth and freedom. It is when the church, out of faith in Christ and in hope for the kingdom, sees itself as the messianic fellowship that it will logically understand its presence and its path in the presence and the process of the Holy Spirit.

The traditional doctrine of the Holy Spirit follows the structure of the Apostles' Creed. The presence and future of redemption,

the church and the kingdom of God are framed and comprehended by belief in the Holy Spirit. History and eschatology are
therefore parts of pneumatology. This means, conversely, that
pneumatology is developed historically and eschatologically, in the
sense that the history of the church, the communion of saints and
the forgiveness of sins are to be interpreted as the history of the
future; while the eschatology of the resurrection of the body and
life everlasting are to be seen as the future of history. That is why
we understand this mediation of eschatology and history as the
presence of the Holy Spirit.

It is the doctrine of the Holy Spirit in particular that depicts
the processes and experiences in which and through which the
church becomes comprehensible to itself as the messianic fellowship in the world and for the world. These processes and experiences are on the one hand the 'means of salvation' – proclamation,
baptism, the Lord's supper, worship, prayer, acts of blessing and
the way in which individual and fellowship live. On the other hand
they are the 'charismata', the ministries, gifts and tasks (or offices,
as they are often called) in this fellowship, or which flow from this
fellowship for society. If these 'means of salvation' and these
ministries of the church are understood as mediations and ministries of the messianic fellowship in the world, then they cannot be
misinterpreted in a clerical sense; nor will it be permissible to
represent them merely in the context of the inner mutual relationship between Christ and the church, or between the church and
Christ. As the mediations and powers of the Holy Spirit, they
lead the church beyond itself, out into the suffering of the world
and into the divine future. It is precisely in its character as a
fellowship in word and sacrament, and as a charismatic fellowship,
that the church will understand itself as a messianic fellowship of
service for the kingdom of God. For the mediations and powers of
the Holy Spirit are open for the things they seek to mediate and
bring about, and they open people for the future of the new creation through newly awakened faith and fresh hope.

In the following chapters, therefore, we shall be presenting the
'means of salvation' and the 'ministries of the church' in the
framework of the doctrine of the Holy Spirit. Within the all-
embracing framework of the trinitarian history of God, we shall
have to unfold both the eschatological understanding of the
historical reality of the church in its mediations of salvation and

its ministries, and the historical interpretation of the eschatology of the kingdom and God's glorification in the world which that framework implies. Although the doctrine of word and sacrament and the doctrine of the ministry are interwoven and cannot be separated, we shall present them one after another, although we shall continually be relating the individual statements to each other, so that their unity in the messianic fellowship becomes perceptible.

1. *The Sending of the Spirit as the Sacrament of the Kingdom*

The expression 'sacrament' has become open to misunderstanding through the development of different theological traditions.[1] What is usually meant are 'the means of grace', the visible signs which mediate the invisible grace, and the 'sacred rites' through which, according to Christ's ordinance and promise, salvation is consummated to men, or by which man is assured of salvation.

The Eastern church has not fixed the number of these sacraments or sacred rites, though concentrating on the church's worship, the sacred liturgy, which stands at the centre of its life. Here, in the form of 'living dogmatics', the great saving mysteries of the Trinity and christology are celebrated and related to the event of the eucharist.[2]

Since its medieval reform, the Roman Catholic church has confined itself to seven sacraments, 'no more and no less', as the Council of Trent said, following Peter Lombard.[3] Historically this can be understood in the light of the struggle to free the church from the power of the Christian imperium, for through these seven sacraments the former imperial sacraments of anointing and consecration lost their status, investiture with the ecclesiastical offices being reserved for the church alone. On the other hand the symbolism of the perfect number may have played a part in the differentiation and limitation of the sacraments to seven. In actual fact the question of the number of the sacraments has no particular significance, for the special position of baptism and the Lord's supper (the eucharist) compared with the other sacraments or sacramentals is undisputed.[4] According to their inner order, the seven sacraments can easily be concentrated on baptism and the eucharist. At the same time, churches with a plurality of sacraments must be asked about the unified ground to which these sacraments are related, and why these acts in particular are called sacraments, and others are not.

The Protestant traditions have another difficulty. The heading *de mediis salutis* covers the proclamation of the word, baptism and the Lord's supper. Then follows, under the heading *de sacramentis in genere*, the exposition of a concept of the sacraments which is particularly designed to take in baptism and the Lord's supper.[5] Proclamation, baptism and the Lord's supper are 'means of salvation', but only baptism and the Lord's supper count as 'sacraments'. That is to say, the proclamation of the Word can take place without baptism and the Lord's supper; but the latter cannot take place without the proclamation of the Word. But this raises the question of what binds the 'means of salvation' together and what differentiates them from one another. Finally, the question of the number of the sacraments was substantiated in early Protestant orthodoxy through a 'founder' christology. What can be traced back to an express ordinance of Christ and is bound up with his especial promise counts as a sacrament. If we are not content with this information, then here too we must enquire into the inner connection between christology and the doctrine of the means of salvation and the 'sacraments', baptism and the Lord's supper.

In the three great Christian churches there is a tendency today to trace back most of the sacraments to a single foundation and to seek for a 'primal sacrament'. In the Roman Catholic doctrine of the sacraments, Karl Rahner's teaching about the church as 'the fundamental sacrament of salvation'[6] is helpful here. If the church itself is the 'fundamental sacrament of salvation', then it is no longer possible to set up 'the church of the sacrament and the sacraments' against 'the church of the word' or to play off sacrament and word against one another in controversial theology.[7] If the church itself is 'the fundamental sacrament of salvation', then we will also view the word as the fundamental element of the sacraments and recognize that there is a 'real presence of the Lord who creates salvation' in the word of the proclamation.[8] Finally, if the church is 'the fundamental sacrament' of salvation, it is not so of itself, but only in 'relation, distinction and subordination . . . to Christ as to the historically primal sacrament in which God's promise of himself as forgiveness and glorification comes to historical appearance and irreversible completion'.[9]

In modern Protestant theology Karl Barth in particular developed a christological concept of the sacraments.[10] The incarnation is 'the great Christian mystery or sacrament'.[11] 'The humanity of Jesus as such is the first sacrament.'[12] Whereas in the first volumes of the *Church Dogmatics* the other sacraments are supposed to find their substantiation in the thesis that Christ is *the* sacrament, or the *first* sacrament, in the volume on *The Doctrine of Reconciliation* Barth explained the incarnation as 'the one and only sacrament, fulfilled once and for all', whose reality is to be attested to the world in proclamation, baptism and the Lord's supper, but whose reality can neither be represented nor repeated in baptism, the Lord's supper, preaching or anywhere else; and which is not to be put into effect through the activity of the church itself.[13] In this way Barth radically called in question the concept of the sacraments which has become customary in the various Christian confessions and supported the exclusively christological use of the term – after an initially open christological substantiation of the sacraments. In so doing he picked up theses of Luther and Melanchthon from the early Reformation period.[14] But if we follow Barth's exclusively christological use of the concept of the sacrament, we are compelled to choose other terms for the events which are traditionally so termed.[15] Proclamation, baptism and the Lord's supper are then 'attestations', 'celebrations' or 'responses' made by man to the one and only divine sacrament, which is Christ. If sacrament means 'the theological concept of a mediation which does not merely mediate something, but mediates itself as well',[16] then we must certainly accept other mediations in addition to the one and only mediation of God in and through Jesus Christ – mediations through which this unique mediation is itself mediated.

In the face of these reflections, it is possible to talk about converging tendencies. Karl Rahner traces back the sacraments of the church to the church as the fundamental sacrament of salvation, and this fundamental sacrament to the primal sacrament of God's promise of himself in Christ; while Karl Barth starts with the primal sacrament, preserves the qualitative priority of Christ before his church through the exclusively christological use of the word sacrament, and relates the attestations through word, baptism and Lord's supper just as exclusively to God's promise of himself in Christ. This 'turn towards christology' on both sides in fact makes clear the uniform origin and unique content of the church's rites; but it leaves untouched the question why the attestation of Christ and the mediation of salvation has to take these precise forms and not others. The present different theological traditions remain untouched; they are simply newly, and christologically, interpreted. This is certainly of considerable importance, both for the renewal of the church from its single foundation, and for the ecumenical fellowship between divided confessions. But does it lead any further than a better mutual understanding of our particular characteristics in each given case? Orthodox observers of the Protestant-Catholic convergence can gain the impression that the Western churches are now escaping from the danger of legalistic ecclesiastical positivism into the danger of Christomonism.[17] Granted the remaining difference in the Protestant-Catholic convergence – Christ as the exclusive sacrament of God, or the church as the fundamental sacrament and Christ as the primal sacrament – could this not be overcome through the Trinitarian understanding of the eschatological gift of the Holy Spirit as the sacrament?

As we know, the expression 'sacrament' for baptism and the Lord's supper, or for other rites in the church, is not found in the New Testament.[18] The New Testament knows no such overall term for these proceedings in the church. When the Greek word *mysterion* is translated by the Latin *sacramentum*, what is meant is not baptism and the Lord's supper, but the divine eschatological secret.

> In Daniel *mysterion* takes on for the first time a sense which is important for the further development of the word, namely, that of an eschatological mystery, a concealed intimation of divinely ordained future events whose disclosure and interpretation is reserved for God alone . . . and for those inspired by his Spirit.[19]

According to the apocalyptic writings, everything that is going to happen is already present in heaven in concealed form. At the end what God has already determined in eternity is revealed. His 'secrets' are the divine decrees destined for the final revelation. The apocalyptic mysteries do not refer to a fate suffered by the deity or the heavenly redeemer, but to a destiny which the deity determines and which is at his disposal. The reception of the mysteries is not understood by the apocalyptic writings as deification. The mysteries point towards an eschatological cosmic revelation. In the New Testament 'the secret of the kingdom of God' lies in the appearance of Jesus himself 'as the Messiah', according to the interpretation of the parable in Mark 4.11ff. The 'secret of the kingdom of God' is the dawn of the messianic era through Jesus. In the Pauline and Deutero-Pauline epistles, the concept of 'mystery' has entered into firm association with the kerygma of Christ. Christ is the divine secret. To proclaim him as the one who was crucified means to proclaim God's secret. God's hidden, eschatological decree becomes manifest on the Lord's cross and embraces the glorification of those who believe. The proclamation of Christ does not only bring tidings of the revelation of the divine secret which has taken place; the proclamation itself is part of the event of the secret and the event of its revelation. The conversion of the Gentiles (Eph. 3.4ff.) and the uniting of Gentiles and Jews in one body under Christ, the head, is also called the divine mystery. Through the proclamation of Christ and the faith of the Gentiles, the eschatological mystery of the summing up of the cosmos in Christ becomes manifest. The revelation of the eschatological divine secret (*apokalypsis*) takes place in veiled and hidden form, out of faith to faith, in the struggle between those who love God and the lords of the world; and it proclaims the coming glorification of believers and the consummation of God's decree of salvation.

> The term mysterion does not everywhere in the New Testament take its content from the Christ revelation, nor is it always part of the *kerygma*. But it always has an eschatological sense.[20]

Paul terms it the gift of the Spirit to penetrate the mysteries of God (I Cor. 14.2). He also calls the future of Israel, whose heart is now hardened, a divine mystery (Rom. 11.25). For Paul an especial mystery is the transformation of believers at the Lord's parousia (I Cor. 15.51). The second epistle to the Thessalonians (2.3ff.) calls the revelation of Antichrist the 'mystery of iniquity' (AV – 'mystery of lawlessness', RSV). Similarly Rev. 17.5, 7 talks about the 'mystery' of the whore of Babylon. If we sum up the varied New Testament usages we arrive at the following range for the term 'mystery':

1. *Mysterion* is an apocalyptic term for the future already resolved on by God, for the end of history. The mystery is the divine resolve. Its revelation in history has the character of a veiled

announcement, of a promise of the future, and of anticipation. Its revelation at the end of history takes place when it is openly put into effect.

2. In the New Testament Jesus is the revelation of the eschatological mystery of God through his mission, his death and his resurrection from the dead. The future determined by God for the world becomes manifest through his messianic mission. The final salvation resolved on by God becomes efficacious through Jesus' death and resurrection. But future and salvation only become manifest to faith as a mystery through the proclamation and the gift of the Holy Spirit. Salvation and future are disclosed to faith through the Spirit and the Word. The Spirit and the Word therefore point beyond themselves to the consummation.

3. Precisely on the basis of this eschatological christology, which sees the coming of Christ as the dawn of the revelation of the divine secret or mystery in the last days, we are justified in finding (and not merely as 'a mythological survival') the eschatological transition to the expectation of the future revelation of this mystery. The riches of God revealed in Christ are overflowing and spread beyond themselves. The use of the word 'mystery' therefore spreads beyond christology and flows into pneumatology, ecclesiology and the eschatology of world history.[21] They are, as it were, fluid transitions which necessarily arise from eschatological christology. In so far as Jesus as the Messiah is the mystery of the rule of God, the signs of the messianic era are also part of his mystery. In so far as the crucified and risen Jesus manifests the salvation of the world determined on by God, proclamation and faith and the outpouring of the Holy Spirit on the Gentiles are also part of this salvation. The revelation of the divine mystery which is veiled in word and sign stands ultimately, on the basis of this concealment, in the context of the mystery of the last days, the conversion of Israel, the revelation of Antichrist and the 'changing' of believers.

It follows from this that an exclusively christological rendering of the concept mystery or 'sacrament' does, indeed, touch the heart of the New Testament statements, but is too narrow, especially when christology is so concentrated on the incarnation that it does not embrace the messianically open history of the incarnate, crucified, exalted and coming Christ. It also follows that a christological-ecclesiological rendering of the term – Christ and the church as the primal and fundamental sacrament of salvation – certainly touches on a further sphere covered by the New Testament but does not go far enough, especially if the church of Christ is only understood in its sacraments and not at the same time in the context of the eschatology of world history. The term 'mystery' and the concept of the 'apocalypse' which goes with it lead to a christology which has to be understood eschatologically and to an ecclesiology which takes its bearings from eschatology. Even if Christ is termed the one, unique mediation of God, yet this mediation presses forward to its self-mediation in the world; for this self-mediation seeks to complete itself. That means that Jesus as the Messiah is open for the messianic era and that as the Christ who has come he is open for the future of his rule. Even if the church is termed the 'fundamental sacrament', the thing that makes it so points beyond itself. 'The eschatologically victorious grace of God' leads the church beyond its own present existence into the world and drives it towards the perfected kingdom of God. If, therefore, the term mystery allows Christ and the church to be understood eschatologically – if it leads in addition to an eschatological understanding of world history – then it would seem obvious to introduce a trinitarian concept of mystery or 'sacrament'. This brings us back to the inclusive doctrine of the Trinity which we developed in chapter II, § 4; the presence of the kingdom of God and the revelation of the divine mystery of the last days are to be found in the eschatological gift of the Holy Spirit. He reveals Christ and creates faith. Proclamation, fellowship and the emblematic messianic acts take place in the power of the Holy Spirit.[22] He is the power of the divine future and the one who completes the divine history. He glorifies Christ in believers and is the power of the new creation of the world. Not Christ for himself but Christ in the Holy Spirit, not the church for itself but Christ's church in the Holy Spirit, must be called the mystery or 'sacrament'. This trinitarian concept of the sacrament includes on the one hand the eschatological history of God's dealings with the world in the 'signs and wonders' of the Holy Spirit, and in the 'signs of the end'. In the eschatological gift of the Holy Spirit 'word and sacrament', 'ministries and charismata' become comprehensible as the revelations and powers of Christ and his future. As the emblematic revelations of Christ they are the messianic mediations of salvation. As glorifications of Christ they are actions of hope pointing towards the kingdom. In the framework of the trinitarian concept of the sacraments we therefore understand the proclamation, the 'sacraments' and the charismata as the 'signs and wonders' of the history of the Spirit who creates salvation and brings about the new creation, and who through Christ unites us with the Father and glorifies him.[23] In our account we shall begin in detail with the prophetic and apocalyptic promises and announcements of the divine future, and establish the grounds of the gospel and its signs, as well as the powers and ministries of the church, in the person and history of Christ, in order finally to unfold them as historical forms of the Spirit.

2. *The Gospel*

The Christian church grew out of the apostolic proclamation of the gospel and is alive in the act of proclamation. But the expression 'proclamation' does not reproduce the full breadth of the church's linguistic communication, especially if it is limited to the public discourse of a preacher who is commissioned for the purpose. By the proclamation of the gospel we therefore mean here all expressions of the church and of Christians made through language which have as their content the history of Christ and the freedom of man for the kingdom which that history opens up. This includes preaching, teaching, conversations with groups and individuals, story-telling, comforting, encouraging and liberating, through the publicity of the media. Instead of proclamation we could also talk about verbal witness in the different relationships of life. In any case, what matters is that public preaching and the preacher should not be isolated from the simple, everyday and matter-of-course language of the congregation's faith, the language used by Christians in the world. In order to indicate the breadth of the verbal communication of the gospel we can talk about proclaiming a promise and liberating by story-telling.[24]

The theological problem of proclamation in this comprehensive sense is the determining of the relationship between *word and truth*, or to put it in traditional terms – the relationship between *Word and Spirit*. The practical problem is not whether anyone can preach or tell a story; the question is, how is he freed and authorized to use the language both of preaching and of story-telling. Much has been written about the crisis of language in general and the crisis of preaching in particular, at a time when we are flooded with words in public and are personally inarticulate. People have lamented the powerlessness of language in a period where words are not supposed to decide anything. The 'visual age' is supposed to have replaced the age of language and the book. The language of the Christian church undoubtedly always shares the fate of language in its society, and of course it can make use of new forms of communication. But the inner powerlessness to proclaim and the freedom to do so will not be decided by outward circumstances; it will be tested against the truth of the proclamation itself and the authority to proclaim in the power of the Spirit. As long as there is a prevailing impression that the sign is not the thing it stands for, the name is not the thing, the idea is not the deed, the dream is not the action, 'the true world (is) unattainable, unprovable, unpromisable',[25] Christian proclamation and liberating narration is impossible. It would be better to be silent if only silence did not lie as well. It is only the truth of the proclamation that makes us free for the proclamation, and it is only the liberation that has been experienced which gives authority for liberating narration. Recent Protestant theology has therefore put the question of word and truth, Word and Spirit at the centre of its endeavours. That is the meaning of the 'Word of God theology' or 'kerygmatic theology'. Its question about the theological interpretation of the proclamation is at heart the question about its criterion of truth; hence it is also the question about the liberation of men and women for proclamation.[26]

(i) God and His Word

Karl Barth has interpreted the proclamation of the gospel as the proclamation of the Word of God. His whole programme is implicit in this expression. The task of theology is the Word of God. The proclamation is not supposed to interpret the world religiously or to give religious articulation to the personal feelings of men and women; it has to express the Word of God. This seems to be an impossible claim:

> As ministers we ought to speak of God. We are human, however, and so cannot speak of God. We ought therefore to recognize our obligation and our inability, and by that very recognition give God the glory.[27]

Yet for Barth this is the only possible starting point; for how else can we speak about God, if God himself has not spoken? How else can we proclaim God if not in the name of God? The Word of God is hence not a discourse about a history which God reveals, nor is it a personal talk about our own faith; it is God's own Word. It is the Word which God himself utters and in which God corresponds to himself, and that therefore for its part corresponds to God. But this cannot be a concept, an image or a symbol; it can only be the name of God itself. There is consequently no definition of the Word of God other than the name of God.[28] *Nomen Dei est Deus ipse* (Calovius). In his name God reveals himself. In his name people have to do with God himself. Consequently in the divine revelation the Word of God is identical with God himself. Understood as God's name the Word of God is the 'self-manifestation' or the 'self-word' of God.[29] For the correctness of this view one can point to the 'self-introductory formulas' in the Old Testament: 'I am the Lord your God'; 'and they shall know: I am the Lord.'[30] The corresponding sayings in the New Testament are the 'I am' sayings of Jesus in the gospel of John.[31] The criterion of truth applied is important theologically: the proclamation of the Word of God takes place in the name of God, and the premise is therefore that the person and the name correspond and that hence speech in the name of the person also corresponds to this person. The criterion for the truth of the Christian proclamation is accordingly: God himself has spoken. God has revealed himself in Christ. Jesus Christ is the name in which God corresponds to himself. Christian proclamation testifies at heart to this divine name in which God himself is revealed and 'is with us'. 'According to the Bible God's being with us is the event of revelation.'[32] As the name of God, God's Word is the revelatory event. In the name of Jesus Christ God's Word is the reconciling event. The human preaching of the Word of God in the name of God stands in an indirect identity with this self as indication, likeness, echo, testimony and answer to this event. The Word of God is hence not verified against anything else, either the external events of history or the inner experiences of man; it verifies itself, enforces its own claim, illuminates through its own being. The criterion of proclamation's truth is a criterion which God himself handles and which is in no other hands than his own.[33] Liberation for proclamation and for the telling of the gospel comes from the certainty that as God's Word it corresponds to God himself. This inner correspondence is that *adaequatio* which we call truth. Outwardly we can draw on Spinoza's definition of truth here: *veritas est index sui et falsi*. The truth verifies itself and falsifies what is untrue.

Important and central though this theological insight into the inner correspondence between the Word of God and God himself is, it must not be stressed exclusively. In the Old Testament God's self-manifestation is always associated with a story which has to be told in order to say who God is. It is, as the first commandment shows, the history of liberation which is constitutive for God's people. Moreover in the Old Testament the Word of God and the name of God are not identical. The two never occur side by side in the same sentence, nor are they interchangeable. The name denotes God himself in his person and his nature. The Word of God is historically the expression of God's thoughts or his will. A divine name reveals God himself, whereas a multiplicity of divine words create and stamp history. The name of God receives from the historical words of God the specific ideas which are associated with it. The Word of God designates the act of revelation, whereas the name denotes the God who is revealing himself. The Word of God is historical and creates history, whereas the name of God will be universally glorified at the end of history.[34] In the New Testament too the trinitarian formulas do not exclusively delineate God's self-revelation in Christ; they inclusively describe the history of God, whose centre represents the Christ event, as the event of God's revelation and man's reconciliation, but whose horizons span the beginning and end of history. The truth of Jesus' proclamation, his preaching of the gospel to the poor, his forgiveness of sins and his healing of the sick is ratified through his giving himself up to death and his resurrection from the dead. The apostolic preaching of the calling, justification and liberation of men comes from this event of truth. But it is directed for its part towards the parousia and the resurrection of the dead, that is, the new creation. Its verification takes place between the remembrance of Christ and hope for the kingdom through the presence of the Spirit and the power of the resurrection.

This historical and eschatological dimension of the gospel and its proclamation is, however, sustained by the inner correspondence of God's Word to God himself. Christian proclamation is in essence the proclamation of God's name and the reconciliation which lies in God's fellowship with the godless through Christ. But just because of this it besets the earthly future with restless hope, letting us wait for the redemption of the world and the glorification of God through the whole liberated creation. It is the very peace with God which the Christian proclamation conveys that brings discontent with an unpeaceful world. The inner correspondence between the Word of God and God himself leads to contradiction with a God-contradictory world and is directed towards a world corresponding to him. The self-revelation of God in Christ therefore does not end history but opens up the history of the future, because it lets us hope for God's glorification in the world and lets us fight against man's humiliation. For the presence of God in Christ is not merely a 'being that is moved within itself'; it is also a being that moves and liberates all being.

(ii) Kerygma and Existence

Rudolf Bultmann has interpreted the proclamation of the gospel as kerygma, as an eschatological call to decision and as a summons which affects existence. This does not necessarily contradict Barth's Word of God concept; it can be seen as its complement. Whereas the concept of the 'Word of God' illuminates the gospel's power of expression, God's self-revelation and self-utterance, the kerygmatic interpretation explains its power of address, which makes possible that existential decision which we call faith. In the event of proclamation and faith the two coincide; but factually statement and summons must be distinguished from one another, for they do not cover exactly the same ground.

Bultmann has brought out the character of the concept of kerygma in the New Testament by comparing it with the Greek concept of the logos.[35] In Greek, logos means the content of meaning in what is said. The word is conceived of, not primarily as the event of a summons, but as the utterance of a comprehensible meaning. Its point is not the summons but the uncovering and revealing of certain facts. It is true that the logos also has an effect rhetorically, but this is secondary. One should assent to what the philosopher says, not because of his authority, but because of the truth of his statements. His person and his words ought to retreat behind the knowledge of the truth he communicates. But the New Testament (analogously to the Old) understands the Word of God

as the Word of the Creator, the Word of the Judge, as commandment and promise – i.e., as the action of creative speech. It
challenges us to hear and obey and is accepted or rejected. It is
understood as the Word of God where it is heard as an authoritative summons which provokes a person's decision. To perceive it
therefore means to accept it. It is legitimated and verified in the
very event of its being heard and believed. That is why this faith
cannot demand any legitimation of the kerygma in the objective
sphere or in the realm of objective knowledge. That has nothing
to do with blind acceptance of unproved (and therefore 'authorita-
tively' postulated) assertions. Nor has it anything to do with outside clerical influence on people. If it were not comprehensible
the kerygma would not be a summons; it would be speaking with
tongues. To what does the comprehensibility of the kerygma
extend? What is the person summoned going to understand?

> To be true summons, a word must necessarily reveal man to himself,
> teach him to understand himself – but not as a theoretical instruction
> about the self. The event of the summons discloses to the man a
> situation of existential self-understanding, a possibility of self-
> understanding which must be grasped in action. Such a summons . . .
> requires decision, it gives me the choice of myself, the choice of who
> I will be through the summons and my response to it.[36]

In this respect the Word's potentiality for being understood coincides with man's potentiality for understanding himself. In the
Old Testament the event of the Word and the story which reminds
us of it, or promises it, are separate. But in the New Testament
'the Word of the Christian proclamation and the history which
communicates it coincide, are one', because it is the eschatological
event of the Word, or rather the event of the eschatological Word.
Word and history 'coincide' in the eschatological event of the
Word. The comprehensibility of the Word as God's Word 'coincides' with the true self-understanding of the hearer who believes.
Although this 'coincidence', as Bultmann calls it, is open to misunderstanding in a number of ways, it is none the less clear that
the verification of the kerygma through the faith which brings a
man to his truth has the truth of this Word as the Word of God for
its premise. Conversely, the Word that corresponds to God
proves itself by bringing men through faith into correspondence
with itself, i.e., its nature, its identity and assurance. This correspondence is again that *adaequatio* which we call truth. The

criterion of truth which Bultmann applies can be called the *adae-quatio existentiae et essentiae*.

Important and central though this theological insight into the correspondence of kerygma, faith and essential truth is, yet this must not be exclusively stressed. Similar questions arise particularly if we see this anthropological verification of the gospel, understood as kerygma, as complementary to the theological verification of the gospel, understood as the Word of God. The history of Christ and the proclaimed Word of Christ do, it is true, coincide noetically in the New Testament in so far as there is no access to the understanding of this history except through the history's proclamation. But they still do not therefore coincide ontically. It is rather the case that the history of Christ precedes proclamation and faith not only in time but also factually and theologically as their foundation, something that took place once and for all. The proclamation and the history of Christ which opens up faith is not a past history in the historical sense; but in the eschatological sense it is an event of the past which opens up the divine future, thus making possible the history of proclamation and faith and giving it its bearings. The gospel therefore teaches more than the mere fact that 'in [Jesus'] historical life the event had its beginning and the event continues in the preaching of the community'.[37] It teaches that 'while we were yet sinners Christ died for us' (Rom. 5.8). It teaches, therefore, that this history of Christ took place without us, for us. This enters into the kerygma in so far as the kerygma proclaims Christ 'for us'; but it is not totally absorbed by the kerygma and does not coincide with it. That is why the gospel is more than merely kerygmatic address. It is also a liberating telling of the history of Christ at the same time. The difference between the history of Christ and its proclamation allows us to hope for the kingdom of God; it makes the kerygma the messianic mediation of this future and makes faith hope for the seeing face to face.

On the other hand man's identity in faith leads to perception of the world's non-identity. The certainty of faith does not separate men and women from the world, but leads them into deeper solidarity with unredeemed creation, in so far as this faith is itself hope for the redemption of the body. It is just when man comes to himself in faith that he sees that this world in which he lives is alienated from its true nature. It is just when man, through the kerygma, learns to understand himself again as God's creation that he will suffer over the disfigurement of enslaved creation and will hope for and work for the new creation. Just as the event of reconciliation lets us hope for the redemption of this unredeemed world, just as the event of revelation lets us wait for the glorification of God through the new creation, so the kerygma as kerygma also becomes the remembrance of Christ and the promise of the kingdom, and faith as faith also becomes hope in the trials that come through variance with the world. It does not detract from the truth of the insights of dialectical theology if we dispense with the degree of enthusiasm with which it translates eschatology into the here and now, by confronting that eschatology with the world's history of suffering, which experience can confirm.

(iii) The Christian Tradition in Universal Historical Intention

Over against Barth and Bultmann, Wolfhart Pannenberg has suggested that we should once again understand the Christian proclamation as a statement about the history that precedes it, in which God was revealed, and only after that as an element in God's history of revelation.[38] As a 'report' of the fate of Jesus, in which God is manifest, the proclamation is entirely related to this event. Its content of truth must therefore be measured against that event.

> The kerygma is to be understood solely on the basis of its content, on the basis of the event that it reports and explicates. In this sense the kerygma is not to be thought of as bringing something to the event. The events in which God demonstrates his deity are self-evident as they stand within the framework of their own history. [Consequently] the sermon as an event by itself is not revelation, but the report of the revealing history and an explication of the language of fact which is implicit in this history.[39]

If the proclamation of the history is related to that history in such a way that it itself retreats behind the history and its 'language of fact', then the necessity for this account through proclamation only emerges out of the universal significance of the history that is to be reported. In the destiny of Jesus God reveals himself indirectly in so far as he anticipates the 'end of history' in him through the resurrection from the dead. The Christian proclamation therefore reports, not a self-contained event, but the prolepsis of the end of history in Jesus' fate – that is, an event which is both open to the future and opens up the future. Hence, as a report, it 'breaks into every situation as call and consolation'. It is not a 'neutral chronicle' but the proclamation of God's decisive eschatological act of salvation. As an account entirely related to the fate of Jesus, it is one element in the completion of the coming event of revelation. On the basis of insight into the history of Jesus, which reveals God and anticipates the end of history, it conveys a universal historical view of the world which must prove to be the true understanding of reality.

In this way Pannenberg has again abolished the confrontation between logos and kerygma found in Bultmann. As an account of the history in which God reveals himself, the Christian tradition lets something be seen and understood. Because God reveals himself proleptically in Jesus' destiny, this seeing and this understanding itself takes on the character of an anticipation of the end of history. But because all historical knowledge is anticipatory knowledge, and only grasps the meaning of past and present in the context of the future, the Christian knowledge of history proves itself the true one. The criterion of the truth of the Christian proclamation which Pannenberg employs is the old definition of *adaequatio rei et intellectus*. In that the Christian proclamation tells of the fate of Jesus, in whom God manifests himself, and in that its account corresponds to the facts, it is true. But in so far as it proclaims this fate of Jesus in the eschatological framework of universal history, it is dependent on eschatological verification through the end of history.

Over against the correspondence of God's Word to God himself and the self-correspondence of believing existence in the kerygma, Pannenberg has drawn attention to the correspondence of the Christian proclamation to the fate of Jesus in the framework of universal history. This historical dimension of the Christian proclamation could be a perspective to supplement the two other aspects, if it were not put forward together with a denial of these aspects. The reproach levied against Barth and Bultmann is directed against the so-called 'authoritarian principle' on which their 'dialectical theology' has allegedly based their theory of the Word of God.[40] By an 'authoritarian principle' Pannenberg apparently means 'assertions' which evade a rational justification of their truth, so as to spread their seeming truth through an appeal either to the higher authority of God or to the authority of the proclaimer. Even though anti-authoritarian gestures are occasionally effective, they neither touch Barth's Word of God theology nor the kerygma theology of Bultmann. As we have seen, both start from the problem of verification, but apply altered forms of the simple criterion of *adaequatio rei et intellectus*. In so far as man exists and is more than a thing, for his existence truth can only mean the correspondence between essence and existence. In so far as God is God and more than a thing and a person – in so far, that is to say, as he is himself the source of truth – the truth of God can only lie in God's self-manifestation, i.e., in the correspondence between the Word of God and God himself. Why should the different versions of the one criterion of truth, and with them the different aspects of the Christian proclamation, contradict one another?

Modern criticism of 'authoritarian' proclamation has the fatal tendency to be silent about its own inclination towards totalitarian ideology. But it is not a useful exchange, nor does it promote the freedom of man, when the supposed deification of authority is replaced by a deification of totality, and when the authoritarian principle is replaced by the totalitarian one. It is not a liberating change when belief in God's promise and pardon is replaced by a world view based on a Christian version of universal history which seeks to exact faith through pressure for a logical assent in the wake of information; and this is the case whether the pressure be exerted through the argument that 'Christianity' is and remains simply our European destiny, or whether through the claim that Christianity is 'the true religion', theology is 'the true philosophy' and the church is 'the true society'.[41] Christian proclamation can neither set up authoritarian assertions and demand blind faith, nor can it offer 'total' interpretations of the world and seek to compel agreement. The Christian proclamation is the messianic message of joy and as such it is the language of liberation.

(iv) The Gospel and the Messianic Era

The expression 'gospel' (which is the term used in the New Testament both for the apostolic proclamation of Christ and for the history of Christ) is not an arbitrary one. It cannot easily be translated by any other term. Expressions such as the Word of God, preaching, proclamation, account or tradition only reproduce partial aspects. They do not lay hold of the full content and whole aura of the gospel and its practice, which is evangelization – that is to say, the liberation of the world in the future of God. Here we shall pick up what we have already said about 'Jesus the prophet and the exodus community' in chapter III, § 2, developing it further.

The history of New Testament interpretation in the last hundred years has turned away from the 'didactic and doctrinaire use of the term gospel'. Nor have attempts at a Hellenistic derivation made by students of comparative religion taken us any further. On the other hand, the Semitic derivation of the term drawn from the prophecy of Deutero-Isaiah and the apocalyptic writings has evidently proved fruitful. Let us sum this up briefly, in order to draw considerable systematic conclusions from it.[42]

Deutero-Isaiah, together with the literature influenced by him, is of the greatest importance for the understanding of the New Testament concept of gospel. Whereas the Psalms talk about individual acts of Yahweh – acts which are proclaimed and praised – the prophet expects from the future Yahweh's final and decisive victory: his enthronement, his final rule without opposition and without end; and with it the dawn of the new era, the era of salvation. Before the coming rule of God the one eschatological messenger of joy appears, proclaiming the royal rule of God and the final liberation of his people. As he announces the rule of God and the liberation of man, and with them the eschatological era, his joyful message puts this era into effect and is, like the word of creation at the beginning, the word that creates the era of salvation. The new era begins for the world of the nations as well. The rule of Yahweh is proclaimed and the wonders of his liberation are praised among the Gentiles. The vision of the pilgrimage of the nations to Zion (Isa. 60.6) and the glorifying of Yahweh by the Gentiles shows the universality of hope in the 'one who brings good tidings' in the last days.[43]

The apocalyptic thinking which follows on Deutero-Isaiah conceived of the gospel of the last days as 'a revealed mystery'. Here the term stands in the context of the apocalyptic concept of revelation. The gospel reveals the eschatological divine secret. In addition, apocalyptic reckons with a twofold concept of revelation: in this age through special revelation to the righteous, while it is still hidden from the world; in the last days when God's decrees come into universal effect.[44] The gospel, then, is what the deutero-

Pauline writers call 'the *mysterion*'. With it there begins the epiphany of the secrets of the time of salvation, which have hitherto been concealed. Against this apocalyptic background, the New Testament gospel therefore has the character of a 'hidden power of revelation already breaking into the present from the end of the world'. It is 'the epiphany of the eschatological divine power *per se*'. In the gospel what will one day finally and visibly be revealed in Christ's parousia is already revealed in a provisional way (ἐν μυστηρίῳ, says Paul, I Cor. 2.7). But this means that the gospel is nothing less than the preliminary presence, veiled in the Word, of the Christ who is finally to come without concealment. 'Where the gospel is proclaimed, the exalted Lord hastens ahead of his appearance in his word in man's mouth; there he anticipates his future in the announcement of himself as the one who is to come.'[45]

According to this, gospel and evangelization are eschatological concepts. Prophecy and apocalyptic let us wait for the messianic messenger of good tidings who will speak 'the word' which, in the power of God's Spirit, will open up the new era and the new creation. It will be the word in which God reveals his coming and makes his victory and final lordship over his creation known. It will be the word which frees captives and brings the nations to peace. In this word and its proclamation the time and the world of salvation become manifest as gospel. The end of history dawns in the midst of history, bringing it to its saving end. That is why the gospel of the last days is to come about 'in power' and is to be accompanied by 'signs and wonders'.

The formula 'the gospel of the kingdom' is found for the first time in the New Testament.[46] According to the synoptic gospels Jesus saw himself as the promised messenger of good tidings of the last days, since he proclaimed his message as 'the gospel of the kingdom'. This includes the certainty that the eschatological 'enthronement of God' is imminent and that Jesus is sent ahead of it to bring about the turning point of time and the world. 'Thus the joyful message of the enthronement of God and the gospel which is fulfilled with Jesus Christ are inextricably linked with one another.'[47] If the kingdom of God is 'at hand' then 'the time is fulfilled' as well. The messianic era dawns in the presence of the messianic messenger of joy with the 'signs and wonders' of men's liberation. The history of Jesus is depicted by the synoptic gospels as the eschatological event of the gospel. The unique character and the scope of this event is, however, described in various ways. In Q the meaning is still predominantly Jewish: the gospel is the message about the coming of the rule of God, which brings salvation to the repentant (i.e., the community of the Son of man) but brings disaster and judgment to the people who are not prepared to repent. The good tidings of the rule of God brought about by the coming of the Son of man belongs to the lost sheep of the house of Israel; it is only when the Son of man comes that the pilgrimage of the nations to Zion will begin. But the gospel of the kingdom also belongs already, in advance, to the humiliated and insulted, although verbally this is obscured. Although it is uncertain whether Jesus himself talked about 'the gospel', the community which beheld in Jesus the prophet of the last days could appeal to the special features of his message and his ministry.[48]

The connection between the apostolic gospel in Paul and the gospels of the synoptic writers is an open question. When Paul uses τὸ εὐαγγέλιον in an absolute sense, he means the 'saving message of Jesus Christ, crucified and risen'.[49] Its content is Christ himself, the Son of God, the Lord, his death and resurrection as an eschatological saving event. Here too the apocalyptic framework seems to be preserved, as in the terminology of the primitive Christian mission, but it is preserved because now it is rooted in this history of Christ and no longer in Israel's Torah. 'The gospel' now means the redeeming message of salvation, which brings to expression and makes credible the salvation which comes from God through Christ and has now at last become universal and open to all. 'The apocalyptic structure of the gospel therefore remains beyond the revolution brought about by the beginning of the mission to the Gentiles and the genesis of a Gentile Christendom. But the gospel now . . . has a decidedly christological focus and is just as decidedly understood as a saving event which presses on the present and presses into it out of the future.'[50] This is shown by the new conjunctions of the gospel as the gospel of God and the gospel of Christ. It is no longer described as 'the gospel of the kingdom' (βασιλεία). It is called 'the gospel of the Son', 'the Word of the cross', and related to the eschatologically interpreted history of Christ in his crucifixion and resurrection. But just because of this it manifests the saving divine righteousness, effects salvation, creates peace, liberates for final freedom and reveals the coming glory of God. As the revelation of

Christ the gospel is the messianic sign of the new era and the charismatic power of the new creation. The gospel glorifies God and liberates man and is the 'sacrament' of the future. In the gospel and in the evangelization of the world this future becomes present in the Word. In the faith and hope which it brings this future of salvation becomes mighty towards the misery of the present.

We can here only mention more recent research into the gospels. Willi Marxsen has undertaken the interesting attempt at interpreting the 'real' gospel of Mark as a 'commentary' on the Pauline concept of gospel.

> The gospel [i.e. the Pauline gospel[51]] can therefore be described as standing between Easter and the *parousia*. The *euangelion* [of Mark] represents the life of Jesus from his first appearance in public up to the Cross as a proclamation; since Easter it has been possible to proclaim this event in Messianic terms (9.9). It is Easter that determines the account of the past as a secret epiphany – and in the same way the proclamation itself becomes a secret epiphany – and this is continued right up to the *parousia*. . . . The evangelist proclaims the One who once appeared as the One who is to come, and who – in secret epiphany – is present now as the proclamation is made.[52]

Ernst Käsemann has also pointed to the theologically essential connection between gospel and gospels. Without the gospels the gospel is in danger of running into gnostic 'enthusiasm'. 'Present eschatology without this reference back to the past of salvation is delivered over defenceless to enthusiasm. . . .'[53] But without the gospel, the gospels are in danger of becoming merely historical reminiscences of the life of Jesus. 'The earthly Jesus had to keep the preached Jesus from dissolving into the projection of an eschatological self-consciousness and becoming the object of a religious ideology.'[54] Whatever historical judgments we may form about these ideas (which rather belong to the sphere of systematic theology) the gospels about the earthly Jesus as the eschatological messenger of good tidings can be understood as hope in the mode of remembrance; while the apostolic gospel of Christ can be understood as remembrance in the mode of hope. Then the telling of the story of Christ implies proclaimed hope and the proclaimed hope of the risen one contains an actualizing remembrance of the one who was crucified. The gospels and the apostolic gospel complement one another, and not merely in this theologically necessary way; they also interpret one another and are mutually intertwined. If it is correct to see the celebration of the Lord's supper as the centre of the life of the primitive Christian churches, then the telling of the story of the passion and the proclamation of Jesus' saving death 'until he comes' coincide in this celebration.

Summing up, we can say that eschatology becomes effective in history whenever the gospel of Christ is proclaimed as the eschatological 'message of good tidings' expected by prophecy and apocalyptic. There the future glory of God and the liberation of man take on historical form; now, indeed, only as the Word that opens up the future and as hoping faith, but already in the power of God. In this way – a way that must be called messianic – the eschatological future casts its light ahead on history, and righteousness, the liberation of captives and the glorification of God are already realized. Consequently, in its very character as the proclamation of Christ the gospel is the revelation of the divine future; and the actual *fact* of this happening must be termed the presence of the Holy Spirit.

1. The prophetic and apocalyptic framework for the gospel and evangelization maintains that this 'message of good tidings' is not possible at all times and in all places, but belongs to the messianic era at the end of history. 'The gospel of the kingdom is proclaimed to the poor' ushers in the time when God takes possession of his dominion over his creation and man becomes free. When 'the gospel of Christ' is proclaimed to the whole world, Jews and Gentiles alike, this initiates the future in which God's creative righteousness will become manifest and God will be all in all. The gospel of Christ proclaims that this era has dawned and this future has already begun with the passion and resurrection of the crucified Jesus. It has already become accessible for everyone in faith; and it can be experienced in the new potentialities of the Spirit. In love people can already live from the powers of the new creation and in the potentialities of the messianic era. But just because the gospel has the eschatologically interpreted history of Christ as its content, the history of Christ is also the presupposition for the public proclamation of the gospel. Every living thing has its particular atmosphere, its aura and its time. If we rob the gospel of its messianic aura – that is, the certainty that with and through Christ the messianic fulfilment of poor, expectant and empty-handed life has dawned – then the proclamation will become sterile, morally, religiously or ideologically. It has then been uprooted

from its time and is no longer 'timely'; or, to be more precise, then
it is 'not yet' timely. We have to be silent, not because there is
nothing to say but because the 'eschatological message of good
tidings' is not yet to be spoken and must not be spoken. The
history of Christ, his suffering to set the world free and his resurrection for its justification, are the guarantee that it is time to
proclaim the gospel of the kingdom to the poor, as well as a blessing on those that mourn, the forgiveness of sins and the liberation
of captives. The proclamation of the gospel of Christ has the
history of Christ both as its content and as its presupposition. The
gospel proclaims Christ as the Lord of the messianic kingdom and
all its possibilities and is itself the first possibility and the first
sign of the messianic era.

Jews and atheists do not really dispute the gospel itself; they
dispute its possibility and its timeliness. 'Morning comes, and also
the night. If you will inquire, inquire; come back again' (Isa. 21.12).
Against this the Christian assurance in its proclamation of the
good tidings of the last days says that the time has come because
God's future, like man's liberation, is manifest in the history of
Christ and its proclamation. It does not deny that the state of the
world fails to display any marked messianic beauty and that there
is little to be seen of the righteousness of the messianic era. But it
sees the world's evil and suffering summed up, revealed and overcome in Christ's passion. That is why it discovers in the resurrection of this crucified Christ the turn of the age and the hidden
dawn of the messianic future. That is why the gospel of Christ
brings a saving future into the disastrous present, speaking of God
in the face of godlessness, of our brotherhood in the face of enmity, and of the new creation in the face of a threatened earth. The
gospel of Christ in the messianic era of Christ is at heart 'the word
of the cross' and the contradiction in practice of a world which
contradicts its Creator and itself. It is only out of this protest
against the contradiction that the correspondences will be created
which, as 'signs and wonders', are the proof of the messianic era.
The exegetical and theological problem of the 'delay' of the
parousia (which basically reproaches Jesus and Christianity with
an outmoded enthusiasm and an illegitimate anticipation of the
future) is solved christologically through the cross of the risen one
and the resurrection of the one who was crucified. For the remembrance of the passion of the Lord and discipleship of the crucified

Jesus keep the Christian faith alive in the contradiction of the time and fill it with protest against that contradiction. The Christian theology of the cross is the true reason for the messianic assurance of faith and the proclamation of the gospel.

2. It follows from this that the Christian proclamation cannot be supported by analogies in the cosmos or historical events. A damaged world and the history of guilt and death do not in themselves reflect any messianic light. Even human reason (which corresponds to the state of this world) and the interests which guide its perception cannot be drawn upon here. According to Paul the saving righteousness of God in the gospel (Rom. 1.17) is revealed in time inasmuch as the wrath of God is revealed against 'all ungodliness and wickedness of men' (v. 18). At the same time as the proclamation of the good tidings of the last days, the world moves into the growing shadow of the judgment which lies in the Godforsakenness of the godless who are surrendered to their self-chosen way. Romans 8.19ff. also sees the suffering which is anonymously enslaving the world, and not the beauty and righteousness of creation, as being the sign of the Creator's struggle for the liberation of the world – a struggle initiated by Christ. In the context of Christ's passion and resurrection this suffering of creation is interpreted messianically as 'the birthpangs of the last days'. When the power of the resurrection becomes effective in the gospel of Christ, then the gospel belongs to the people who stand in the fellowship of Christ's sufferings, for whom the suffering Christ has become a brother, and for whom the crucified one died. The hermeneutical circle therefore does not close exclusively round word and reality or round word and faith. Faith and reality belong rather to the life which is stamped by Spirit and suffering. Just as the gospel of God's kingdom is proclaimed to the poor, so the gospel of Christ is proclaimed to sinners, that is to say, to the Godforsaken godless. The messianic era opened up through the crucified Jesus and revealed through the gospel is no longer exclusively the era of the righteous and of righteous acts, as it was in Jewish expectation; it is first of all the era of the justification of the godless, the forgiveness of sins, the liberation of the humiliated and the reconciliation of enemies.[55] Hope in action in the sign of the crucified Jesus is the messianic protest against godlessness and unrighteousness in this period of death; a protest which liberates men for response to and fellowship with God, and for righteous-

ness. Wherever the liberating protest in the face of resistance leads
to such responses, fragments and anticipations of the new creation
come into being. They are to be understood as 'signs and wonders'
of the Holy Spirit. In this sense the Spirit verifies the proclamation
of the gospel.[56] This comes about in the assent of faith, which says
'amen' to its messianic liberation. It comes about in the initial
new obedience and in the forms of the new fellowship.

Consequently, although Christianity certainly has to understand the gospel and the evangelization of the world messianically
in its eschatological context, it must equally substantiate its
messianism christologically, from the cross of the Lord of the
future. But how is this messianism to be practised in the form of a
theology of the cross?

3. The gospel is the liberating word in the name of the God who
is to come. Just as the coming kingdom is universal, so the gospel
brings the liberation of men to universal expression. It seeks to
liberate the soul and the body, individuals and social conditions,
human systems and the systems of nature from the closedness of
reserve, from self-righteousness, and from godless and inhuman
pressures. It takes place in the word, in language, for the purpose
of hearing and believing; but the freedom to which it calls reaches
further and seeks to place the whole of life in the sphere of the
hope of the kingdom. By preaching Christ the liberator, who was
crucified and raised for us, the gospel heralds his kingdom and at
the same time cancels the ties with sin, law and death – gives
notice *of* the one and gives notice *to* the other. The proclamation of
Christ is the proclamation of the new covenant. When the new
covenant 'in the blood of Christ' with the coming God is proclaimed, the old ties of idolatry, superstition and self-justification
are thereby abolished. When the 'covenant with life' is made, the
'covenant with death' is ended. Consequently the divine pardon
stands at the centre of every proclamation of the gospel, the pardon
that liberates men and women from the compulsion of evil, from
the control of 'the powers', from fear of forsakenness, and from
the apathy of the empty life, and that gives them courage for a new
life for the kingdom in fellowship with Christ.

Every Christian proclamation is an expression in one way or
another of 'I absolve thee'. Redemption is properly only expressed
in language that sets free, and freedom is only expressed in a
language which does not determine, pin down, define and accuse,

but acquits in the liberating word, makes new life possible and allows frontiers to be crossed.

(v) *The Gospel and the Messianic Fellowship*

The proclamation of the gospel always belongs within a community, for every language lives in a community or creates one. As public proclamation, the gospel is part of a society's public activity and it alters its form when the society's public character alters. In the Christianized societies of Europe, the proclamation long counted as the public ministry. Priests and pastors had a status which was analogous to that of the other public offices. Their proclamation to the people corresponded to the hierarchical, vertical pattern that public life takes in a class society – from the top downwards. For when society was Christianized the Christian church took over the functions of the socially essential 'state religion'. The community of Christians and the community of citizens coincided. Parishes followed residential districts. The church took over the pastoral care of individuals and families and administered the religious framework of meaning of society. In a framework of this kind the gospel is in danger of losing its critical and liberating power and of being reduced to religious consolation, to morality and the teaching of the people. At the beginning of modern times voluntary religious fellowships of believers then grew up in Germany out of the pietistic movement. This Evangelical revival movement broke through the class order and the parochial divisions of the institutionalized church and organized itself into voluntary groups. The pattern of pastoral welfare was replaced by personal adherence to the faith; the public ministry gave way to the personal witness of the brethren; and prayer meetings took the place of public worship. Faith no longer meant being one of the recipients of the pastoral care exercised by the church; it meant personal experience and decision. Here the old vertical scheme of proclamation was replaced by a horizontal scheme of communication among the group of believers. In place of the pastoral care of the whole population, the fellowship of believers developed a missionary relationship to non-believers. At the beginning of modern times a new dialogistic relationship to the church also simultaneously developed among the educated classes. Faith is neither participation in the church nor personal decision but a kind of permanent reflection of Christianity in the form of critical religiosity. It is not the authority of the church and tradition that makes the religious system of thought acceptable; it is well-founded information. Free, interested discussion with the church takes the place of church-going and the decision of faith. The church becomes a forum and platform for dialogue with Christianity. The 'public' work performed by academies, church assemblies, radio, social work, work among men, women, school children and students reflects this form of proclamation. But whereas the pietistic 'revival movement', with its separatist tendencies, threatens to cut the gospel off from the very world to which it seeks to proclaim liberation in the name of the coming God, 'enlightened' Christianity threatens to rob the gospel of its character of commitment.

The fellowship which corresponds to the gospel in its original interpretation is the messianic community. It is the fellowship which narrates the story of Christ, and its own story with that story, because its own existence, fellowship and activity springs from that story of liberation. It is a 'story-telling fellowship', which continually wins its own freedom from the stories and myths of the society in which it lives, from the present realization of this story of Christ. It is a fellowship of hope, which finds freedom from the perspectives of its society through the perspectives of the kingdom of God. Finally, it is a fellowship which, by virtue of its remembrance of the story of Christ and its hope for the kingdom of man, liberates men and women from the compulsive actions of existing society and from the inner attitudes that correspond to them, freeing them for a life which takes on a messianic character. In Christianized societies this does not merely lead to the critical freedom of faith towards the respective social systems; it leads to critical freedom towards the church which is tied up with the social system, and towards Christianity in general. In this liberating society the language of liberation finds a correspondence that is seldom possible in the religious 'pastoral' church, or in the exclusive society of the converted, or in Christian society. The messianic community belongs to the Messiah and the messianic word; and this community, with the powers that it has, already realizes the possibilities of the messianic era, which brings the gospel of the kingdom to the poor, which proclaims the lifting up of the downtrodden to the lowly, and begins the glorification of the coming God through actions of hope in the fellowship of the poor, the sad and those condemned to silence, so that it may lay hold on all men. In the traditions of the established churches the important thing is to build up independent communities, capable of action. In the minority churches it is openness to the world in missionary and charitable activity that has to be developed.

'The sign is not the thing it stands for, the name is not the thing, the idea is not the deed, the dream is not the action. The true world (is) unattainable, unprovable, unpromisable', said Nietzsche. Is it really? Where the gospel corresponds to Christ, and the messianic fellowship of the people corresponds to the gospel, the truth of the proclamation is recognizable from the freedom it creates. The 'true world' is promised in the gospel of Christ and is made accessible in the power of the Holy Spirit.

3. *Baptism*

Just as the Christian church is called into being through the proclamation of the gospel, so through baptism it is called to the freedom of the messianic era. Through baptism it demonstrates the dawn of the rule of God in personal life and the common conversion to the future of that rule. Through baptism in Christ's name believers are publicly set in Christ's fellowship; and through baptism in the name of the triune God they are thereby simultaneously set in the trinitarian history of God. In the framework of the concept of the sacraments which underlies our reflections here we understand baptism as a sign bound up with the gospel which is also the public sign of life of the Holy Spirit, who unites believers with Christ and brings about the new creation.

When we understand baptism in the context of this promise, however, the churches' present baptismal practice and theology becomes problematical in a number of ways. We shall therefore begin with a brief account of the theory and practice of baptism in the Protestant tradition, so as to scrutinize it in its dogmatic, missionary, ecumenical and political aspects. The baptismal tradition ought to be reflected in the messianic light of the story of Christ's history.

(*i*) *Protestant Baptismal Practice and Baptismal Theology*

The renewal of the church at the Reformation assumed its largely binding form in the age of Protestant orthodoxy.[57] Every

alteration in Protestantism must digest this tradition. The dogmatic theologians put baptism in the framework of soteriology.
The 'principles of salvation' in which christology is developed are
followed by the 'order of salvation' in which the gift of the Holy
Spirit is unfolded in faith, justification, calling, illumination, conversion, mystical union and glorification; and then comes the
doctrine of the 'means of salvation'. The grace of the Holy
Spirit, which appropriates salvation in Christ, is mediated through
the word, baptism and the Lord's supper. The salvation which is
objectively obtained through Christ is subjectively appropriated
through the Holy Spirit. Salvation itself is spiritual, invisible and
inward. It is mediated, therefore, through the audible and visible
means of salvation, that is, through word and sacraments. Christ
counts as the efficient cause of salvation, whereas baptism in the
power of the Spirit is the instrument. The mediation through the
word thus has pre-eminent importance, because the word can
exist without the sacraments but the sacraments cannot exist
without the word. Sacraments count as 'holy rites or actions'
ordained by God through which saving grace is appropriated or
people are given the certainty of that grace through the medium of
visible signs. Baptism and the Lord's supper are subject to an
express divine intention. Over both are the promises of Christ's
presence. These promises are understood both as words of institution and as binding assurances to the receiver. A 'holy rite'
becomes efficacious as a 'sacrament' when it is performed through
the church and in the church, in accordance with its institution.
Baptism is justified through a founder christology and legitimated
by the fact that it was instituted by Christ himself. As a means of
salvation it is part of the ground of salvation and participates in the
power of its efficacy. As a 'holy rite' it links the visible and invisible reality in a metaphorical way. In the order of the means of
salvation, baptism precedes the Lord's supper. It is the sacrament
of initiation and the door of grace. The Lord's supper is the sacrament of confirmation and the path of grace. Through baptism men
and women are born again to eternal life. Through the Lord's
supper they are sustained in that life. Accepted into the covenant
of grace through baptism, believers are sustained in it through the
Lord's supper. Baptism is therefore by nature a holy rite com-
manded by Christ and invested with his promise. His word of
institution and promise effects saving grace through the waters of

baptism. According to its form, baptism effects what it says and promises, provided it is performed in accordance with its institution. Its purpose is to make saving grace efficacious in men and women. In adults, proclamation and faith precede baptism. In the case of children they are supposed to follow it. Since baptism is acceptance into an 'eternal covenant', it can only be performed once. But because it is valid once and for all, its efficacy is not restricted to the actual moment of baptism. Consequently the baptized person acquires the means of repentance, through which he can regain baptismal grace daily. Repentance is continual life in baptismal grace on the basis of the baptism that has been performed once and for all. That is why repetitions of baptism are inadmissible.

What baptismal practice lies behind early Protestant baptismal theology? Since the Reformers decided against the 'Baptists' in favour of the preservation of infant baptism, early Protestant baptismal theology was not only applied to infant baptism, but also served to justify it against Baptist attacks. It is true that it talks about adult baptism, but the trend of its comments is directed towards the justification of the baptism of infants. When the efficacy of baptism is based on its performance in accordance with its ordinance, when non-resistance is presupposed on the recipient's part, when we speak of the vicarious efficacy of the faith of the parents or of the church, or even about a 'seed of faith' in infants – then this sacramental objectivism is ministering to the practice of infant baptism. For this practice requires the proof that baptism can not only follow on faith, but that it can also precede faith and the profession of faith, and can bring about both.

Infant baptism, as the attempts to justify it theologically show, is an open theological problem as long as the churches that practise it appeal to its origin in the history of Christ. The primitive Christian churches (like all missionary churches) spread through calling men and women and through their being born again; but churches with infant baptism propagate themselves from generation to generation by means of birth and tradition: everyone born of Christian parents is also born into the Christian church. The perpetual actualization of the New Testament continually calls this practice in question. Every baptismal theology is therefore forced to a critical comparison between the proclaimed story of Christ and the baptismal practice in question, whether it justifies the present baptismal practice from the history of its origin, or whether it criticizes the history of this activity in the light of its origin.

The practice of infant baptism is also an open political problem connected with the form of the church in its particular society. Infant baptism is without any doubt the basic pillar of the *corpus christianum*, the 'Christian society' which acknowledges – or at least does not reject – Christianity in the widest sense of the word as its tradition. Infant baptism is the foundation of a national church. Through it 'Christian society' regenerates itself in the bond that links one generation to another. Anyone who affirms infant baptism, for whatever theological reason, thereby affirms at the same time this public form of the church, or Christianity. Anyone who condemns it, for whatever theological reason, must also have in mind and want another social form for the church. A change of baptismal practice without a change in the public form and function of the church in society is not possible. Let us first examine the traditional theological arguments for infant baptism.

1. 'He who believes and is baptized will be saved' (Mark 16.16). The order of the New Testament churches is: first faith, then baptism. But the practice of infant baptism compels this to be reversed: first baptism, then faith. Generally, however, this reversal is not carried through theologically. In infant baptism faith comes first too – namely the faith of the parents, the godparents and the church. By virtue of the natural representative function of parents and community for children, their preceding faith must therefore intervene and be put to the children's account, representatively and in hope for the children's faith, which cannot yet be presumed. Now it is undoubtedly correct that believers are not baptized merely as individuals and private persons; through baptism their gifts, the tasks assigned to them and their responsibilities are also put at the service of Christ and his kingdom. It follows from this that parenthood is also accepted into this service through baptism. Parents have a messianic function towards their children too, being to a special degree their missionaries and evangelists. Children are not foundlings, so to speak, shut out from their parents' faith and condemned to find it for themselves. But children are not, either, 'a something from the father, as it were, an extension of his fatherly person', as Thomas Aquinas put it, and hence able to be automatically integrated into their parents' baptism. The

baptism of the parents and their Christian responsibility for their children does not lead to any compulsive necessity for the children themselves, or to any justification of infant baptism either; though what it does lead to is undoubtedly the charge of proclamation to the children, prayer for them and the lived testimony of freedom in fellowship with them. The natural link between the generations has relevance for the proclamation of the gospel and for the ministry of liberation in the sequence of time. But it cannot compel the sequel of baptism and does not justify the baptism of infants. Faith and baptism commit to service in the natural relations of life, but they are not themselves passed on through these natural relations.

2. This also invalidates the other argument, that infant baptism represents in a particularly cogent way the unconditional justification of sinners and God's prevenient grace. The justification of the sinner and prevenient grace come about when a person believes, not directly at baptism. The pure passivity of receiving, pardoned, liberated men and women is a creative receptivity, and it is at most metaphorically that it has anything to do with the defencelessness of new-born babes. If baptism were to effect grace *ex opere operato*, as an unconditionally effective means of salvation, then all children without distinction would have to be baptized. But only children of Christian parents who have been baptized themselves were and are baptized – by no means all the 'heathen children' one could lay hands on. Why are only the children of Christians baptized? Not because of prevenient grace, but because faith does in fact precede baptism – in this case the faith of the parents on behalf of their children. Infant baptism is not a token of prevenient grace; it is a sign of the prevenient faith of the parents. Consequently this argument too falls back on the first one, and is equally lacking in cogency. Baptism cannot be without faith. Faith commits us to representative service, but it cannot be taken as being representative for the faith of another person or as a temporary substitute for that faith. The faith of the fellowship is necessary, but it does not diminish the freedom of the child who is baptized to believe for himself; on the contrary, it is a challenge for him to do so.

Let us go on to examine the political arguments for infant baptism.

In the framework of 'Christian society' infant baptism is understood as a rite of initiation and accordingly as an analogy to circumcision among the people of Israel. Children are received into society at birth. Through baptism they are accepted into the religious bond of this society. Infant baptism then counts as the first act of pastoral care performed by this religious system, to which society assigns the custody of the feeling for the life of individuals and society as a whole. Earlier, people liked to see baptism and the Lord's supper as analogies to circumcision and passover in the Old Testament. The Mosaic system, the law and order of the ancient people of the covenant, counted as the prefiguration of the Christian society, not the church in particular but the public form of God's rule on earth in church and society. This picture of 'Christian society' as the successor to Israel and as the earthly anticipation of the kingdom of God has in essence persisted, even if the impress of the Old Testament has been lost. 'Christian society' allots to the church, as religious functions, functions of socialization and integration. It claims the care of the church as the custodian of the significance at the central moments and turning points of life: baptism at birth; confirmation at puberty; the wedding at the beginning of married life; extreme unction before death; and church burial afterwards. If the religious system of significance becomes looser, more pluralistic and more diffuse, then baptism loses its original binding character as well. Calvin still called it a *seminarium civitatis coelestium*. It then developed into a *seminarium civitatis christianae* and finally into a merely private *seminarium familiae*. Erosions of the Christian society chiefly appear in individuals at puberty and the age of independence. This gives rise to the curious situation that religion is still considered necessary and helpful for children, whereas for adults it is thought of as a 'private affair'. Consequently the religious ideas of adults often remain in their childish phase. Through this practice the original promise of Christian baptism is distorted to the point of unrecognizability. Here the theological question of the relevance of the social bond for Christian baptism arises. Because every individual person lives not merely for himself but in a community, churches and missionaries have often baptized whole families, villages, tribes and peoples. If rulers and chiefs were baptized, the whole society was baptized in principle. for the previous cults were abolished, the 'national' religion was Christianized and baptism was made obligatory for all. If it is impossible to ignore the links between the generations, it is just as impossible to disregard the social groupings in which people actually live. But a society which is open for Christianity always allots religious functions to the church as well and it has to fulfil these whether they correspond to its origin and nature or not. The church can be persecuted; but it can also be alienated from its foundation, and its Christian rites and symbols can be misused. A society's leanings towards infant baptism and the religious education of children is always based on more than one motive and cannot merely be assessed as an opportunity for baptism; it must also be seen as a hindrance to the real meaning of baptism. The social structure can encourage baptism through the pressure of the public aspect of religion – adult baptism as well as infant baptism, but pre-eminently the latter. Then, however, the form and interpretation of baptism takes on the impress of the society's predominating interests. The social structure can constrain baptism, but it does not justify it. Faith and baptism impose an obligation to service in the social structures of life; so much we can say here too. But they cannot be passed on through the social structure. The freedom of faith takes form in the freedom to be baptized. This freedom must be observed, both in the face of a society's resistance and in the face of a society's misuse of baptism. Baptism can only be practised in accordance with its proper meaning if the church's public form and function in society is altered at the same time, and if the church becomes recognizable and active as the messianic fellowship of Christ. A convincing baptismal practice can only be acquired together with a convincing church. There can be no reform of baptism without a reform of the church, and no church reform without a reform of baptism. If we abide by the bourgeois religious form of the church in a 'Christian society', as we have described it, then if infant baptism is the general rule, the individual baptism of an adult on the basis of a personal profession of faith would only lead to baptism's becoming a matter of the inner, personal life, which would have to be lived in private; or it would lead to a life in the exclusive circle of the converted. In both cases baptism would lose the character of a public, confessional sign of resistance and hope.

(ii) The Christian Meaning of Baptism[58]

Early Christian baptism is connected genetically with *John the Baptist*'s repentance movement, and with Jesus' baptism by John.

It has no genetic connection at all with Israelite circumcision or the purification rites of the mystery religions, although analogies can be discovered. John baptized 'in the wilderness' at Jordan.[59] He called the people to repent of their unrighteousness and to come out from bondage, because the judgment of God on the mighty and the compromises made with them was at hand: anyone who now lived the righteousness of God, radically and without any compromise, anyone who repented and went 'into the wilderness' could be saved from the coming divine wrath. The 'desert preacher' introduced a movement for repentance in Israel whose critical social and political consequences were such that he was considered dangerous and was executed. John's baptism in Jordan was intended to symbolize the new exodus from bondage, and the eschatological entry into the promised land of the divine kingdom. In this respect the baptism of John was particular and unique. It differed from the daily lustrations of the Essenes through its eschatological finality. It was not an initiation rite for an existing society; it was the eschatological sign of the setting forth out of present oppression towards the immediately imminent freedom of the divine rule. Going down into the waters of the Jordan is to be understood as the step out of the old life of unrighteousness into the new life with the righteous God. This baptism is 'an expression of repentance and guarantees salvation from judgment. It is an eschatological sacrament of repentance':[60] the kingdom of God is at hand. But the kingdom is breaking in as judgment. Anyone who wants to stand the test must let the judgment be anticipated on himself. John the Baptist did not apparently found any new sect, but preached to the people the kind of repentance that was only aware that the open space of the imminent divine rule was ahead of it.

John's baptism of *Jesus of Nazareth* is relatively well authenticated, historically. We can assume that Jesus was one of John's disciples for a time, and only began his public ministry after John's imprisonment. Some of Jesus' disciples probably also came to him from John. On the other hand we know nothing about any baptismal practice on the part of Jesus and his disciples. He himself did not baptize. It was evidently only after Easter that the community received the command to baptize, on the occasion of their sending forth by the risen Christ. At all events, in the apostolic period we find no appeal to the earthly Jesus' own establishment of baptism, or to his institution of it as a sacrament.

But Jesus' baptism by John was from the very beginning constitutive for the acceptance and taking over of John the Baptist's eschatology – his teaching about the coming rule of God – by Jesus and the Christian community. The Christian church's acceptance and heightening of John's baptism does not go back to a particular institution on the part of Jesus, but it does follow from Jesus' acceptance and alteration of John's eschatology. The fact that Jesus parted from John in order to begin preaching his own message can be taken as a sign of the fact that his eschatological gospel deviated from John's eschatology of judgment.[61] Where John proclaimed the kingdom of God as judgment, with a view to repentance, Jesus evidently proclaimed the kingdom of God as the justice of grace and demonstrated it by acts of forgiving sins. For Jesus the gospel of the kingdom was an eschatological message of joy. Unlike John's disciples, the disciples of Jesus did not fast. Nor did they emigrate from the oppression under which the country was living 'into the wilderness'; they went into the villages and taught the people. Jesus' parting from John therefore points to his new version of John's eschatological message. But he took over the imminent eschatological expectation, with its provocation of the powerful and the collaborators, and the call to freedom it addressed to the people. Now, however, the threat of judgment was replaced by the liberating good tidings of grace. Because the earthly Jesus and his gospel cannot be understood without Jesus' baptism by John and his parting from him, Christian baptism follows, with inner cogency, from the eschatology of Jesus and is founded on the church's eschatological profession of faith in Jesus as the Christ of God. In conjunction with John's eschatology, Christian baptism is comprehensible as being a sign of the coming of God into a person's life and his turning to the future. That is why 'the baptism of John' is to be preached as well.

The primitive church evidently baptized very soon after Easter. Remembering Jesus' baptism by John, they understood their baptism eschatologically. Under the impression of Jesus' resurrection and in the experience of the Spirit, they proclaimed their baptism with the Holy Spirit. They 'Christianized' the eschatological sealing of the repentant for the coming kingdom of God by baptism in the name and into the name of Christ. When they baptized 'in the power of the Holy Spirit', they understood this event as the earnest and dawn of the glory of God in the story of a person's life. As a matter of fact we can see the baptism with the eschatological gift of the Holy Spirit after Easter as corresponding to the earthly Jesus' turning from John's threat of judgment to the revelation of the gospel of the kingdom in the forgiveness of sins. Historically, it seems likely that after Easter some of the disciples of Jesus who had been baptized by John began to baptize believers. We may also suspect that there was competition between Jesus' disciples and John's, and that this led Christians to proclaim the crucified and risen Jesus as the one whom John had promised was to come, and to their outdoing John's baptism with water through their baptism with the Spirit, which they represented as being the fulfilment of John's. The period after Easter shows that baptism corresponded to the understanding of the new fellowship in any given case. Where the Christian community understood itself as 'the holy remnant' and therefore as the beginning of Israel in its eschatological renewal, Christian baptism counted as being the symbol of this messianic renewal of God's people. Where they conceived of themselves as 'the new people of God', made up of Jews and Gentiles, baptism became the emblem of the 'new creation' in Christ. At all events, in I Cor. 12.13 Paul assumes as a matter of course that all Christians are baptized, although he himself was sent not to baptize but to preach the gospel (I Cor. 1.17) and only baptized occasionally.

On the foundation of Easter, in the experience of the Holy Spirit and together with the proclamation of the gospel, believers were baptized into the name of Christ, the Lord of the coming divine kingdom. Like the proclamation of the gospel of the last days, Christian baptism is eschatology put into practice. It manifests the advent of the coming God through Christ in human life and is the sign of life's conversion to the life of Easter. Like the proclamation of the gospel of the last days, Christian baptism is Christian hope in action. The Christian meaning of baptism follows from the eschatological understanding of the gospel of Jesus and the gospel about Jesus, the Christ of the God who is to come. An eschatologically open christology explains why baptism was taken over from John and was reformed. Its own eschatological and pneumatic character can only be maintained if the connection with John's baptism is preserved. Without baptism in this sense the eschatological history of Christ would be incomprehensible. That is why baptism for Christ's sake is necessary, even if we cannot say that it is 'necessary for salvation' in any further sense.

The intertwining before and after Easter of eschatology and gospel, or christology and eschatology, can also be interpreted pneumatologically: after his baptism in Jordan, Jesus was anointed with the Spirit (Mark 1.10ff.) and equipped for his messianic mission. His public ministry stands in the sign of the Spirit (Luke 4.14, 18 et passim). The Spirit leads and drives him on his way (Mark 1.12). His signs and wonders count as the signs and wonders of the Spirit. In the Spirit he offers himself up for death on the cross (Heb. 9.14). Through the power of the Spirit, God has raised him from the dead (Rom. 8.11) and exalted him to be a life-giving spirit (I Cor. 15.45). In so far as the life, death and resurrection of Jesus are formed by the Spirit, the Holy Spirit reveals, glorifies and completes the lordship of Christ in believers, in the church and in the world. It is not that the gift of the Holy Spirit is merely the subjective side of the objective divine acts of salvation in Christ, nor is it as if its dispensation and intercession for us could be added to the salvation really gained on the cross. The history of Christ and the history of the Holy Spirit are so interwoven that a pneumatic christology leads with inner cogency to a christological pneumatology. We shall therefore have to see baptism, as well, as part of the trinitarian relations of the eschatological history of God's dealings with the world.

(iii) The Fundamentals of Baptismal Theology

The multiplicity of the notions about baptism found in the New Testament makes it difficult to ascertain the fundamental ideas which can be justified theologically today. Every choice is one-sided. We must therefore try to discover the fundamental problems which gave rise to the different answers, and then go on to seek an answer of our own. The central problem is the relationship of the baptismal event to the history of Christ.

Mark found the reason for Christian baptism in the baptism of Jesus, which in its turn points forward to Jesus' passion and death.[62] The meaning of Jesus' baptism is his election to be Son of God and his messianic equipping with the power of the Holy Spirit. The divine sonship of Jesus is confirmed in the story of the transfiguration (9.7) and is finally acknowledged by Jesus during his cross-examination (14.61f.) and by the centurion at the foot of

the cross (15.39). The divine sonship of Jesus includes Jesus'
mission and his self-giving. In the passage about the sons of
Zebedee (10.38ff.), baptism also points towards martyrdom. Jesus'
baptism points forward to his passion and includes the whole of
his path to death on the cross. This link between baptism and the
death of Jesus is important for Mark.

Matthew, on the other hand, found the reason for Christian
baptism in the missionary charge of the exalted Lord; but he
understood Jesus' own baptism as an eschatological epoch.[63]
John's baptism is completed with the baptism of Jesus, for in
Jesus the one who fulfils righteousness has come (3.14ff.). This
gives Jesus' baptism an exclusively christological meaning. It does
not as yet tell us anything about Christian baptism. Christian
baptism, according to Matthew, is based not on Jesus' own baptism
but on the missionary charge of the exalted Christ, which includes
the whole world of the nations, because the risen one has been
given all power by God (Matt. 28.18).

Luke, finally, finds the reason for Christian baptism in what
happened at Pentecost. He distinguishes it from John's baptism
with water as being a baptism with the Spirit. John is the forerunner of the era of Jesus, and his baptism is the prefiguration of
the era of the church.[64] Luke therefore stresses the conferring of the
Spirit at Jesus' baptism (3.21ff.). Whereas Mark found the justification for baptism in Jesus' death, and whereas Matthew found it in
the missionary charge of the exalted Christ, Luke explains baptism in
the light of the miracle of the outpouring of the Spirit at Pentecost
(Acts 1.5–8), which is then further explained in Peter's sermon
(2.38ff.). It takes place for the forgiveness of sins and is linked with
the receiving of the Spirit.

For *Paul* Christian baptism gives tangible form to Christ's
fellowship of believers.[65] He consequently makes baptism's relation to the Christ event thematic. Baptism is the expression of
belonging. Christ is crucified for you, you are baptized in Christ's
name (I Cor. 1.10–18). The saving event is not baptism through
Cephas or Apollos itself, but the cross of Christ, baptism being a
link with the cross's saving significance. That is why in this context he also calls his gospel 'the word of the cross'. According to
Romans 6, those who are baptized into the name of Christ are
'baptized into his death' and 'buried with him in baptism'. In this
way they have died to the power of sin. Just as all accusations and

claims fall when they are brought against the dead, so those who
are baptized are out of reach of the accusations of the law and the
claims of power. Baptism into the death of Christ thus demonstrates the liberation of believers from the power of sin. They
have the death of sin behind them and life in the divine righteousness ahead. Just as burial is a final declaration of death, so dying
to sin in the death of Christ is also valid once and for all. Since
baptism into the death of Christ is the mark of the whole of
Christ's fellowship of faith, it also demonstrates fellowship with
the risen one. But fellowship with the death of Christ is in the
perfect tense, while fellowship with his resurrection is in the
future. The perfect tense of the 'having died into Christ' opens the
future of eternal life with Christ, which has already dawned here
and which will be completed at the resurrection of the dead. It is
new life in the Spirit, in the dawn of the new creation and the glory
of God. It is new life in the service of righteousness, and therefore
in discipleship of the crucified Jesus. But it is also new life in the
community of Christ. In I Corinthians 12 Paul sets baptism in the
charismatic community. Just as this community lived in the manifestation of the Spirit, which sets every one in his particular ministry
and makes him a member of the whole, so through baptism people
are integrated into this community and are entrusted with their
particular ministry. Through baptism the believer is called into
this messianic community and is called to liberating creative
service for the kingdom. Baptism is in this sense a 'call'. In
Galatians 3 Paul puts baptism in the same context as justification and the right to hope for the future rule of God. Baptism
therefore gives concrete form to the divine righteousness manifest
in the gospel, as this touches a single person, making the universal
future of Christ effective in his particular life.

If we try to sum up the different aspects of New Testament
baptismal theology, we shall have to see the baptismal event in the
framework of the whole history of Christ – that is to say, in the
framework of the baptized, crucified, risen and coming Christ.
The baptismal event is not something that stands over against this
history of Christ; it must be seen as an integral part of this history
itself. In this perspective, the theological dispute as to whether
baptism is a cognitive, or a causative and generative means of
salvation ought to be open to solution.

In his writings on baptism, Karl Barth has stressed the saving event completed and perfected in Christ, thus denying to baptism the character of a means of salvation which is sacramental, or necessary for salvation, or which supplements or prolongs salvation.[66] In the power of the Holy Spirit baptism is entirely and exclusively related to the Christ event and must therefore be understood as the representation, witness, sign and illumination of this event. It points away from itself and its own happening in the direction of Christ alone. In so far it has cognitive meaning. Barth deduces from this the inadmissibility of infant baptism and pleads for the baptism of believers.

On the other hand Heinrich Schlier maintains that baptism is a sacramental action, which effects the salvation of the person baptized in a causative sense.[67] It is true that it does not effect salvation itself, since that has already been brought about in Christ; but it does effect salvation in the case of the baptismal candidate. Baptism is, indeed, a figurative action in Christ's name, but as an instrumental sign it effects the thing it denotes, through the actual fact of its performance. It is consequently, according to Schlier, 'necessary for salvation' in the sense of a necessary means. Between Pentecost and the parousia Christ linked his efficacy with baptism. As a result, Schlier says, infant baptism is not only possible but necessary. Through infant baptism the church – the body of Christ growing through the cosmos – is to incorporate people of every age, just as it is also to incorporate all nations and institutions.

If we leave infant baptism on one side in this dispute (because in my view it cannot be justified even by Schlier's arguments, unless he wants to incorporate all children, not merely the children of Christians, into the church through baptism) certain extremes, even in Barth, could become superfluous in the theological justification of baptism. The dispute between an exclusively christological orientation and an ecclesiological justification of baptism can be solved if baptism is understood in a trinitarian sense in the light of the eschatological gift of the Holy Spirit. As 'representation' and 'recognition' of the reconciliation brought about through Christ's giving of himself to death 'for us', baptism manifests the creative power of the Spirit. As a leading back into the death of Christ it is the anticipation of the resurrection in this life. Together with the 'word of the cross', it belongs to the spirit of the resurrection and the power of the new creation.[68] Just because it is a cognitive event it is a creative one, for knowledge of Christ is knowledge that changes existence. Because baptism is a call in faith, it also stands in the power of the one who calls into being the thing that is not. For that reason it demonstrates the believer's new identity in the fellowship of Christ and proves him to be an heir of the divine future. Baptism points to the liberation of man which took place once and for all in the death of Christ. At the same time it reveals the crucified Lord's claim to new life and anticipates in man the future of God's universal glory. In this context there can be no talk about the efficacy of baptism *ex opere operato*. Baptism is efficacious *ex verbo vocante*.[69] Its word of promise is the word through which it calls. But the calling gospel is a call to faith, to the new obedience of righteousness, to freedom and to hope. It is hence perceived by faith and laid hold of in hope. It is a creative event, but it creates nothing without faith. In so far as faith is a call, baptism is necessary. But we cannot say that it is necessary for salvation.

(iv) Suggestions for a New Baptismal Practice

The way to a new, more authentic baptismal practice will be the way from infant to adult baptism. By adult baptism we mean the baptism of those who believe, are called and confess their faith. The usages of centuries cannot be suddenly altered. The path proposed means a learning process for the Christian church which has many implications.

As a first step the time of baptism should be made a matter of free decision and left to the parents.[70] Church law and church order would have to be altered in this sense. The clergy and the church's 'full-time workers' should not be forced to have their children baptized either. But for their part they must not compel anyone to postpone baptism, or prevent parents from having their children baptized. They should preach and teach the Christian meaning of baptism and make it comprehensible, and not only at baptismal services themselves. Responsibility for children lies in the parents' hands in the first instance. This responsibility must be impressed on the parents as regards baptism, but it cannot be taken from them.

Infant baptism should be replaced by the blessing of the children in the congregation's service of worship and by the 'ordination' – the public and explicit commissioning of parents and congregation – for their messianic service to the children. The baptism of parents is a call covering their family, social and political relationships as well. The Christian ought to follow his call in his secular profession too, and act accordingly. That is why it is important to make this call clear in the vocation of parenthood. Parenthood is a charisma, and becomes a living charisma in faith. The calling of the community is then realized in missionary service to the children and in their instruction. 'Confirmation' classes can then be directed towards baptism, which people approach when they feel able to confess their faith before the congregation and desire the assurance of their calling. Through the birth of children to Christian parents, the church is called to the service of reconciliation and liberation on their behalf. This progression from infant baptism to baptism as a call cannot be pursued unless we note the implications for the history of the individual life and for the church of Christ.

In the history of the individual life the religious festival of birth and name-giving would be replaced by a call event, which would make clear the believer's Christian identity. The person's natural identifications through family, nation and society then recede into the background. The new identity of Christ's fellowship frees the believer from those natural identifications for representative, liberating service on their behalf. So-called voluntary baptism does not really make baptism a matter of choice, but is essentially a baptism into the liberty of Christ. It is a liberating event. In the history of a person's life this means the pain of alienation from his present associations and groups, and often enough an exodus like the exodus of Abraham. But it leads him into a freedom in which he can 'be there for others'. In baptism as a call, the important thing is to stress not merely the alienation from the existing groups and associations of life, but even more the commission to service for their reconciliation and liberation. This baptism must not become the symbol of inner emigration and resignation in the face of 'the wicked world'. It is the sign of the dawn of hope for this world and of messianic service in it. It is a missionary sign. Through a baptism of this kind the meaning of one's own life is comprehended in the wider framework of God's history with the world. Baptism joins a fragmentary and incomplete human life with the fullness of life and the perfect glory of God.

Without new fellowship in a supporting group, this way cannot

be pursued by individuals. It is only in the degree in which the
church ceases to be a non-committal religious society and turns into
a recognizable messianic fellowship of service for the kingdom of
God that individuals can realize their calling in the sense we have
described. Conversely, however, such a fellowship only develops
out of professing believers.[71] Here we are concerned with a reciprocal relationship which has to be given effect from the individual
and the social side simultaneously. If individuals go over to voca-
tional baptism from infant baptism, then the church must develop
at the same time from the religious welfare institution to a social
body built up on firm fellowship. It must stop being a church of
ministers functioning on behalf of laymen, and become a charismatic fellowship in which everyone recognizes his ministry and
lays hold on his charisma. People then become 'subjects' within
the church, losing their position as 'objects' of religious welfare.
Just as believers' baptism can lead to inner emigration, so a confessing community of this kind can of course turn into an introvert
group in a self-made ghetto. That is why this development must
be accompanied by increased stress on the individual's call to
liberating service for society and on the fellowship's openness to
the world. If a 'worldly' church were merely to become an 'unworldly' one, nothing would be gained. The church's detachment
from worldly influence must lead to the 'church for the world',
which renders service to society and the individual out of the things
that are its own: the proclamation of the gospel and the new turning to the future. Common baptism binds together the fragmentary form of this church with the perfection of the coming kingdom
of God. Baptism as the calling event in the life of the individual
person corresponds only to a church that follows Christ's call, the
'call to freedom'. Baptism as the liberating event in a person's life
corresponds only to a church which spreads the liberty of Christ.
This must not be confused with a liberalization of religious usages
in a 'Christian society'. A liberal church may make adult baptism
'voluntary'. A church of liberation lives from baptism as liberating
event. That is something different.

4. *The Lord's Supper*

The messianic proclamation of the gospel calls faith into life. The
call which the believer hears leads him to baptism in Christ's

church. This fellowship assembles in worship at the Lord's table, celebrating its bond with Christ and with one another in the Lord's supper. Just as baptism is the eschatological *sign of starting out*, valid once and for all, so the regular and constant fellowship at the table of the Lord is the eschatological *sign of being on the way*. If baptism is called the unique *sign of grace*, then the Lord's supper must be understood as the repeatable *sign of hope*. Baptism and the Lord's supper belong essentially together and are linked with one another in the messianic community. In the baptismal event the community is linked to the individual who enters the fellowship of Christ and confesses it publicly. In eating and drinking at the Lord's table individuals are linked to the community which is visible in these acts. Baptism and the Lord's supper are the signs of the church's life,[72] because they are the signs of the one who *is* their life. They are in this way the public signs of the church's confession of faith because they show the one who leads the world into the liberty of the divine life.

Just as the gospel is the language of the messianic era, so we may call baptism and the Lord's supper the signs of the messianic era. For the Lord's supper is the sign of the actualizing remembrance of the liberating suffering of Christ (*signum rememorativum*). As such it is the prefiguration of Christ's redeeming future and glory (*signum prognosticum*). In the coincidence of remembrance and hope, history and eschatology, it is the sign of present grace, which confers liberty and fellowship (*signum demonstrativum*).[73] In the Lord's supper Christ's redeeming future is anticipated and this hope celebrated in remembrance of his passion. In this meal his past and his future are simultaneously made present. This present actualization frees the assembled congregation from the powers of the world which lead to sin and gives it the assurance of the divine future. The Lord's supper is an eschatological *sign of history*.[74] The Christian experience of time and the corresponding theological understanding of time will consequently take their bearings from the Lord's supper, and only cautiously look for other experiences of history.[75] It is only in the light of the Lord's supper that the interpretation of 'the signs of the time' is possible and has any point – the point being for the church and its individual members to perceive their tasks for the world amid the opportunities of history. The fellowship at the Lord's table involves fellowship with one another, and in the framework of that fellowship conversation about the current problems and tasks of our daily work in the world. In the messianic understanding of it, the Lord's supper is not a mystery cult which the initiated celebrate in separation from their surroundings; it is a public and open meal of fellowship for the peace and the righteousness of God in the world.

(i) The Open Invitation

Because the Lord's supper has always stood at the centre of the Christian life, it has acquired a great wealth of meaning in the course of history. It is difficult to sum this up. But today everything depends on our grasping the Lord's supper in its nature as a unified event, and on our understanding its different perspectives in the light of its common ground, so that it confers fellowship and not division. For though the Lord's supper in itself is fundamental to the wealth of the church, in history it has unfortunately also been the occasion for the misery of schism and denominational conflict. The very names by which it is called are an expression of the different aspects on which emphasis has been laid and which – when they have been held with rigid absolutism – have destroyed fellowship. Whereas the expressions 'the Mass' and 'the sacrifice of the Mass' point to Christ's sacrifice, the sacrifice of the church and of believers, the Protestant expression 'the Lord's supper' stresses the link with Jesus' last meal with his disciples. The name 'Eucharist' puts the meal in the context of divine worship, of praise and thanksgiving. In the ecumenical movement the name 'Lord's supper' has become established usage in recent years, because it points to the common christological foundation of the different church traditions. We shall adopt it here.

Before arriving at a theology of the Lord's supper we must be clear about what a theological doctrine of this kind is supposed to achieve, and whom it is supposed to serve.[76] The doctrine of the Lord's supper is the theological theory behind a particular practice. But the Lord's supper is not the practice of a theological theory. Communion with Christ in his supper is obeying Christ's own invitation, not a christological dogma. For it is the *Lord's* supper, not something organized by a church or denomination.[77] The church owes its life to the Lord and its fellowship to his supper, not the other way round. Its invitation goes out to all whom he is sent to invite. If a church were to limit the openness of his invitation of its own accord, it would be turning the Lord's supper into the church's supper and putting its own fellowship at the centre, not fellowship with him. By using the expression 'the Lord's supper' we are therefore stressing the pre-eminence of Christ above his earthly church and are calling in question every denominationally limited 'church supper'. The theological doctrine of the Lord's supper must consequently not be allowed to exercise any controversial theological function through which Christians are separated from Christians. If it represents the supper as being the supper of the Lord, then it is setting itself in the sphere of interest of his open invitation and is giving effect to that invitation. The theological doctrine of the Lord's supper includes the understanding of it as a task in the service of the Lord and his universal liberation, and therefore as a task belonging to his true church. In view of the divided church – divided by, of all things, its concept of the Lord's supper! – it is essential to stress this. Just as the Lord's supper is a sign of fellowship and not of division, so the corresponding theology will have to present what is in common and not what divides.

What is true of theology applies to church discipline as well. The Lord's supper is not the place to practise church discipline; it is first of all the place where the liberating presence of the crucified Lord is celebrated.[78] But in many churches the admission of one person to communion is practically linked with the excommunication of others, so that the Lord's supper is preceded by a 'test' of the individual's worthiness or unworthiness. The question of 'admission' to the meal becomes burdensome. Confession and absolution often precede the Lord's supper, so that the open, prevenient invitation of Christ is linked with legalistic injunctions and moral conditions for 'admission'. Christ's original feast of joy is then unfortunately transformed into a meal of repentance where people beat their breasts and gnash their teeth. It is then no wonder if many people excommunicate themselves from this meal, and if even serious Christians experience an unholy dread before the Lord's supper. This moral legalism spoils the evangelical character of the meal just as much as dogmatic legalism. We should therefore start from the Lord's supper as something done together and openly, and try to explain the moral questions on the basis of this action and this fellowship.

Finally, what is true of church discipline applies to the ministry as well. Can acknowledgment of a special priestly ministry (and, with it, of bishops and pope) be made the condition for recognition of the legitimacy and efficacy of the communion?[79] In the Lord's supper Christ exercises his 'ministry' as prophet, priest and king. He exercises it in the same way that he gave himself for the redeeming liberation of many. His invitation involves no condition about the acknowledgment of ministries in the church. It is gracious, unconditional and prevenient like the love of God itself. Everyone whom he calls and who follows his call has the authority to break the bread and dispense the wine. The administration of the supper is the 'ministry' of the whole congregation and every person who is called. The acknowledgment of a 'special' ministry obscures Christ's giving of himself 'for all' and the fellowship of brothers and sisters into which all are to enter. Hierarchical legalism spoils the evangelical character of the Lord's supper just as much as dogmatic and moral legalism.

Life is more than knowledge about the laws of life; and in the same way the fellowship of Christ and fellowship with one another are more than knowledge about its conditions. The Lord's supper takes place on the basis of an invitation which is as open as the outstretched arms of Christ on the cross. Because he died for the reconciliation of 'the world', the world is invited to reconciliation in the supper. It is not the openness of this invitation, it is the restrictive measures of the churches which have to be justified before the face of the crucified Jesus. But which of us can justify them in his sight? The openness of the crucified Lord's invitation to his supper and his fellowship reaches beyond the frontiers of the different denominations. It even reaches beyond the frontiers of Christianity; for it is addressed to 'all nations' and to 'tax-collectors and sinners' first of all. Consequently we understand Christ's invitation as being open, not merely to the churches but to the whole world.[80]

(ii) The Sign of Remembered Hope

The meal whose theological interpretation we are discussing has particular characteristics and elements.[81] It is a real fellowship at table of the whole assembly. People meet in order to eat and drink together. It is not a matter of an individual giving and taking. Eating and drinking together are physical actions which point beyond themselves, by virtue of Christ's promise. They do not serve to satisfy the body, but they do embrace (I Cor. 11.23ff.) the common meal. The fellowship gathers round the table for the sake of the bread and wine (which originally, no doubt, was not particular bread – wafers – or wine mixed with water), breaking bread with one another in Christ's name and with his words, and with his words offering one another the cup of wine. While it does this and in the action of so doing the fellowship relates the messianic story of the passion, proclaims the representative death of Christ and announces its hope for his coming in glory to fulfil God's rule in the world. During the meal it prays for the whole church and the whole world. It thanks God the Father for the creation and redemption of the world and glorifies the triune God in its song of joy. It prays for the eschatological gift of the Holy Spirit, so that the Spirit may fill it with the powers of the new creation and may descend on 'all flesh'. It prays for the coming of his kingdom. The congregation gathered at the Lord's table discusses, in the common meal that precedes or follows, the specific needs of the community and of the world around it, the tasks of the community and of each of its members in the world. It is the Lord's supper above all that ought to show in its eschatological openness the openness to the world of Christian mission. And it ought moreover to have room for comforting and encouraging, and for planning actions and offerings. It was not for nothing that the primitive Christian pareneses had their *Sitz im Leben* at the common meal.

With these elements and characteristics of the Lord's supper before our eyes, let us consider its historical origin and what the meal really makes present in the act of remembrance. Of course many religious communities have solemn cultic and sacral meals. In daily life too eating and drinking together is a sign of fellowship and friendship. But the nature of the Lord's supper and the unique character of the Christian fellowship cannot be derived from these things. The Lord's supper has never been celebrated by the church in any other way than as a pointing back to Jesus' own feast. It has its origin in Christ's particular history. Because in its own way it makes this history of Christ present in the act of remembrance, Jesus' own feast remains constitutive for 'the Lord's supper'.

The earthly Jesus celebrated the feast with *tax-collectors and sinners*.[82] These common meals of Jesus are to be understood as anticipations of the sacred banquet of the last days. They have their particular meaning in the context of the prophetic promise of the great feast of joy celebrated by the nations in Zion:

> On this mountain the Lord of hosts will make for all peoples a feast of fat things, a feast of wine on the lees, of fat things full of marrow, of wine on the lees well refined. And he will destroy on this mountain the covering that is cast over all peoples, the veil that is spread over all nations. He will swallow up death for ever . . . (Isa. 25.6–8).

This prophetic vision talks about the eschatological feast of peace and joy shared by the nations in the kingdom of God.[83] According to the gospel of the kingdom proclaimed by Jesus, many will 'sit at table' in God's kingdom (Matt. 8.11; Luke 13.29). 'Blessed is he who shall eat bread in the kingdom of God' (Luke 14.14). The synoptic parable of the 'great supper' (Matt. 22.2–10) clearly shows the unity of the kingdom of God and the fellowship of the table. The kingdom of God is a physical reality, not a kingdom of ghosts. When Jesus eats with publicans and sinners, this must be understood in the context of his gospel of the kingdom as an anticipation of this eating and drinking in the kingdom of God. But just as the special thing about Jesus' gospel of the kingdom is to be seen in the prevenient justice of God's grace on the unjust, so here the special thing about his sitting at table with tax-collectors and sinners is its anticipation of the 'feast of the righteous' with the unrighteous, who are made righteous through his presence. Just as Jesus demonstrates his message of the kingdom through the forgiveness of sins, so he also shows it through his acceptance of tax-collectors and sinners: 'This man receives sinners and eats with them' (Luke 15.2). Jesus' fellowship of the common meal is therefore inseparable from his gospel of the nearness of the kingdom and his acceptance of sinners. His message about the kingdom and his forgiveness of sins are incomprehensible without this fellowship of the table. The feast of the messianic era and the community of the saved was anticipated by Jesus, and anticipated with tax-collectors and sinners. That is why his feasts are joyful 'wedding' feasts in the dawn of the divine rule as demonstrations of God's undeserved, prevenient and astounding grace (cf. Luke 15.22ff.; 19.1–10).

Jesus' meals *with his disciples* are to be understood in the same context. Through these too he anticipates the eating and drinking in the kingdom of God, in correspondence with his gospel of the kingdom. This is shown by his renunciatory words at the Last

Supper (Mark 14.25ff.): 'Truly, I say to you, I shall not drink again of the fruit of the vine until that day when I drink it new in the kingdom of God.' The special thing about Jesus' eating together with his disciples is that not only does it give effect to Jesus' messianic mission in the disciples themselves (as in the case of the tax-collectors and sinners), but they are also drawn actively into his messianic mission and participate in it. That is why the meal with the disciples has a different significance from the meal with the tax-collectors and sinners, although they are related. The meal with the disciples is not an exclusive meal enjoyed by the righteous; it is the meal of Jesus' friends, who participate in his mission 'to seek that which was lost'.

The Christian supper of the Lord therefore has its origin in the messianic history of Jesus and his messianic feasts with his disciples and with tax-collectors and sinners. It follows from this that, in the first place, without common feasts of this kind the messianic history of Christ cannot be actualized properly and appropriately. A community without the common table loses its messianic spirit and its eschatological meaning. It also follows however, that the fellowship at table of the men and women who follow Jesus and enter into his messianic mission must be open for the meal which accepts and justifies 'tax-collectors and sinners', and must be seen in the perspective of the universal banquet of the nations in the coming kingdom. In this sense the Christian fellowship of the table needs no especial institutional command on the part of the historical Jesus. Like baptism, the Lord's supper emerges of its own accord from the messianic history of Christ. The 'evangelist' of the poor is also the messianic 'host' who invites the hungry to eat and drink in the kingdom of God and brings them into the divine fellowship.

Jesus' Last Supper with his disciples before his crucifixion has always had a particular significance for the Lord's supper.[84] According to I Corinthians 11, the church never celebrated the feast without pointing back to Jesus' Last Supper. The backward reference to 'the night in which he was betrayed' is not a reconstruction of the situation on Maundy Thursday. But Jesus' supper the night before his death has its particular importance in the fact that, according to the gospels and to Paul, it anticipates his death as a sacrificial death for many. In this way the messianic anticipation of eating and drinking in the kingdom of God are linked with Christ's giving of himself to death for the world's salvation. The breaking of the bread and the pouring out of the wine acquire a unique significance through the self-giving of the Messiah. They make the kingdom of God present in the form of Christ's body broken 'for us' and Christ's blood shed 'for us'. They make the kingdom of God present in Christ's person and his self-giving. He is both the giver of the feast and the gift itself. The gift, the kingdom of God, is he himself in person. By joining us with him and his self-giving, the feast is a bond with the kingdom, for through his death the kingdom he proclaimed and anticipated has become a historical reality. Again we can say that without his giving up of himself to death the messianic feast of the kingdom is not properly understood, just as, conversely, his offering of himself 'for many' is not fully understood without the messianic feast. His death is to be understood eucharistically, and the eucharist is to be understood in the light of his death.

Although the Lord's supper has its historical origin in Jesus' feasts, it itself none the less makes present the crucified and risen Lord. It is not the historical remembrance as such which provides the foundation for the Lord's supper, but the presence of the crucified one in the Spirit of the resurrection. As the one who is risen, Christ through his Easter appearances makes his earthly ministry binding, and reveals the meaning of his death for salvation. The church therefore remembers Jesus' earthly ministry and makes his death present in the presence of the risen Lord. 'The Lord's supper is the feast of the community of the saved, who wait but wait with assurance; the community which is grounded on the dying of Jesus and lives from his living presence.'[85] This is proved on the one hand by the injunction to repeat the rite 'in remembrance' (I Cor. 11.24f.; Luke 22.19); and on the other hand by the Pauline phrase about the 'new covenant' of Christ's body and blood (I Cor. 11.23ff.). Both statements are eschatologically motivated; the first is linked with Jesus' renunciatory vow (Luke 22.18 par.) and the second with the perspective 'until he comes' (I Cor. 11.26). The Lord's supper must not be understood solely in the light of the passion, but in the light of Easter as well. It mediates communion with the crucified one in the presence of the risen one. On the basis of Christ's giving himself up to death, it is itself the eschatological banquet of life. Through his body given to death for all, and his blood shed for all, the exalted Lord gives those who are already his a share in the future fellowship of the kingdom of God. According to Luke and John, the Easter appearances of the risen Christ and the eschatological banquet were already intimately connected with one another in primitive Christian thought. They interpret one another mutually. It is true that this fact shows certain analogies with the experience of the exodus and the feast of the passover in Israel. But it corresponds much more closely to the festival of the *todah*, the feast of thanksgiving celebrated by the person who had been preserved from death, according to Psalm 22.[86] For Old Testament thinking the experience of salvation had necessarily to be followed by the feast of the *todah*. Consequently the proclamation of the resurrection can only be fully valid in the *todah* feast. The breaking-in of God's sovereignty into this world is realized in Jesus' death and resurrection. That is why this feast is the eschatological feast of the divine lordship in him.

If we follow this reasoning, we can understand why the history of Christ's passion is proclaimed in the Lord's supper and why this takes place in the joy over his resurrection and in the hope of his coming. The connection between eating and drinking in the kingdom of God and the gift of his given body and his shed blood becomes clear. At long last we no longer have any need to seek for a historically dated institution for the Lord's supper, nor must we confine its christology to a founder christology. The Lord's supper is, with inner, factual cogency, the expression of the eschatological history of Christ – that is to say, the dawn of the kingdom of God in his self-giving and his resurrection from the dead. The fellowship with Christ made effective in the supper is the fellowship of the coming kingdom, and the fellowship of the kingdom of God is present in the fellowship of Christ in the midst of the history of evil and suffering. The Lord's supper is the eschatological sign of the coming kingdom in history. In the Lord's supper the coming kingdom is present in the form of the body given for us and the blood shed for us. The Lord's supper is not an unmediated messianic anticipation of the banquet of the nations, although it points towards that. Nor is it simply the continuation of the fellowship at table of the earthly Jesus, as this is to be seen in the daily 'breaking of bread' of the primitive churches, although it cannot be separated from that. Nor is the Lord's supper a sacred meal in remembrance of the dead; or a sacrificial meal; or a

Christian passover meal. As the joyful feast of the Christ given for us and raised before us, it gives a foretaste of the coming kingdom, because the coming kingdom has become history in Christ's crucifixion and resurrection. Because Christ's cross and resurrection stand in the sign of the eschatological eucharist, the Christian eucharist stands in the sign of cross and resurrection.

The Lord's supper is the eschatological sign of remembrance of this hope. It mediates the power of Christ's passion, and redemption from sin and the powers through his death. It mediates the Spirit and the power of the resurrection. It confers the new covenant. Finally, it confers fellowship in the body of Christ, a fellowship which overcomes separation and enmity through the self-giving of Christ for all men, and which creates solidarity among people who are in themselves different. This new covenant and this new fellowship are in tendency universal, all-embracing and exclusive of no one; they are open to the world because they point to the banquet of the nations.

(iii) The Presence of the One Who is to Come

The Lord's supper, with the bread and the wine, can be understood as a sign in a number of different ways. It can be an evident *sign of spiritual recollection*. The feast is then a remembrance feast. It recalls to our memory the history of redemption, which took place on the cross of Christ for us. The remembrance bridges the difference between the history there and the event here. Christ is therefore present in the Spirit that recalls him to us, and the bread and the wine are merely the outward signs of our spiritual communion with Christ. Zwingli interpreted the Lord's supper in this sense. He rightly stressed what happened on Golgotha, which took place once and for all, compared with its actualization in the supper. But his Platonic concept of spirit hindered him from perceiving the presence of the crucified one in the Spirit of the resurrection.[87]

The Lord's supper can further be understood as the earthly *sign of the presence* of the God who has become man and of the man who has been exalted to God. Then the bread and wine signify that which they are according to Christ's promise – the body and blood of Christ. Christ's body and blood are present *in* the bread and wine. Because the Son of God has become flesh the bread and the wine are part of the humanity he has assumed, like the manger and the cross. But because, on the other hand, the crucified Jesus has been exalted 'to the right hand of God', he is also, according to his humanity, bodily present in the divine presence that permeates all things. Luther interpreted the Lord's supper in the framework of these ideas. If we understand Christ's presence in the Lord's supper along the same lines as the incarnation, then the christological difference between what happened on Golgotha and what happens on the altar can easily be overlooked; while if we understand it in the framework of his exaltation, then it is easy to ignore the eschatological difference between the supper in history and the feast in the kingdom of God.

Finally, the Lord's supper can be *a token of the future*. Then the bread and the wine are the symbols of the great future *shalom* feast of the nations and are understood as the beginning of the universal banquet of the kingdom. The supper of the hoping church is a 'foretaste' of the messianic banquet of all mankind. The bread that is broken counts as a fore-token of peace for all men. The wine that is poured out counts as a fore-token of the hope of the nations. The groups which celebrate the supper in this sense understand it as a love feast for the celebration of life, fellowship, hope and work for peace and righteousness in the world. The remembrance on which this hope is based reaches back to Old Testament prophecy. But if it does not, at the same time and at its very core, reach back to Christ's giving himself up to death, this hope loses its fermenting power and its stability.

Historical orientation and prophetic orientation only faintly bring the presence of Christ in the meal to expression. The christological unity of God and man, eternity and history makes it almost impossible to understand the relation of his presence in the feast to his past on the cross and his future in the kingdom. The difficulties lie basically in the spatial concepts which people used in their attempts to understand Christ's presence. 'Every spatial interpretation of the event of the supper represents a one-sided view. For the primary problem is the problem of time.'[88] But how can Christ's presence in the feast be understood in terms of time?

The risen and exalted Christ manifests and confers his presence solely in his character as the one who was crucified. The Lord's supper confers fellowship with the crucified Jesus, his body given on Golgotha and his blood shed there, not with any heavenly body of Christ. The Lord's supper points expressly to the one who was crucified. The presence of the exalted one can therefore be nothing other than the manifestation of the one who was crucified. Conversely, however, the manifestation of the crucified Jesus in the fellowship of his body and his blood takes place in no other way than through himself, the exalted one. But the risen Jesus who is exalted to be Lord is 'the one who is to come'. The fellowship of the table with the one who was crucified for us once and for all, takes place in the presence of the one who is to come; and it is therefore, as fellowship with the crucified Jesus, the anticipation of the coming kingdom. In the one who is to come the one who died for us is present in our midst. The Christ who has torn down the dividing wall once and for all manifests himself as our future. The fellowship of the table with the one who was crucified therefore becomes the foretaste of the eschaton.

What is gained by these temporal and eschatological categories? 'The present' is not something absolute; it is always the being present of something or someone. *Prae-sentia* really means being in advance. In the eschatological sense the one who was once crucified on Golgotha is now himself present with the power of his suffering and the fruit of his death, in his giving of himself for many. This happening in the past is not a past event; it is an event which liberates, opens up the future, and therefore determines the present. In the temporal sense the crucified Jesus is present as the One who is to come in the Spirit of the new creation and final redemption. His future is not a future happening; it is a power that liberates, determines the future and opens up new possibilities. In this eschatological context the feast can be termed a sacrament of time, for in the presence of Christ, understood in this way, the experience of time is itself transformed. It no longer flows, as a stream of transience, from the future through the present into the past; on the contrary, through the Christ event it is opened up once and for all, in order to be consummated in his parousia. Time has become eschatological time and flows, as it were – to keep the image – out of his past through his presence into his future. The images of evanescence are evening and parting. The image of eschatologically transformed time is morning and the greeting of hope. In this sense the Lord's supper in Christ's presence is the real anticipation in common of the coming fullness of time. The eschatological presence of Christ then embraces the material elements, the personal fellowship, the proclamation and the spirit of the feast, so that there is no need to localize it any further.

We must learn to think in a new way here: not – Christ is present in the feast here or there, but – the feast is held in his presence and carries those who partake of it into the eschatological history of Christ, into the time between the cross and the kingdom which takes its quality from his presence.[89]

The words of institution and promise can then be understood in a similar sense: 'This is my body which was broken for you.' The identifying 'is' in this sentence must not be separated from the promise 'for you'. Fact and purpose are a unity. Consequently we ought not to make a division between a word of consecration addressed to the elements and a word of promise addressed to the congregation. The presence of Christ is, in that it happens; for it is his presence 'for us'. Both sentences are expressions of the promise of Christ's presence: I will be there as the one I will be there as. I will be there for you. I will be with you thus, and in this mode of self-giving. The presence of Christ's body and blood in the bread and the wine is the presence of Christ in person, and his person in its self-giving for us. But it is his presence in something different, in signs, by virtue of his identification with them. In that Christ makes himself present in bread and wine, the difference between the event of the cross and the event of the Lord's supper is preserved. Golgotha is not the equivalent of the Lord's supper. The Lord's supper, which can be repeated, signifies the history of Christ which has taken place once and for all and is therefore un-repeatable. Nor does Golgotha become a mere prefiguration of a 'sacrifice' continued on the altar. The concept of 'making present' preserves the difference in the unity. The presence of Christ in the Lord's supper is credible simply on the basis of his promise, in which he identifies himself; not on the basis of metaphysical specu-lations. But the reason that makes this promise possible lies in his resurrection and his future. That is why his promise to be present in the meal is at the same time the anticipation of his parousia in glory.[90] What he makes present is the meaning of his death for salvation, as the coming redeemer. If we understand his presence in the feast as the anticipation of his coming kingdom, then the difference between the unity of his presence in the feast and in his kingdom will be preserved. In the unity between difference and unity we understand the feast as a messianic mediation between the Christ event, which opens up and creates freedom, and his king-dom, which completes this freedom universally. As a messianic mediation the feast strengthens and preserves the freedom of faith, the courage of hope and the fellowship of love.

(iv) The Sign of the Trinitarian History of God's Dealings with the World

In the presence of Christ the Lord's supper joins the past and the future, history and eschatology in a unique way, and becomes the token of liberating grace. For the participants this means that in this meal they *remember* the death of Christ, through which God reconciled the world once and for all; *acknowledge* the presence of the risen Lord in their midst; and *hope* with joy for the coming of his kingdom in glory. Whenever they do this they are responding through their own free gratitude to the grace that frees them. The *charis* experienced corresponds to joy in pardoned existence, and therefore to the eucharist. The glorification of God on earth, which is to lay hold on the whole of creation, begins in the feast of gratitude. Joy in freedom and fellowship anticipates the joy of the new creation and its universal fellowship. Understood as a eucharist in this sense, the feast of Christ's fellowship is the great thanksgiving to the Father for everything he has made in creation and has achieved in the reconciliation of the world, and has promised to accomplish in its redemption. In the eucharist the congregation thanks the triune God for all his acts of goodness and sets itself in his trinitarian history with the world. The universal meaning of the eucharist becomes comprehensible because, and in so far as, it brings to expression the song of praise through which the whole creation honours its creator, singing the hymn with which all things rejoice in him.

> For the world which God reconciles with himself is present at every eucharist: in the bread and the wine, in the believers and in the prayers which they offer for all men. Because believers and their prayers are joined with the person of our Lord and his intercession, they are transformed and accepted. Thus the eucharist reveals to the world what it is to be.[91]

This aspect of the Lord's supper has been chiefly stressed in the liturgy of the Eastern churches. It does not obscure the fellowship with the self-giving and future of Christ, which stands in the forefront in the Western church's tradition; but it sets the christological foundation and the eschatological direction of the feast in its trinitarian context. Just because the fellowship in the supper is a remembrance of Christ's death as the ground of liberation and reconciliation, this remembrance can only be gratitude; and this gratitude will be as wide and as all-embracing as the liberating reconciliation itself. It comprehends the whole of creation in representative thanksgiving and intercession and awaits its coming redemption. Through the fellowship of Christ which the Lord's supper mediates, God the Father is glorified in thanksgiving, praise, delight and joy. The meal becomes a feast when this gratitude is expressed not only in official liturgies but in the free utterance of those who meet at the table and their spontaneous joy.

The prayer for the Holy Spirit (*epiclesis*) is also an inseparable part of this feast, for the feast itself is celebrated as the gift of the Holy Spirit. It is the Spirit who allows Christ to be truly present in the meal and gives us fellowship with him in bread and wine in accordance with the words of institution. It is the Spirit who, as the power of the kingdom, gives a foretaste of the new creation in the feast. Through him the fellowship of the table receives the life and the powers of the new creation and the assurance of the coming kingdom. The eschatological bearings of the meal and its messianic character find particularly clear expression in the *epiclesis*, the prayer for the eschatological gift of the Holy Spirit and the assurance of his presence. Here the liturgical position of this prayer for the Spirit is not as important as our understanding of the whole feast and the assembled fellowship as actually being this prayer. In the prayer for the coming of the Spirit the fellowship opens and prepares itself for his coming. It becomes conscious of its charismatic renewal and commission. It is therefore part of the movement through which the Spirit descends 'on all flesh', in order to make it live eternally. Just as the remembrance of Christ's death makes the fellowship conscious of the 'openness' of his self-giving, so the prayer for the Spirit opens it for the perfecting power of his glory. In this way the Lord's supper becomes the mark of the history of the Spirit.[92]

Because the fellowship of the table unites believers with the triune God through Christ, it also causes men to unite with one another in messianic fellowship. The common bread and the common cup point to the oneness of the people who partake in the one Christ, and in him with all participants at all times and in all places. Every individual fellowship of the table therefore confesses its fellowship with the whole of Christendom on earth. Every feast is understood as the fellowship of the body of Christ. Every individual congregation knows itself to be a member of the whole people of God. The open invitation of the crucified one to his supper is what fundamentally overcomes all tendencies towards alienation, separation and segregation. For through his giving himself up to death for the fellowship of men with God and with one another, the godless and inhuman divisions and enmities between races, nations, civilizations and classes are overcome. Churches which permit these deadly divisions in themselves are making the cross of Christ a mockery. The fellowship of the table is the visible sign of the church's catholicity. But because this catholicity is messianically open for the uniting of mankind in the presence of God, the fellowship of the table is open to the world too. This fact finds expression best of all when – following the custom of the early church – the Lord's supper is followed by an *agape* meal. For this the participants brought their gifts with them, gifts which were then distributed by deacons to the needy members of the fellowship. This does not mean that it was a 'charitable' feast. It is rather that the common meal and the fellowship of the table have directly charitable consequences for the hungry and the sick. As the supper with Jesus and his disciples demonstrates fellowship with his mission to the poor, the imprisoned, the sick and the despised, so in the same way the Lord's supper leads to mission and missionary tasks for the conquest of need, the liberation of prisoners and the acceptance of the despised. The fellowship of the table strengthens and encourages the sense of mission in all who partake, opening their eyes to specific hardships and the opportunities to overcome them. Anyone who celebrates the Lord's supper in a world of hunger and oppression does so in complete solidarity with the sufferings and hopes of all men, because he believes that the Messiah invites all men to his table and because he hopes that they will all sit at table with him.[93] In the mysteries, the feast separates the initiated from the rest of the world. But Christ's messianic feast makes its participants one with the physically and spiritually hungry all over the world.

(v) The Open Feast

We have tried to understand the different perspectives of the Lord's supper in the light of the unified, eschatological nature of

Christ's history, and in the all-embracing trinitarian history of God's dealings with the world; and now suggestions for the actual practice of the Lord's supper would seem to be indicated.

(*a*) The fellowship of the table must be central for the assembled congregation, just as much as the proclamation of the gospel. The Lord's supper must be integrated into the service of worship. It must no longer be celebrated as a coda to it. The communion must be in bread *and wine*, and the whole congregation must communicate. The more the church becomes a fellowship church belonging to the people, the more important the fellowship in the Lord's supper will be. It will celebrate this fellowship of the table at all its assemblies. It will extend it in time so that it does not merely consist of a common liturgy, but so that spontaneous fellowship in the mutual exchange of the experiences and problems of everyday life becomes possible.

(*b*) Because this fellowship comes into being on the basis of Christ's unconditional and prevenient invitation, the fellowship will be an open one. It cannot limit Christ's invitation on its own account. Everyone can participate who wants to participate in the fellowship of Christ. The communion is the answer to Christ's open invitation. Talk about the 'intercommunion' of Christians belonging to different churches and denominations is misleading if it draws away attention from communion with Christ. What this means is obvious on the basis of Christ's invitation to everyone. The traditionally varying interpretations of the Lord's supper can only be clarified when we all follow Christ's open invitation together. The contradictions can be solved through a common practice, because then they *have* to be solved.

(*c*) Because of Christ's prevenient and unconditional invitation, the fellowship of the table cannot be restricted to people who are 'faithful to the church', or to the 'inner circle' of the community. For it is not the feast of the particularly righteous, or the people who think that they are particularly devout; it is the feast of the weary and heavy-laden, who have heard the call to refreshment. We must ask ourselves whether baptism and confirmation ought to go on counting as the presuppositions for 'admittance' to the Lord's supper. If we remember that Jesus' meal with tax-collectors and sinners is also present in the Lord's supper, then the open invitation to it should also be carried 'into the highways and by-ways'. It will then lose its 'mystery' character, but it will not become an ordinary, everyday meal for all that, because the invitation is a call to the fellowship of the crucified one and an invitation in his name to reconciliation with God (I Cor. 11.27).

(*d*) In a congregation which sees itself as a messianic fellowship, one person will offer another bread and wine with Christ's words of promise. Everyone who tells the gospel story and proclaims faith will distribute the bread and wine as well. The celebration of the supper is not bound to any particular ministry, though it is bound to the 'ministry' in the sense of the calling and mission of the whole congregation and every individual Christian.

(*e*) The meal's character of fellowship is brought out when the person performing the liturgy stands behind the altar, so making it the table, and celebrates facing the people. It is demonstrated even more clearly when the congregation sits round a table. But for this the body of the church has to be altered; the traditional church form, designed for a number of people facing the front, has to be changed to a 'common room' in which the participants can see and talk to one another.

(*f*) This will also make it externally possible to celebrate divine worship as the assembly of the community, to follow the Lord's supper by a common meal, and the proclamation of the gospel by a common discussion of people's real needs and the specific tasks of Christian mission. The *agape* meal that follows shows the Lord's supper's openness to the future. Between the feast with Christ and the great banquet of the nations in the kingdom of God lies the world's hunger and misery. In this tension we become aware of this and accept it as our task in the hope for the kingdom founded on the fellowship of Christ. This means that the *agape* will not be a friendly appendage to the Lord's supper; it will be a *shalom* meal to express, in the promises of the prophets, the eschatological hope which is the ground for the Lord's supper.[94]

As a feast open to the churches, Christ's supper demonstrates the community's catholicity. As a feast open to the world it demonstrates the community's mission to the world. As a feast open to the future it demonstrates the community's universal hope. It acquires this character from the prevenient, liberating and unifying invitation of Christ.

5. Worship

(i) Worship as a Messianic Feast

The messianic feast is part of the language of the messianic era and its signs.[95] It is a feast of the assembled community, which proclaims the gospel, responds to the liberation experienced, baptizes with the token of the new beginning and, at the table of the Lord, anticipates the fellowship of God's kingdom. The divine lordship which is manifest in the history of Christ and is experienced in the Spirit gives a new quality to the whole of life. It itself is the feast of freedom in the presence of the triune God and is here therefore celebrated and experienced in feasts.

Understood as a messianic feast, the Christian service of worship is entirely determined by the history of God and by what takes place in it. The assembled community perceives anew the complete history of Christ, his giving himself up to death for the salvation of creation, and his glorification in the life of God for creation's future. The messianic feast renews the remembrance of Christ and awakens hope for his kingdom.[96] In this way it sets everyday life in the great arc spanning this remembrance and this hope. In this history of Christ the assembled community perceives the trinitarian history of God, his love's openness to the world and the perfection of all things in his joy. The liberation it experiences in the present moment seeks harmony with the joy of all creation in being, and lays anticipatory hold on the joy of redeemed existence.[97] The messianic feast sets the assembled community, with its daily pains and joys, in the broad context of the trinitarian history of God with the world. This is what is meant when Christian meetings and services are begun in Christ's name and in the name of the triune God. The church satisfies itself about its own history in the history of Christ, the history of God with the world. In this it acquires and demonstrates freedom – freedom from the alienations of existence, freedom for the alternative of new life, and freedom for the acceptance of existence in the present.[98]

Just because it experiences the freedom of the messianic era in the feast, the things that are in contrast with this – the pains, omissions and failures of everyday life – are brought to expression in the service of worship. The messianic feast is not an ecstasy that transports us into another world; it is the experience of the

qualitative alteration of this world.[99] Joy in the divine liberation is
therefore accompanied by the expression of suffering over the
godlessness that restricts life; rejoicing in the presence of the
Spirit is accompanied by the utterance of the sighs of expectant
creation; while knowledge of the Son of man is linked with a
sense of society's inhumanity. The service of worship reveals the
heights of life, but also the poverty of the depths of our own lives.
These dissonances are part of its harmony. They make it at once
realistic and hopeful. 'How shall we sing the Lord's song in a
foreign land?' asks Psalm 137. The messianic feast is the Lord's
song 'in a foreign land'.[100] Its melodies mingle thoughts of home
with the sighs of exile. For it is the feast of the lordship of God
under the cross of Christ, and at the point where Christ's discipleship in the world belongs. But it has an unmistakable trend and a
clear direction towards the victory of life and the consummation
of freedom in God's coming. The liberating feast 'in the foreign
land' is the fragmentary anticipation of God's free and festal
world.

The assembled community comes to know itself as the messianic fellowship in the messianic feast. But for that very reason it
must also critically re-examine the outward functions of its
services in relation to the life of the individual and the public life
of society. Like preaching, baptism and the Lord's supper, the
service of worship also stands at the point of intersection between
very different interests and functions. The important point is that
the assembled community should not merely give its worship the
character of a messianic feast, but should also give its everyday individual and social functions the impress of messianic
impulses.[101]

(ii) The Feast as Ritual

Before anyone speaks or sings in church, the church has already
spoken and sung through its ritual. Sermons and liturgies may
change, but the ritual remains and speaks its own language. It
draws religious needs and acknowledged expectations into itself.
If the priest or minister has not preached a good sermon, he can
comfort himself with the thought that at least the hymns were well
chosen; and if the hymns were unfamiliar, church attendance still
has the functions ascribed to it by the people who go. An effective
church reform begins first of all by altering the rituals. But these

are so hard to change that they have caused more than one split in the church.

The ritual of the service of worship is fixed. In the succession of the Sundays and in the rhythm of the church's year, the services form a seasonal ritual. Every human society is familiar with rituals of time which give order to time's flux and in the yearly cycle awake particular memories which are fundamental for the community. Through these memories tradition and continuity is grafted into life's changes and chances. Without a temporal order and repetitions of this kind it would seem to be impossible for man to live in 'the terrors of history'. In its outward order the Christian service of worship is institutionalized by its setting in time. Through the church's year the unique and eschatologically open history of Christ is brought to expression in a recurrent cycle (even if the church year does not quite coincide with the calendar one): from Christmas by way of Good Friday and Easter to Pentecost; from Advent to All Saints, All Souls and – in the Lutheran church – 'the Sunday of the dead' – the last Sunday before Advent. What does this mean? Does it spring from the divine history celebrated in the Christian services, or from the history of our culture, or from the very nature of man?

Human life – like animal life too, incidentally – is to a great extent ritually ordered and constituted. A functional analysis shows that ritual has four fundamental purposes:[102]

(*a*) Every ritual creates historical *continuity*. It regulates the course of the year, as well as the course of the individual life and society, by relating particular seasons and turning points to the past, by means of anniversaries, birthdays, days of remembrance, jubilees, and so forth. In this way it also orders the future by mediating values and patterns of behaviour that have been handed down by tradition. The presupposition for historical continuity is the repeatability of the past through rites. Without ritual there is no tradition. The participant in the ritual does not find the repetition in any way boring; it is solemn and of decisive importance for his life, and he associates it with personal commitment.

(*b*) Every ritual has an *indicative* character. Through the binding together of the different levels, the sign and the thing denoted, ritual becomes the symbol that points beyond itself, expresses something different and invites us to remembrance, to hope, or to a new page in life. Through the ritual representation, the thing represented becomes present in an accentuated way.

(*c*) Every ritual stands in *a framework of social coherences* and also establishes social coherences. Through ritual a group assures itself of its own character, integrates itself and portrays itself. Because rituals socialize, they are also joined with sanctions against outsiders and against deviating behaviour. Common rituals and symbolic interactions give a group form. Taboos protect it against others, and against intrusions.

(*d*) If, then, ritual has the function of temporal integration through the formation of tradition; of spatial integration through the forming of a social group; and of an overriding indicative character, it follows that the functions of ritual are primarily *ordering functions*. Rituals regulate the group in the face of the chaos of diverging interests and anti-social behaviour. They establish stable patterns of thinking and behaviour for constitutionally unstable man. They are necessary for the building up of individual and collective identity. Free, spontaneous and creative life, whose effect is not destructive, only becomes possible out of the security ritual confers.

It is not difficult to see that Christian worship and ecclesiastical 'rites' fulfil these ritual functions, and in what way, and how they are consequently related to the ritual constitution of human existence. A special functional analysis of the church's feasts and celebrations can show this in its anthropological necessity. But any other religious and ideological content can invade these functions and fulfil them. Initiation rites, maturity ceremonies, wedding and burial rites, rituals of tradition and integration are to be found everywhere. They can be religious, but they do not have to be. They can be Christian, but they are not necessarily so.

The functional analysis of ritual enquires into its necessity and sees the ritualization of life against the background of the needs of the anthropological situation of man, that 'undetermined animal', world-open, flooded with stimuli and unstable as he is. It easily overlooks the 'play' element in the rituals, especially the religious ones – their 'non-essential' character, free and exuberant. In everything that people have to *produce*, economically, socially and ritually, in order to survive, they also *portray* themselves.[103] Anyone who produces and reproduces presents himself for inspection at the same time. He introduces himself. Rituals do not merely have the necessary functions we have mentioned; they always express a demonstrative existential value as well.[104] It is not expedient in the functional sense, but it is meaningful. Religious rituals in particular show a creative play of expression, of free self-portrayal and an excess of joy in existence that cannot be calculated in terms of purpose and utility. This play makes the ritual a feast beyond what necessity demands of it. In religious ritual people do not merely order their time and their community against chaos, so as to master the necessities of their situation; they also present themselves before the 'wholly other' of the gods in prayer, song, thanksgiving, intercession, sacrifice and dance. This orientation turns ritual, purposive though it still is, into something free, playful, demonstrative and festal.

In religious ritual the cult is celebrated as the feast of the gods and is performed together with the gods.[105] Religion is not at all 'the sigh of the oppressed creature, the feeling of a heartless world and the soul of soulless circumstances'.[106] It is not 'the opium of the people'. It can become that in a particular social situation. But from the point of view of the history of religion the cult can hardly be explained as an illusory compensation for material and psychological deprivation. It is to be understood as the expression of ecstasy, of orgy and exuberance. Far from having to be termed religious in the sense of the great pagan festal religions, Christianity, and especially Protestantism in its modern workaday world, must rather be termed their opposite pole.

> One has to be very coarse in order not to feel the presence of Christians and Christian values as an oppression beneath which all genuine festive feelings go to the devil. . . . The feast is paganism *par excellence*.[107]

In this respect Marxism, with its religious criticism of Christianity and with its transformation of religious energy into its revolutionary counterpart, is entirely in line with the prophets and the Christian Puritans. Its constraint plays the devil with the festal mood, and the feast as 'paganism *par excellence*' is driven out altogether.

(iii) The Feast in the Modern Workaday World

In pre-Christian and non-Christian cultures the cult is the feast of the gods. In this feast the pure primal origin of the world returns and renews time past and the life that has been expended. The place of the cult is the centre of its civilization, and it orders the space round the universal centre which it symbolizes. The cultic seasons order fleeting time into a cycle of eternal recurrence, a cycle of time's origin. At the sacred places and at sacred seasons gods and men again meet as in their unscathed beginnings. The myth relates the primal event of the world's beginning; the cultic liturgy depicts it. The feast lifts men up to their origin, where all is as it was on the day of creation. The feast therefore has the character of renewal. It regenerates time, people and society. What is celebrated is the *restitutio in integrum*.[108] 'Time will run back, and fetch the age of gold.'[109] People wish one another 'a happy New Year', even if it is only another year like the last that is coming; and this is a survival of the old feast of yearly renewal.

The modern workaday world has taken away from the religious feast this sense of life's renewal from its source. The reproduction of life through work has replaced its festal renewal from its transcendental foundation. Consequently the world has come to ascribe different functions to feast days and holidays.[110] These functions are no longer the original religious ones, nor are they the general anthropological ones. Formally, feast days and holidays have acquired the role of a temporary suspension of the laws and ways of behaviour that regulate daily work. People are to 'have a break'; they are to rest from the compulsion of action, relax and recuperate. What is the purpose? Because the modern working world demands a disciplined orientation of life towards utility, means directed to an end, and success, it has to sacrifice a great deal in the renunciation of its natural urges. Without temporary and controlled safety valves the psychological balance can hardly be preserved and the self-control which is necessary can hardly be endured. Leisure, feasts and celebrations turn into a safety-valve for the pent-up pressure of emotions and aggressions. But where they function in this way they are ministering to a domination that is irreconcilable with freedom, either in personal life (where spontaneity and self-control cannot be reduced to a single common denominator) or in public life, where the people dominated are prescribed 'bread and circuses' so that they can 'live it up' for once. Because daily life is stamped by tension, stress and the pressure to produce 'results', it needs suspensions and safety valves for relaxation, and relief from its burdens in order to make the burdens bearable and the tensions endurable. One must have a holiday in order to recover one's resilience. One looks for some 'compensation for everyday working life'. Hand in hand with reliefs and relaxations of this kind go the compensations which make all free time a function of the time that is not free and offer 'ersatz' pleasures for the joyless features of the working world. One might call it the advertisers' philosophy: 'Have a break', they say, meaning: life really consists of work and we are not in the world to enjoy ourselves. But there are intervals in which we ought to refresh ourselves so that we can work all the better afterwards. There are leisure 'activities' as well. Because 'keeping fit' is all-important, towns lay on sports and recreation grounds, and 'health farms' are opened for 'the top people' who really make the grade in the economic world.

Christian worship on Sunday, the 'day off', is no exception, for it is used by the harassed people of our society in the way we have described, even if it cannot offer the same 'leisure activities' and 'fun'. What people mainly look for in it is therefore mainly inner, spiritual relaxation and a religious lifting of the burden of responsibility they have to carry during the week. It is not by chance that here the church service is finding increasing competition from new practices of religious meditation of what is thought to be an Eastern kind. In modern society religious functions in the form of suspension, outlet, relief and compensation can, but do not have to be, taken over by Christian worship. Consequently the church must ask itself whether its services are expressing messianic freedom when they fulfil these functions.

(iv) The Feast of the History of God

From the very beginning the biblical traditions show a particular, and in many respects a unique, understanding of the feast. It was as a nomadic people that Israel entered the cultivated land of Canaan, with its fixed cultic sites. It settled down, planted the fields, bred cattle and took over the cultic forms of the agrarian religion of the country, which expressed the yearly cycle of seedtime and harvest. But Israel did not change its gods, as so many other peoples did, when it changed from a nomadic to a settled existence. The tension between Yahweh, the 'God of Abraham, Isaac and Jacob', and the country's Baals remained and led to continual new conflicts, as the Old Testament shows. Protest and criticism were directed both against the Baal cult and against the baalization of Yahweh.

The difference between Yahweh and Baal can be typologically described as follows: the nomad does not live in the cycle of seed-time and harvest. He is continually on the move in search of pastures and hunting grounds. His gods are moving, guiding gods, who go ahead, journeying with the people, and are themselves wayfarers.[111] Nomadic religion is a religion of promise. The god who inspires, leads and journeys with the people differs from the gods of agrarian peoples because he is not territorially bound and possesses no cultic sites where he dwells. Under the guidance of the wayfaring God, therefore, life is experienced as history. The future sought is not a repetition of the past, nor is it a confirmation of the present. It is the goal of a journey. It gives the journey its meaning and makes the experiences of privation on the way endurable. A settled people, on the other hand, does not live in time so much as in the space of a particular country. It is dependent on the circulatory movement of nature and has to observe the annually recurring seasons of spring and autumn, summer and winter, rains and drought. It therefore celebrates the festivals of the gods in the cycle of the year, thus celebrating the cyclical renewal of life. Its future lies in the eternal recurrence of the same thing. In addition to this temporal order, a settled people needs an order for the space in which it lives. That is why a country's civilization is ordered round the cultic site. It is the centre of its culture, symbolically representing the centre of the ordered world, over against chaos. The festal seasons hallow the time and the cultic places hallow the space where man lives and tills the ground.

When the Israelite tribes came into the cultivated lands, they adopted the cult in the yearly cycle, but gave its content a new function. In the feast held at the beginning of the barley harvest they remembered the historic exodus from Egypt, at the great vintage festival in autumn, the period in the wilderness and the unsettled life in tabernacles, or leafy huts. In this way the Israelites related the cyclical festivals of the year to the history of their relations with God and to the God of their history. They historicized the agricultural festivals, no longer celebrating the eternal recurrence of the same thing, but the unique, unrepeatable history of their relations with the God of the promise. The feasts no longer carried participants back to the primal origin of the world; they set them in the historical era of the patriarchs, their exodus from bondage and their long march through the desert.

Israel also gave a future dimension to the feasts which it took over.
Just as they made present the historical faithfulness of God to the
patriarchs, they also awoke trust in the future faithfulness of this
same God. They did not point to their own repetition the following year; they pointed to the future history of God's dealings with
the people. The historical uniqueness of the divine history that
was remembered corresponded to the future finality of the divine
history that was hoped for. It was certainly a lengthy and complex
process, but its trend and its result can be seen in the fact that the
God of the promise, who went ahead of his people through the
space of the wilderness, became in the land of Canaan the God of
history, who goes ahead of his settled people through time. The
experience of history was not dissolved in the experience of the
space of a particular time; it integrated the experience of space in
times that transcend it. Yet it remains an open question how the
feasts of the divine history can enter the annual cycle without being
dissolved in that cycle. Does the cycle serve to give an assurance of
the unique divine history, or does it dominate that history and con-
fuse the one with the other?

This question can be answered on the basis of the Israelite and
Jewish understanding of the sabbath. The sabbath goes back to the
story of creation. The seventh day is the festival of creation. On
that day God 'rested' and took pleasure in his creation because
'everything was very good'. According to the creation accounts
this cannot be understood as a resting after strenuous work. It is
the goal of the divine creation and its completion. The rest and
pleasure are the quality of the divine life. The sabbath is not there
for the sake of the work; the work is there for the sake of the feast.
The festival of creation is the goal of the whole history of God's
dealings with the world, from the creation in the beginning to the
creation of the last days. The sabbath, therefore, simultaneously
reaches forward to the messianic era. The messianic era is often
called the 'era of the endless sabbath', so the weekly sabbath is
understood as an anticipation and foretaste of this time. The
sabbath brings 'the central idea of Judaism' to expression, the idea
of freedom and complete harmony between man and man as well
as between man and nature. That is 'the idea of the anticipation of
the messianic time and of man's defeat of time, sadness and
death'.[112] Since all work is an interference with nature on man's
part, sabbath rest means the state of peace between man and

nature. The weekly sabbath is not merely ritual and symbol but an anticipation of the *shalom*, even if it is on the 'exceptional day'. The sabbath is certainly part of the weekly cycle but in its content it interrupts the cyclical rebirth of time by anticipating the messianic era. It stands in the cycle of time, yet it is the sign of freedom from time's cycle, since it anticipates the victory over time and death. 'Time is suspended; Saturn is dethroned on his very day, Saturn's-day. Death is suspended and life rules on the Sabbath day.'[113]

Jesus' attitude to the sabbath is often reduced to his polemic against its ritualization: 'The sabbath was made for man, not man for the sabbath; so the Son of man is lord even of the sabbath' (Mark 2.27f.). With this he justifies the healing of the sick on the sabbath. The sabbath is made for man's sake, not for work's sake. Jesus does not orientate it towards the working days. The fact that 'the blind receive their sight, the deaf hear and the dead are raised up' is actually part of Jesus' messianic mission. According to Luke this begins with the proclamation of the final 'acceptable year of the Lord' through Jesus of Nazareth (Luke 4.18ff.). According to Leviticus 25 this is the sabbatical year; and according to the prophets (Isa. 61.1ff.) it is the final dawn of the messianic era – in other words the fulfilment of the weekly sabbath's anticipations and promises. Jesus did not therefore 'make the sabbath a matter of indifference'.[114] Like the prophets, he attacked the confining of the divine history and law to the cult and to cultic seasons. But when he abolished the division between the cultic and the secular, the pure and the impure, sabbath and the ordinary days, it was not in favour of everyday secularity, but in favour of the messianic festiveness of all life. If his mission is a messianic one, then it is also the beginning of the sabbath of the last days. The whole of life becomes a feast.[115]

It is true that we know of no special pilgrimages made by Jesus to cultic festivals; but the journey to Jerusalem which ended with his passion and crucifixion can be understood in this sense as his festal procession. If his suffering and dying manifests the lordship of God, and with it the liberation of man, then his self-giving must be understood as the end of the special cult and the beginning of a new quality of life in the feast of the divine rule. As the end of the particular sabbath the history of Jesus is the beginning of the all-embracing eschatological sabbath.

The 'Christian cult' consists of Christ's person and history, and the history of the church's relationship to Christ in the Spirit. Apart from that there is no special 'Christian cult'.[116] Paul understood this new quality of the whole of life through Christ and his history, and upheld it in his congregations against Judaism and enthusiasm. The freedom for which Christ set us free cannot put up with any cultic legalism (Gal. 5.1ff.). He considered that the observance of holy days, months and festal occasions showed lack of knowledge of the true God. For the man who knows God, all days are alike (Gal. 4.10; Col. 2.16; Rom. 14.5). 'I appeal to you therefore, brethren, by the mercies of God, to present your bodies as a living sacrifice, holy and acceptable to God, which is your spiritual worship' (AV: reasonable service; Rom. 12.1). When he describes the surrender and obedience of our bodies on the ground of God's mercy – Christ's giving of himself for us – as 'worship' then 'the doctrines of worship and Christian "ethics" converge'.[117] But worship is not replaced by ethics; ethics are turned into worship. The new unity of worship and ethics which abolishes the division between ordinary days and feast days cannot be interpreted ethically, or in a secular and everyday way; for the feast of God's lordship is lived in the secularity of everyday. Bodily obedience in resistance to the powers of the passing world and its laws becomes 'the offering of self-sacrifice'. The service of reconciliation in the forum of the world becomes an expression of joy in God's rule. That is why worship has priority over ethics.

In the early church Chrysostom once gave a definition of festivity which is in line with this: '*Ubi caritas gaudet, ibi est festivitas.*'[118] The love that serves our neighbour without having any personal axe to grind is joy. It is the feast of the new life. Here no special festal times and periods of leisure are required. Wherever it comes into being there is the sabbath, God's sabbatical year, the messianic era. To preach the gospel of the kingdom to the poor, to heal the sick, to receive the despised, free prisoners, and eat and drink with the hungry is the feast of Christ in the history of God's dealings with the world.

It is understandable that John saw no temple in his visions of the new heaven and the new earth and the Jerusalem coming down from heaven. What the temple in the sacred precinct represented – namely, the cultic indwelling of God – becomes superfluous when the glory of God fills everything. For John too the separation between the temple and the street, Sunday and weekday, is overcome by the one whom the temple and Sunday stand for. He then overcomes even the temple and Sunday itself.

(v) 'The Messianic Intermezzo'

What we have said up to now has shown that in their intention and their tendency both the Jewish sabbath and the Christian Sunday aim to overcome the division between the feast day and the ordinary day. The messianic era is to be the era of the eternal sabbath. For Christians the whole of life is to be a perpetual feast of love and joy. But wherever the polemic against particular holy days, places and rituals is detached from this messianic hope it becomes moralistic – even when its arguments are political – and puts the feast at the service of everyday life. The Reformers proclaimed man's justification by faith alone, and therefore abolished the 'meritorious' cults and festivals. The Christian's whole life was to become the reasonable service, or spiritual worship, of love. But by so doing they merely multiplied the number of working days and encouraged an unpleasant rationalization of everyday life – a result they did not aim at at all. Marxist criticism of religion completed this development. The worker was to be freed from his various forms of alienation. But the overcoming of his religious alienation was followed by the abolition of the feast days, and in some countries by an increase in the number of working shifts. This way of overcoming the difference between the feast day and the working day in favour of the latter cannot be called messianic. It is merely sad. Sunday can be made a working day, but the working day just cannot, within history, become Sunday.[119] But the difference can already be overcome here if worship on Sunday is consciously directed towards a stimulation of the festal life in everyday existence. Since, as messianic feasts, they are open for the divine future, they will also be open to the world for the pains and joys of life in love. They then bring hope into the world and everyday life. If they are to do this the following elements should be noted when we mould our services of worship:

(*a*) As ritual, divine service is a celebration. Only a relatively closed group, after years of practice, can inwardly join in the ceremonies and symbols which have been formed through long tradition. But as a feast the service is closer to an unsolemn and open game. A celebration is simply disturbed by anything unexpected.

But the feast is open for spontaneous ideas and for accidents coming from outside. There are no disturbances in it, only surprises. Strangers can participate in the feast too. For a feast, only the framework is planned in advance. What happens in it depends on the participants themselves. The feast therefore expands the traditional elements of the celebration in order to leave scope for spontaneous and creative contributions. If we interpret the Christian service messianically, we will have to expand its ceremonies with elements of the feast, and its dignified ceremonial with spontaneous festivity. Then it has an infectious influence on the festiveness of everyday life.[120]

(*b*) The Christian service was originally and still is the feast of Christ's resurrection. That is why it was celebrated on the first day of the Jewish week, at sunrise. The resurrection feast is a feast with the risen Christ. It reveals and demonstrates in him the eschatological alternative to this world of work, guilt and death. The inescapability of history is broken through, the compulsion of wickedness is abolished and death is disarmed. As such an alternative resurrection is celebrated in a festive way and is carried into unfree and alienated life as an anticipation. That is why the Easter character of the Christian service also contains the contradiction of the powers of death that oppress life and the apathy that gives way to them. This disarming of the powers and the rebirth of hope out of apathy should be stressed more strongly than hitherto, so as to free church worship from misuse as a safety valve and compensation. As an action of hope in the resurrection, worship is, in a crucial sense, a liberating, public matter.

(*c*) The Christian service of worship, as the feast of the risen one, is always at the same time the making present of the one who was crucified. Together with joy in the freedom manifested, it also expresses pain over the failures and omissions of life. Where the nearness of God is experienced in the Spirit, there is also awareness of life's godlessness. Where people begin to live in the kingdom of the Son of man, inhuman relationships and inhuman behaviour become painfully obvious. In this sense the service will also express the laments of the Psalms and the cry from the depths of the assailed life. If it is expanded from a ceremony into a feast, this cannot be done merely through pre-formulated psalms and prayers; it must also emerge through spontaneous laments springing from the actual situation of individuals and groups. The feast of the resurrection makes room for the cry of the crucified Jesus to God, and for the outcry of the dumb, imprisoned, suffering people. 'And if man in his torment falls dumb, a God taught me to say how I suffer,' said Goethe. The human, suffering, crucified God, whose presence is celebrated in worship, lets us cry out and utter what we suffer. If he breaks the spell of silence he will also bring the cry of the peoples who have been politically silenced. A celebration cannot endure the unanswered cry out of the depths or unsolaced pain; but the feast with the crucified Christ in the presence of the Christ who is risen can be open for these things.

(*d*) Though worship in the name of the crucified and risen Christ makes a stand against life's inward and outward oppressions, its criticism of the state of the world is still none the less bound up with man's justification and the assent to creation. Just because it is the leaven of liberation it mediates the power to accept existence. It does not justify the existing state of affairs or ruling circumstances; but it does justify creation.

Right through its criticism of evil, the feast will be an affirmation of existence, and hence an expression of joy in that existence. The 'Yes' of God's incarnation implies the 'No' of the cross. Right through the 'No' of the cross the 'Yes' of the kingdom is to be heard and cannot be mistaken for any other extorted affirmations of things that are not 'very good'.

(*e*) Through the presence of the risen Christ the feast of the resurrection always has elements of rapture. The new messianic life is not merely changed life; it is life of new quality. The rapture of the divine future will first of all be felt and celebrated in festal ecstasy. It can only be transferred into practice fragmentarily and as a beginning. But this does not make the liberating feast senseless or superfluous. Its very superfluity in the literal sense – its overflowing character – produces continually new attitudes of resistance to the different forms of repression and unfree life. It provokes and stimulates companions in the feast to bring freedom and more freedom into everyday life, in accordance with the powers they receive and the potentialities they recognize. The feast of Christ's freedom and serene joy in him are not a contradiction of struggle and labour and do not paralyse energies. Through the spirit of the feast the struggle for the liberation of the poor is guarded against narrow-mindedness and daemonism, and preserved from resignation in the face of resistance and the sense of our own helplessness. Understood as a liberating feast, Christian worship becomes 'the messianic intermezzo'[121] in the history of God's dealings with men and women and on the path of the fellowship which follows Jesus' messianic mission, taking up its cross in the world.

(*f*) The messianic feast is dependent on a fellowship which sees itself as a messianic fellowship. A 'religious' church which aims to 'look after' people will always stylize its services into fixed ceremonials and will understand them quite generally as being anthropologically founded rituals with social functions, adapted to people's particular needs in certain social situations. But a messianic fellowship of the people will see itself as the subject of its assemblies, and will hence mould them into feasts of the divine history. The reform of church worship and reform of the church therefore belong together. No reform of worship succeeds without a new building up of the congregation 'from below', that is, its own organization of itself in accordance with the gospel, its promises and its challenges.

6. *The Messianic Way of Life*

(*i*) *The* façon de vivre

Wherever people experience and hold on to the meaning of human life, a certain way of living comes into being. Man attempts to direct his life in accordance with its meaning. He 'leads' his life in its changing situations and demands by trying to make it correspond to the sense he has extracted from it. The meaning of life gives man a firm, inner support and this then gives its stamp to his outward attitude as well. Life which is consciously lived forms itself and acquires stature. Man absorbs his experiences and projects himself towards his future. The personality comes into being in the mutual play of person and history, in suffering and action. It acquires a profile in the mutual play between individual and community, in being there for himself and for others. In the great cultural revolutions and in life's crises, ways or styles of life decay because they are no longer capable of putting their stamp on experiences and actions and have lost their power of lending orientation. Then 'breaks in style' come about. A new 'style' of life has to be worked out, because a person cannot live without style, which is to say formlessly. One can 'lose face' but one cannot live without a face. 'Let your manner of life be worthy of – or, in accordance with – the gospel of Christ', demands Paul (Phil. 1.27). His exhortations to the Christian churches are directed towards a conduct of life which receives its messianic quality from Christ's gospel.[122]

In the history of Christianity Christian theology has taken its bearings from the Christian life – even if not always consciously. Where it did this consciously, it did not merely see itself as a science but as 'an art of living' as well; for 'the theory of a practice' belongs to the sphere of art. Under the influence of humanist educational ideals, Huguenot theologians declared theology to be the *ars Deo vivendi*.[123] The practical *façon de vivre* stood at the centre of their endeavours and they set up the motto of *recte vivere* (which took its impress from the Old Testament) as against the eudaemonistic ideal of *beate vivere*. It is not the striving for earthly happiness and eternal bliss that ought to mark the Christian's life, but the struggle for divine and human righteousness. Catholic traditions have a theology of the monastic life. Its centre is spirituality, which is brought out particularly clearly and influentially in Ignatius Loyola's *Spiritual Exercises*. Spirituality does not only mean the inner life of devotion and prayer, cut off from the world; it is also the conduct of life in distinguishing one spirit from another, and in making decisions under the guidance of the Holy Spirit. Spirituality includes the whole of life, soul and body, individual and community, the inner life and the outward one. Loyala's spirituality influenced the *façon de vivre* of theologians more than an initial glance into their theological works would suggest.[124] It is therefore necessary to investigate and understand the history of theology, not merely in the context of the history of thought, but also as part of the history of life.[125] On the Lutheran side, we shall discover that the Reformation hymns and catechisms have given their stamp to the style of life and thought of theologians for generations. The experiences of faith shared by communities in the Thirty Years' War (which find classic expression in Paul Gerhardt's hymns), the pietistic awakening of the revival movement, the youth movement, the Confessing Church, as these are reflected in hymns, biographies, poems, forms of fellowship and church buildings, have made history and influence our life and thinking even today. These are only a few examples of the interdependence of theology and devotion, the history of life and the history of the Spirit. When theology thinks in terms of the experiences of the Christian life, it also interprets the experiences of this life. If theology does not consciously take hold of this task, far-reaching differences can arise, which are themselves already the mark of a 'break in style'. In this case theology is no longer expressing and defining the experiences of Christian life in the present, but is only reproducing the definition of earlier experiences. Its scholarship then divides it from the life of the people and that life will separate itself from theology. Then rival styles arise which are more influenced by the 'place' where life is lived than by its meaning. This finds expression in talk about 'university theology' and 'community theology'; or 'professional theology' and 'lay theology'. The community of theology and the Christian life is an urgent task in situations of this kind.

When we talk about the style, the forms and the conduct of the Christian life, we enter the complex sphere of mutually contradictory prejudices. Many people reject a Christian life in its established form and yet have a profound longing for its clear lines. The generations which still knew (or thought they did) how one could live a Christian life and die a Christian death, whose prayers and devotional forms followed the course of the day and the week, and the progress of life itself, the generations which encountered the changes and chances of life with a time-tested outlook and a firm attitude, frighten many people and yet at the same time fascinate them. Why?

The Christian way of life as it has been handed down obviously has many legalistic features. It often takes more account of life's prohibitions than its injunctions. This life is not always viewed as conduct 'worthy of – or in accordance with – the gospel of Christ', but often more as conduct in accordance with the law of Moses and the Stoics, or the rules of church and society. Every established form of life is stamped, not merely by the meaning of life which people hold, but by the circumstances of the time as well. But this cannot lead to the gospel's being turned into a law. A common law demands uniformity, but the gospel spreads individuality in fellowship. Legalism makes a Christian way of life (and the church's way of life too) pervasively timid and narrow-minded. Self-discipline and continual control over the natural urges and feelings are its way of life. It says nothing about self-affirmation and an acceptance of one's own individuality, about the liberation of natural and physical life. Because people have no courage for spontaneity they are continually forced to ask what is permissible and whether they are 'allowed' to do what they want to do.

Of course people's individuality rebels against the moral pressure of this legalism, especially in the adolescent years, when a person is finding himself, has to arrive at himself and become responsible for his own life. The firmly established faith of his parents then becomes for him a set of 'childish beliefs' which he has outgrown. But the freedom for which 'Christ has set us free' (Gal. 5.1ff.) also rebels against this legalism. That freedom is not identical with the natural rebelliousness of youth, but it has importance for it. For legalism certainly cannot be replaced by lawlessness, and firm obligations can by no means be replaced by libertinism. That does not lead to freedom but merely replaces the ties of the generations by the ties exerted by groups. Their solidarity can have just as legalistic an effect as loyalty to fathers and mothers. Life 'in accordance with the gospel' is life in recognized and accepted personal individuality, but an individuality that is charismatically alive, a personality that is lived in and for the community, and an independence that does not suppress originality but sets it free and develops it in relationship to forefathers and contemporaries. A life 'in accordance with the gospel of Christ' seeks the individual and common messianic way of life. It cannot have anything to do with either legalism or lawlessness, for it looks for forms of the liberated life in experience and for forms of life's liberation in practice. The messianic gospel liberates oppressed life. It gives it bearings and meaning. It gives its stamp to life in the Spirit.

(ii) Born again to a Living Hope

Before we consider the life which is stamped for freedom by the gospel, it may be helpful to look round for the theological concept which expresses this experience of faith. Here we shall take the concept of 'rebirth'.[126] *Regeneratio, renovatio* – '*incipit vita nova*' seem to capture the sense of what is meant better than sanctification, with its many levels of meaning. The actual word 'rebirth' is seldom used in the New Testament (Matt. 19.28; Titus 3.5). But the fact is often treated in the context of baptism. Like all related concepts, rebirth is to be understood eschatologically. Matthew

19.28 means by it the renewal and rebirth of the world in the future of the Son of man and his glory. Titus 3.5 talks about the rebirth (regeneration) of believers in the Holy Spirit according to the mercy of God through Jesus Christ, which makes them already heirs of eternal life 'in hope'. When the Johannine writings talk about new birth 'from God' and 'from the Spirit' they are talking about the new source of new life.[127] Born again of the Spirit, believers acquire a share in the kingdom of God. The first epistle of Peter talks about being born again 'to a living hope' (1.3) by the mercy of God through the resurrection of Jesus Christ from the dead. In the rebirth of life the new creation of the world into the kingdom of God in an individual life is already experienced and anticipated *here*. This has its foundation in the prevenient mercy of God; it is manifest in the resurrection of Christ from the dead; and it is efficacious in the Spirit, which moulds life in faith to the living hope. Theological tradition has seldom taken account of this eschatological character of rebirth. But it is just this that makes it clear that the rebirth of an individual means his orientation towards the new creation: 'The one who is born again is, as it were, ahead of himself; he lives from the thing that is coming to him, not from what is already in him.'[128] The one who is born again cannot, therefore, be scrupulously and anxiously preoccupied with himself, although he lives in this experience. His life has become new because, being orientated towards the new creation, he lives in the presence of the Spirit and under his influence, the 'earnest of glory'. At the same time the eschatological orientation of the individual's rebirth opens him for the community and for the world. The experience is his own – irreplaceably so; but it sets him in the movement of hope and in the fellowship of the messianic community. Re-birth does not isolate a person, even though it affects the individual in his unrepeatable character. On the contrary, it links his life with the future, giving that life, limited as it is, a meaning that transcends it. Rebirth does not isolate the individual, even though it makes him a person, but sets him in the common movement of the Spirit which is poured out 'on all flesh'. Where the messianic gospel is heard and evokes faith, life is born again 'to a living hope' and – in however fragmentary a form – the rebirth of the world is anticipated. The 'new man', the heir of the future and citizen of the kingdom, takes form. As the concepts which are related to 'rebirth' show, this means that the

Messiah takes form in the individual and in the community, in the soul and in the body.

(iii) The Meaningful History of the Individual Life

What form does rebirth take in a person's life? Its eschatological orientation cannot endure any legalism which makes man his own overseer. On the contrary, it manifests itself in the new spontaneity in which a man lets himself go and entrusts himself to the Spirit – that is to say, acquires self-confidence through his confidence in God.[129] It shows itself in the openness of an otherwise timidly withdrawn existence, an openness which nevertheless forms personality and does not surrender man to what he encounters at any given moment without any will-power of his own. But its eschatological orientation cannot endure lawlessness and formlessness, for what is visualized is not redemption *from* the body, but the redemption *of* the body.

The problem of the form taken by the reborn life really lies in experience, and our dealings with experience. The new life style cannot be set up as a programme and carried through without any interference. 'Man makes something, and history makes something out of him.'[130] When he entrusts himself in faith to the history of God, then his way of life takes the impress of this history. The form of the new life is experienced and *suffered*, and is only recognizable subsequently for what it is. Life history in faith is the history of enduring God: 'Not my will, but thine, be done.' This is a challenge to wise dealing with inward and outward experience. There is no such thing as experience *per se*. Experiences are always remembered, digested and actualized, and their meaning is evaluated afresh in every new situation. Certain experiences are grasped as being fundamental ones, if they alter the whole of life and give it new perspectives. External, shared experiences – war, the collapse of the state, captivity or revolution – have put their stamp on the life of whole generations. Inner personal experiences, conversions, inspirations, sufferings and decisions influence certain periods, and more than that, in the life of individuals. Daily experiences are generally interpreted in the light of these fundamental experiences, and these test their viability and power of lending orientation against this interpretation. It is hardly possible to re-examine one's life and to make existential decisions every minute. Even faith cannot be the 'ever new decision'. In the history of a life, faith is also loyalty to the experience that one has once had and the decision that has once been taken. Only this loyalty must not be confused with a security which is ready to hand. Our dealings with the experiences and decisions of faith are stamped by living faith themselves.

Here we can distinguish between the work of memory and the work of hope.[131] This is the two-sided hermeneutical process in the history of a person's life. With the aid of memory we return to past experiences and disperse possible repressions and bitternesses, such as grow up in connection with painful and embarrassing experiences, for example. We expose ourselves to these experiences again, rediscovering ourselves in them as being moulded by them. Thanks to memory we actualize these experiences and the 'I', which is affected by them, links them with experiences and decisions which have to be made in the present. The work of memory creates continuity. There is no identity which is not also continuity, stretched over a period of time and held fast through memory. But identity in the history of life is always historical and open to the future. A life can only be surveyed as a whole when it has reached its end.[132] But it is questionable whether the hour of death is this end in which a life is completed and becomes surveyable as a whole. For the whole of life is more than the sum of its parts and periods; it is the whole for which this life was led and from which it took its meaning. The work of memory on life's past is bound up with the work of hope on its future. The meaning which we see in our future determines the significance we ascribe to the past. The continuity of life history therefore involves the design planned with a view to a meaningful whole. Remembered experiences and decisions become significant in the present in so far as they open up for us angles of approach to the potentialities of the future. We then remember past experiences, not under any compulsion to repeat them, but in freedom, so as to be certain of our destination.

If the experiences of the Christian faith are called the rebirth of life to a living hope, then the natural work of memory stands in the light of this work of hope. The power of continuity won through memory is directed towards the rebirth of the whole. Life, temporally limited and historically forgetful and fickle as it is, is set in this perspective. The incompletable fragments of a human life become fragments of the rebirth of the whole creation. Memory will in this light understand all the experiences of faith as open experiences pointing beyond themselves and as changing signs which point in the same direction – that is, as fragments and prefigurations of the new creation. It is not death that completes life but the kingdom of God. The hermeneutics of the history of an individual life are hermeneutics of the cyphers of rebirth. It is only one part of the hermeneutics of the Spirit's history, but it is a necessary and irremissible part.

The bourgeois age of personalities and biographies may be at an end. But if its end is not to be 'the death of man',[133] then courage must be awakened for our own lives in their narrow limitations and for our own life histories in their banalities. Without the eschatological orientation of his rebirth man can lose his 'I', letting it be dispersed into mere reactions to actions from outside. Without it he can also crawl into the story of his own private life and lose himself just because he wants to save himself by this method. 'Non-eschatological man loses his humanity as a power that he consciously experiences. He will be exposed to external control to the very centre of his person.'[134] The perspective of rebirth we have described is absorbed neither by private nor by collective biography. It is able to reconcile the personal as what is uniquely one's own with the common element of the uniquely other, because it orientates both sides of life, the individual and the collective, to the new creation of the whole.

(iv) Creative Tensions

The style of life that is reborn and new comes into being from creative tensions. There are times in which these tensions allow themselves to be brought harmoniously into a form which appears consistent. Today they are tensions which often enough produce disharmonies and lack of consistency and lead to forms of life which display the points of fragmentation rather than the unity of the whole. We mean by this the tensions between prayer and faithfulness to the earth, between contemplation and political struggle, between transcendental religion and the religion of solidarity. Today many people are carrying out the experiment of Christian life between these poles. But polarizations threaten the rebirth of life. We must therefore seek pointers for a way of life which springs from the endurance of these tensions.

(a) The dialectical unity between *prayer and earthiness* was the fascinating secret of Dietrich Bonhoeffer's spirituality.[135] His *Letters and Papers from Prison* have become the breviary of committed Christians all over the world. He fought passionately against the withdrawn piety of those who put up with every injustice on earth because they have long since resigned themselves to it and only live life here in a half-hearted way. But he opposed with equal passion the flat and trivial this-worldliness of those who consider themselves enlightened, who want to enjoy the present, resign themselves in the face of the future, and therefore only live half-heartedly and without fervour. An other-worldly piety, which wants God without his kingdom and the blessedness of the soul without the new earth, is really just as atheistic as the this-worldliness which wants its kingdom without God, and the earth without the horizon of salvation. God without the world and the world without God, faith without hope and hope without faith are merely a mutual corroboration of one another. They are the products of the disintegration of a Christianity without Christ. 'Brethren, remain true to the earth!' With this cry from Nietzsche's Zarathustra Bonhoeffer fought against resigned, half-hearted Christianity in its flight from the world.

In the same way, earlier than Bonhoeffer, the Blumhardts attacked the liberal bourgeois attitude which limited faith to God and the soul, and in opposition to both made their central watchword: 'Seek first the kingdom of God and his righteousness and all these things shall be yours as well.' 'Yes indeed, Christian, by all means see to it that you die in a state of blessedness. But the Lord Jesus wants more than that. He does not want my redemption and yours; he wants the redemption of the whole world. He wants to put an end to evil altogether. He wants to make the whole world, in its utter godlessness, free.'[136] Christoph Blumhardt, Kutter and Ragaz therefore also took the practical step away from religion to the kingdom of God, away from the church to the world, away from concern for the individual self to hope for the whole.[137] They became religious socialists and Social Democrats because they looked for the coming of the kingdom of God in the world among the poor and oppressed. But this investment of one's own life, experience and strength in preparing the way for the coming Lord in the world presupposes (as Christoph Blumhardt made unmistakably clear) 'the ceaseless prayer for the spirit of perseverance'. It is only self-forgetful trust in the faithfulness of God that creates freedom for selfless service for the world's liberation.

'Only the man who loves the earth and God as a single unity can believe in the kingdom of God', declared Bonhoeffer as early as 1932.[138] 'Christ does not lead man into the backwoods of religion's flight from the world; he gives the world back to him as her faithful son. . . . The hour in which the church prays for the kingdom today forces it completely, for good or ill, into the comradeship of the children of the earth and the world; it swears the church to faithfulness to the earth, to misery, to hunger and to dying.' The person who really hopes for the kingdom of God endures the conflicts and defeats of history. He remains true to the earth and does not give it up, because he directs his gaze unswervingly towards the point where the curse is broken and God's 'Yes' to the world can be perceived: 'the resurrection of Christ'. Bonhoeffer's notion of the profound this-worldliness of the Christian life takes its whole colouring from the present actualization of the crucified and risen Liberator and has as little to do with bourgeois secularization as it has with a religious moderation of the feelings. The more intensely a man loves the earth, the more strongly he feels the injustice done to it, its fatal self-destruction and the way it is forsaken, and the more spontaneously he laments with the suffering and cries out with the wounded – which is to say prays, if praying means crying out to God the lament of the people, the cry of the oppressed and the hunger of those who hope. The more spontaneous and worldly a man's prayer is in this sense, the more deeply he is drawn into the people's suffering and will participate in it as God's suffering over the world.[139] Praying in the Spirit and interest in life drive one another on, if both are concentrated on the crucified Christ and his messianic kingdom. Then prayer is not a compensation for disappointed love; it makes love ready to absorb the pain into itself and to love more fiercely than before. Then faithfulness to the earth is not a dispensation from praying and crying, but increases their passion. Bonhoeffer's life, his resistance, his faith and the way he died are an example of a way of life which has its genesis in the creative tension of prayer and faithfulness to the earth. It remained a fragment and was broken off in 1945 at the place of execution in a concentration camp; but just because of that it points beyond itself. The way of life of the messianic era is stamped by messianic suffering. It is hardly ever recognizable in any other way, for 'dying, and behold we live'.

(*b*) The dialectical unity between *contemplation and political struggle* is the secret of Taizé's way of life. Here prayer is not an inner tranquillizing of the self, or a religious flight from the world. It is interpreted messianically. 'Prayer is first of all waiting. It is allowing the "Come, Lord" of the Apocalypse to well up in oneself, day after day. Come for mankind! Come for us all! Come for me!'[140] Whoever prays takes up the world's cry of hunger. Whoever prays abides in the hope of Christ. Whoever prays opens himself for the world and the future of Christ, uniting both in himself. Contemplation is linked with prayer, but it is not the same as prayer. In contemplation the lament falls silent and the heart is open to receive. Man becomes free for others, free from egoistical desires and his own ideals. Contemplation and meditation are not directly 'practical'. But meditation on Christ's passion and contemplation of the presence of his Spirit alter practice more fundamentally than all the alternatives which the active man sees as being at his disposal. They lead his practical faith away from the trivializing of the idea of God and the future hope, setting both face to face with God's hard reality. To know God means to suffer God, and anyone who 'suffers' God experiences the reversal of his existence, the pains of his life's rebirth. He becomes a different person. He dies, as Paul says, to the demands and compulsions of 'this world' and awakes to new life for God and his kingdom. Only meditation without any object can lead to flight from action, not Christian meditation. That is at heart *meditatio crucis*. Turning to Christ and turning to the men and women for whom he died are part of a single movement. Contemplation in the presence of his Spirit destroys man's own will more thoroughly than anything else and makes the messianic will of God the meaning of one's own life. Contemplation concentrates on the one thing that is needful, the seeking for the kingdom of God. It reduces life, which struggle has inevitably diffused and confused, to a single common denominator.

Just as meditation cannot be a flight from action, so, conversely, action cannot be a flight from meditation. Anyone who falls back on activity because he cannot come to terms with himself, and who praises action because he is afraid of theory, achieves nothing at all, but is merely a burden to other people. Activity and political commitment for the liberation of the oppressed are not a panacea against feebleness of the personality and lazy thinking. It is only the person who finds himself who can give himself. It is only the one who has become free that can free others without taking away their capacity for ideologically free decision. But there is no 'I' which I can hold fast to in myself. There is only the 'I' in the context of a history, in which it finds its place and its task. Christian meditation and contemplation allow the real 'I' to be discovered as an 'I' accepted, liberated and redeemed by God in the context of its call to partake in the messianic liberation of the whole. We are told that we must not merely discover *who we are* but also *where we belong*. In meditating on the history of Christ and in becoming conscious, in the Spirit, of our own history in relation to this history of Christ, we discover ourselves and our tasks in the process of this open history. This can only be the reverse side of the practical life in which we try to realize ourselves and our destiny in the messianic history of God's dealings with the world. Meditation and liberating practice in the different spheres of life complement one another and deepen one another mutually. The style of the Christian – which is to say the messianic – life comes into being from the tension between meditation and struggle. In this field of tension too we find fragments, fractures and inconsistencies. The new life is seldom experienced in any other way than as: 'We are afflicted in every way, but not crushed' (II Cor. 4.8).

(*c*) Today *transcendental religion and the religion of solidarity* have polarized wide groups in Christianity. Anyone who prays is standing aloof from politics, is evidently concerned with himself and 'his God' and makes no protest. Anyone who publicly protests is standing aloof from traditional devotionalism, is concerned with the world, and no longer prays. The unforgettable picture when Martin Luther King, with his black and white civil-rights supporters on the march to Selma, knelt down in the road in front of the rifles and prayed, is as off-putting for many devout people as it is for many who are politically committed. There are student societies which now see themselves solely as part of the political movement for liberation and have relinquished their Christian identity. They leave the Bible, prayer and mission to the conservative groups, and ultimately have nothing to offer their left-wing comrades except their solidarity, without any ideas, visions and initiatives of their own. On the other hand there are devout student groups which meet together for Bible classes and prayer meetings and are concerned in a more traditional way with God and the soul or, to put it in more modern terms, with the experience of the transcendental and the self. Their self-styled detachment from politics usually exerts a conservative political influence, to preserve the privileges of their class, country and society. Generally the dispute between the two is fought out in the pusillanimous and stupid alternatives of a 'vertical' dimension of faith and a 'horizontal' dimension of love. This does not preserve the tension between prayer and political effort, reading the Bible and reading the newspaper; it puts an end to it altogether. Transcendence is not the transcendence of the risen Christ if it does not lead to solidarity with those he came to free and for whose salvation he died. Solidarity is not the solidarity of the crucified Jesus if it does not lead to the transcendence of that future into which he was raised. The religion of transcendence and the religion of solidarity are two sides of the Christian way of life. If they are separated and polarized in opposition to one another, the new life is either hindered or destroyed.

No one who prays in Christ's name and cries out for redemption can put up with oppression. No one who fights against injustice can dispense with prayer for redemption. The more Christians intervene for the life of the hungry, the human rights of the oppressed and the fellowship of the forsaken, the deeper they will be led into continual prayer. It sounds paradoxical, but the more their actions are related to this world, and the more passionately they love life, the more strongly they will believe, if they want to remain true to the hope which Jesus brought into the world.

Prayer for the Spirit makes people watchful and sensitive. It makes them vulnerable and stimulates all the powers of the imagination to perceive the coming of God in the liberation of man and to move into accord with it. This prayer therefore leads to political watchfulness, and political watchfulness leads to prayer. The spirituality of fellowship with Christ grows up between solitude with Christ and fellowship with others. It is seldom manifested in any other way than: 'We are always carrying in the body the death of Jesus, so that the life of Jesus may be manifested in our mortal flesh' (II Cor. 4.10).

We cannot 'make' a messianic way of life. It is not practice that makes perfect here; it is suffering and hope. This way of life is created by the Spirit where people, personally and collectively, discover their life and the history of their lives in the comprehensive

history of Christ, and participate in the history of God's dealings with the world. The rebirth of the individual and the
fellowship then becomes the sign and foretaste of the coming
rebirth of the whole creation. Fellowship with the crucified Jesus
leads to the fellowship of the world's messianic suffering. Fellowship with the risen Christ leads to the dawn of the liberty of the
messianic era. In the light of the messianic history of God the life
reborn in pain begins to shine – but not of its own power. Its fragments and beginnings become lived and suffered signposts of hope
for others. Anyone who enquires seriously about 'the sacrament of
the Spirit' and its signs will not pass over this sign of the lived life.
In life together with the Messiah his life will itself be forged into
a messianic sign.

VI

THE CHURCH IN THE POWER OF THE HOLY SPIRIT

When it listens to the language of the messianic era and celebrates the signs of dawn and hope in baptism and the Lord's supper, the church sees itself in the presence of the Holy Spirit as the messianic people destined for the coming kingdom. In the messianic feast it becomes conscious of its freedom and its charge. In the power of the Holy Spirit the church experiences itself as the messianic fellowship of service for the kingdom of God in the world. Having considered the 'sacraments' of the church in chapter V, we shall now turn to the church's ministries and functions, its gifts and the tasks assigned to it. When we considered the sacraments, we did not see the Spirit in the sacraments, but the sacraments in the movement and the presence of the Spirit; and here too the Spirit is not to be apprehended in the ministries of the church, but the church, with its manifold ministries and tasks, is to be conceived in the movement and presence of the Spirit. There is no 'Spirit of the sacraments' and no 'Spirit of the ministry', there are sacraments and ministries of the Spirit. In this context we are calling the church a 'congregation', because we are thinking of the definite and specific event of its gathering together and its mission in the world.

Discussion about the relationships between 'ministry and the community' or 'ministry and charisma' often suffer from being pursued along too narrow lines, because the participants in the discussion do not see the wider context – the manifestations of the church's life in the eschatological history of Christ and the trinitarian history of God. If these are ignored the church's determining conditions are easily reduced to the dignities and functions of the church's office bearers. Ecclesiology becomes hierarchology if we do not start from the fact that every believer, whether he be an office-bearer or not, is a member of the messianic people of God.[1] The ministry is turned into an insipid – a 'spiritless' – kind of civil service, and the charisma becomes a cult of the religious genius, if we do not make the one charismatically living community our point of departure.[2] Many problems can be solved if ministry and congregation, ministry and charisma are understood in the eschatological history of God with the world. We then no longer proceed from the state of the church but from its future, as that is opened up by the history of Christ. The question of which came first, the ministry or the community, and which of them has priority, and the question whether ministry or free charisma has priority, can be answered out of this wider context.

It is necessary to reflect theologically on the mission of the community and every individual Christian, and on the congregation's order and special ministry; for before anyone actually speaks and acts in the church or in its name, the church has already spoken and acted through its very existence, its visible organization and its public functions. The forms of its fellowship and public functions, and the shape of its order and its ministries, are not merely externals and inessentials; they are no less important than the word and the sacraments.[3] The church's institutions and its traditional congregational forms can become a stumbling block for many people, even if – and especially if – they do not thereby make the things of Christianity itself a stumbling block. People demand 'the witness of existence' – and rightly so. Through its order, its ministries and its organizations the church either confesses or denies the thing that it has to represent. So it cannot leave its visible form to the power of the state or the requirements of its particular social order, if it wants to be recognizable as the church of Christ and as the people of the coming kingdom. It is of course true that every historical form the church takes also bears the stamp of its particular environment. But that is not a reason for accepting that stamp passively and for leaving it to external influences. As the church of Christ, the congregation with all its own powers has to realize the social, political and cultural potentialities of a particular period in a way that is in accordance with the cause it maintains; so that through its physical and public profile as well people will be confronted with the freedom of Christ and will be invited to the messianic kingdom. When bourgeois liberals separate Spirit from law, this makes the Spirit lawless and the law spiritless, just as it also makes love lawless and law loveless.[4] The division between theology and church organization makes the public life of the church schizophrenic. The interpretation of the church in the process of the Spirit cannot be merely spiritualistic or lead to a despising of the public form of its life. In church history the ecclesiastical differences and disputes did not only belong to the sphere of dogma; disputes in the field of church order, church leadership and the ministry were just as frequent and just as important, as the names of the various historical movements and denominations show: papalism, episcopalianism, presbyterianism, synodicalism, conciliarism, congregationalism, independency, and the rest. Church unions do not come about in this sphere through joint doctrinal formulas but through new fellowship, in the mutual recognition of ministries and through the uniting of the church's leadership in the field of organization. These so-called 'institutional questions' are questions of faith and are of the greatest theological importance. They cannot be solved pragmatically. For they are not inessentials; they are matters of our actual and present profession of faith. This makes church law 'confessing church law' and church order part of the church's living witness.[5]

1. *The Community in the Process of the Holy Spirit*

(i) God is not a God of 'disorder', but of peace (I Cor. 14.33). In the New Testament peace does not mean bringing order out of chaos in specific cases, nor is it merely the elimination of conflict. It is the eschatological 'new order of all things'; and consequently the eschatological salvation of the new creation.[6] The community's life and actions are to correspond to the peace of God in this world of conflict (I Cor. 7.15) and anticipate them (Eph. 4.3) because the community lives from the peace of God through the lordship of Christ (Rom. 5.1). The life-style and the actions of the community do not therefore follow the general principles of order which obtain in its particular constitution but conform to the 'principles' of this divine peace. The ecclesiastical orders of Christ's church are historical portrayals of God's eschatological *order of peace*. What follows from this as far as state and society is concerned (as well as man's will to power in state and society) is the form taken by the contrast and alternative: 'You know that those who are supposed to rule over the Gentiles lord it over them, and their great men exercise authority over them. But it shall not be so among you; but whoever would be great among you must be your servant, and whoever would be first among you must be slave of all. For the Son of man also came not to be served but to serve, and to give his life a ransom for many' (Mark 10.42–45). Through Christ's self-giving, the rule of violence and oppression has been repealed in his fellowship. The coming peace of the kingdom will be lived in the discipleship of Christ and in mutual service for freedom. The community's order of freedom will in this way become the sign and point of departure for the conquest of godless and inhuman conditions of rule and oppression in society.

(ii) The community is to stand fast in the freedom for which 'Christ has set us free' (Gal. 5.1). It is the fellowship of the free. In its order eschatological freedom is to acquire stability. The order of Christ's church must therefore be an *order of freedom*, already showing man's redemption from sin, law and death. In the fellowship of Christ, people are freed from the oppression which separates them from others – freed for free fellowship with one another. That is why it can be stated that there is here 'neither Jew nor Greek, there is neither slave nor free, there is neither male nor female; for you are all one in Christ Jesus' (Gal. 3.28). Man's eschatological destiny to be heir of the kingdom and his destiny to be free here on earth comes into play, surmounting the lack of freedom which the historical struggle for power brings with it. The justification of sinners places believers in the eschatological heritage of the divine future, which also means the heritage of their own freedom. 'The new man' becomes manifest, not merely inwardly but outwardly too, so that we can say: 'Here there cannot be Greek and Jew, circumcised and uncircumcised, barbarian, Scythian, slave, free man, but Christ is all, and in all' (Col. 3.11). In Christ a person appears as God's person, not as a Greek, a Scythian, a slave or a freeman. The social, historical and natural identifications recede and decay. The constitution of Christ's community ought to represent this *eschatological divine right* of true man. In so doing it will abolish unjust constitutions and the privileges of absolute supremacy in the church. The constitution of Christ's community is the constitution of new life in the midst of the old, of true life in the midst of what is false. 'Because Jesus Christ is present in the community in the Holy Spirit, the new thing which he brings about for *the world* is already visible there.'[7]

(iii) If the community is the sign, the instrument and the breaking-in of Christ's lordship, and therefore the sign, instrument and breaking-in of 'the new order of all things', then it will direct its life and actions towards these things. The community lives from the kingdom of Christ. It lives from it as from the one who is to come. All rule in the church is only legitimated by its correspondence to *the rule of Christ*; but through this it is also truly legitimated. But what is 'the rule of Christ'? Is it a theocracy, which legitimates a hierarchy, or the authority of a value confined to religion and the inner life of the soul? The charismatic rule of Christ in the community is essentially liberation from the violence and pressure of 'the powers of this world'.[8] Ephesians 4 makes this connection clear: by virtue of his resurrection, Christ 'led a host of captives and gave gifts to men' (4.8). The community's gifts and tasks are the powers of the victorious Christ who went through hell and heaven to save all things. As the cosmocrator, he fulfils all things, 'and his gifts were that some should be apostles, some prophets, some evangelists, some pastors and teachers, for the equipment of the saints, for the work of ministry, for building up the body of Christ' (4.10–12). The gifts and tasks which the exalted Christ gives and appoints are the powers of the life liberated from prison. The risen Christ has taken away power from the 'elemental spirits of the universe' (Gal. 4.3). He has not merely led believers out of prison subjectively, but has also broken down the prison in the objective sense. He has not merely snatched individuals from the grasp of the pernicious forces of the universe, but has dethroned these forces themselves. The community which is filled with different energies of Christ's liberating power is therefore not an exclusive community of the saved, but the initial and inclusive materialization of the world freed by the risen Christ. If the prison has been stormed, if the powers have had their power taken from them, then the world has become different. This is perceived first of all in the fellowship of Christ through faith and hope, discipleship and new fellowship; but it affects the whole world and puts Christ's church at the service of the manifestations of the world freed by Christ.

Christ's 'church government' belongs within the framework of

his rule over the world. All the gifts and powers of his liberating
Spirit in the church are directed towards the world freed from the
'elemental spirits'. The church is therefore not a restricted religious community; if it were, the risen Christ would be merely the
Lord of its cult. Nor is it a fellowship of like-minded people; in
that case the Lord would only be there to give value to its mental
attitude. The church, with its cult and its attitude, is the earthly
form of Christ's lordship, which overcomes the world, and the
instrument of his liberation of that world. This can be called
'theocracy' if the nature of the rule is entirely and solely identified
from the way in which Christ freed men through his self-giving.
In that case, however, this Christocracy cannot be represented by
a hierarchy separated from the people, but only through the
brotherly order of a charismatic community. Its purport and its
promise is Christ's redeeming pantocracy.

(iv) For Paul the congregation is the place where the Spirit
manifests itself (I Cor. 14) in an overflowing wealth of spiritual
powers (charismata). According to Old Testament prophecy the
spirit counts as being the gift of the last days (Isa. 44.3; 63.14;
Ezek. 36.27; Zech. 4.6). In the messianic era not only the chosen
prophets and kings but the whole people of God will be filled by
the living force and newly creating power of God. According to
Joel 2.28f., this is the beginning of the outpouring of the Spirit of
God 'on all flesh'. That means the new creation of all things for
the eternal life of the kingdom, and it means at the same time the
glorifying of God; for God himself is present in the Spirit. By
virtue of the Spirit God himself takes up his dwelling in his
creation. Early Christianity understood its experiences with the
appearances of the risen Christ and his presence as being experiences in this messianic Spirit. The promise of Joel is fulfilled in
what happened at Pentecost (Acts 2.14–21). The Spirit of the
last days and the eschatological community of the saved belong
together. The new people of God see themselves in their existence
and form as being 'the creation of the Spirit',[9] and therefore as the
initial fulfilment of the new creation of all things and the glorification of God. The Spirit calls them into life; the Spirit gives the
community the authority for its mission; the Spirit makes its
living powers and the ministries that spring from them effective;
the Spirit unites, orders and preserves it. It therefore sees itself
and its powers and tasks as deriving from and existing in the es-

chatological history of the Spirit. In this it experiences not only what it itself is, but also where it belongs. It discovers the redeeming future of the world in the overriding span of the Spirit's history.

The New Testament knows no technical term for what we call 'the church's ministry'.[10] Paul talks about *charismata*, meaning the *energies* of the new life (I Cor. 12.6, 11), which is to say the powers of the Spirit. These are designations of what is, not of what ought to be. They are the gifts of grace springing from the creative grace of God. When he talks about the use of these new living energies, on the other hand, he evidently avoids all the words expressing conditions of rule. He does not talk about 'holy rule' (hierarchy) but chooses the expression *diakonia*. Creative grace leads to new obedience; and the gifts of grace and the energies of the Spirit lead to ready, courteous service. Claims and privileges cannot be deduced from them. The source of life's new forces is the new life itself. 'The charisma of God is eternal life in Christ Jesus our Lord' (Rom. 6.23). Just as the new life becomes manifest and efficacious in life's new powers, so the eschatological gift of the Holy Spirit also becomes manifest and efficacious in the powers of the Spirit. The charismata can be understood as the crystallization and individuation of the one charis given in Christ.[11] Through the powers of the Spirit, the one Spirit gives every individual his specific share and calling, which is exactly cut out for him, in the process of the new creation. Because the word 'spirit' is exposed to traditional misunderstandings, we must remember that for Paul the Spirit is 'the power of the resurrection' and thus the divine power of creation and new creation (Rom. 8.11; Rom. 4.17). The Spirit is not an ideal, over against what is physical and mortal, but is God himself, who calls into being the thing that is not, makes the godless righteous, and raises the dead. He is the 'life-giving' Spirit, giving life to everything that is mortal (I Cor. 15.45). The community's spiritual powers must be correspondingly understood as creative powers endowed with life. As the power of resurrection, the Spirit is the reviving presence of the future of eternal life in the midst of the history of death; he is the presence of the future of the new creation in the midst of the dying life of this world and its evil state. In the Spirit and through the Spirit's powers the eschatological new thing – 'Behold I make all things new' – becomes the new thing in history, reaching, at least in tendency, over the whole breadth of creation in its present

wretchedness. That is why the energies of new life in the Spirit
are as manifold and motley as creation itself. Nothing is to be
passed over, pushed aside or given up. On the contrary, everything
is to be made eternally alive. That is why Paul and the epistle to
the Ephesians talk about the charismata with such assurance. They
overflow in an abundance whose extent cannot be fixed once and
for all.

On the one hand the charismata serve to build up the eschatological community. Here Paul talks about kerygmatic powers,
gifts of utterance, to which category apostles, prophets, evangelists,
teachers and comforters or admonishers belong. But inspirations
and ecstasies belong to the same category. He also mentions dia-
conic powers, gifts of service, which move deacons, both men and
women, almsgivers and the people who care for the sick. Miraculous healings and the expulsion of demons are included here too.
Finally, when he is talking about the leaders of assemblies, the
elders and overseers (*episkopoi*) he mentions cybernetic powers,
gifts of rule. But the apostolic experiences of suffering are charismatic as well. It is not merely action that has a charismatic efficacy
but suffering too.

The charismata are by no means to be seen merely in the 'special
ministries' of the gathered community. Every member of the messianic community is a charismatic, not only in the community's
solemn assemblies but every day, when members are scattered and
isolated in the world. That is why in I Cor. 7.7 Paul also uses
charisma for the historical place where a person is called, with his
potentialities and powers. The call to the fellowship of Christ and
the gift of the Holy Spirit makes a charisma out of bondage and
freedom, marriage and celibacy, manhood and womanhood,
Jewish and Gentile existence. For the call puts the person's
particular situation at the service of the new creation. The Spirit
makes the whole biological, cultural and religious life history of a
person charismatically alive: 'Let every one lead the life which the
Lord has assigned to him' – 'every one in the state in which he was
called' (I Cor. 7.17, 20, 24). This expansion of the doctrine of the
charismata is not merely of interest where it affects the slaves and
the free; it is even more so where it touches on the circumcised and
the uncircumcised. Everyone is to bring into the church and the
process of new creation everything he has, whatever he brings with
him and whatever he can do. The foundation and goal of the

charismatic enlivening make it clear that this does not mean any justification of existing circumstances and conflicts: 'You were bought with a price; do not become slaves of men' (I Cor. 7.23). This is particularly important for the people who are called as slaves. All are to 'deal with the world as though they had no dealings with it' – that is, use it as though they did not need it – and should not misuse it, 'for the form of this world is passing away' (I Cor. 7.31). Our dealings with the particular social, biological, cultural and religious conditions into which we are called are therefore to be free, determined by the eschatological freedom which overcomes this world and makes the new creation obedient. In principle every human potentiality and capacity can become charismatic through a person's call, if only they are used in Christ. It is not the facticity that decides what a charisma is; it is the modality. And this modality is stamped by the congregation's organization and by new obedience in the lordship of Christ. It is not the gift itself that is important, but its use.

Paul expresses *the universal trend* of the eschatological outpouring of the divine Spirit on all flesh when his account of the charismata within the congregation in I Cor. 12 flows over into his description of the 'more excellent way of love' in I Cor. 13, and when he passes from the list of the congregation's functions in Rom. 12.9ff. to the 'catalogue of virtues' for Christians living in the world. The admonitions expressed in his maxims reveal his idea of the new creation in its charismatic life.[12] Everywhere Christians stand face to face with the coming Lord of the world – not merely in their assemblies but in their dispersion as well. This outlook determines not only the life and powers of the apostles, pastors, deacons and congregational leaders, but the ministries performed by Christians in everyday life also.

> God gives life to the dead and, through the invasion of grace, sets up his kingdom where before demons and demonic energies held sway; thus, the various lists of charismatic gifts are enumerated as counterblasts to the catalogue of vices.[13]

It follows that

> Charisma is no longer the distinguishing mark of elect individuals but that which is the common endowment of all who call upon the name of the Lord, or . . . a demonstration of the fact that the Spirit of God has been poured out on all flesh.[14]

The *unity* of all the charismata is fore-given in Christ. *What they have in common* lies in the one Spirit, the one calling, the one baptism. Their criterion is the lordship of the crucified Jesus. Their measure is the fellowship of the Holy Spirit. All the members of the messianic community have the gift of the Spirit and are therefore 'office-bearers'. There is no division between office bearers and the people. There is no division between the Spirit of the ministry and the free Spirit. There is no essential difference, either, between the different charismatics and the tasks appointed them. The widow who exercises mercy is acting just as charismatically as a 'bishop'. But there are functional differences, for there is no equality in the sense of uniformity. The powers of the Spirit in the new creation are just as protean as the creation itself. If this were not the case, its charismatic enlivening would be impossible. Consequently freedom, diversity and brotherliness prevail in the community. It is our 'legal' equality before God which opens up the varied riches of his pleasure. So we might formulate the principle: to each his own; all for each other; testifying together to the world the saving life of Christ.

If we try to formulate a provisional result, the essential thing is to hear in Paul's doctrine of the charismata the proclamation which has its foundation in Christ and is still relevant today.

1. Paul's outline of a charismatic common order is not the only one in the New Testament. Another picture is traced by Luke and in the Pastoral Epistles. There does not seem to be much point in weighing up these concepts against one another or in linking them with the history of the tradition. As a doctrine of the charismata, Paul's outline is not a law; it is a crystallization of the gospel. We shall therefore have to enquire about correspondences in our own situation if we are looking for the form of the eschatological community of the saved which follows the messianic gospel. But this is the presupposition. The number of ministries in the congregation and their particular character is not left to the personal choice of the congregation itself. Nor can it be extracted as a rule or regulation from the tradition of earlier congregations. It is founded and forged by Christ through the present gathering and sending forth of the messianic community.

2. Paul's outline is founded on his acknowledgment of the lordship of Christ, is evolved out of his experience of the powers of the Spirit, and is developed in the perspective of the eschatological

history of God's dealings. Wherever the church loses this justification, this experience and this perspective, the diversity of the charismata and the unity of the charismatic community is lost. Then hierarchies and monarchical episcopates grow up on the one hand, and merely passive church members, incapable of independent decision and action, on the other. This is when apathy develops and outbreaks of 'enthusiasm' take place. Then the common hope for the kingdom, and common service in preparing its way in the world, give way to institutions designed for the pastoral care of the whole community. The Christian church will be open for the diversity of the Spirit's gifts (and will have the corresponding experiences) to the degree in which it wins back its original eschatological orientation towards the new creation. The struggles for power in the church – which are, after all, very provisional and secondary – will subside in the degree to which the church is concerned solely about the lordship of the crucified Jesus and his future. These two elements of the Pauline doctrine of the charismata are not historically conditioned. They remain the foundations of the gospel that calls and gathers its people.

3. The Pauline doctrine of the charismata has been called enthusiastic. It is true that an *enthusiasm* of the Spirit and the assurance of the Spirit's gifts is implicit in it. But formally Paul was against enthusiasm. The Spirit of the last days is the Spirit of Christ, and Christ is the Christ who was crucified. The assurance of the Spirit does not lead to a dream of worlds beyond this world; it leads ever more deeply into Christ's sufferings and into earthly discipleship. The crucified Jesus is the measure of the fervency of the charismata. If we want to follow Paul today, we must not make a dogma out of his criticism of the enthusiasts in Corinth in the name of the crucified Jesus; we must be alive to its premises. There are a great many churches and congregations today which are anything but threatened by enthusiasm. On the contrary, they suffer from a quenching of the Spirit. There are churches which by no means suffer from an over-fervent diversity of callings and ministries – too many to co-ordinate – but which, on the contrary, suffer from the usurpation of all offices and tasks by a hierarchy of 'spiritual office-bearers' or an aristocracy of pastors. No one will be desirous of surrendering the source of the outpouring of the Spirit in the risen Christ, that is to say the binding of every power to Christ himself. But – in line with Paul's

gospel, even if moving in the reverse direction – ought we not to do away with the quenching of the Spirit in communities of this kind, and discover the free abundance of the Spirit's gifts? It would be showing lack of faith if we wanted to acquiesce in the romantic historical picture, according which the abundance of the Spirit's gifts was only present in the first flowering of the apostolic spring, becoming more and more reduced and stunted in the channels of historical evolution. It would be no less romantic if we wanted to wait for 'a second Pentecost' – as people have done again and again in the church's history. In the dawn of the messianic era there are no longer any periods devoid of the Spirit. But the Spirit can be 'grieved' and 'quenched'; his powers can be 'hindered' and dispersed. This is not what Paul meant.

2. *The Charge to the Community and the Assignments within the Community*

From what we have said up to now it is clear that in determining the particular callings in a community we have to proceed from the calling of the community as a whole. The various ministries in the church have the church's single and common ministry as their presupposition and basis. The various forms of service presuppose the general service of the kingdom of God, to which every believer belongs. The various assignments in the community, which can be distinguished from one another, are related to the common charge through Christ, the charge which reaches everyone.[15] The traditional word 'ministry' has in some traditions an undertone of hierarchy and bureaucracy and has become open to misunderstanding. The more modern expression, 'service', is supposed to exclude claims to rule, though it can of course conceal these. Here, in order to put the actual function above status and person, we have chosen to describe what is meant by both expressions by the terms 'charge', 'commission' or 'assignment'. An assignment is always aimed as something particular; it is always specific. It depends on the person who gives the assignment, or it is verified through its carrying out. Before we can talk about the individual, special and distinguishable 'assignments' or 'charges' in the community and for the community, it is important to remember the one general charge to the community as a whole and every one of its members.

(i) *The charge to the community* lies in the calling of believers through Christ to the kingdom of God through the power of the Holy Spirit. This charge is made visible through the sign of baptism. The community of the baptized is the community of those who have been called. There are no differences here. All are called and commissioned for eternal life, the glory of the kingdom and messianic fellowship, charged to live in the messianic presence of this eschatological future and to bear witness to it. That becomes especially clear when we enquire into priesthood in the New Testament.[16] When the New Testament uses the word 'priest' it does not mean any special priestly class. According to the Epistle to the Hebrews (which uses priestly terminology) Jesus himself is the one, unique 'high priest'; through his vicarious surrender of himself on the cross and his continual intercession with the Father he has fulfilled the special priesthood of the old covenant, and has thus abolished and ended it on earth. In his fellowship the separation between priest and people is overcome and discarded. His giving of himself for the reconciliation of the world is the 'offering' which is valid once and for all (Heb. 10.10–14). This brings the daily and annual sacrificial cult to an end. He is the messianic mediator (Heb. 8.6) and the single guarantor of the new covenant (Heb. 9.15). No further mediator and guarantor is necessary. Consequently the people of the new covenant no longer remain on profane ground outside the sanctuary. In the fellowship of Christ they have become 'a chosen race, a royal priesthood, a holy nation, God's own people', so that they 'may declare the wonderful deeds of him who called you out of darkness into his marvellous light' (I Peter 2.9ff.). That is to say, the whole people, being imbued with the Spirit, has become 'spiritual' and called to the prophetic proclamation of the coming kingdom. It is only in its undivided entirety that it will become the revelation of the Spirit of the last days which descends 'on all flesh'.

It is *the prophetic people* which through its life and the style of that life bears witness before the world to God's promise and its future. Moreover, the whole people lives from the self-giving of Christ and freely gives itself to the will of God. It is therefore only in its undivided entirety that it testifies to the one reconciliation of the world with God. It is *the priestly people*, which intercedes for others and bears witness before the world to the liberating representation of Christ. The whole people has been finally freed for new life through the lordship of Christ. It is only as an undivided entirety that it can make the entire and total character of the life of the new creation manifest. Because they serve the liberation of the whole in common, and each in his own way, they are *the kingly people* and participate in the divine rule (Rev. 1.5; 5.10; 20.6). Through fellowship with Christ the whole people becomes the subject of the history of freedom, which takes its stamp from the history of God. Consequently this *messianic people* is no longer 'subject' to special prophets, priests and kings. It has 'found itself' and its destiny through the workings of the risen Christ. So it cannot be a dumb and passive crowd. Every individual and all individuals together live from the Spirit in which they experience their identity, finding their place and their charge in the history of God's kingdom. The 'service of the kingdom of God' (*ministerium regni dei*) gives them all 'equal rights' and points them towards their common goal in solidarity.[17] Factually, the presence of Christ in his church precedes his presence in particular assignments. The gift of the Holy Spirit is the one common ground for the experience of his diverse powers. This can be called the 'general' or 'universal' 'priesthood of all believers'. This expression is justified if we consider the one priesthood of Christ, which relates to everyone; but it has only limited value if it is merely used to mean the polemical spearhead of Reformation theology, directed against a special priesthood. We should then have to speak with equal emphasis about the general prophetic office and general kingship of all believers. But really it is only the particular offices which ecclesiastical tradition once cut off from the people which are given back to it again through this expression. The phrase does not yet explain the difficult relationship between the common commissioning of all believers and special assignments within the community.

(ii) *The various* distinguishable *assignments within the community* only come into being by virtue of the common commissioning of the community itself. As Christ's messianic community, it passes on these assignments in Christ's name. But we must note here that its assignments are not assignments made by an existing fellowship but are given by Christ.[18] They are not a matter of the community's choice and cannot be produced *out* of the fellowship either. They have nothing to do with any 'imperative mandate' belonging to the fellowship, but solely with the conscience which has been liberated by Christ and is therefore bound to him. The special assignments in the church are within and under Christ's liberty and authority, and are therefore not simply an expression of the ideas of the existing fellowship. They lie within the power of the Holy Spirit and cannot therefore be the uncritical expression of the forces of any particular community spirit. They serve the kingdom of God and not the interests of the existing church and the different human interests contained in it. We cannot say that Christ's assignments are 'a sacred rule' imposed upon the community; but neither can we say either that they spring *from the fellowship in any given case*. In order properly to understand the relationship of these assignments to the community and of the community to the assignments, we can take our bearings from the simple, visible procedure: the community gathers to hear the proclamation, or for a baptism, for the common meal, for the feast and to talk together. Then one person or more gets up in front of the congregation in order to preach the Gospel, to baptize, to prepare the meal, to arrange the feast, and to make his contribution to the discussion. These people come from the community but come forward in front of it and act in Christ's name. It is not they as 'office bearers' who 'confront' the congregation; it is Christ. What they do and say is in the name of the triune God.

How, then, are we to understand the position of these people, with their particular charges or assignments? They come from God's people, stand up in front of God's people and act in God's name. Their commission does not separate them from the people and does not set them above the people either, for it is exercised in fellowship with and by commission of the whole people and in the name of that people's commissioning. But the thing for which the people are commissioned does nct come from them themselves; it comes from their God, in whose name they speak and act. After all, the commissioned and commissioning community does not want to listen to itself and project its own image of itself; it wants to hear Christ's voice, celebrate his fellowship, and have the assurance of his commission. As the messianic congregation the people of God cannot recognize the sovereignty of a priestly caste or special ministerial class. If it did it would be giving up its own freedom, which Christ has brought about. But as Christ's church the people cannot ascribe any 'popular sovereignty' to itself either; to do so would be to surrender the sovereign rights of its liberator. The common experience of Christ's sovereignty in his church therefore presents itself in such a way that the people for the special assignments come from the community, but not the content of these assignments themselves – and neither do the rules and directives according to which they are to be carried out. The charismata are the powers of the Spirit from whom they proceed, and the assignments or commissions are determined by the kingdom which they are intended to serve. They are functions of the messianic rule of Christ.

Any member of the community who stands up in front of it is therefore commissioned by it to act in Christ's name. This means that the community keeps the right to recall him, and to commission someone else. But it has not the right to stop assigning the commisions themselves – to put an end to the preaching of the gospel or to charitable work; to stop baptizing or holding the Lord's supper; or no longer to meet together. If it did this it would be abandoning its own existence. Nor has it any right to insist that the people who minister to it and to society in Christ's name act in a way which is in its own interests but is not legitimated by faith and is in contradiction to the Gospel. The member of the community who is called by it is, as one commissioned by Christ, answerable to Christ and to all the people who appeal to him in Christ's name about the kingdom which he is supposed to serve. But the preacher commissioned by the community is not the 'spokesman' of the fellowship. The leader whom the community has commissioned to lead its assemblies is not a 'chairman' to express its prevailing opinions. The deacon appointed by the community is not a servant of its dominant interests. If the community understands itself as Christ's community in the full sense of the word, then there is no difference between the particular assignments and the rank and file, because both stand in the service of the kingdom. But in practice it is advisable to note the inner differentiation between the fellowship, the whole people and the individuals commissioned, as those commissioned by Christ. The interlocking between the commissioned community and the different commissions within the community, which is evident in the visible procedure (out of the community – in front of the community – for the kingdom of God – in Christ's name) is appropriate to the people as the people of God and to the community as Christ's messianic community; for it sets the freedom of the people and the freedom of those with particular commissions in the common freedom of Christ.

(iii) The commissioning of the community as a whole and the various distinguishable assignments in the community have a *genetic connection* with one another. Here there is no temporal priority, and no priority of value. For there is no community without special assignments and no special assignments apart from a community. Community and particular assignments grow up *simultaneously*, *together*, and are therefore *dependent* on one another. Assignments can only be given and carried out in the fellowship of God's people. It is only at Christ's charge that the people of God is gathered together. Anyone who fails to recognize this genetic connection destroys the charismatic congregation. For a long time people in the church thought in a quite one-sided way from Christ to the office, and from the office to the Christian fellowship.[19] That led to the separation of the ministry from the people and reduced the people of God to the status of the church's lay rank and file – people deprived of the right to responsible decision. The monarchical justification of the ministry, which has been usual in the mainstream church since Ignatius of Antioch was: one God, one Christ, one bishop, one church. This may have had pragmatical reasons in its favour in its own time, but theologically it is wrong, and ecclesiologically it led to a false development. This unified hierarchy reflects a clerical monotheism which corresponded to contemporary 'political monotheism', but which is in contradiction to the trinitarian understanding of God and his people.[20] The development of the monarchical episcopate led to a quenching of the Spirit and was an impediment to the charismatic church. It is no wonder that at the same time as this hierarchical official church developed, Christian spiritualism grew up parallel to it. It spread, and is spreading still, in the church's 'underground' of sects, movements and brotherhoods. The growth of the monarchical episcopate broke up the genetic relationship between the commissioned church and its special commissions in a way that was totally one-sided. The aristocratic justification of the ministry of a 'vénérable compagnie des pasteurs' – a group that reproduces itself through co-optation and only recognizes brotherhood on the level of 'brothers in office' – can hardly be judged as progress, qualitatively speaking.[21] A democratic justification of the ministry is undoubtedly conceivable and would certainly be in accord with people in general, but hardly to the people of God.[22] It would presuppose a kind of pantheism of the Spirit which gives everyone 'the same' but not 'what is his own'. It is only the trinitarian under-standing of the commissioned community and the commissions in the community which is in a position to express the dignity, both of the people as a whole, and of its special ministries – and also the genetic connection of the two. Socialization and individuation are two sides of one and the same operation in the history of the Spirit. The Spirit leads men and women into the fellowship of the messianic people, at the same time giving everyone his own place and his particular charge. In messianic history everyone finds his new identity in Christ and the place to which he personally be-longs. By socializing, the Spirit individualizes; and by individualiz-ing, he socializes. Here we live both with and for one another. The particular commission strengthens the common commissioning and the common commissioning presents itself in the special commis-sions, and in no other way. The general 'priesthood of all believers' cannot be set up over against the particular commissions, and the particular 'ministries' cannot be set up over against the priesthood of all believers, if we take account of the fellowship of the Holy Spirit, which is 'with all'.

(iv) Because the different assignments are functions of the messi-anic liberation of the world, the form they take is historically *variable*. Their number and form can be fixed neither through the myth of a transfigured past, nor through the ideal of an Utopian future. Nor can any law laying claim to completeness be set up; for the assignments to be fulfilled by a community are dependent on the powers of the Spirit which are livingly present in it, and are determined in accordance with the tasks with which it is con-fronted. But because the community is itself the messianic people commissioned by Christ, there are *essentials* without which it can-not properly be what it is designed to be. Churches which put the celebration of the Eucharist at the centre of their life consider serving at the altar (and hence the priestly ministry) to be essential. Churches which put the preaching of God's word at the centre of their assemblies and their mission consider the preaching ministry essential. There are other Christian fellowships which hold common prayer, or the healing of the sick, or charitable work to be essential; and they gather together round activities of this kind. Wherever a community may find its powers and its tasks to lie, the important thing is always that the charges or commissions that are held to be essential and central should be carried by the whole community; because they are part of the commission of the community itself. It would be perverse for the community to make a virtue of necessity, and deduce all other commissions from the one commission which it holds to be essential; or to lay on the holder of the assignment it considers essential all the other assignments as well.[23] The community would then no longer be considering itself charismatically gifted and alive but would be delegating its own commission to the single holder of the central office. It is therefore not advisable to proceed from the one priestly ministry over against the congregation, and then go on to split this up into a differentiated *ordo*.Nor is it helpful to proceed from a preaching ministry over against the community, in order to divide this into a series of distinguishable pastoral activities, for which 'workers' from the community have to be sought. Again, it does not take us any further if we give priorities and values to the divisions of the ministry and pastoral activities according to their closeness to the centre, whether this centre be the Eucharist or the proclamation. If, on the other hand, we proceed in the reverse direction, from the commissioning of the whole community and the eschatological gift of the Holy Spirit, who lays hold on everyone, we then have to ask what special charges assigned by the community and directed towards it are necessary and of essential importance. Here we must name the following, but without order of precedence or value: (i) The charge to proclaim the gospel; (ii) the charge to baptize and celebrate the Lord's supper; (iii) the charge to lead the community's assemblies; (iv) the charge to carry out charitable work. What are essential for the community are: *kerygma*, *koinonia* and *diakonia*. For these the congregation needs preachers, presbyters and deacons. The task of proclamation can be distributed between preacher, teacher, pastor, sick-visitor and missionary. The task of leadership in the community can be distributed between elders and other leading members. The charge to carry out charitable work in the congregation and in society can be defined according to the situation. But the church cannot do justice to the mission for which Christ sends it forth without the proclamation of the gospel, without baptism and the Lord's supper, without gathering together and without charitable work.

In defining these charges the freedom and fullness of the Spirit must be taken into account, as well as the particular situation.[24] The charges we have named can be assumed for a certain time or

for life. The difference is not an essential one, for as charges given
by God they always claim the whole of existence and total commitment. Even ordination, which takes place once and for all and
determines the whole of life, makes no difference here, for the 'call'
event of baptism is already once and for all and determines the
whole of life. Ordination, with its conferring of a particular charge,
cannot enter into competition with baptism and cannot outdo it.
The person who is commissioned therefore still has liberty to say:
'If I can no longer preach or no longer want to, then I will join the
common group again, will be like the rest of you, and will let
someone else preach.'[25] Where the exercise of a commission comes
to an end, the person's commissioning ends as well, and the
difference in the charismata lapses. But the commission itself does
not end. It is a gift of the gospel to the whole church and must not
therefore be made a law. According to the powers and possibilities
available, the charges we have named can be full-time or part-time.
They can be carried out by men and women, by the married and the
unmarried, by the theologically trained and people without any
theological training. They can be exercised by individuals and
groups. None of these circumstances and aptitudes amount to a
law. The community must continually ask itself how its messianic
commission can be fulfilled in its particular situation and with its
particular powers. Traditional prejudices must not be allowed to
quench the Spirit and hinder the charismatic powers from their
service for the kingdom. The specific shaping of the different
charges in the community, and in face of it, must take their
function into account and must therefore be flexible; but they must
always be grounded on the mission of the whole congregation and
directed towards the kingdom of God. It is high time for churches
where there is a traditional monopoly of the ministry to open
themselves to the diversity of the different charges. The traditional
fear of a chaos of spiritual gifts is, in the face of their present
poverty, without foundation.

(v) *The unity of the charismatic community* turns on the fellowship of the commissioned community and the specially commissioned individuals. It is first of all the question of the fellowship of
'all in one place'. The starting assumption is that every person
called, whether he be an ordinary member or one with a special
commission, has the same dignity and the same rights. But though
everyone has his own commission, not everyone has the same one;

and consequently it is not the people but the commissions that stand in the forefront. As a result, in the fellowship weight and votes (though not rank and dignity) must be so apportioned that the common cause will be promoted. The general commissioning of the whole congregation will go on to concede a special position and responsibility to the people with special charges, because otherwise the charges cannot be fulfilled. Where the charismata are concerned, the brotherliness of the messianic community does not find expression through uniformity, but through diversity. The one fellowship of the Holy Spirit is expressed in the fellowship of those who are commissioned, which is a fellowship of brothers and colleagues. The demand for a special office and the demand for a 'democratization' of the church must continually have in view the foundation on which the church is gathered and the goal of its mission. Democracy and hierarchy, simply as patterns, do not in themselves bring this to expression. If the charismatic community does not present itself in any other way than in and through its special commissions, then it forms this fellowship as it renders these services. It will neither wish to dissolve it completely in what is common to everyone, nor be able to see itself merely in the people who have special charges. If we take our bearings again from the visible activities of the assembled community, then the mutual relationship of this with these commissioned by it will be clear. The people who have been commissioned for special tasks co-operate with the community and with one another. The two areas of co-operation belong together and ought not to be separated. In the parochial church council, elders' meeting, deacons' meeting, or whatever it may be called, the people who are specially commissioned ought to form a fellowship of service. Mere dignitaries have no place here. But everyone who exercises a public function in the congregation, before it and on its behalf – the church sister or deaconess as well as the deacon or the youth leader, the teacher or the sick visitor – ought to participate in these practical discussions. This fellowship of special services ought to be led in a 'brotherly' or collegial fashion by a president. He should be chosen for his aptitude, but his task is to stand in the service of Christ's church. The isolation and separation of the fellowship of service from the whole community and its commission can only be overcome if the community meets publicly with equal regularity and keenness. The differentiation can only be one of function, not one of rank. It is of vital importance both for the special services themselves and for the community that the people with special charges and their fellowship of service should have a 'feed back' to the people and the whole community. The *presbyteral leadership* of the congregation cannot be without its synodal fellowship. Here colleagues on different levels cannot be kept separate. Without a permanent relationship to the rank and file the particular commissions and services lose their power. The priest or 'minister of the word' can take over the leadership both of the practical discussions and of the congregational meetings, if his commission is assigned particular importance. But the charisma of leadership and responsibility for the fellowship can be found in someone else as well. It can also be carried out by a 'council of brethren'. The only important thing is that the community should be united and that the leadership of its assemblies should which is directed towards that unity. It is only because the community gathers together for the proclamation of the gospel and for the fellowship of hearing the Word, here finding its unity in Christ, that the commissioned preacher can be charged with further services which will contribute to its unity.[26] And it is in so far as the community celebrates its fellowship with Christ in the Lord's supper that those commissioned for the table of the Lord can be charged with further services directed towards its unity.[27] The association of the ministry of leadership with the ministries of word and sacrament makes it absolutely clear that the point of the ministries of leadership lies in the unity of the congregation. But this is not a law. The charisma of leadership and the keeping the community together can be carried out by other people as well; and in many congregations is in fact often enough carried out by non-ordained members of the congregation, even though a leading priestly or pastoral office is exercised.

The unity of individual local or 'gathered' congregations with other congregations in the neighbourhood and further afield is also part of the unity of the congregation meeting in a particular place. The church of Christ exists in one particular place and also in many places. It must therefore present its unity supra-regionally. Every individual congregation needs here the fellowship and concord with the church as a whole, which ultimately means concord in proclamation, sacraments and brotherhood with the church universal. This can be portrayed through a representative office of unity, whether it is linked with the name of Peter or not. It can also be represented by a presbyteral-synodal structure built up from below, that is, in conciliar form. If the unity of the church is presented through a *representative office*, this office is judged as it serves the whole of Christianity and functions for the unity of the whole church. To put it in another way: anyone who speaks on behalf of the whole of Christendom is exercising this commission. Here too the road goes from charisma to recognition and commissioning, not the other way round. If the unity of the church is presented through *councils*, what they say too will have to prove itself against its function for the church's unity. But when an individual community already exists in its assemblies gathered round the word and the sacraments, when those it has commissioned present its fellowship with one another and with the community in assemblies, the conciliar way of representing the church universal would seem obvious; for *concilium* comes from *con-calare*.[28] Just as the latter means 'calling out' and 'calling together', so *concilium* means 'assembly'. The assembling and coming together on the basis of the jointly heard call of God is the church's fundamental act. It is the *assembled people of God*. Consequently it will present its unity through assemblies in local, regional and universal spheres. To serve the unity of Christ's church is, therefore, to serve its assemblies. The service extends as widely as the assemblies themselves do. They are universal and ecumenical, in accordance with the mission of Christ and the tendency of the Spirit's operations. As a result the community needs these wider ecumenical and conciliar ministries, will discover the charismata for them, and will bestow the appropriate commissions.

(vi) *The unity of the charismatic church*, however, does not only cover everyone in all the various places at a particular period. It also embraces people in different periods of history. The account of the assembled church in space must therefore also be coupled with the temporal portrayal of its unity throughout history. Its *fellowship in time* with those who have gone before and those who are to come is traditionally expressed in the idea of the *apostolic succession* and is preserved through the practice of the laying on of hands. This term is often too narrowly defined. What is meant, in the first place, is that the apostles, as the eyewitnesses of the risen Christ, have a unique and fundamental importance for the church at all times and in all places. The church is built on the foundation of the apostles and prophets. But the call of the first witnesses of the risen Christ and those who were sent out by him first of all is also unrepeatable. To describe what happened quite simply: they saw and believed. But they proclaimed because they believed. The people whom their message reached heard the gospel and believed. The Easter appearances and the visions that called the disciples do not spread beyond themselves and are not communicable. But the gospel is spread and faith in the Word continually repeats itself and is transmitted. The apostles' role as eyewitnesses is not transferable, but their service for the gospel is passed on to the whole church and every believer. We must therefore distinguish the beginning of the church in those who were called first of all from the permanent missionary charge of the church and every Christian. The apostolic succession can consequently only relate to the apostles' charge to proclaim; it cannot refer to the Easter appearance through which they were called. The power and the command of apostolic succession belongs 'to the church as a whole and with it to every individual member for the ministry in which he is placed through the gift of the Spirit'.[29] The expression 'succession' is intended to preserve the continuing proclamation and the continuing ministries of the church in faithfulness to the apostolic proclamation and the apostolic ministry; so that the message remains Christ's message, without falsification, and the ministries are directed towards the kingdom of God, without deviation. Faithfulness to the beginning, however, is nothing other than faithfulness to the origin, for it is only as the church of Christ that the church is an apostolic church. As faithfulness to the beginning and origin, the apostolic succession also means faithfulness to the promise and mission. The church does not already become apostolic simply through remembrance of the first apostles and faithfulness to their message; it only becomes so when it fulfils its own missionary charge. It is only in fulfilling the mission itself that the church can be called apostolic. For the apostolic church is the church of the apostolate of the coming kingdom. In this sense it would be better to talk about the church's apostolic procession 'to the end of time'. The apostolic succession is not only a category of the church's legitimation; it is a category of its commission. It does not only point backwards, but forwards as well.

Apostolic succession and procession are the terms used to convey the unique nature of the messianic community as a whole. They therefore affect the unique character of the different charges or commissions in and before the congregation. According to the view we have developed up to now, the apostolic succession of the whole church and the apostolic succession of particular offices cannot be alternatives. But it is true that the reduction of the apostolic succession to only one office appears to be a narrowing down both of the succession of the people, and of its various other ministries. The sequence of the episcopal laying on of hands cannot be the sole condition for the recognition of a church's apostolic succession. It may be understood as a visible sign of the fellowship of the church in time; but the succession of church baptism, the fellowship of the Lord's supper and the unbroken proclamation of Christ – 'the same yesterday today and for ever' – are signs too, in at least equal measure. The fellowship of the church in time and through time is before all else an article of faith.[30] The church is preserved in its identity and continuity by Christ's faithfulness to his promises and through the presence of the Holy Spirit. It is given the assurance that 'the gates of hell' will not prevail against it and that it 'will endure to the end' through Christ's self-giving and his continual intercession with the Father (Luke 22.31f.). This perseverance both of God's faithfulness and of our faith can be realized through signs in the historical fellowship of the church; but whatever its historical continuity may be, it is not the historical continuity that secures the continuity of God's faithfulness. Even a succession of bishops is no guarantee of the permanent identity of faith, nor of faithfulness to the apostolic gospel. Historically demonstrable continuity is a gift of grace. In face of the wreckage and revolutions of history we should gratefully acknowledge it. The believed and acknowledged continuity of God's faithfulness is itself the grace from which the messianic community lives and for which it hopes. It is only the basis of its faith in its own preservation through God's faithfulness that gives the church the ability and the will to strive for historical faithfulness. And here its relationship to its 'fathers and mothers' will simply be the same, basically speaking, as its relationship to its 'sisters and brothers'. It is a free relationship of recognition and criticism in the fellowship of faith. Throughout the whole of time, the church is a charismatic fellowship in which everyone experiences what is 'his own' and all are there 'together' for the coming kingdom. Traditions, successions and historical continuity are to be seen in this wider context as foretastes, portions bestowed as advance gifts. But they must not narrow down and petrify the all-surrounding framework of the history of the one Spirit, or be used in an exclusive way.

The special stress on ordination and a sacred ministry – to the point of raising it to the rank of sacrament – apparently always crops up when the church goes over to the practice of infant baptism. The baptism of those who are not of age is always in danger of making the community spiritual babes too, for no special value in the sense of a call can be ascribed to infant baptism as such. Just as confirmation must supplement it, so too must ordination (if applicable), as the visible act of the call to a special ministry. But actually confirmation and ordination can only display and emphasize in visible terms what is already implicit in baptism both as a confession of faith and a call. In a congregation of baptized believers, baptism and confirmation coincide, and ordination approaches baptism directly, as the conferring of a special charge. It does not confer any higher dignity than baptism and merely gives specific form to the person's special call.

3. *The Form of the Church as Fellowship*

When the congregation gathers at the table, understands its own charge and confers special charges on its members, fellowship comes into being. How are we to interpret this new fellowship of believers with one another and for other people? Does it merely grow up by the way, beneath the word and at the sacraments, through the particular ministries? Or are word, sacraments and the special ministries directed towards the life of the new fellowship?

(i) *The Task: a Fellowship of Friends*

The Apostles' Creed talks about the 'communion of saints' immediately after it has mentioned the church. The *communio sanctorum* was interpreted in a twofold sense: it can mean, concretely, communion or fellowship in the sacred things, the sacraments. It can also mean, in personal terms, the fellowship of sanctified people, the called and the justified.[31] Whereas in the middle ages the phrase formulated in the neuter meant participation partly in the sacraments and partly in the merits of the saints, Luther understood it in personal terms. The *congregatio sanctorum* is the 'assembly', the 'congregation', 'Christian people', who live in mutual concern for one another and mutual self-giving. Article

VII of the Augsburg Confession therefore translates the expression *congregatio sanctorum* as 'the assembly of all believers'; but it defines this assembly solely through the event of the pure preaching of the gospel and the right use of the sacraments.[32] The assembly of believers and the event of the word and the sacraments constitute and interpret one another mutually. The Confession goes on to state that it is enough for the true unity of the church if it agrees in the proclamation of the gospel and the use of the sacraments. It is not necessary for there to be identical ceremonies everywhere, since these are introduced by men.[33] In the context of the conflict between the Reformed churches and the Roman Catholic churches at that time, this must be understood as an offer of unity. But for the closer definition of the fellowship of believers the statement is not sufficient. Word and sacrament certainly constitute the communion or fellowship; but this fellowship itself must be stressed in mutual concern and self-devotion. The terms 'communion of saints' and assembly of believers are not enough to express the fellowship of Christians with one another in the spirit of love.

That is why the third article of the Barmen Theological Declaration, while repeating the content of article VII of the Augsburg Confession, said, in place of *congregatio sanctorum*: 'The Christian church is the *community of brethren*'.[34] A 'community of brethren' lives in the spirit of brotherliness, showing its fellowship with God's Son, 'the first-born among many brethren' (Rom. 8.29), through a brotherly common life. This goes further than an assembly of believers for the purpose of proclaiming the gospel and partaking in the sacraments (although that is its source) and embraces the whole of life, our dealings with one another, our representation for others and our common actions. The 'community of brethren' means the new, visible way of life. In the New Testament this is often contrasted with social conditions in the surrounding world. In the community of brethren there is no more lordship or slavery: 'It shall not be so among you' (Matt. 20.26). In the community of brethren the greed for possessions and the claim to personal property come to an end: 'And all who believed were together and had all things in common; and they sold their possessions and goods and distributed them to all, as any had need. And day by day, [they attended] the temple together and [broke] bread in their homes' (Acts 2.44–46). In the community of brethren social, cultural, racial and sexual privileges lose their validity: 'You are all one in Christ Jesus . . . heirs according to promise' (Gal. 3.28f.). The community of brethren proclaims the kingdom of God through its way of life, which provides an alternative to the life of the world surrounding it.

The expression 'brotherliness' surmounts the language of rule and privilege, but it only extends to the male sex, although it is of course designed to reach further, and means the fellowship of all believers, both men and women, and the promised fellowship of all people on earth. For that reason the term friendship seems to be an apter expression for what is meant. Friendship is a free association. Friendship is a new relationship, which goes beyond the social roles of those involved. Friendship is an open relationship which spreads friendliness, because it combines affection with respect. The *congregatio sanctorum*, the community of brethren, is really the fellowship of friends who live in the friendship of Jesus and spread friendliness in the fellowship, by meeting the forsaken with affection and the despised with respect.[35] Its brothers and sisters cannot choose each other. Brotherliness is not terminable. Brother remains brother, even in conflict. We become friends by our own free decision and we look for our friends ourselves. Humanly speaking, friendship can be terminated. But life in the friendship of Jesus is rooted in the free giving of his life 'for his friends'. That is why even unfriendliness cannot destroy this friendship of Jesus. Those who belong to him remain in his friendship when they themselves become the friends of other people. The freedom out of which this friendship springs is therefore not a private and arbitrary affair; it is the liberation for new life itself, without which all the other freedoms cannot go on existing. The friendship to which this friendship leads is the 'practical concept of freedom' without which all other friendships become powerless. Compared with the concept of the friend, the concept 'brother' implies the inescapable destiny to brotherhood – even in conflicts. It makes brotherly love necessary. Compared with the concept of brother, the concept 'friend' stresses freedom. Rightly understood, the friend is the person who 'loves in freedom'.[36] That is why the concept of friendship is the best way of expressing the liberating relationship with God, and the fellowship of men and women in the spirit of freedom.

But how are fellowship and friendship realized in the church?

What form have they taken and what form can they take? The church grew up out of Christ's fellowship. Out of his fellowship it is born anew. The community of the brethren springs from the brotherhood of Christ, and from brotherliness it will acquire a new form. As friends they live from the friendship of Jesus. From the spirit of friendship they will form themselves anew. The church will not overcome its present crisis through reform of the administration of the sacraments, or from the reform of its ministries. It will overcome this crisis through the rebirth of practical fellowship. The reforms of evangelization and the administration of the sacraments, and the inescapable reform of the church's ministries, will spring from the rebirth of fellowship and friendship among the rank and file. The one certainly cannot take place without the other, but the starting point lies in the congregation and its form as fellowship. Fellowship in word and sacrament, fellowship in the profession of faith, fellowship in the institution and the hierarchy, become lifeless and are petrified into formalities with which people can no longer identify themselves, if fellowship among the congregation's rank and file is lost, and if friendship is not recovered from the 'grass-roots'.

(ii) The State Church and the Sects

Early Christianity began as 'the Nazarene heresy' (Acts 24.5, 14; 28.22) and was viewed as a religious school or party belonging to Judaism, like the Pharisees, Sadducees or Essenes.[37] It was only when Christianity went outside the frontiers of the Judaism of the synagogue that it acquired an independent form of its own. Christianity adopted the concept of the *ecclesia*, which originally meant the popular political assembly of full citizens. It saw itself neither as a Christian synagogue nor as one religious community among the many other cults of the ancient world. By calling itself *ecclesia* Christianity emerged as a *tertium genus* between the Jews and the Gentiles, and formed a community of its own. Christians emigrated in spirit and practice, both from the synagogue and from the popular, state and private religions, and formed something new: the church. By doing this they brought on themselves the reproach of sectarianism from the side of the synagogue, and the accusation of atheism from the Gentile side. But the early Jewish-Christian community, and the communities made up of both Jews and Gentiles that followed, soon became the genesis of purely

Gentile Christian communities. Mission and the spread of Christianity among the Gentiles therefore quickly led to the fundamental decision which we might call the decision in favour of a church open to the world. Because, apart from border regions, the inhabited world ruled by the Roman empire presented itself as 'the world' *per se*, the transition under Constantine to the church of the Roman empire was not understood as being a dangerous innovation, although the results were serious enough. To such a church, the Roman empire stood open for mission and the spread of Christianity. But for this the church was compelled to take over the role of the public state religion, which was politically necessary for the integration of the different peoples in the Roman empire.[38] The church became the religion of society and as such an integrated element in the social order. In Christianizing the Roman empire the church lost the particular and visible form of Christian society. The Christian community and the civil community coincided. Consequently the church was no longer organized in independent and voluntary fellowships; it was ordered according to regions and territories, sees and parishes, for the care and welfare of the people. The two things are closely connected. According to ancient social doctrine, the highest task of society is to show the gods of the *polis* the necessary reverence, since the country's welfare and peace is dependent on their favour. If the Christian church becomes the religious institution of the whole of society, it takes over this function, becoming the *cultus publicus* and the guardian of society's public rites. Its organization therefore adapts itself to the social organization. Church districts are ordered according to the residential areas in which people live. Its meetings are a part of public social life. The offices of clergy and bishops become authoritative in character. The faith of the people is then only practised through participation in the church's public meetings and events. Church fellowship becomes not so much fellowship *in* the church as fellowship *with* the church. The sacraments of the messianic fellowship – baptism and the Lord's supper – recede behind the clerical ministrations of infant baptism, confirmation, the marriage ceremony, and burial; or they are interpreted in the sense of being part of the pastoral care of the people.

This transition from the church open to the world to the imperial church still determines the church's structure and organization today in what were for long 'Christian' countries. It is true that, in opposition to it, the Reformation discovered the *congregational principle* and was also prepared to drop the expression 'church' in favour of 'congregation'. But the consolidation of the Reformation in Protestant state churches, and the religious wars that followed, led to a different principle: *cuius regio, eius religio.* Outwardly, this kept the warring confessions apart; but inwardly they became the political religions of their respective territories. The ruler, the state church and the state university determined the confessional allegeance of the unified state. The unity of the Christian community and the civil community remained. The long trail from the church which was a fellowship, open to the world, to the territorially and socially closed church, designed for the care of the whole people, still determines the present condition of Christianity in these countries. In the course of this development the special form of the church as a fellowship was lost, for there can be little talk about fellowship, brotherliness and friendship in this 'church for the whole people'.

From the very beginning, Christianity, which was itself termed a Jewish heresy, was familiar with heresies in its own domain, as Paul's letters show. There are frequent warnings about false prophets and teachers in the New Testament. But it was only with the establishment of the church of the empire that forcible measures were taken against heretics with the state's help. In our present context, the heresies and sects which fought against the imperial church are particularly important.[39] On its way to becoming the church of the empire, Christianity was forced to detach itself more and more from the conditions of its beginnings. That is why reforming sects grew up in the course of this development. These wanted the restoration of the congregation in its pure form and condemned the conformity to the world of the large-scale church in its self-assimilation to emperor and empire. On its way to becoming the church of the empire, Christianity surrendered the passion of its messianic hope. Hope was turned into the inner hope of the soul and its fulfilment was postponed to the next world. That is why the prophetic sects came into being in the course of this development. By virtue of their imminent expectation, these sects called people to resistance and denial of the world. And their criticism of 'the world' included the church in the world. Both types of sect cultivated an exceptional life of fellowship.

Their members were conscious of themselves as being the elect, and would rather suffer persecution than exclusion from their fellowship.

The reforming sects glorified the golden age of the primitive church and protested against the takeover of the church by the state. In these groups a direct relationship to Jesus through the charismatic experience of the Spirit was lived in a consistent ethic of discipleship. The sermon on the mount, interpreted as 'the law of Christ', permitted no compromises with state morality. The objective authority of the priest was challenged on the basis of the inner authority of the Spirit, and the value of the objective means of grace on the basis of personal faith. These fellowships saw the church of the empire not as the bride of Christ, but as the whore of Antichrist. In the dispute between the reforming sects and the mainstream church, the point at issue was 'the true church', the true fellowship of Jesus. There has never been an imperial, national or established church without these simultaneous alternatives provided by reforming sects active under the surface.

The prophetic sects did not go back from the decadent forms of Christianity to its pristine beginnings, but claimed to anticipate Christianity's consummation, beyond its beginnings and its history. The promise of the Spirit, who will finally accomplish the cause of Jesus, led to Christian spiritualism. From Montanus onwards, new prophets continually sprang up as the bearers of the Spirit promised by Christ. The promise of the kingdom of God, in which the church was to come to an end, led to Christian and post-Christian messianism. These sects see themselves as the forerunners of Christianity's self-realization in the Spirit and hence as the self-dissolution of the church in the kingdom of God. Because Christianity, by virtue of its messianic hope, points beyond itself and the church, prophetic and messianic sects always come to the fore whenever the church surrenders its hope for the coming kingdom. The conflict between the imperial church and the prophetic sects is the conflict about the authentic form of the Christian hope. There has never been an established church without the simultaneous existence of sects under the surface who have formulated this alternative.

The conflict between the mainstream church and the sects was never purely theoretical. In the age before Constantine it broke out in the Christian persecutions. The conflict about the true church,

Christian discipleship and faithfulness to the Christian hope was fought out in the different attitudes of the Christians who were persecuted by the state. The conflict also arose in the revolutions of the social structures to which the church had adapted itself. In the eleventh century, during the transition from feudalism to a middle-class society, lay reform movements sprang up in the towns of Lombardy and the south of France. The Cathars, Waldenses and Albigenses set up fellowship churches which, seeking to be consistent disciples of Jesus, rose against the alliance of pope and emperor. In the age of rising absolutism, the reforming and prophetic sects proliferated. With the flowering of bourgeois society from the beginning of the Enlightenment onwards, both types of sect became so common that they have become the hallmark of modern Christianity. Denominational situations, social revolutions and cultural changes are eroding the confidence of the 'pastoral' church; and the situation is apparently bringing those Christian fellowships which from the very beginning represented the alternative to mainstream Christianity out of obscurity and into the public eye.

The decision in favour of the universal church and the church of the empire has been a continual matter of dispute in Christianity. There has always been the one or the other alternative. In order to understand Christianity as a whole, therefore, it is useful to read church history and the history of the sects at the same time, and to see both forms of Christianity together. A Christianity that departs from its beginnings in order to adapt itself to the present-day state is bound to evoke the Christianity of reform. A Christianity that surrenders its messianic hope is bound to evoke the Christianity of prophecy. In the schism between the mainstream church and the sects, the church itself becomes sectarian, because it represses fundamental elements of the Christian truth. On the other hand, both the reforming and the prophetic sects, with their criticism of the church's worldliness, always repress the elements of Christian mission and love which are open to the world. If we see it in this way, however, the conclusion to be drawn cannot lie in a sum of the different elements of truth, but only in the design of a form of Christ's church as a fellowship which is authentic in the present. The dissolution of the one church of Christ in a multiplicity of sects is no answer to this question, for the major churches and the sects live from their mutual conflict and hinder the development of an authentic fellowship of Christ just because of it.

(ii) The World Church and the Religious Communities

Early Christianity gathered together as a church under the apostolic proclamation of the gospel. The gospels, however, tell the story of the earthly Jesus, who called his followers to discipleship and a common life, and demanded of them that they break with all other social ties (Matt. 10.3ff.).[40] The call to the new community of the risen Christ and the call to discipleship of the Christ who was crucified, the call to the new people of God and the call to the discipleship of Jesus are heard with equal distinctness in Christ's proclamation and must be realized in one and the same mode of life.[41] This became more difficult in the degree in which the congregations grew. That is why asceticism and the eremitical form of the Christian life grew up side by side with the decision for the church open to the world. Examples of a discipleship of Jesus demonstrated through renunciation of the world are to be found from the very beginning in the Christian communities. Christianity has always existed in both forms of life: as a world-wide church, and in the consistent discipleship of Jesus. Here the example of the disciples – 'We have left everything and followed you' (Matt. 19.27) – worked as a critical leaven in the church as a whole. The early wandering ascetics (Didache 11.5ff.) saw themselves as Jesus' disciples and became the vehicles of mission. In their homelessness they followed the fate of the Son of man. Their celibacy gave them freedom to devote themselves completely to the service of Christ. Taking the sermon on the mount as their rule, they sought absolute righteousness in undivided self-surrender to the mission for which Christ sent them forth.

The Christian hermits left the inhabited world, in accordance with the model of St Antony, in order to take up the fight with the demons, like Jesus 'in the wilderness', and to win access to the heavenly world. Their flight from the world was intended as part of this struggle. Pachomius inspired the first forms of the communal life in monasteries. Common worship, common property, common meals, common prayer and work regulated the life of these Christian communes. Although non-Christian ideas deriving from stoicism, gnosticism and Manichaeism were to be found in early Christian monasticism, the essential impulse none the less came from the picture of the fellowship of the disciples as it is depicted in the gospels. The monastic life in complete poverty, complete obedience, complete continence and unceasing worship realized fellowship with Christ more clearly than did mere participation in the public activities of the church by the bulk of its members. In the West the monasteries became the centre of church life and church order. Whereas the itinerant monks carried on the work of Christian mission, the monastic communities worked for the Christianization of the people through instruction, pastoral care and education. This was the great importance of the 'stability of residence' required of the monks by Benedict of Nursia in the unquiet times of the barbarian invasions. From the time of the Cluniac reform in the tenth century, the orders also worked for the liberation of the church from the domination of territorial rulers and the Christian emperor. The mediaeval struggle for the freedom of the church was primarily carried on by the monasteries. In this struggle the celibacy of the clergy took on political importance, because it made undivided obedience to church and pope possible. The 'common life' of the monasteries also had its effect on the laity. Religious lay brotherhoods grew up which took over the economic form of common property from the monasteries. Other lay brotherhoods devoted themselves to the care of the sick or the poor, burial and other social needs. In the towns 'the brethren of the common life' formed cells of Christian communes.

In the eleventh century the demands for evangelical poverty and consistent discipleship were raised by the Cathars and Waldenses to a norm for life in Christian communities; though they were forced to put their ideas into practice outside the structure of the mainstream church and in opposition to the political powers. The mendicant orders then picked up these ideas and put them into practice among the lay members of the church. The ideals of simple discipleship and a common life were introduced among the people as a whole in order to bring the laity into full membership of the church. Thus the call to follow Jesus and the call to full commitment to the common life through the religious orders and monasteries had their effect on the rest of the church too, continually stimulating new reforms of the form of the church as a fellowship. Whatever ideas about an élite group may have been bound up with this 'more excellent way' to Christian perfection (compared with the ways of simple believers), as far as the historical development goes, the hermits and coenobites, the wandering ascetics, the monastic communities and the lay brotherhoods must be seen as innovatory groups in the mainstream church. Without them the church open to the world would probably have been transformed without resistance into the religion of a society. But through this consistently lived discipleship, resistance in the name of the Christ crucified by the ruling powers, and hope for the world-transforming kingdom of God, remained alive in it.

The Reformation brought monasticism and the monastic life to a crisis which in Protestant countries led to its dissolution altogether. The reason for this was not the decay of monastic discipline but the Reformers' doctrine of justification: every baptized Christian, every believer, is called to the status of a true Christian. Consequently there are not two different ways of Christian existence. Justifying faith puts an end to the difference in status between the laity and the monastic orders. Every Christian receives his calling from his call, alike in worldly affairs and in his tasks in the church. The call to discipleship, to the common life and to special ministries, which the religious orders claimed for themselves, therefore applies to the whole church. The principle of the single Christian community grew up in place of the two ways of Christian life, in the monastery and the world. The rejection of monasticism and the monastic life at the Reformation was not intended to lead to the secularization of Christianity. On the contrary, it saw itself as the sharpest attack on the world. Discipleship, asceticism and brotherhood were to be lived in the midst of the world, not separated from it. Yet the Reformation churches, apart from 'the churches under the cross' and refugee communities, have hardly been able to realize the principle of the voluntary congregation. The clear and concerted rejection of monasticism and the cloistered life did not correspond to an equally clear and concerted rejection of the territorial church designed for the care of the whole people. It did not succeed in surmounting the double form of Christian life, or in creating the community as a single, simple way of life. The established Protestant churches, against their will, became more deeply dependent on society and the ruling authorities than before. The alternative to established Christianity, represented by radical discipleship groups, was lacking. It was the Pietist revival movement which first attempted a reforming renewal of the established Protestant churches in Germany.

It follows from this brief historical survey that the more Christianity develops ways of life appropriate to a national or established church, the more it is dependent on the existence and example of radical discipleship groups. In churches which are organized accolding to political territories, a person belongs to the church by virtue of his birth. But discipleship and the common life are a matter for voluntary decision. 'Establishment' Christianity can only be lived by making a compromise with family, professional, social and political laws and duties. What is lived in the Christian communes is the attempt at uncompromising self-surrender. In the parishes of the established church it is hard to put Christian brotherhood and friendship into practice, because people hardly know each other and only trust and confide in one another in crises and emergencies. But in communities of a surveyable size, people's individual potentialities and powers can be released and activated. In the 'parishes' and 'pastorates' of the church which provides 'welfare', those who have no authority are kept in leading strings by means of one-sided communication from 'the top'; and this is hard to overcome. In 'fellowships', discussion between the members and mutual sympathy and participation stands in the forefront.

The world-wide church has always seen itself as a power immanent within the governing system, a power for Christianizing the people and changing the conditions in which it lives; and in this respect it was unable to get along without compromises. In world-wide Christianity this has often enough led to the church's suspension of the sermon on the mount. If it is impossible to rule a country by means of the sermon on the mount (as Bismarck said) then it is also hard to live by the sermon on the mount in a political state. Churches on a national scale are compelled to make concordats with society and the state if they want to operate publicly. Moreover, they must adapt themselves to the average opinion prevailing among their members. Consequently they are relatively inflexible. The church has always had its 'heroes', but there has not often been a 'heroic church' (K. Rahner). For its orientation towards Christ and the kingdom of God, the world-wide church needs the example of the groups committed to consistent discipleship, which demonstrate the liberty of Christ more unhesitatingly than church leaders and more radically than the masses. Every power of alteration which is immanent in a given system needs orientation towards an alternative which transcends that system. So as long as large-scale church organizations exist, we have to reckon with alternative forms of the Christian life. They and their criticism must be recognized by the established churches. They must not be pushed into the underground as irregular fringe groups. They are of quite vital importance for the mainstream churches, and must be accepted as 'pacemakers'. But on the other hand every alternative that transcends the given system – an alternative based on renunciation of the world and on resistance – remains ineffective if it is not related to the forces of alteration immanent in the system itself. Regulated discipleship groups and spontaneous movements for Christian action are putting themselves in a social ghetto of their own accord if they do not want to have a reforming effect on church and society. Without the large-scale churches these groups have no basis in the rank and file. Unless it affects the church which is open to the world, the practice of denying the world loses its relationship to the world altogether. The organizations of the mainstream church should not therefore attempt to bring these groups under their own control. To do so would be to destroy the forces of their own renewal. But these groups must not deny the mainstream church and emigrate from it altogether. To do so would be to rob themselves of their own destiny. The mainstream churches and the discipleship groups remain dependent on one another in a kind of double strategy until the community principle can be realized.

(iv) Double Strategies and the Community Principle

There is nothing new about the fact that the major territorial churches have today arrived at a crisis. The established churches of old do, it is true, still possess a large organization for the care of the people, with trained experts for many different ministries; but they have less and less hold on the people. Indifference towards the church is growing; the silent falling away is spreading. People's identification with this church is diminishing step by step. Church services are attended less and less. People are leaving the established church, in Germany because of the church tax, or for other really non-essential reasons. The church's chances of influencing society are visibly lessening. The clergy no longer feel themselves 'supported' by their congregations and are often fighting a lonely battle to 'get at' people. In many churches the number of new applicants for ordination no longer covers the needs of the parishes and congregations. The population's mobility in the industrial countries, and mass immigration to the new cities of the developing countries, are making the territorially organized 'welfare' church increasingly ineffective. The more people are educated and the more independent they are, the less they can put up with their merely passive role of listener and onlooker in church services. Even in the village the old unity of civil community and Christian community is beginning to break up.

These symptoms of recession in the church would have to be described solely in terms of crisis if corresponding counter-movements were not also becoming evident in Christianity. Although the quantity of the church's life is less, in many churches we can discover a new and increasing quality in the Christian life. It is true that the number of church-goers is diminishing, but the number of communicants is growing. The number of passive members is decreasing, but the number of active participants in religious seminars, theological courses, spiritual exercises and retreats is on the increase, as well as the number of people who are engaged in charitable activity and liturgical, pastoral, social and political work in their communities. The 'pastoral' church is losing its effectiveness and its capacity for influencing and directing the whole of Christian life; but to the same degree processes of growing independence are apparently developing, and many Christians are grasping chances of personal responsibility. The erosion within the established church (which is intended to embrace the whole of the people) is being balanced out by 'a market of potentialities' for free and specific Christian commitment in many problematical spheres of life.[42] Is this already the beginning of a therapy for the crisis of the established church? Will this development lead to the replacement of the traditional, national church by a voluntary fellowship church? Does this mean that Christianity is taking the self-chosen path into the social ghetto of 'the little flock'?

The first attempts to answer the crises of the 'territorial' church came through *church reform from above*. The programmes 'church for the world', 'church for others' and 'church for the people' were intended to open the institutions of the state church for people's new needs. The intention, indeed, was that the church should be freed from concern about its institutional survival in order to turn without reserve to the needs of men and women. But as the

formulas show, those concerned still started from a division between the church and 'the others', 'the world' and 'the people', and
then went on to try to overcome this gap. The undertones of 'the
élite' are clearly audible. The church approached the changed
situation with action programmes for mission to the people and
charitable work. Pastoral functions were specialized, and specialized pastorates were grouped together. Special pastorates for
hospitals, prisons, radio, television, the armed forces, the police,
seamen, men, women, young people, mission, the ecumenical
movement, charitable work, and so forth, grew up. The presence
of the church – that is, the official church – was split up in accordance with the differentiation of modern life. This church reform
started from a reform of the church's ministries, not from the
community. If the church is still to be conceived as a church for
the care of the people, then these adaptations to people's differentiated needs are inescapable. But it can hardly be said that these endeavours have brought people back into the church, or have really
brought the church to the people. The lethargy of the large number of passive church members has seldom been overcome. It is
often even increased, because their own responsibility is taken from
them even further by full-time church workers. But on the other
hand the very differentiation from above of what the church has to
offer has released processes of growing independence on the part
of the people who are involved 'at the bottom'; and these have led
to a multiplicity of new groupings.

It is true that the impression of the established churches remains,
that the privatization of the Christian life on the one hand and the
institutionalization of the national and other large churches on the
other mutually condition and strengthen one another, and threaten
the real life of the actual individual congregation. But between the
individual and the organizations of these large churches (which the
individual simply cannot survey as a whole) there is also a wealth of
interest, participation and commitment in fields whose extent can
be seen and grasped.

Other attempts at entering into the crises of ecclesiastical insti-
tuitions come from *reform of the community from below*. There is a
wide diversity of attempts and approaches here, but we will pick
out as examples the 'grass-roots communities' and community
work. In recent years 'grass-roots communities' have grown up
almost simultaneously in different countries and denominations.[43]

Their centre of gravity is Latin America. Brazilian experiments with such communities, which have achieved a lay apostolate for evangelization and adult instruction, were the genesis of a movement that is spreading over the whole continent. There are individual parishes which have more than forty such communities within their area. These communities fill with their own life areas which are merely delimited by the organized church. The second General Assembly of the Latin American episcopate at Medellin in 1968 judged these communities as follows:

> The 'grass-roots' community is the primary, fundamental core of the church. On its own level it must take responsibility for the riches of faith and for its propagation, as well as for the cult, which brings faith to expression. It is consequently the initial cell of the church's structure, the focus of evangelization, and at present the main point of departure for man's improvement and development.[44]

The characteristics of such communities are hard to sum up, because they vary so much. But the following seem to be essential to all of them:

1. The voluntary association of members in a Christian fellowship.
2. The fellowship of a manageable size, in which life in mutual friendship and common devotion to a specific task is possible.
3. The awakening of creative powers in every individual and the surrender of privileges that members bring with them.
4. Autonomy in forming the spiritual life of the community and its life of fellowship.
5. Common concentration on special Christian tasks in society, whether it be in the field of evangelization, or the liberation of the under-privileged and oppressed.
6. The deliberate return to a simple Christo-centricism in the devotional life and to a reflection of new Christian practice in theology.

Many of these communities are led by laymen, occasionally helped by a priest. Most of them are to be found among the poor, a few in the middle-class milieu, and none at all in upper-class areas. They began with common services of worship and preaching, common prayer and mutual help; but now the sacraments are celebrated in these fellowships as well. They seem to be influenced both by the charismatic Pentecostal movements and by cultural, social and political movements existing among the people. In these communities people are the subject of their own Christian fellowship. In place of 'the church for the people' we have the beginnings of 'the church of the people', which lives, suffers and acts among the people themselves and with them.[45] The Argentinian episcopate has therefore declared in its 'Medellin Conclusions':

> The church has to examine its liberating, salvation-creating action from the point of view of the people and their interests. . . . Consequently the action of the church should not merely be directed *towards* the people but should also, and above all, permit itself to be directed *by* the people.[46]

These 'grass-roots' communities have been called 'a prophetic leaven' for the renewal of church and society. People have talked about the 'bricks for the church of tomorrow'. If they have the chance to be this, then the 'grass-roots' must not be put at the service of the organization of the established church; the latter must be put at the service of the former.[47] As long as these communities do not remain in a state of complete flux, or become élitist sects, they really do have the chance to overcome the double form of the Christian life of fellowship as we have described it, and to live the simple 'communion of saints' – or fellowship of believers – in a convincing way through open friendship among the people. They can avoid the danger of esoteric self-isolation by living down on the people's level. If they really offer people the common opportunity for friendship free of domination, in which they can find themselves and their own creative potentialities and emerge from their loneliness, helplessness and dependency – then these communities will be letting the people become the subject of their own history in the liberating history of God.[48] In this case they will not be the bricks for a church of an élite; they will be the bricks for a people's church worthy of the name. Just as in the seventeenth century the Calvinist 'right to community' (compared with the state and the state church) provided motive power for the democratic development of the political polity, so the 'grass-roots' communities among the people can provide impulses for a fundamental and democratic social reconstruction.[49] So that we may arrive at this point, it is important for these communities to develop a new theological concept of the church and its tasks in the social process. Without a concept of this kind it can easily lose itself in particularist actions and fall a victim to either sectarian or political movements.

The community work which was originally developed in American and English slums as ways of community organization shows parallels to the 'grass-roots' communities in the social and political sphere, and can also be drawn on as an aid in reforming the church from below.[50] Its activity has led to the citizens' action groups which have become popular in Germany, though the two things are not identical. 'The concept of community work is the term for a process, in the course of which a community determines its needs and goals, orders them, or brings them into a sequence of priorities; develops the confidence and the will to do something about them; mobilizes inward and outward resources in order to satisfy the needs facing it – is, in fact, active, in this direction and in this way encourages the attitudes of co-operation and common endeavour, and their actual practice.'[51] Community work aims to put people in a position where they can shape their fortunes for themselves, through initiatives for self-help, in the local sphere, and where they can acquire influence on the wider processes of planning and decision. In this way, in manageable areas and problems of limited extent, people will cease to be an object of planning and administration and will become the subject of their own lives. Community work does not aim to be a new form of welfare work. It wants to be a help to self-help. Its actions reach from the organization of new residential areas, measures to improve the living conditions of the homeless, actions in the educational field (kindergartens, schools and adult education), down to consumer boycotts, rent strikes, electoral initiatives and protests against the building of nuclear power stations. Wherever a community begins to determine its fortunes for itself, a new consciousness of their own dignity and their own strength grows up among the people involved. The passive, subservient attitude towards 'the people at the top' gives way to an independent sense of freedom and responsibility. Community work might therefore be formally defined as 'the technique of activation and participation'.[52] But a definition of this kind remains an abstraction. In the case of every action we have to ask who is exerting his energies for whom and for what. Civil initiatives can act progressively for more freedom and personal initiative, and they can also be reactionary and minister to the egoistical personal interests of property-owners and the well-to-do. They can be mobilized in favour of the homeless, and against them; in favour of the handicapped, and against them. Consequently, though in the citizen action groups people are discovering their own power and dignity (which is essential for man's humanity) and are finding fulfilment of life's meaning, in a local and limited but none the less specific way, these things must be set in the wider context of the conflicts and hopes of society as a whole. Spontaneity and self-realization, as they are experienced here, only anticipate a more human society if they are won, not in the face of other people but with others and for them. Here conflict among the rank and file must be expected. Without a total social perspective community work loses itself in pragmatism, and citizens' action groups remain ambivalent. But without the initiatives in the local, direct sphere these perspectives remain abstract and empty.

In the field of community work it is important, if the situation permits, for the church's congregations to accept and participate in the specific actions of community work as their own. The concept of the charismatic community leads in this direction, for there everyone finds his assignments, and no sphere of life is left without the practical witness of liberating action. On the other hand community workers in the church of Christ will see their own challenging activities in the context of the gospel and hope for the kingdom. Community work helps the church that understands itself as a community to commit itself as community on behalf of the people and among them. It can preserve the local church from threatening self-isolation and remind it of its practical apostolate.

The different approaches of church reform from above and from below are often combined at the congregational level in a kind of double strategy. Through a deepened growth of faith and through the growth of fellowship and social practice, core groups are built up in the parishes. Unlike the people on the fringe of the church, they are prepared to identify themselves strongly with the church. These core communities and core groups are expected to give new life to the congregations of the established church and at the same time to strike out new paths linking the church to society as a whole. But at the same time the established church of old days is preserved because it is open to the whole people and also includes passive members, fringe members, and the Christians who only go to church on major festivals. The established church seems to keep the threshold of entry low because – by virtue of infant baptism and the Christian cultural tradition – it reckons with almost all members of society. If Christianity were to tie itself down to the congregation in a one-sided way the church's openness to the world would be threatened. The voluntary church, with its willing members, would almost inevitably involve the condemnation of the unwilling. But if one is prepared for this form of double strategy, it is almost impossible to do justice to either of the two forms of Christianity's life. Wherever the activities of the core groups are at all unusual, they will be hindered by the silent majority in the established church. On the other hand, a parish will see new hierarchical groupings of laymen springing up from the core to the fringe, according to the measure of these people's identification with the church. And if in this way we make identification with the church the classifying criterion, we are really back in the old official church pattern, in which the priest or pastor comes to stand at the innermost core of Christianity. Identification with the church then becomes graduated participation in the functions of the particular ministry which represents the church's identity. When we talk about a double strategy we must ultimately ask about the direction the strategy is to take. Is the activation of the congregation to serve the traditional church organizations, or vice versa?

On the theological level the double strategy is popularly formulated in the double ecclesiological concept of 'the church as an institution' and 'the church as an event'. But the two are related to one another with the help of the notion of complementarity.[53] 'The church as an event', as fellowship and action, needs the church as an institution, because of its historical continuity and the extra-territorial solidarity of its groups. On the other hand 'the church as an institution' needs 'the church as an event' because of its practical vitality. Of course this is merely a notional and typical allocation of characteristics. The concepts which are reconciled with one another in this complementary way (such as institution and event) do not coincide with any reality. There are no institutions without events and no events without institutions. One might as well try first to divide the static and the dynamic from one another, and then to relate them to each other again, as being complementary. Like other social institutions, the church is a living process. Basically this theological and conceptual terminology merely reflects the problematical situation of the traditional, national churches. To use these terms really means to enquire about the building up of independent communities capable of

acting independently under the conditions and continued main-
tainance of the territorial church. For communities that live under
the conditions of non-Christian national and state religions, this
question does not arise. The double ecclesiology – the church as an
institution and an event – corresponds to the double strategy
practised. It partakes of the indecisiveness of the double strategy
we have mentioned, because the complementarity striven for lacks
direction, intention and definite trend. In this question the decision
cannot be a pragmatic one. It must be a theological decision, which
can be put into practice under the given historical conditions of
what is possible.

The present crises of the territorial churches and the therapy
from below which is just beginning point to their initial lack: lack
of cultivated fellowship. But the *ecclesia* is, by definition and
nature, the community that gathers together. 'The visible coming
together of visible people in a special place to do something
particular'[54] stands at the centre of the church. Without the actual,
visible procedure of meeting together there is no church. That is
why everything in the church is concentrated on this procedure.
Where the community gathers round the gospel and the Lord's
table, it becomes recognizable in the world and unmistakably the
people of Christ, the messianic community of the coming kingdom.
In and through its actual assemblies it is free from those political
powers and laws which the Barmen Declaration, article II, assigned
to 'the godless ties of this world'. In the fellowship of Christ it
becomes a community capable of action. The facts are simple
enough: without assembly no fellowship, without fellowship no
freedom, without freedom no capacity for action. Because the
invitation of the gospel and the invitation to the messianic banquet
are open, and reach further than the group of those who are
assembled, this group can never form a closed circle. It is open,
and will practise this openness for other people through evangelization and practical acts of liberation. If the assembled community
were not to be an 'open church' it would neither be the church of
Christ nor the people of the coming kingdom. But if its openness to
the world meant that it no longer gathered together, then it would
not be a community or a people. There is no need for the institution of a general, established church in order to practise the openness of the gospel and of love. Its unqualified openness for everyone
has only a remote connection with the qualified openness of Christ

and the kingdom of God. Nor is it as such the institutional form of God's prevenient grace or the visible expression of the forgiveness of the sins of the whole people. The congregation, on the other hand, is very well able to avoid seeing itself as the elect company of 'the children of light' which condemns 'the children of darkness' and cuts itself off from them. It is certainly able to turn to others, and especially the underprivileged and rejected, in evangelically defined openness. The problematical conditions of the established church can hardly be justified by pointing to the dangers of an élitist or voluntary church. A congregation must by no means exclude the passive, fringe members or degrade them to the level of mere 'fellow-travellers'. The principle of the committed congregation seems to me, not an easy but perhaps a hopeful solution, as a direction for the double strategy and double ecclesiologies, which today, and in Germany, are unavoidable. Church reforms and church reconstruction will begin at the point where people in congregations of manageable size hear, discuss and profess the gospel; where, at the Lord's table, they become friends and perform their tasks in mutual sympathy and co-operation. Of course conflicts will arise here too, but then they are conflicts in the proper place. The restriction of faith to private life leads to the powerlessness of the individual's faith and is a continual source of doubt. Church organizations above the local level deprive the individual congregations of their independence, and often of their own responsibility. They lead to an abstract unity which, when it actually comes to the point, cannot put up any resistance. Individuals and church organizations can really only find themselves in one place: in the committed congregation. It is only in the committed congregation that Christianity becomes capable of action and resistance. That is a matter of experience. The committed congregation is not an 'event' without an 'institution', any more than it is an 'institution' without an 'event'. It lives both in tradition with the church at all times and in communication with the church at all places. Not the isolated Christian and not the huge, lavish 'pastoral' church, but the congregation gathered together in the openness of Christ, which everyone can see as his own affair: this is the living hope in the conflicts of society today – living hope, because it is also lived and enlivening hope.

1. Church reform from above, which begins with the church's ministries, can serve the committed congregation if it relates these

ministries to the one common ministry of the congregation. It will make the build-up of the living congregational church its priority, not the extension of supra-regional offices.

2. The 'grass-roots' communities and community work supplement one another mutually in the committed congregation, which is conscious of the fullness of its creative powers for the kingdom of God. They would be surrendering their own best intentions if they did not make use of Christianity's right to community. They are to be seen as a stimulus, not as a substitute for the gathered congregation.

3. Whether the double strategies and the double ecclesiologies will one day dissolve in favour of the one, common form of Christian life in the committed congregation, depends ultimately, not merely on what Christianity wants, but also on the state of the society in which Christianity is involved. In a 'closed society' the reforming forces and the forces of mystical negation in Christianity will present themselves in twofold form. In an open society, the committed congregation can live its life without double strategies of this kind. We shall therefore only be able to realize the right to the committed congregation if we press for an 'open society' at the same time. The goal of all strategies is the building up of mature responsible congregation.

4. If the trends within the church take their bearings from the committed congregation, then there will be an ecumenical convergence between the churches in 'Christian' countries and the churches in 'non-Christian' countries. The conditions under which the congregation becomes effective are different, but the direction of this practical effect will then be the same. That is of considerable importance for what goes on ecumenically and in the church all over the world.

VII

THE MARKS OF THE CHURCH

1. *The One, Holy, Catholic and Apostolic Church*

The Apostles' Creed acknowledges the 'one, holy, catholic church'. The Nicene-Constantinopolitan Creed (dating from the Council of Constantinople in 381) talks about the 'one, holy, catholic and apostolic church'. The true church is described in these three or four attributes. But how are we to understand them? Are they meant to be the church's essential elements? Are they the church's landmarks? Are they the criteria for the church's truth? Are they the church's own credal marks for the kingdom of God in the world? And if they are to be interpreted in this light, do these four attributes characterize the church completely?

These questions are important for the fellowship of the different churches.[1] They are more important still for the visible form of the church in the world.[2] If we see them as the conditions (*criteria*) of the true church, then we look for what distinguishes it from the false church, and ask what the premises are for fellowship between the different churches. If we see them as the signs (*signa*) or characteristics (*notae*) of the church, then we ask about the form by which it can be recognized in the world and their character as testimony. It is therefore important to substantiate these statements about the church theologically and fully if we are to legitimate their use and avoid one-sidedness.

(i) The statements about the church are a component part of the creed. They are made by faith, and unless they are made in faith they lose their meaning. They are integrated components of the confession of the triune God, and cannot be detached from this context. They belong to the article about faith in the Holy Spirit, and are only justified and comprehensible in the framework of the creative workings of that Spirit. This distinguishes the 'characteristics' of the church named here from the characteristics of any other object of experience. We can only know them for signs through perception in which we are inwardly and actively involved. They make sense if we see the church in the context of the divine history in which the acknowledgment of the triune God puts it. They are consequently not merely distinguishing marks, but credal marks as well. They are not the characteristics of an object *per se*; they are characteristics which this object receives through a history external to itself. The church receives the attributes named from the activity of Christ in the workings of the Spirit for the coming kingdom. But as these extend and link together, the attributes become the inalienable signs of the true church, which is to say the church in the truth of God.

(ii) If the church acquires its existence through the activity of Christ, then her characteristics, too, are characteristics of Christ's activity first of all. The acknowledgment of the 'one, holy, catholic and apostolic church' is acknowledgment of the uniting, sanctifying, comprehensive and commissioning lordship of Christ. In so far they are *statements of faith*. 'The *unity* of the church is not primarily the unity of her members, but the unity of Christ who acts upon them all, in all places and at all times.'[3] Christ gathers his church. Consequently the unity of the church lies in his uniting activity. The result of his gathering activity is the unity of believers in Christ (Gal. 3.28) and their unity of mind in the Spirit (Eph. 4.1ff.). The *holiness* of the church is not initially the holiness of her members or her cultic assemblies; it is the holiness of the Christ who acts on sinners. Christ sanctifies his church by justifying it. Consequently the holiness of the church lies in his sanctifying activity. The result of his justifying activity is 'the communion of saints'. The *catholicity* of the church is not initially her spatial extent or the fact that she is in principle open to the world; it is the limitless lordship of Christ, to whom 'all authority is given in heaven and on earth'. Where, and so far as, Christ rules, there, consequently, the church is to be found. She acquires her openness to the world in the breadth of his rule. 'She is catholic on the strength of the catholicity of her Lord, which is imputed to her.'[4] Her *apostolic character* is also to be understood in the framework of the mission of Christ and the Spirit. Founded by Christ's apostles in the Spirit, her charge is the apostolate in the world. As the church of Christ the church is bound to be the one, holy, catholic and apostolic church.

(iii) If the church acquires her existence from Christ's messianic mission and the eschatological gift of the Spirit, then her characteristics are messianic predicates at the same time. In so far these are *statements of hope*. The *unity* of the church is a 'predicate of the time of salvation',[5] for in the Old Testament the restoration of the unity of God's people and the unity of mankind are prophetic promises. The Messiah of the last days will 'gather' those who have been dispersed, unite the divided and bring about the kingdom of peace. As the Messiah of the time of salvation Christ gathers and unites Jews and Gentiles, Greeks and barbarians, masters and slaves, men and women, making them the new people of the *one* kingdom. According to the prophetic promise, *holiness* is part of the inmost nature of the coming divine glory that is going to fill the earth. 'The Holy One of Israel' will redeem his people. When the church is called 'holy' in the New Testament, this means that it has become the new creation in Christ and therefore partakes of the holiness of the new creation, which the holy God brings about through his Spirit. The church is holy because it is the 'community of the last days'. The apostles and the church's *apostolate* belong to the beginning of the messianic era, like the gospel and evangelization. Finally, the church is catholic to the extent in which it partakes of the *catholicity* of the coming kingdom. In its openness for the kingdom of God it is also open to the world, encompassing it with its mission and intercession. The four characteristics of the church are therefore to be seen as messianic predicates of the church in the perspective of the coming kingdom, for which it exists and which in the church acquires form and testimony. As the church of the kingdom of God, the church is bound to be the one, holy, catholic and apostolic church.

(iv) If the characteristics of the church are statements of faith and hope, they also lead to *statements of action*. Because in Christ the church is one, it ought *to be* one.[6] Those who receive its unity in Christ ought to seek its unity. The one people of the one kingdom ought to lay the foundations of unity among men. Because in Christ the church is holy, its members ought to fight sin and sanctify its life through righteousness. Because they are sanctified through the Spirit, they ought in obedience to sanctify all things for the new creation. Because in Christ it is open to the world, it ought to be catholic, testifying everywhere to the all-embracing kingdom. As the church of the Spirit, the one church is the unifying church. The holy church is the church that sanctifies or makes holy. The catholic church is the peace-giving, and so the all-embracing, church. The apostolic church is – through the gospel – the liberating church in the world.

The church's essential nature is given, promised and laid upon it in the characteristics we have named. Faith, hope and action are the genesis of the form of the church visible to the world in unity, holiness, catholicity and apostolicity. That is why theology cannot withdraw to 'the invisible church', 'the church of the future', or 'the church of pure demands'. The church lives in the one, holy, catholic and apostolic rule of Christ through faith, hope and action.

(v) Although the creed limits itself to these three or four marks of the church, this has never been seen in history as a restriction, but always as a pointer to the essentials. Theological doctrines of the church therefore include a wealth of other signs. Luther, for example, named seven: (i) the preaching of the true word of God; (ii) the right administration of baptism; (iii) the right form of the Lord's supper; (iv) the power of the keys; (v) the rightful calling and ordination of the church's ministers; (vi) prayer and hymn-singing in the vernacular; (vii) suffering and persecution.[7] The church's creeds, however, always stopped short at the four classical attributes. These are undoubtedly the essential ones. But it must be noted that they were formulated and laid down for the first time at the great imperial synods of the early church and we therefore have to see them in the context of the church's development into the church of the empire. At that period there was considerable political pressure for the church's unity and universality, so that it might be in a position to administer the unified religion for the Roman empire. To make this historical observation is not to deny the truth of these statements about the church. But it gives us liberty to move other marks of the true church into the foreground in a changed world situation, and to link these with the traditional ones.

Theological recognition is not in itself a creed. It is not therefore bound to the formulated creed either. We shall permit ourselves to add other characteristics to the theological interpretation of the classical marks of the true church and to show their essential connection with the latter today. The church's unity is its *unity in freedom*. The church's holiness is its *holiness in poverty*. The church's apostolicity bears *the sign of the cross*, and its catholicity is linked with its *partisan support for the oppressed*.

(vi) Finally, we must draw attention to a denominational difference in the doctrine about the marks of the church (*notae ecclesiae*) which grew up in the Reformation period. The Reformers did not reject the four attributes of the church, but they saw the marks of the true church in the pure – i.e., scriptural – proclamation of the gospel and the right administration of the sacraments; that is to say, an administration in accordance with the charge to the church and the promises conferred on it. It is these signs of the church which make it the church, practically speaking, for they are its real foundations. They cannot therefore be set up contrary to the four other predicates, any more than these can be set up against these two signs. A church in which the gospel is purely preached and the sacraments are rightly used is the one, holy, catholic and apostolic church. The two Reformation signs of the church really only show from within what the traditional attributes of the church describe from without, so to speak. Without the pure proclamation there is no messianic church, gathered together for unity in Christ. Without the fellowship of the table and the one baptism the church has no catholicity. But then the reverse is true as well: without unity, holiness, catholicity and apostolicity there is no pure proclamation and no right use of the sacraments. There is no real difference here; there is only a mutual complementing. The four attributes of the church point to the proclamation and the sacraments and cannot be maintained apart from them. But word and sacrament point to the church's four attributes and cannot be purely and rightly ordered without the fellowship which faith sees as having these attributes.

The matter only becomes difficult – because more controversial – when the one, holy, catholic church gathered round word and sacrament considers its situation in our divided, fought over, unjust, inhuman world.[8] Is not the Christ proclaimed in the church the one who preaches the gospel to the poor? Is not the Christ of its Eucharist also the brother of the one who is persecuted outside the church? What form is to be taken by Christ in the church in a world of hostility? By the church sanctified in the Spirit in a world of poverty? By the catholic church as it testifies to the kingdom in a world of violence? By the apostolic church in the world of the cross? Is the situation in which the church finds itself in this society not bound to stamp it with the signs of poverty, suffering, liberation and partisanship? If the church were to ignore its social and political *Sitz im Leben* – its situation in the life of mankind – then it would be forsaking the cross of its Lord and would be turning into the illusionary church, occupied merely with itself. We cannot therefore merely give the marks of the church bearings that tend in an inward direction, understanding them in the light of word and sacrament; we must to the same degree give them an outward direction and see them in reference to the world. They are not merely important for the internal activities of the church; they are even more important for the witness of the church's form in the world. The marks of the church will then become confessional signs in the conflicts which today are really splitting and dividing mankind. Let us therefore extend the ecclesiology of tradition, which is orientated towards unity, into an ecclesiology oriented towards conflict in the world situation of today.

2. *Unity in Freedom*

(i) The unity of the church is experienced first of all in the gathered congregation.[9] The congregation is gathered through proclamation and calling. It gathers for the one baptism (Eph. 4.5; I Cor. 12.13) and for the common Lord's supper (I Cor. 12.13; 10.17). It lives in the spirit of mutual acceptance (Rom. 15.7) and maintains the unity of the Spirit through 'the bond of peace' (Eph. 4.3). In the church people of different social, religious and cultural origins become friends who 'forbear one another in love' (Eph. 4.3), do not judge one another, but stand up for each other, especially for the weak among them. The unity of the gathered congregation is visible and experienced in the fellowship of people who are in themselves different. It is in no way a fortuitous result of the proclamation and the administration of the sacraments, but is, in association with these, itself the sign of hope. The fact that Jews and Gentiles, Greeks and barbarians, masters and slaves, men and women surrender their privileges, or are freed from oppression as the case may be, is – like the gathering of the new people of God itself – the sacrament of the kingdom and the beginning of the messianic era.

The unity of the congregation is a unity in freedom. It must not be confused with unanimity, let alone uniformity in perception, feeling or morals. No one must be regimented, or forced into conformity with conditions prevailing in the church. Everyone must be accepted with his gifts and tasks, his weaknesses and handicaps. This unity is an evangelical unity, not a legal one. The charismatic congregation gives everyone the room he needs to be free in his dealings with other people and to be at their disposal when they need him. Because it is Christ who gathers it and the Spirit of the new creation who gives it life, nothing that serves the kingdom of God and the freedom of man must be suppressed in it. It is a unity in diversity and freedom.

But the congregation's unity is also freedom and diversity in unity. Where old enmities flare up again in it, where people insist on getting their own way and want to make their perceptions or experiences a law for other people, not only is the fellowship between people threatened, but so (in a deeper sense) is the fellowship with God himself. Through claims to domination and divisions of this kind Christ himself is divided (I. Cor. 1.13). Anyone who uses freedom in order to destroy freedom is not acting in accordance with that freedom. Freedom can be destroyed through the mania for uniformity, just as it can be killed by ruthless pluralism. In both these dangers, the important thing for the committed congregation is to return to the foundation of its unity in diversity, and to experience the open fellowship of Christ in his supper. For the committed congregation is *his* people and it is only in *his* Spirit that unity and diversity can be so intertwined that they do not destroy one another.

(ii) Every congregation gathered together in one place is one in Christ with every other congregation gathered together in other places and at other times. A community which does not see the suffering and testimony of other communities as its own suffering and its own testimony is dividing the one Christ who suffers and acts in all places and at all times. Communities which are divided in space and time recognize one another through their identity in Christ and the common Spirit. They will therefore experience this common identity of theirs and make it visible through fellowship and friendship with one another. They will recognize one another as members of the one church of Christ. 'If one member suffers, all suffer together; if one member is honoured, all rejoice together'

(I Cor. 12.26). This demands a solidarity beyond the limits of one's own community and must be proved in times of persecution. Every repression of a single Christian or a single community in the world affects all Christians and the whole church. It is only through this living solidarity and full identification with its persecuted members that the church will be able to resist the oppressor's tactics of 'divide and rule'. That is why it is not enough for the fellowship between the individual communities to exist merely in an organization over a large area.

The hierarchical build-up of large-scale church units and of administrations over a large area becomes abstract if it loses its contact with the 'grass roots'. It is true that many of the community's tasks can be carried out regionally or territorially by the church authorities: questions of finance, schools, dealings with government departments. But this does not affect the *specific* tasks of the local community – proclamation, mission, charitable work, fellowship, and so forth. Individual communities cannot delegate their specific duties to supra-regional units, and so shed their own responsibility for them. If they did so they would become poverty-stricken and reduce their work at the 'grass-roots'. Even fellowship at the local level is one of the community's own specific duties. It must be performed by the community itself and cannot be delegated.

The community can assign particular charges connected with their mutual fellowship. The apostles performed this function in the early Christian churches. Later it was given to bishops. In state churches it was possible to leave this task to the state authorities. On the other hand regional and territorial synods grew up which represented and expressed practically the common fellowship between the different congregations. But the episcopal organization is in danger of absorbing the actual congregation into abstract units under the name, in Germany, of *Landeskirchen* (churches belonging to a particular federal *Land*, or state); and on the other hand the synodal organization is in danger of seeing itself solely as the representative of the congregations, over against a central church government. In both cases organizations above the local level lose the character of the 'committed congregation'. The governing bodies and the synods then see themselves as institutions for the support of the congregations, or even as 'the church' compared with 'the congregations'. The all-important thing is therefore to present and organize the fellowship between local churches not from above but from below. Church governments and synods cannot set themselves up 'above' the congregations; they themselves can only be again the congregation gathered round word and sacrament. The unity of the congregations depends on what the congregations do. The fellowship of the fellowships should be lived as fellowship. The open friendship of Jesus, which is experienced and lived in the gathered congregation, and 'the unity of the Spirit in the bond of peace', cannot be surpassed. It is only when the unity of the congregations with one another is itself realized as a congregation that unity in freedom and freedom in unity can be experienced. For all inter-congregational fellowships and organizations, therefore, the fellowship in word and sacrament is fundamental, and the things that have to be administered and the affairs that have to be ordered must be settled in the fellowship of the Spirit.

(iii) Unity in freedom is not merely a mark of Christ's church; it is also a confessional mark, a sign of the church's creed in a divided and estranged world, 'that the world may believe' (John 17.21). The word and the sacraments have a power that gives fellowship and freedom in the church and – through the church – in the whole world of men and women as well. As a unifying force, the church is the messianic people of Christ, for unity is not merely an attribute of the church; it is the church's task in the world as well. If the assembled church is the confessing church, then it will represent the unity in Christ and the Spirit that makes all things new in the midst of the conflicts of its social and political situation. That is why the unifying power of the sacraments cannot be separated from the tasks and forces of social and political justice. The unity of Christ, which must not be divided, is not only unity with his disciples and the fellowship of believers but, based on that, is also his unity and fellowship with the oppressed, humiliated and forsaken.[10] The church would not witness to the whole Christ if it were not a fellowship of believers with the poor, a fellowship of the hopeful with the sick, and a fellowship of the loving with the oppressed. Its unity would no longer be a 'predicate of the time of salvation' if it were not to achieve liberation for the downtrodden, justice for those without rights, and peace in social conflicts. It is not 'one' for itself; it is one for the peace of divided mankind in the coming kingdom of God. In this respect 'unity in freedom' and 'freedom in unity' become particularly important.

The church itself acquires its practical unity as it experiences and lives in liberation from claims to domination in the society in which it exists. It is only a church liberated in this sense that portrays that unity. But this also means, as experience shows, that a church that suffers because of its resistance to claims of this kind becomes assured of its unity in Christ in a particular degree. The church will seize every opportunity to work for unity through liberation, and for peace through justice, in social and political conflicts. It does this when it works for the liberation of people whose rights have been taken from them and who have to suffer injustice helplessly. It does this when it offers open friendship to the people who have to suffer enmity and contempt. It testifies to the fellowship of the crucified Christ when it offers this fellowship and helps the people who are poor, oppressed and rejected to find fellowship themselves.

But when the church believes, hopes and practises unity in, with and beneath the real conflicts of society, it is also taking new conflicts on itself. The church's inward orientation towards its own unity would remain abstract and remote from its messianic mission if this political trend of its unity were not discerned and accepted. The ecumenical movement of the separated churches has made great progress in the field of dogma, and has been able to overcome traditional conflicts about baptism, the Lord's supper and the ministry. But for a number of years a growing sense of the social and political tasks of messianic action has introduced new conflicts into these endeavours on the part of the church for unity and fellowship. It is no longer merely true that 'doctrine divides but service unites'; now it is often the case that 'doctrine unites but politics divide'. Here the question of which kind of unity has priority is especially delicate. Is it the fellowship in word and sacrament that unites a person with his political enemies, or is it fellowship with the poor and all those who are standing up for them that divides the one from the other? When does a political situation become so acute that it becomes a matter of creed? Does Christian fellowship exist between the hangman and his victims? Can there be Christian fellowship with both the hangman and his victims at the same time? How far can the church settle conflicts of this kind within itself, and when does Christian fellowship run aground on them? Can we witness to our unity even through confrontation and conflict about the truth? Can the church confine itself to word and sacrament, and keep out of the quarrel altogether as an institution, while individual Christians take different and opposing sides in the various conflicts? Can political enemies 'remain one under the gospel'? How long can they do this? And what does it mean for their conflict itself? Does this not make 'the gospel' an abstract and ineffective power? These are some of the practical questions facing the church and many individual Christians today. If we only have the church's internal unity in view, we will push these questions off into the field of ethics. If we are looking towards messianic unity, they are questions of faith as well. If we only look at the unity without taking account of the freedom, reconciliation for fellowship easily becomes a policy of appeasement – a mere prevention of conflicts without any search for a solution. If we only look at the freedom without taking account of the unity, then we easily overlook the irreparable sacrifice required by conflict as a means to liberation and peace. Neither the unity as such nor the conflict as such is creative. The only creative thing is the strength that accepts the conflicts and seeks for unity in freedom, and freedom in unity. As far as the practical and personal questions in these conflicts are concerned, the primary question is not whether fellowship with the church or fellowship with the oppressed and persecuted is more important. The question of really pre-eminent importance is where the assured and consistent *fellowship of Christ* is to be found. For this alone is, after all, the foundation of the fellowship with our Christian brethren, and with the least of men. It will therefore also be the yardstick for church fellowship and political fellowship. Unity and division, conflict and reconciliation, confrontation and co-operation must be tested against the cross of Christ; for his cross is the first and last sign of the one kingdom.

3. *Catholicity and Partisanship*

(i) The expression 'catholic', καθολικός (which comes from the adverbial usage καθ' ὅλου, 'generally', 'universally') is not as yet applied to the church in the New Testament. It was first used in that context by Ignatius of Antioch:

> Let that be considered a valid eucharist which is celebrated by the bishop, or by one whom he appoints. Wherever the bishop appears,

let the congregation be present; just as wherever Jesus Christ is, there is the catholic church (*Smyrn.* 8.1f.).

'Catholic' means, first of all, what is general, universal, linked with everything, compared with the particular and individual.[11] Applied to the church, it meant the main church, the bishop's church in a province, compared with the local churches. If, as Ignatius stresses, the bishop represents Christ and hence the unity of the church, then the church's catholicity is determined by the universal, all-uniting presence of Christ. In this case what is meant is the church whole and entire, as it is in Christ. That includes its spatial catholicity – its presence in all parts of the inhabited earth (the *oikumene*) and its temporal catholicity – its presence in all periods of history. It was only in the quarrels with the heretics and schismatics in the first centuries that 'catholic' was used as the mark of 'the true church', the sole and rightful church. The term then included its quality – its fullness of truth, its unity and holiness in Christ, and its apostolic legitimation.

The church's catholicity is a correlative term to its unity. Whereas its unity means its catholicity in intention and trend, its catholicity means its unity in extent. Qualitatively, its catholicity means the church's inner wholeness, compared with the splitting off of individual elements of truth, which are then given an absolute validity of their own. It we put the spatial and the inner meaning of the word together, then the church with its inner wholeness is related to the whole of the world. This follows inevitably from its definition as the church of Christ. Being entirely related to Christ, it is related to the whole world, for whose reconciliation Christ was sacrificed by God, and for whose liberation and unification all power was given him in heaven and on eaith (cf. Eph. 1.2off.). When, in the conflicts of the Reformation period, 'Catholic' became the party name for one particular church, the Reformers also replaced the word 'catholic' in the German creed by 'general' or 'Christian' church.

(ii) The claim made in talking about the church's spatial, temporal and inner catholicity is a large one, and has given rise to misunderstandings. Consequently we must make some theological distinctions here. The church is not universal, general and related to the whole in itself, but solely in and through Christ. That is why Ignatius was right (if we leave his episcopalism on one side) when he said: 'Wherever Jesus Christ is, there is the catholic church.' For in the fullest sense of the word, the attribute 'catholic' applies to the lordship of Christ, through which the universe is summed up and united, and the kingdom of God, which the lordship of Christ serves.[12] Even in its comprehensive form, the historical church is particular and not yet *the whole*. Just because it is the people of the coming kingdom, it is not yet the new humanity itself. It is not yet itself the summing-up and unification of the universe, but is only its witness in the divided world. It cannot therefore be its duty to combine everything syncretistically and to incorporate everything in itself. But at the same time the church of Christ and the coming kingdom is *related to the whole*. Its catholicity lies in the universal and, in principle, unlimited breadth of its apostolic mission. Its participation in the catholicity of the kingdom is realized through its mission to the world – 'to the end of the earth' (Acts 1.8) and 'to the close of the age' (Matt. 28.20). The church is catholic in its mission, because in its proclamation it appeals to people who do not belong to it, and because it does not accept that there is any sphere which Christ would not have claimed for his own from the beginning.[13] Thanks to its hope it cannot surrender any individual person or any part of creation. 'Catholic' is therefore not an adjective describing the church's state; it is an attribute describing its movement, its mission and its hope. We may remind ourselves in this connection that before the word became a predicate of the church Justin talked about the 'catholic . . . resurrection' (*Dial.* 81.4) and that early liturgies called the prayer of intercession for all men and all situations in life 'the catholic prayer'.[14] The church is related in a missionary way to the whole of mankind, because its resurrection hope and its eucharistic prayer include everyone. 'Catholic' is therefore an eminently eschatological definition of the church.

(iii) But how are we to interpret this eschatological definition of the church? If it is related to the whole by virtue of its universal mission, then the catholicity of God's kingdom is manifested in this movement of the church and the openness to the world of its prayer. If it is itself the beginning of the kingdom of God on earth in the particular sense, then in the eschatological consummation it will itself *be the whole* and realize its catholicity. The perfected church is then to be the 'truly catholic, perfect society' and conversely, the church which is incomplete in its particularity must represent nothing other than the future universal society.[15] But the second postulate, like most other interpretations of the word catholic, overlooks the historical differences between the church and Israel, as well as the distinction between the church and the political orders of society.

The church in history is limited not merely by its inadequate extent. It does not merely remain limited because it cannot, fundamentally speaking, live for everyone at the same time. It is above all limited, non-universal and non-Catholic as long as Israel exists parallel to it.[16] An incorporation of Israel is neither promised, nor enjoined upon it, though what is laid on it is the missionary task of 'making Israel jealous' for salvation (Rom. 11.11ff.). If the acceptance of Israel will be like 'life from the dead' (Rom 11.15), then that is the point when the general resurrection of the dead acquires the predicate 'catholic' for the first time, as the description of a state of affairs. In the sense of the missionary relation 'to the whole', the church must be called catholic from the moment of its decision in favour of the mission to the Gentiles and the nations of the world. Yet this very decision leaves Israel's hope and the hope for Israel eschatologically open. The church of Christ is 'catholic' as regards Israel in an extremely dialectical sense, precisely through the decision for the unilateral mission to the Gentiles, so that through the salvation of the Gentiles Israel too might ultimately be saved.

Moreover the church in history remains limited, non-universal and non-catholic until 'every rule and every authority and power' is destroyed (I Cor. 15.24).[17] An incorporation of this earthly rule is neither promised nor enjoined upon the church; what is laid on it indeed is to bear witness to and practise brotherhood, friendship and freedom in fellowship in its own midst. If God will only be 'all in all' when the rule of Christ is consummated in the rule of God, then the kingdom of glory can only be called catholic in the fullest sense at that point. The church in history cannot therefore be 'catholic' in the sense of the incorporation of all people and conditions in the church, including Israel and the nations. It is catholic in the eschatological context we have described, in its mission. Its world-wide mission points everything towards the catholic kingdom of God and relates the whole, which is fragmented and divided here, to the future total salvation.

(iv) If the church finds its historical catholicity, which is related to the coming kingdom, in its apostolate, then it also acquires freedom from those enthusiastic dreams of realizing the universality of God's kingdom through a universal Christian state or by supplanting Israel. It will also be free from the Christian 'integralism' which forces it to be there 'for everyone' in the same way at all times and in all places.[18] It will then be flexible in its apostolate for the universal kingdom. That is important for the actual putting into effect of the mission and policies that are related to the whole.

If the church, being catholic, 'is there for all' it will be inclined to keep out of the conflict between one person or group and another. It will either confine itself to a purely religious ministry addressed to people of whatever party, or will offer itself as a 'third power', as a neutral platform or as a meeting point in the conflict. It will admonish the warring parties to peace and reconciliation but will remain above the conflict and will not intervene itself.

If, on the other hand, the church sees its catholicity in its apostolate, it can serve the universality of God's kingdom in a different way. The goal of the church's mission remains universal. In the new people of God the divisions that destroy mankind will already be deprived of their force here and now. The barriers which people set up against each other, in order to maintain their own position and to put down others, will be broken down through mission and fellowship. But the path that leads to this goal begins at the bottom. According to Isaiah 40.4f., 'every valley shall be lifted up, and every mountain and hill be made low. . . . And the glory of the Lord shall be revealed, and all flesh shall see it together.' In the words of Luke 1.51ff., 'He has shown strength with his arm, he has scattered the proud in the imagination of their hearts, he has put down the mighty from their thrones, and exalted those of low degree; he has filled the hungry with good things, and the rich he has sent empty away.' According to I Cor. 1.26ff. this path manifests itself in the church itself through the preaching of the crucified Jesus. God chooses the people who in the eyes of the world are foolish, weak, 'low and despised', in order to judge the wise, the strong, and the people who count for something in the world, 'so that no human being might boast. . . . Let him who boasts, boast of the Lord.' The goal of glory is intended for all men. But because not all are 'people' in the same way, as far as their means, rights and freedom to live are concerned, the fellowship in which all are to see the glory of God 'together' is created, through the choosing of the humble and through judgment on the violent. This form of partisanship does not destroy Christian universalism, nor does it deny God's love for all men; it is the historical form of universal love in a world in which people oppress and hate each other. Jesus turned to the sinners, tax-collectors and lepers in order to save the Pharisees and the healthy as well. Paul turned to the Gentiles in order to save Israel too. Christian partisan support for the oppressed is intentional and its goal is to save the oppressor also. The 'mountains' are not made low as an end in itself, but in order to reveal the glory of God to all flesh 'together'. The rich and the mighty are not rejected out of revenge but in order to save them. Masters are rejected because of their oppression, so that they may experience the fullness of the common humanity, of which they are depriving themselves and others. Christian universalism will therefore be realized in particular conflict situations in a partisanship of this kind; otherwise it is still in danger of being abstract and of dissolving the community itself. Conversely, however, any partisan intervention in power struggles loses its Christian legitimation if it loses sight of the universal goal. The church is not yet itself the glory of God; it is the way and the historical movement towards the goal whereby all flesh should see it *together*. Universality and partisanship are not opposites when they are historically intertwined in this way. The church is related to the whole and is catholic in so far as, in the fragmentation of the whole, it primarily seeks and restores to favour the lost, the rejected and the oppressed.

4. *Holiness in Poverty*

(i) The creed uses the term 'holy' twice – for the 'holy' church and for what our creed calls 'the communion of saints', i.e., the fellowship of the holy. The 'fellowship of the holy' can be seen as the comprehensive definition of the church and can mean the fellowship of 'the holy things' as well as fellowship with holy people and their merits. The Reformers, however, thought of the *congregatio sanctorum*, and understood the 'one, holy, catholic church' as the community of holy people. Thus the first phrase calls the church in its unity and wholeness holy, whereas the second talks about the holiness of all and each of its members. Whatever the authors of the Apostles' Creed may have meant, this interpretation is in accordance with New Testament usage.[19]

The church is holy in its unity and in all its members, not in itself but in Christ, 'whom God made our . . . sanctification and redemption' (I Cor 1.30ff.). 'You were sanctified . . . in the name of the Lord Jesus Christ and in the Spirit of our God' (I Cor. 6.11). That is why the apostle addresses the church in his letters as 'sanctified in Christ Jesus' (I Cor. 1.2), as 'saints in Christ Jesus' (Phil. 1.1), and as 'God's chosen ones, holy and beloved' (Col. 3.12). The church is holy because it is sanctified through Christ's activity in and on it. Holiness means here not a higher sphere of divine power, before which people shudder and shrink back; it must be understood as a verbal noun. Holiness consists of being made holy, in sanctification, the subject of the activity being God (I Thess. 5.23; II Thess. 2.13). God sanctifies his church by calling the godless through Christ, by justifying sinners, and by accepting the lost. The communion or community of the saints – or the holy or sanctified – is therefore always at the same time the community of sinners; and the sanctified church is always at the same time the sinful church. Through its continual prayer 'forgive us our trespasses,' it recognizes itself as being in sin and at the same time as being holy in the divine forgiveness of sins. 'If we say we have no sin, we deceive ourselves, and the truth is not in us' (I John 1.8). In the confession of sin and faith in justification the church is simultaneously *communio peccatorum* and *communio sanctorum*.[20] It is in this very thing that its sanctification, and consequently its holiness, consists.

Holiness does not divide the church and Christians substantially from sinful humanity, and does not remove it to a position above the mass of sinners. If God's justifying grace is believed in the church, then that grace also manifests the true and whole misery of men and women. That misery, which is described by the word sin, can only be perceived and acknowledged undisguised and without self-justification, where the divine forgiveness, justification and sanctification is historically manifest. The church is therefore holy precisely at the point where it acknowledges its sins and the sins of mankind and trusts to justification through God. This does not merely apply to individual Christians; as we said at the beginning, it is true for the church as a whole.

The public admission of guilt made by the Protestant churches in Germany and Japan after the Second World War, and the public admission of guilt made by the churches in the former colonial countries and in countries where there is slavery and racialism, are to be viewed as signs of the churches' sanctification.[21] They reach beyond the churches to the whole people and therefore serve the liberation and sanctification of the nations. It must be noted, however, that they do not merely contain impeachments and self-impeachments and are not the expression of a guilty conscience which lets itself be put under pressure by other people. They are rather public manifestations of the liberating divine righteousness, and of a conversion to a new, different future. Just as liberating grace determines the whole church, and not only its individual members, so the whole church also lives from the forgiveness of guilt. Guilt is personal and social at the same time, and so, therefore, is liberating grace as well.

(ii) The church is holy because God shows himself to be holy in the grace of the crucified Christ acting on it.[22] The revelation of his holiness means redemption. In the New Testament the Holy Spirit, as the eschatological 'advance gift' of glory and the power of the new creation, is determinative for the idea of holiness. The people who are called through the gospel and are chosen, justified and sanctified are 'led by the Spirit of God' (Rom. 8.14). Being united through the Spirit they are given life through the fullness of the Spirit's different gifts. They live, suffer and act from the Spirit of the last days. The church is therefore holy in the dawn of the new era and the new creation. We are continually told that the goal of sanctification is bringing forth fruit to eternal life and glory. Consequently the fellowship of justified sinners is at the same time the fellowship of the people called to service for the kingdom of God and the believers who are equipped with the powers of the Spirit. They are set apart and destined, not for themselves but for the service of the kingdom of God. As the sanctified they therefore sanctify the world. They themselves set apart and destine for the kingdom of God whatever they reach. The non-Christian partner in a marriage is 'sanctified' by the Christian partner, and so are the children of the marriage (I Cor. 7.14). Everything that love reaches and destines for love is sanctified for the kingdom of God, and so filled with hope and charismatically enlivened.

This means for the church as a whole that the *communio peccatorum* it acknowledges in the confession of guilt is its past, and the *communio sanctorum* that it believes when it believes in the forgiveness of sin is its future. It testifies to the fellowship of justified sinners, which acknowledges both, in the perpetual conversion from that past to this future. In this sense the holy church is the converting church of the new beginnings. It is *ecclesia reformata et semper reformanda*.[23] Its faith becomes trustworthy in its *reformatio perennis*.[24] Through continual new conversion and permanent reformation it testifies to the coming *reformatio mundi* which is already present in the Spirit – the 'new order of all things' in the kingdom of God, and the sanctification of the whole creation in the glory of God. Its sanctification puts the church and all its members on the road to universal glory. In the context of the fellowship of sinners, the sanctification of the church lies in justification. In the context of the coming kingdom of glory its sanctification lies in its call to service, to suffering and to poverty.

(iii) 'To be a Church in splendour, without spot or wrinkle, is the ultimate goal to which we are being led by the passion of Christ. This, then, will come about in heaven, not on earth.'[25] This remark indicates that sanctification does not only come about through active service in the world but is also – and even more – suffered. It is experienced and suffered in the fellowship of Christ's sufferings. The signs of the sanctification of the church and its members are in a particular way the signs of its suffering, its persecution because of its resistance, and its poverty in the ground of its hope. The saints who were revered by the church in a particular way were the martyrs, who in the visible fellowship of the crucified Jesus testified to his invisible glory. The friends of Jesus who were called to discipleship and the messianic mission left everything and became poor for the kingdom's sake. The church in Jerusalem was called 'the poor saints at Jerusalem' (Rom. 15.26). Paul collected money for them in Macedonia and Achaia. Christ himself, 'whom God made our . . . sanctification' 'for your sake . . . became poor, so that by his poverty you might become rich' (II Cor. 8.9). The church is therefore sanctified wherever it participates in the lowliness, helplessness, poverty and suffering of Christ. Its glory is manifest through the sign of poverty. When believers take up their cross, the kingdom of God is manifested to the world. In this sense we can say that the church is sanctified in this 'perverse world' through the signs of poverty, suffering and oppression. These are the birth pangs of the new creation in the midst of the creation that is still enslaved. What the apostle says about himself is also true of the apostolic church in a corresponding degree: 'As unknown, and yet well known; as dying, and behold we live; as punished, and yet not killed; as sorrowful, yet always rejoicing; as poor, yet making many rich; as having nothing, and yet possessing everything' (II Cor. 6.9–10).

If God's strength 'is made perfect in weakness' (II Cor. 12.9) then his holiness is also mighty in poverty. Because these statements stand in the context of the fellowship of Christ and the apostolate, they cannot be isolated from the world in which the church lives. Poverty would otherwise easily become an attitude of humility limited to the inner and spiritual life. We would enthuse about 'a church poor in the poverty of Christ' without perceiving the real poverty in the world and the riches of the glory for the sake of which Christ and his followers 'become poor'. The church is not as yet sanctified by poverty if it does not become 'the church for the poor' and especially honour alms given for the poor. If it only praises 'the dignity of the poor in the church', then it is not yet moving in this direction.[26] Christ became poor in order through his poverty to make many rich. The disciples became poor in order to fill the world with the gospel. So the church too will only be poor in this sense if it consecrates everything it has to service for the kingdom of God, investing it in the messianic mission to the world (I Cor. 15. 43). It will be poor in a both spiritual and material sense if it becomes the church of the poor and if the real poor find themselves and their hope in the church. Poverty is not a virtue unless it leads to the fellowship of the really poor. Humility is not an attitude unless it leads to the fellowship of the humiliated. The poor church will therefore have to be understood as the church of the poor – as the fellowship, that is, in which the poor arrive at freedom and become the upholders of the kingdom. Christian poverty therefore means the fellowship of the poor and fellowship with the poor – but as the fellowship of the messianic mission and the hope for the kingdom. In this sense Christian poverty, as 'an expression of love is solidarity with the poor and is a protest *against poverty*'.[27]

In a world where there is an unjust division between the riches in the power of a few and the poverty in the empty hands of the many, the church's poverty becomes the witness of the messianic kingdom. Sanctified through its poverty in the fellowship of the poor, and in protest against poverty, it becomes the sign of the glory of God which fills all flesh. It is then sanctified through the spirit of the Beatitudes. The true fellowship of the poor is of more value than all the alms and development aid of the rich. The problem of poverty in the world is not solved by programmes which mobilize 'the church for the poor' or try to win 'the poor for the church', but only through the church of the poor itself. Whatever state churches and other rich and well-organized churches can do in the way of help, the apostolic charge remains central: to found congregations at the lowest level, congregations which independently discover their powers and potentialities in the liberating history of Christ; for the fellowship of the poor and suffering Christ is the secret of the 'holy church' and the 'communion of saints'. In his fellowship the church becomes the poor people of the coming kingdom and so becomes holy and blessed.

5. *The Apostolate in Suffering*

(i) The apostolicity of the church has a special place among its four characteristics. On the one hand the church which in Christ is holy and catholic only encounters man in history through the apostolic witness. 'Without the apostolic witness He would simply be hidden, and only on the basis of this witness is He really known.'[28] Historically, therefore, the three other characteristics of the church are manifest and assured from its apostolate. But on the other hand, apostolicity is the church's special historical designation. It is the mark of its messianic mission in the name of Christ for the coming kingdom. Whereas the three other characteristics continue in eternity, and are also the characteristics of the church when it is glorified in the kingdom, the apostolic mission will come to an end when it is fulfilled. The three other attributes are designations of the kingdom and are transferred to the people of the kingdom as 'designations of the time of salvation'. But apostolicity is a designation for the kingdom. It is not an eschatological term, but a term related to the eschaton, because it is not a characteristic of the eschaton itself. In respect of the kingdom of glory the apostolate is provisional, the forerunner of what is to come, just as the apostles saw themselves as forerunners of the coming Lord and hence sought to fill the whole world with his gospel. The unity, catholicity and holiness of the people of God, on the other hand, are final designations, because they describe the one, all-embracing and holy kingdom of God. We can therefore say that the historical church *will be* the one, holy, catholic church through the apostolic witness of Christ, and in carrying out that witness; whereas the church glorified in the kingdom of God *is* the one, holy and catholic church, through the fulfilment of its apostolate. Historically the church has its being in carrying out the apostolate. In eternity the church has its being in the fulfilment of the apostolate, that is, in the seeing face to face.

(ii) The historical church must be called 'apostolic' in a double sense: its gospel and its doctrine are founded on the testimony of the first apostles, the eyewitnesses of the risen Christ, and it exists in the carrying out of the apostolic proclamation, the missionary charge. The expression 'apostolic' therefore denotes both the church's foundation and its commission.

If the historical church is founded on the witness of Christ's apostles, then the word has first of all the simple meaning: 'deriving from the apostles', 'relating to the apostles', 'dating from the period of the apostles'. In this sense the church fathers later greeted the churches 'in the apostolic manner', and talked about 'the apostolic age' and 'the fellowship of the apostles'.[29] In the conflict with heretics and schismatics the word acquired the character of legitimation, the legitimation of true doctrine, the whole unadulterated gospel; and became a category of tradition. Correspondingly, the word was used in the dispute about ministry and charisma to legitimate the bishops as the successors of the apostles. Irenaeus, for example, talks about 'those who were appointed bishops in the church by the apostles and those who are their successors down to our own time'.[30] The apostolicity of the church therefore meant the claim to an unbroken, unaltered and unadulterated bond between the present church and the apostles in faith and practice, proclamation and office.

But we must go beyond the use of the word as a category of legitimation. For the apostles, to whom the church appeals, were the eyewitnesses of the risen Lord. 'The first Christian apostolate was founded through the appearances of the risen Christ.'[31] Luke talks about the 'twelve apostles' (Luke 6.13; Acts 1.21ff.). But Paul talked about all the apostles, and did not only mean the twelve. What constitute the apostolate are the appearance and commission of the risen Christ, not merely the discipleship of the earthly Jesus. And here the Easter appearances have a threefold meaning: (*a*) They reveal the Jesus crucified on Golgotha as the one raised by God and exalted to be Lord. They therefore found and provoke the proclamation and the faith: 'Jesus – the Christ', 'Jesus – the Lord'. (*b*) They reveal the crucified Jesus in the splendour of the coming divine glory and bring the victory of life to light. They therefore substantiate the promise of coming glory and eschatological hope. (*c*) They are appearances which convey a call, through which those affected are designated witnesses of Christ and his future. Knowledge of Christ, hope for the future, and mission coincide in the Easter appearances. In the light of the appearances of the crucified and risen Christ the first Christian apostolate therefore takes on an eschatological meaning.[32] The messianic hope was given practical expression in the mission to Israel of the first Jewish-Christian church. The prophetic hope for the salvation of the nations was given practical expression in the apostle Paul's mission to the Gentiles. Because the apostolate has its foundation in the eschatological event of the raising of the crucified Christ, it lays advance hold on Christ's universal future. The coming Lord of glory reveals himself and gathers his people in the apostolic gospel. If, therefore, the historical church looks back to its beginnings in its appeal to the apostles, in this way it also actualizes its eschatological hope and becomes assured of its own messianic mission. If we understand the apostolate in the light of the Easter appearances, it is not enough merely to see it in the history of the tradition and to trace back the apostolic church to its earthly founder and the 'apostolic age'. Its apostolicity is not merely a category of legitimation; it is even more a category of promise and commission. Nor is it enough to affirm the bond with the apostles merely through the proofs of tradition and succession. The apostolic succession is, in fact and in truth, the evangelical succession, the continuing and unadulterated proclamation of the gospel of the risen Christ. The Reformers therefore demanded that the proclamation of Christ be made the criterion of apostolicity. They understood the scriptures as the true *apostolos*, that is to say as the apostolic testimony to the continuing apostolic proclamation and the expanding messianic church.

(iii) It follows from the unique character of the first Christian apostolate that the church can only appeal to the apostles when it lays hold on its own apostolic and missionary charge. In the history of God's dealings with the world the church has a particular commission. It is to testify by means of word, deed and fellowship to the liberating lordship of Christ, to the ends of the earth and to the end of time. That is the nature of its apostolate, and for that reason the apostolate is also its historical nature.[33] It is the church of the apostolate. The apostolate is its subject. In the apostolic movement it evangelizes the peoples and, as a new fellowship, itself becomes the form the kingdom of God takes in the world. It calls men and women to repentance and, as an open fellowship, itself becomes the form this repentance takes. It witnesses to the enlivening hope for the kingdom and as a fellowship of poverty becomes a lived hope. In this apostolic movement the church must continually assure itself of its origin in the appearances of the risen Christ, and therefore of the proclamation of the apostles as well. But it does not therefore need to idealize the apostolic age for all that. It does not have to maintain its apostolic identity slavishly, through repetition. The important thing is equivalence, not identity. In this apostolic movement the church must continually orientate itself towards the future – the future of Christ which the first Christian apostolate talks about. Where the retrospective bond with the apostles is concerned, the historical church will ask about continuity and strive for continuity. But where the future its apostolate serves is concerned it will be open to leap forward to what is new and surprising. Here 'the most characteristic thing is not the old things that are preserved but the new ones that take place and come into being'.[34] The apostolic church is the missionary church. Something new, individual and independent is always springing up. So the missionary church will not aim to spread its own form and found 'daughter churches' everywhere. A 'young church' is not the subsidiary branch of an old church, which the old one has to look after. It is 'a new church' of the same apostolate. It preserves its unity when it fulfils Christ's apostolic mission in its own historical situation. The risen Christ is called 'the life-giving Spirit'. He is the creative Spirit who makes something new everywhere, uniting it in himself. The Christian apostolate participates in this and must therefore not be quenched by outward regimentation.

(iv) Up to now we have understood the apostolate of the apostles and the church as *active mission*. But if the apostolate is the mission of the gospel, the call to freedom, the call to messianic fellowship, then the apostolate in the world is never undisputed. The powers and laws of unfreedom and timid reserve contradict and resist it, as they contradicted and resisted the mission of Christ. Participation in the apostolic mission of Christ therefore leads inescapably into *tribulation, contradiction and suffering*. The apostolate is carried out in the weakness and poverty of Christ, not through force or the strategies of force. Reserved and withdrawn men and women and closed societies are opened through the witness of apostolic suffering, and can only through this be converted to the future of the kingdom. Just as the apostle Paul pointed to his persecutions, tribulations, wounds and scars in order to prove his apostolate (II Cor. 6 and 7), so persecutions and sufferings will also be the proof of the apostolic church. 'The blood of the martyrs is the seed of the church', said the early church. The numbers of martyrs in the 'young' missionary churches meanwhile exceeds the number of martyrs in the early church. There are many countries in which the apostolic witness is predominantly heard in prison, and nowhere so distinctly as there.

Even though the apostolate is so strongly eschatologically determined by the Easter appearances of the risen Christ, it is equally strongly determined by suffering and sacrifice in disciple-ship of the Christ who was crucified. The one cannot be without the other if the whole Christ is to be witnessed to. The fellowship of Christ does not only determine the content of the apostolate; it determines its form in history as well. We shall therefore have to understand the apostolate essentially – not merely fortuitously – as active suffering and as suffering activity. The church is apostolic when it takes up its cross. It then witnesses to the glory of the risen Christ in its fellowship with those who suffer, and his future in its fellowship with the imprisoned. In our godless and inhuman world 'the church under the cross' shows itself to be the *true* apostolic church. Its apostolic succession is the succession of the passion of Christ.

The one holy, catholic and apostolic church is the church of Jesus Christ. Fellowship with Christ is its secret. The church of Jesus Christ is the one, holy, catholic and apostolic church. Unity in freedom, holiness in poverty, catholicity in partisan support for the weak, and apostolate in suffering are the marks by which it is known in the world.

ABBREVIATIONS

AV	Authorized Version of the Bible
BWANT	Beiträge zur Wissenschaft des Alten und Neuen Testament, Stuttgart
BZAW	Beiheft sur *Zeitschrift für die alttestamentliche Wissenschaft*, Berlin
EvKomm	*Evangelische Kommentare*, Stuttgart
EvTh	*Evangelische Theologie*, Munich
FRLANT	Forschungen zur Religion und Literatur des Alten und Neuen Testaments, Göttingen
LThK	*Lexikon für Theologie und Kirche*, Freiburg
MPL	Migne, Patrologia Latina, Paris
NEB	New English Bible
NRT	*Nouvelle Revue Théologique*
RAC	*Reallexikon für Antike und Christentum*, Stuttgart
RGG	*Die Religion in Geschichte und Gegenwart*, Tübingen
RSV	Revised Standard Version of the Bible
SBT	Studies in Biblical Theology, London and Naperville
TDNT	*Theological Dictionary of the New Testament*, ed. G. Kittel, ET by G. W. Bromiley, Grand Rapids, Michigan, 1964ff.
ThEx	Theologische Existenz heute, Munich
ThB	Theologische Bücherei, Munich
WA	M. Luther, *Werke*, Weimarer Ausgabe, 1883ff.
WCC	World Council of Churches
ZKG	*Zeitschrift für Kirchengeschichte*, Stuttgart
ZThK	*Zeitschrift für Theologie und Kirche*, Tübingen

NOTES

I The Dimensions of the Doctrine of the Church Today

1. *Bekenntnisschriften und Kirchenordnungen der nach Gottes Wort reformierten Kirche*, ed. W. Niesel, 2nd ed. Zürich 1938, p.335: 'Jesus Christ, as he borne witness to for us in Holy Scripture, is the sole Word of God to which we have to listen and which we have to trust and obey in living and in dying. We reject the false doctrine that the church could and must recognize as the source of her proclamation any other events and powers, persons and truths as God's revelation, apart from or beside this sole Word of God.'

2. These are the condemnatory statements from Theses 2 and 3, op. cit., pp.335f.

3. Karl Barth, *Church Dogmatics*, I.1, ET T. & T. Clark and Scribner 1975², p.3. P. Tillich, *Systematic Theology* I, ET University of Chicago Press 1951, p.3 = Nisbet 1951, p.3; O. Weber, *Grundlagen der Dogmatik* I, Neukirchen 1955, p.30.

4. A. Schlatter, *Der Dienst des Christen in der älteren Dogmatik*, Gütersloh 1897, p.7.

5. Ibid., p.7.

6. H. Hoekendijk, 'Die Welt als Horizont', *EvTh* 25, 1965, p.478.

7. G. F. Vicedom, *Missio Dei. Einführung in eine Theologie der Mission*, Munich 1958, and *Actio Dei. Mission und Reich Gottes*, Munich 1975; H.-W. Genischen, *Glaube für die Welt, Theologische Aspekte der Mission*, Gütersloh 1971; A. M. Aagaard, *Helliganden sendt till Verden*, Aarhus 1973; L. Rütti, *Zur Theologie der Mission. Kritische Analysen und neue Orientierungen*, Munich and Mainz 1972.

8. E. Lange, *Die ökumenische Utopie oder: Was bewegt die ökumenische Bewegung?*, Stuttgart 1972, p.37.

9. J. Moltmann, 'Bringing Peace to a Divided World', in *The Experiment Hope*, ET SCM Press 1975, pp.172ff.

10. Lange, op. cit., pp.39ff. I am following his brilliant account here.

11. *Third World Conference on Faith and Order held at Lund August 15th to 25th, 1952*, ed. O. Tomkins, SCM Press 1953, p.15.

12. *The Uppsala Report 1968*, ed. N. Goodall, Geneva 1968, p.5.

13. *The Documents of Vatican II*, ed. W. M. Abbott, SJ, Geoffrey Chapman and Herder & Herder 1966, p. 79: 'Iam ergo finis saeculorum ad

nos pervenerunt (cf. I. Cor. 10.11) et renovatio mundi irrevocabiliter est constituta atque in hoc saeculo reali quodammodo anticipatur.'

14. J. B. Metz, *Theology of the World*, ET Burns & Oates and Herder & Herder 1969, p.115; cf. also Metz, J. Moltmann and W. Oelmüller, *Kirche im Prozeß der Aufklärung*, Munich and Mainz 1970; *Diskussion zur 'politischen Theologie'*, ed. H. Peuckert, Munich and Mainz 1969.

15. R. Strunk, *Politische Ekklesiologie im Zeitalter der Revolution*, Munich and Mainz 1971.

16. Metz, ibid.

17. The earlier expression 'political theology' comes from Carl Schmitt. Cf. C. Schmitt, *Politische Theologie. Vier Kapital von der Souveränität*, Leipzig 1934, and *Politische Theologie II. Die Legende von der Erledigung jeder Politischen Theologie*, Berlin 1970.

18. R. Shaull, *Befreiung durch Veränderung*, Munich and Mainz 1970; G. Girardi, *Christianisme, libération humaine, lutte des classes*, Paris 1972; H. Gollwitzer, *Die kapitalistische Revolution*, Munich 1974; *Diskussion zur 'Theologie der Revolution'*, ed. E. Feil and R. Weth, Munich and Mainz 1969; T. Rendtorff and H. E. Tödt, *Theologie der Revolution. Analysen und Materialien*, Frankfurt 1968.

19. E. Bloch, *Atheism in Christianity*, ET Herder & Herder 1972; D. Sölle, *Politische Theologie*, Stuttgart 1971.

20. J. B. Metz, 'Kirche und Volk', *Stimmen der Zeit* 192, 1974, pp. 797ff.

21. E. Rosenstock-Huessy proves this in *Die europäischen Revolutionen und der Charakter der Nationen*, Stuttgart 1951.

22. G. Gutiérrez, *A Theology of Liberation*, ET Orbis Books 1973, SCM Press 1974; H. Assmann, *Opresión – Liberación. Desafío a los christianos*, Montevideo 1971; J. Miguez-Bonino, *Doing Theology in a Revolutionary Situation*, Philadelphia 1974.

23. See here J. Moltmann, 'Befreiung im Licht der Hoffnung', *Ökumenische Rundschau* 23, 1974, pp.296ff.

II The Church in History

1. W.-D. Marsch, *Institution im Übergang. Evangelische Kirche zwischen Tradition und Reform*, Göttingen 1970, p.11.

2. H. Diem, *Die Kirche und ihre Praxis*, Munich 1963, p.20. The book takes over concepts from Bultmann.

3. P. Tillich, *Systematic Theology* III, Univ. of Chicago Press 1963, p.165 = Nisbet 1964, p.176.

4. G. Ebeling, 'Towards an ecclesiology', *Theology and Proclamation*, ET Collins and Fortress Press 1966, pp.94ff.

5. H. Küng, *The Church*, ET Burns & Oates and Sheed & Ward 1967, pp.3ff.

6. H. Hild (ed.), *Wie stabil ist die Kirche? Bestand und Erneuerung. Ergebnisse einer Umfrage*, Gelnhausen 1974.

7. K.-W. Dahm, N. Luhmann and D. Stoodt, *Religion-System und Sozialisation*, Sammlung Luchterhand 85, Neuwied 1972.

8. Bultmann developed this formula. See 'Zum Problem der Entmythologisierung' in *Kerygma und Mythos* II, Hamburg 1952, p.197. Cf. D. Sölle, 'Paradoxe Identität', *Monatsschrift für Pastoraltheologie* 53, 1964, pp.366ff.

9. R. Bultmann, *History and Eschatology*, Edinburgh University Press (= *The Presence of Eternity*, Harper & Bros.) 1957, p.154.

10. Ibid.

11. Ibid.

12. G. Hasenhüttl does not seem to have entirely escaped this misunderstanding: see *Der Glaubensvollzug. Eine Begegnung mit R. Bultmann aus katholischem Glaubensverständnis*, Essen 1963.

13. Cf. here R. Hermann, *Luthers These 'Gerecht und Sünder zugleich'*, Gütersloh 1960², esp. pp.234ff.; W. Joest, *Gesetz und Freiheit. Das Problem des Tertius uss legis bei Luther und die neutestamentlichen Parainese*, Göttingen 1961³, esp. pp.55ff., where the writer distinguishes between the 'total aspect of *simul*' and 'the partial aspect of *simul*' and hence between 'being a Christian as *transitus*' and 'being a Christian as *progressus*'.

14. Diem, op. cit., p.23, expresses this fear. But *semper* does not mean 'eternally'.

15. Marsch, op. cit., p.175.

16. Lange, op. cit., p.119.

17. Thus Lange, ibid., p.119. Behind what he says are the distinctions which Ernst Bloch put forward in the category of possibility (*Das Prinzip Hoffnung* I, Frankfurt 1959, pp.258ff.). He distinguishes among other things between 'what is in the range of possibility' and 'what can possibly be'. If this is transferred to the church, we should have to distinguish between the church in the divine possibility and the church which is possible in history.

18. E. Jüngel in 'Die Welt als Möglichkeit und Wirklichkeit. Zum ontologischen Ansatz der Rechtfertigungslehre', *Unterwegs zur Sache. Theologische Bemerkungen*, Munich 1972, pp.206–33, has rightly drawn attention to the difference between the possible world and the possibilities in the world. This distinction in the theology of creation seems to me, however, to be overcome in pneumatology. The Christian hope is not faced with the alternative of either trusting in the divine possibilities or seeking the possibilities of world history. On the contrary, it is pointed to the possibilities and powers of the Spirit of the last days in the history of God with the world. The new creation which is possible for the Holy Spirit works itself out historically through 'the manifestation of the Spirit' in the charismata in the church. Cf. J. Moltmann, *Diskussion über die* Theologie der Hoffnung, Munich 1967, pp.236ff.

19. Tillich, op. cit., p.165 = p.176.

20. Marsch, op. cit., p.201. He adds: 'If we understand the risen Christ in this sense as the future of the church, then it is possible to

formulate its essential character as follows: In the church as a social and political institution, Jesus' proclamation of the kingdom of God continues – not bound to his personal presence, though doubtless bound to the conditions of his fate and only under these conditions still to be expected.' I myself would say: just because of his personal presence, bound to the conditions of his fate, i.e., the cross.

21. Marsch, ibid., p.202.

22. Thus Diem also supplements Bultmann's 'at the same time' through an 'in one another' (op. cit., pp.20f. n.16).

23. Tillich, op. cit., pp.167ff., 172 = pp.178, 180, 183.

24. Küng, op. cit., p.5.

25. Ibid.

26. Ibid., pp.88ff.

27. Ibid., p.95.

28. Ibid., p.96.

29. J. V. Taylor, *The Go-Between God. The Holy Spirit and the Christian Mission*, SCM Press and Fortress Press 1972, esp. pp.42ff.

30. For a more detailed exposition see J. Moltmann, *The Crucified God*, ET SCM Press and Harper & Row 1974, pp.112ff.

31. R. Bultmann, *Glauben and Verstehen* III, Tübingen 1960, p.113.

32. E. Stauffer, 'ἵνα', *TDNT* III, pp.323–33; here pp.324ff., 'Theological Final Clauses'.

33. On this point cf. W. Pannenberg, *Jesus – God and Man*, SCM Press and Westminster Press 1968, §2: Christology und Soteriology, pp. 38ff.

34. Cf. P. Melanchthon, *Apologia Confessionis Augustanae*, in *Die Bekenntnisschriften der evangelisch-lutherischen Kirche*, Göttingen 1971[2], IV, pp.48, 50ff., 62, 101: 'Itaque non satis est credere, quod Christus natus, passus, resuscitatus sit, nisi addimus et hunc articulum, qui est causa finalis historiae: remissionem peccatorum' (p.51).

35. On Luther's concept of *promissio* cf. O. Bayer, *Promissio. Geschichte der reformatorischen Wende in Luthers Theologie*, Göttingen 1971, p.347. Cf. also pp.298ff: 'The new Christology'. I do not understand Bayer's sharp contrasting of Luther's *promissio* concept ('a legally binding promise taking immediate effect') with 'promise' as interpreted by Old Testament theology and the theology of universal history (presumably he is referring to G. von Rad and W. Pannenberg). For there too what is meant is not a 'category of revelation belonging to a philosophy of salvation history' as Bayer maintains (p.347). The following sentence also postulates an alternative which does not exist: 'The unity of God is not first acquired in the totality of a history which is incomplete in each given case, but gives itself entirely in the unambiguousness of its promise and becomes known in specific faith in that promise' (ibid.). For on the basis of a clear promise, the specific faith hopes for the revelation of God's glory.

36. P. Melanchthon, *Loci communes 1521. Melanchthons Werke*, ed. R. Stupperich, II.1, Gütersloh 1952, p.7. As Melanchthon's later

revisions of the *Loci communes* show, he was not thinking of a dissolution of christology in soteriology.

37. The Heidelberg Catechism of 1563, especially questions 36, 43, 45, 49, 51, 57, 58, 59.

38. On the modern concept of 'meaning' cf. H. Gollwitzer, *Krummes Holz – aufrechter Gang. Zur Frage nach dem Sinn des Lebens*, Munich 1970, pp.46ff.

39. E. Stauffer, op. cit., p.328.

40. O. Michel, *Der Brief an die Römer*, Göttingen 1955, p.184.

41. The relationship between Paul's christology and his doctrine of justification is dealt with in detail in E. Käsemann, *Perspectives on Paul*, ET SCM Press and Fortress Press 1971; P. Stuhlmacher, *Gerechtigkeit Gottes bei Paulus*, Göttingen 1965; and above all in G. Eichholz, *Die Theologie des Paulus im Umriß*, Neukirchen 1972.

42. So P. Melanchthon, *Loci praecipui theologici* (1559), *Melanchthons Werke*, ed. Stupperich, II. 2, 1953, p. 359: 'Justificatio significat remissionem peccatorum et reconciliationem seu acceptationem personae ad vitam aeternam.' The modern reduction of justification to the event of man's acceptance by God (a view which is supported by Paul Tillich's theology) is just as one-sided as the reduction of justification to the forgiveness of sins in some sectors of the Lutheran tradition.

43. Karl Barth especially stressed this 'disproportion', over against the one-sidedness of the Lutheran theology of the cross. Cf. *Church Dogmatics* II. 2, pp.389–92; IV.3. 2, pp.515f., 530f., 675f. Cf. also IV.2, p.577: '*Vivificatio* is the meaning and intention of *mortificatio*.'

44. Contrary to Ebeling, for whom what came to expression in Jesus finds its goal in the faith that gives certainty. Cf. *Theology and Proclamation*, pp.89ff.

45. A. Schlatter stressed this particularly, linking it with criticism (though not always apt criticism) of the Reformation's 'restricted' interpretation of justification: cf. *Luthers Deutung des Römerbriefs*, Beiträge zur Förderung christlicher Theologie 21.7, Gütersloh 1917.

46. E. Käsemann, 'On the Subject of Primitive Christian Apocalyptic', *New Testament Questions of Today*, ET SCM Press and Fortress Press 1969, pp.133f.

47. Ibid., p.136.

48. M. Luther, *Kleiner Katechismus*, in *Bekenntnisschriften*, p.520.

49. C. Wordsworth's Easter hymn ('Alleluia! Alleluia! Hearts to heaven and voices raise') echoes closely in this verse the ideas in J. Heermann's hymn 'Frühmorgens, da die Sonn aufgeht . . .':

> Hier ist noch nicht ganz kundgemacht,
> was er aus einem Grab gebracht . . .
> Der jüngste Tag wird's zeigen an,
> was er für Taten hat getan.

50. Stauffer, op. cit., pp.329f., 333: 'For Paul perceives a whole hierarchy of goals in which the provisional must serve the definitive and the salvation of the individual the salvation of the whole. The final goal

which must permeate all our conduct and must impress all lesser goals into its service is again the glorifying of God.'

51. N. A. Nissiotis, *Die Theologie der Ostkirche im ökumenischen Dialog*, Stuttgart 1968, p.60.

52. Cf. here R. Bultmann, *Theology of the New Testament* I, ET SCM Press and Scribner 1952, 38, pp.330ff.

53. Ibid., p.336.

54. Ibid., p.335: 'So Spirit may be called the power of futurity.'

55. Ibid.

56. Ibid., Vol. II, 1955, §41, p. 8: 'Still more important is the fact that Paul's terminology relating specifically to the history of salvation is not encountered in John.'

57. Cf. Nissiotis, op. cit., p.58.

58. Ibid., p.54.

59. M. Luther, *Schmalkaldic Article* II, in *Bekenntnisschriften*, p. 415.

60. Nissiotis, op. cit., pp.64ff.

61. Curiously enough, in his short account of pneumatic christology (ibid., pp.67ff.) Nissiotis does not mention Christ's sacrifice on the cross, which Heb. 9.14 says took place 'through the . . . Spirit'.

62. Cf. H. Blumenberg, *Die Legitimität der Neuzeit*, Frankfurt 1966, p.31.

63. K. Löwith, *Gesammelte Abhandlungen. Zur Kritik der geschichtlichen Existenz*, Stuttgart 1960; *Vorträge und Abhandlungen. Zur Kritik der christlichen Überlieferung*, Stuttgart 1966.

64. Cf. here M.-D. Chenu, 'Les signes des temps', *NRT* 87, 1965, pp. 29–39, and the comment 'Signs of the Times' in *Concilium* vol.5 no.3 (ET of Band 3 Heft 5), May 1967, pp.68–72. Here, however, the writer only talks about the positive signs of salvation and the longing for salvation found in world history. Archetypal pictures are the signs on 'the way to freedom' (Lohfink) – i.e., the exodus in the Old Testament and the exodus' continuing influence in the New. Even when 'the signs of the times' are interpreted as *praeparatio evangelica*, they are interpreted eschatologically.

65. The church's apocalyptic orientation and its focus on world history can already be seen in the medieval chronicles, which are also the first accounts of church history in their period.

66. K. Rengstorf, 'σημεῖον', *TDNT* VII, pp.200ff., here p.216.

67. Ibid., p.216.

68. Ibid., p.232. According to II(4) Esd. 8.63, changes in the firmament are also among 'a great number of the signs which thou art about to do in the last times'. Signs of this kind – eclipses of the sun and comets – are also noted in the Christian chronicles.

69. Ibid., p.233.

70. Ibid., p.237.

71. Ibid.

72. Ibid., p.241.

73. Ibid., p.258. Cf. here also E. Käsemann, 'Die Legitimität des Apostels' in *ZNW* 41, 1942, pp.33–71.

74. Cf. R. Strunk's comprehensive investigation, *Politische Ekklesiologie im Zeitalter der Revolution*, Munich and Mainz 1971. I am following his account here.
75. Strunk, op. cit., pp.102ff.
76. Quoted ibid., pp.236f.
77. Ibid., pp.154ff.
78. Ibid., p.221.
79. A. Vilmar, *Kirche und Welt. Pastoral-theologische Aufsätze*, ed. J. C. Müller, 1872, p.118.
80. Strunk, op. cit., p.249.
81. Vilmar, loc. cit.
82. A. Kuyper, *Reformation wider Revolution. Sechs Vorlesungen über den Calvinismus* (German trans.), Berlin 1904, p.4.
83. Ibid., p.5.
84. Ibid., pp.34, 81; cf. also pp.67, 27 and passim.
85. F. Schlegel, *Athenäumsfragmente*, Nr. 222. Cf. on the following passage J. Moltmann, *Theology of Hope*, ET SCM Press and Harper & Row 1967, ch. IV: Eschatology and History.
86. I. Kant, *Der Streit der Fakultäten*, 1798 (*Philosophische Bibliothek* 252, Hamburg 1959, pp.87, 83).
87. I. Kant, *Religion within the Limits of Reason Alone*, Book III, Div. I, 7, ET Harper & Bros. 1960, pp.105ff.
88. Cf. here C. Walther, *Typen des Reich-Gottes-Verständnisses. Studien zur Eschatologie und Ethik im 19. Jahrhundert*, Munich 1961, pp.117ff.
89. R. Rothe, *Theologische Ethik* III, 1848, §1177, pp.1010f.
90. Cf. Walther, op. cit., p.135.
91. Ibid.
92. T. Rendtorff shows himself a faithful pupil of Rothe's in his *Theorie des Christentums. Historisch-theologische Studien zu seiner neuzeitlichen Verfassung*, Gütersloh 1972. His theories about Christianity in modern times and modern Christianity, which has now entered into its ethical era, i.e., its era in world-history, are a repetition of Rothe's theses.
93. Bultmann, *Theology of the New Testament I*, pp.6f.
94. Cf. Moltmann, *Theology of Hope*, p.263.
95. A. M. K. Müller, *Die präparierte Zeit*, Stuttgart 1972, p.33.
96. So K. Barth, 'Der Christ in der Gesellschaft' in *Anfänge der dialektischen Theologie*, ThB 17, 1962, pp.9ff.
97. So K. Rengstorf, 'ἀποστέλλω', *TDNT* I, p.398.
98. Cf. here also H. Mühlen, *Der Heilige Geist als Person*, Münster 1966², pp.197ff.
99. A. M. Aagaard, 'Missio Dei in katholischer Sicht' in *EvTh* 34, 1974, pp.423f.
100. G. Wagner, 'Der Heilige Geist als offenbarmachende und vollendende Kraft' in C. Heitmann and H. Mühlen, *Erfahrung und Theologie des Heiligen Geistes*, Hamburg 1974, p.216. Following the Orthodox

view, the writer talks about a 'temporal reflection of the eternal life of the Trinity as it is in itself'.

101. On the Orthodox distinction between the 'procession' of the Spirit from the Father and his 'sending forth' by the Son (John 15.26), and the problem of the '*Filioque*' in the Western church, cf. Nissiotis, op. cit., pp.26ff.

102. Barth, *Church Dogmatics* IV. 2, p.342.

103. Wagner, op. cit., p.220: 'In fact in Augustine the life within the Trinity already closes into a self-contained circle, or – to use another image – into a closed triangle. The Spirit closes this circle as the bond of mutual love, the *vinculum amoris* between Father and Son. It was on this foundation that the "*Filioque*" dispute later developed. The East always reflected the speculative Augustinian conception of the Spirit as the bond of mutual love, which closes the circle of trinitarian love inwardly, within itself. "We do not say that the Spirit is from the Son, but we call him the Spirit of the Son", was the way John of Damascus formulated the Eastern church's answer to the Western "*Filioque*". The rejection of the "*Filioque*" implies that, according to the Eastern conception, the Trinity remains fundamentally "open", in order to manifest itself in the coming of the Spirit.'

104. Cf. Moltmann, *The Crucified God*, pp.274ff.

105. For more detail cf. Moltmann, op. cit., pp.112ff.

106. On the following passage cf. G. Kittel, 'δόξα', *TDNT* II, pp. 233ff., 242ff.; H. Urs von Balthasar, *Herrlichkeit. Eine theologische Ästhetik* I–III. 2, Einsiedeln 1961–7; J. Moltmann, *Theology and Joy*, ET SCM Press 1973. For the exegetical substantiation cf. W. Thüsing, *Per Christum in Deum. Studien zum Verhältnis von Christozentrik und Theozentrik in den paulinischen Hauptbriefen*, Münster 1968[2].

107. So according to Aquinas the doctrine of the Trinity is subordinated to the doctrine of the divine nature, for when we abstract from the three divine Persons, the one absolute divine nature remains. For a critical view of this see H. Mühlen, *Der Heilige Geist als Person*, pp.318ff., and 'Soziale Geisterfahrung als Antwort auf eine einseitige Gotteslehre' in C. Heitmann and H. Mühlen, *Erfahrung und Theologie des Heiligen Geistes*, pp.253ff., esp. p.257. The precedence of the doctrine *de Deo uno* over the doctrine of the Trinity and its substantiation by natural theology had disastrous effects for the whole Western doctrine of God, because it gave grounds for the development of atheism and has itself pre-Christian features.

108. F. Rosenzweig, *Der Stern der Erlösung*, Heidelberg 1954[3], Book III, pp.192–4. Cf. also A. Heschel, *The Prophets*, Harper & Row 1962.

109. In the following passage I am picking up ideas of Adrienne von Speyr, which coincide closely with my theology of 'the crucified God'. Cf. B. Albrecht, *Eine Theologie des Katholischen. Einführung in das Werk Adrienne von Speyrs*, Einsiedeln 1972–3, esp. II, pp.155ff., 'Die Sendung der Liebe und ihre Rückwirkung auf Gott.'

110. With this I am taking up the suggestion of R. Bohren, *Fasten und Feiern*, Neukirchen 1973, pp.11f. and n.2.

111. Cf. also H. Gollwitzer, *Die kapitalistische Revolution*, Munich 1974, p. 105: 'Old and New Testaments see humanity as the object and addressee of a great historical undertaking of cosmic scope, in which God finally defines himself, makes himself known and brings himself to full divinity, that is, to his *doxa*. This continually forward-moving process includes the conversion of the individual brought about by the message, and the coming into being of groups of disciples; and from this process these things take on their wider meaning.'

III The Church of Jesus Christ

1. Dietrich Bonhoeffer sought to understand the being of the church ontologically as 'being in' the act of Christ. Cf. *Act and Being*, ET Harper & Row 1961, Collins 1962, pp.117ff.; *Sanctorum Communio*, ET Collins and Harper & Row 1963, pp.106ff.

2. Cf. here also H. de Lubac, *The Splendour of the Church*, ET Sheed and Ward 1956, pp.37ff. and 147ff.

3. This means that the Reformed definition of the church as *creatura verbi* must also be set in the wider framework of the definition of the church as the creation of the Spirit.

4. On the question of the church's and the individual's certainty of perseverance, cf. J. Moltmann, *Prädestination und Perseveranz*, Neukirchen 1961, esp. pp.89ff.

5. Barth also criticizes the same lack in the article on the church (article VII) in the Augsburg Confession.

6. Recently Marsch (*Institution im Übergang*, pp.184ff.) has depicted 'Jesus as the founder of the church' in order to legitimize the church's institutional character. But he too does not get beyond the limitations of this formula – the limitations laid down by the death of the 'founder'. In order to grasp the mystery of the church, which is to be found in the presence of the risen Christ, it is not sufficient to reckon with a continuingly efficacious 'trend' on Christ's part.

7. R. Bultmann, *Faith and Understanding*, ET SCM Press and Harper & Row 1969, p.308.

8. Ibid., p.310.

9. Ibid., pp.310f. 'The word of the Christian proclamation and the history which it communicates coincide, are one' (ibid.). Here it remains unclear whether a temporal or a factual coincidence is meant. This is an ambiguity which occasionally occurs elsewhere in Bultmann.

10. Cf. G. Ebeling, *The Nature of Faith*, ET Collins 1961, Muhlenberg Press 1962.

11. G. Ebeling makes this distinction himself in *Theology and Proclamation. A Discussion with R. Bultmann*, p.96, when he says: 'The basis of the church, i.e. that which makes the church the church, is not the

church itself; in just the same way as it is impossible for the basis of the church to exist without the church, and for the church to exist without its basis.' But this then also applies to the relationship of faith to Christ. Christ as the foundation of faith is indeed only evident to faith; but, equally, as the foundation he has a position independent of faith, thanks to which he calls forth faith without being dependent on it.

12. Pope Pius XII, *Mystici Corporis Christi*, par. 51, ET Catholic Truth Society 1944, p.32.

13. Augustine, *Sermo* 137. 1 (MPL 38, 754): 'Cum ergo sit ille caput Ecclesiae, et sit corpus eius Ecclesia, totus Christus et caput et corpus est.'

14. H. Schlier, *Der Brief an die Epheser*, Düsseldorf 1969⁵, pp.91ff., 206ff.: 'Beneath her inner growth, beneath her approach to Christ, beneath her entry into the fullness of Christ, she permits the universe to grow towards Christ. . . . The ultimate goal is Christ as head of the universe. This goal is achieved in the context of the growth of the church and in no other. . . . The body of Christ sees to its building up and in its building up the growth of the body of the universe towards Christ.'

15. See E. Käsemann's critical view of Schlier in 'Das Interpretations-problem des Epheserbriefs', *Exegetische Versuche und Besinnungen* II, Göttingen 1964, pp.253–61 [no ET].

16. This is E. Käsemann's critical comment on Bultmann; cf. his 'Blind Alleys in the "Jesus of History" Controversy', *New Testament Questions of Today*, ET SCM Press and Fortress Press 1969, pp. 35ff.

17. W. Kramer, *Christ, Lord, Son of God*, ET SBT 50, 1966, §7d, p.37: 'For while the resurrection constitutes, or confirms, Jesus' eschato-logical status, the phrase "for us" interprets his death as the death of this same eschatological figure.'

18. I have borrowed these phrases from Ernst Bloch, *Das Prinzip Hoffnung* I, Frankfurt 1959, p.7: 'In this way the petrified divorces between future and past collapse by themselves; the future which has not come, becomes in the past visible, revenged and inherited – communicated and fulfilled past in the future.'

19. Orthodox Lutheranism put under the heading *de officio Christi*: (i) the *officium propheticum*, the revelation of the divine will towards salvation; (ii) the *officium sacerdotale*, Christ's vicarious atonement (*satisfactio*) and present intercession (*intercessio*); (iii) the *officium regium Christi* in the *regnum potentiae*, *regnum gratiae* and *regnum gloriae*. This certainly does not comprehend all Christ's functions, which are expressed in the multiplicity of the New Testament titles; but it names the most important aspects. The doctrine of Christ's threefold office has a regu-lative function, as the countercheck shows: restriction to Christ's prophetic office leads to liberal Protestantism, which overlooks evil and death; restriction to Christ's priestly office leads to the danger of a religion of consolation which justifies existing injustice; restriction to Christ's kingly office leads to clerical, moral or political triumphalism.

It is noticeable that Küng (*The Church*, pp.43ff.) shows that the eschatological community of the redeemed came into being simply on the basis of Jesus' proclamation, i.e., simply from the *officium propheticum Christi*. He does not draw on the significance of the sacrifice on the cross and Christ's resurrection. In *Strukturen der Kirche*, 1962², p.21, he says: 'In the church all Christians share in the kingly, priestly and prophetic office of Christ.'

20. For the following passage see G. Friedrich, 'εὐαγγελίζομαι', *TDNT* II, pp.707–37; J. Schniewind, *Euangelion. Ursprung und erste Gestalt des Begriffes Evangelium* I and II, Gütersloh 1927, 1931; P. Stuhlmacher, *Das paulinische Evangelium I. Vorgeschichte*, Göttingen 1968.

21. So too H. Schlier, *Wort Gottes. Eine neutestamentliche Besinnung*, Würzburg 1962², p.18: 'Where the gospel is preached the exalted Lord hurries ahead of his appearance, through his word in man's mouth; in that word he anticipates his future in the announcement of himself as the one who is to come.'

22. Here I am deviating from Friedrich's article, since he hardly stresses this aspect at all.

23. Karl Marx, however, believed that petrified conditions could be made to dance if one 'sang them their own melody'. But here it would be truer to say that one sings to realities the melody of their slumbering potentialities, including the potentialities in them open to the creator. The power of the creative potentialities in reality is the power of the Holy Spirit, the Spirit of the new creation.

24. Friedrich, op. cit., p.718.

25. On the concept of poverty cf. Gutiérrez, *A Theology of Liberation*, pp. 287ff. He describes very well the contradiction within the theological concept and would like to depict poverty as solidarity and protest: 'Christian poverty, an expression of love, is solidarity *with the poor* and is a protest *against poverty*' (p.301). For an understanding of the biblical concept, cf. A. Kuschke, 'Arm und Reich im Alten Testament', *ZAW* 16, 1931, pp.3ff.

26. E. Peterson sees this very clearly in 'Was ist der Mensch?', *Theologische Traktate*, Munich 1951, pp.227ff.: 'From the beginning of the Son of man's ministry until near its end, people with every imaginable sickness come to him. From fever to blindness, from paralysis to leprosy. . . . The poor Jesus talks about are so poor that no human society will absorb them any more. The poor who are called blessed in Jesus' words are those who even transcend the term "the proletarian rabble"; they are not even on the fringe of human society; they are on the fringe of the world itself. . . . Christ calls himself the Son of man because he transcends man. The Son of man is the one who comprehends himself in human sickness by taking that sickness on himself. The Son of man is the one who sees himself in the possessed by telling the demons to depart. . . . The Son of man is the one who sees himself in the poor as the one who for our sakes has become poor.'

27. Cf. H. Gollwitzer, *Die kapitalistische Revolution*, Munich 1974,

pp.98ff. Here the total character of conversion and its orientation towards life in the world of death is especially stressed.

28. The Council of Youth at Taizé in 1974 very pertinently reminded the churches that it is only as 'the people of the beatitudes' that they can appeal to Jesus and are legitimized by him.

29. Bultmann, *Faith and Understanding*, p.292.

30. J. Schniewind, 'Messiasgeheimnis und Eschatologie' in *Nachgelassene Reden und Aufsätze*, ed. E. Kähler, Berlin 1952, pp.1ff.

31. Käsemann, 'On the Subject of Primitive Christian Apocalyptic', *New Testament Questions of Today*, p.122.

32. Cf. Moltmann, *Theology of Hope*, ch. V.

33. J. Matthes, *Die Emigration der Kirche aus der Gesellschaft*, Hamburg 1964, has described this dangerous retreat of the church. It has nothing to do with the exodus idea.

34. Thus among the coloured slaves in America the Bible did not have the soothing effect intended; its influence was revolutionary. Cf. J. Cone, *The Spirituals and the Blues*, Seabury Press 1972.

35. *Mystici Corporis* par. 32, p.21.

36. de Lubac, op. cit., p.31.

37. M. Luther, *Von der Freiheit eines Christenmenschen*, ch. 12 (*Luthers Werke in Auswahl*, vol. 2, ed. O. Clemen, Berlin 1929, pp. 15f.).

38. S. Tromp, *De Nativitate Ecclesiae ex Corde in Cruce*, Rome 1932; H. Urs von Balthasar, 'Mysterium Paschale' in *Mysterium Salutis. Grundriß heilsgeschichtlicher Dogmatik*, III/2, Einsiedeln 1969, pp.216ff.

39. For a more detailed discussion here cf. Moltmann, *The Crucified God*, pp.126ff.

40. P. Stuhlmacher, *Gerechtigkeit Gottes bei Paulus*, Göttingen 1965.

41. The Lutheran distinction between law and gospel does not mean that the revolutionary power of the gospel in the world is neutralized; it is an alternative way of bringing out its rigour.

42. Cf. here H. Schlier, *The Relevance of the New Testament*, ET Burns & Oates and Herder & Herder 1968, pp.215ff.

43. For a more detailed consideration of this point cf. J. Moltmann, 'Theologische Kritik der politischen Religion' in J. B. Metz, J. Moltmann and W. Oelmüller, *Kirche im Prozeß der Aufklärung*, Munich and Mainz 1970, pp.11–52.

44. E. Bloch, *Atheism in Christianity*, ET Herder & Herder 1972, pp. 126ff.

45. B. Brecht, *The Good Person of Szechwan*, scene 10 (ET, *Plays* II, Methuen 1962, p.307).

46. G. W. F. Hegel, *Werke* XVI, ed. H. Glockner, Stuttgart 1928, pp. 298f.; ET, *Philosophy of Religion*, London 1895, vol. III, p.90.

47. H. Urs von Balthasar, op. cit., p.220.

48. This aspect ought to be added as a supplementary point to Karl Barth's christological doctrine of election, according to which, on the basis of the rejection of Christ, the choice of grace is in principle and potentially universal. Cf. *Church Dogmatics* II.2.

49. Particularism and universalism, the calling of the humble and the glorifying of all, are apparently not alternatives for biblical thinking. Just as justification applies to everyone who believes, but 'to the Jew first, and also to the Greek' (Rom. 1.16), so all men are to be glorified together in God's coming; but this begins with the calling of the despised and the 'lifting up of the valleys'. This particularist predisposition must hence be understood inclusively and as being in intention universal.

50. Cf. de Lubac, op. cit., pp.226ff.

51. Clement of Rome 16.1, quoted by de Lubac, ibid., p.232.

52. Cf. here the whole passage II Cor. 4.7–18 and the comments by E. Güttgemanns, *Der leidende Apostle und sein Herr*, Göttingen 1966; W. Schrage, 'Leid, Kreuz und Eschaton. Die Peristasenkataloge als Merkmale paulinischer theologia crucis und Eschatologie', *EvTh* 34, 1974, pp.141–75.

53. For a more detailed exposition cf. H. Mühlen, *Die Veränderlichkeit Gottes als Horizont einer zukünftigen Christologie*, Münster 1969; von Balthasar, op. cit., pp.223ff.; B. Albrecht, *Eine Theologie des Katholischen. Einführung in das Werk Adrienne von Speyrs* II, Einsiedeln 1973, pp. 113ff.; Moltmann, *The Crucified God*, pp.235ff.

54. Cf. ch. II, § 4.

55. Cf. ch. VI, § 2, where the particular ministry is given its foundation in the charismatic community, and the 'spiritual office' in the spirit and office of the whole church.

56. D. Bonhoeffer to E. Bethge, 18 July 1944, *Letters and Papers from Prison*, ET, enlarged ed., SCM Press and Macmillan 1971, p.361.

57. Käsemann has stressed this in connection with the gospel narratives. Cf. 'The Beginnings of Christian Theology', *New Testament Questions of Today*, pp.82ff.

58. E. Fuchs is therefore correct in interpreting the resurrection as love and in expounding I Cor. 15 through I Cor. 13. Though the converse must then be true as well.

59. F. Hahn, *Christologische Hoheitstitel. Ihre Geschichte im frühen Christentum*, Göttingen 1963.

60. Pannenberg, *Jesus – God and Man*, esp. pp.74ff.

61. Küng's view in *The Church*, pp.47f.

62. Contrary to Küng's view, op. cit., p.49. By 'purely religious' he intends here a criticism of earthly, national and religio-political theocracy. One must agree with this criticism. But in modern usage the expression 'purely religious' has taken on a meaning which confines it to the religion of 'the heart' and the private sphere; and in this respect the phrase is inappropriate.

63. According to Käsemann, this is the theme of apocalyptic, primitive Christian apocalyptic included. Cf. op. cit., pp.108ff.

64. G. von Rad, 'εἰκών', *TDNT* II, p. 392: 'Thus man in his sphere of rule as God's vice-gerent is summoned to represent the dominion and majesty of God.'

65. K. Koch, 'Spätisraelitisches Geschichtsdenken am Beispiel des Buches Daniel' in *Historische Zeitschrift* 193/1, 1961, pp.1–32.

66. In my view the *'eikon'* idea clearly shows the connection between the lordship of Christ and man's dominion over the earth (Gen. 1.28). On this point cf. G. Kittel, 'εἰκών', *TDNT* II, pp.392ff.; J. Jervell, *Imago Dei. Gen 1.26f.* im *Spätjudentum, in der Gnosis und in den paulinischen Briefen*, Göttingen 1960; W. Thüsing, *Per Christum in Deum. Studien zum Verhältnis von Christozentrik und Theozentrik in den paulinischen Hauptbriefen*, Münster 1968², ch. III: 'Unsere Verbindung mit Christus als dem "Sohn Gottes" und dem "Bild Gottes"', pp.115ff.

67. Cf. Barth, *Church Dogmatics*, IV. 1, pp.157–357; W. Kreck, *Grundfragen der Dogmatik*, Munich 1970, pp.79ff.; W. Kohler, 'Neue Herrschaftsverhältnisse als Grund der Mission' in *EvTh* 34, 1974, pp.462ff.

68. Cf. here Thüsing, op. cit., ch. VI: 'Die Übergabe der Herrschaft an den Vater', pp.238ff.

69. Kohler (op. cit., p.464) has in a very interesting way related Karl Marx's theory of reflection to Karl Barth's christological analogical thinking. His conclusions are critical of the churches.

70. G. Hasenhüttl, *Herrschaftsfreie Kirche, Sozio-theologische Grundlegung*, Düsseldorf 1974, pp.12ff.

71. Cf. E. Brunner, *Dogmatics* III, ET Lutterworth Press and Westminster Press 1962.

72. F. Schleiermacher, *Reden über die Religion* (1799), ET *On Religion: Speeches to its Cultured Despisers*, London 1893; J. Habermas, *Technik und Wissenschaft als Ideologie*, Frankfurt 1968.

73. On the importance of the idea of human rights in the Christian movement for women's emancipation, and in the German women's movement, cf. E. Moltmann-Wendel, *Menschenrechte für die Frau*, Munich and Mainz 1974.

74. H. Rahner, *Man at Play*, ET Burns & Oates 1965; H. Cox, *The Feast of Fools. A Theological Essay on Festivity and Fantasy*, Harvard University Press 1969; G. M. Martin, *Fest und Alltag. Bausteine zu einer Theorie des Festes*, Stuttgart 1973; Moltmann, *Theology and Joy*; also the collection of essays on the theme of 'Politics and Liturgy' in *Concilium* vol. 2 no. 10, February 1974 (= Band 10 Heft 2 in German ed.).

75. R. Schutz, *Festival*, ET SPCK 1974, pp.130f.

76. Rahner, op. cit., p.86.

77. Cf. here W. Hollenweger, *The Pentecostals*, ET SCM Press and Random House 1972.

78. F. Stepun, *Dostojewski. Weltschau und Weltanschauung*, Heidelberg 1950, p.43 (reissued in *Dostojewskij und Tolstoj*, Munich 1961, p.29).

79. I. Kant, *The Metaphysical Principles of Virtue*, Part II of the *Metaphysics of Morals*, §§46f., ET Bobs-Merrill 1964, pp.135ff.

80. G. W. F. Hegel, *Werke* VII, ed. H. Glockner, Stuttgart 1928, p.60, ET, *Hegel's Philosophy of Right*, Clarendon Press 1942, p.228.

81. Cf. here J. Schniewind, *Das Evangelium nach Matthäus*, NTD 2, 1950⁵, pp.146f., on Matt. 11.19.

82. R. Bultmann, *The Gospel of John*, ET Blackwell and Westminster Press 1971, pp.542ff.

83. Barth, *Church Dogmatics* III.3, pp.285f.; cf. also IV.3, pp.796ff.

84. See the article 'Freundschaft' in *Historisches Wörterbuch der Philosophie*, ed. J. Ritter, Basle 1972, 1104ff.

85. E. Peterson, 'Der Gottesfreund. Beiträge zur Geschichte eines religiösen Terminus', *ZKG* 42, NF 5, 1923, pp.161–202.

86. F. Nietzsche's Zarathustra teaches [that it is] 'not the neighbour . . . but the friend', who is to be the 'festival of the earth . . . and a foretaste of the Superman' (*Thus Spake Zarathustra* XVI) and who becomes a friend not through shared suffering, but through 'fellowship in joy' (*Human, Alltoo-human*, I, div. 9, 499).

87. Cf. E. Russell, *History of Quakerism*, Macmillan 1942; T. E. Drake, *Quakers and Slavery in America*, Yale University Press and OUP 1950; Richenda C. Scott, *Die Quäker*, Stuttgart 1974.

88. This thesis is developed in contrast to Ambrose, who said: '*Ubi Petrus, ibi ecclesia*' (de Lubac, op. cit., p.202). M. Tripole subjected it to a critical evaluation, comparing it with statements made by the Second Vatican Council in 'Ecclesiological developments in Moltmann's Theology of Hope', *Theological Studies* 34, 1973, 1, pp.19–35. The thesis itself derives from Ignatius, *Smyrn.* 8.2.

89. On the interpretation of the name JHWH cf. H. Gollwitzer, *Krummes Holz – aufrechter Gang. Zur Frage nach dem Sinn des Lebens*, Munich 1970, pp.303ff.

90. On the relationship between the Johannine 'I am' sayings of Jesus and the Old Testament name for God, cf. G. Gloege, *The Day of his Coming*, ET SCM Press and Fortress Press 1963, p.214.

91. Eichholz, *Die Theologie des Paulus im Umriß*, pp.14ff.

92. Cf. E. Jüngel, 'Die Autorität des bittenden Christus' in *Unterwegs zur Sache. Theologische Bemerkungen*, Munich 1972, pp. 179ff.

93. J. Schniewind's view in *Das Evangelium nach Matthäus*, NTD 2, 1950, p.255.

94. M. Luther, *Von der Freiheit eines Christenmenschen*, ch. 27.

95. R. Bultmann, *Glauben und Verstehen* IV, Tübingen 1965, pp.111f., 125ff.

96. It is only this aspect that is stressed by de Lubac, for example op. cit., pp.147ff.). The same may be said about the books on the church by Nissiotis and Küng.

97. Cf. V. Lanternari, *The Religions of the Oppressed*, Knopf and Mac-Gibbon & Kee 1963; M. Doerne, *Gott und Mensch in Dostojewskijs Werk*, Göttingen 1962²; and in this connection the 'truly overwhelming "rabbinic fable" ' according to which the Messiah is already present in concealed form, sitting among the lepers and beggars at the gates of Rome: G. Scholem, 'Zum Verständnis der messianischen Idee im Judentum', *Judaica*, Frankfurt 1963, pp.28f.

98. I am here referring to distinctions made by Paul Tillich on the one hand and by K. Rahner on the other. Both are designed to make the

frontiers of the church penetrable and to open the church for the greater efficacy of Christ in each case.

99. M. Tripole (op. cit., pp.30ff.) has not perceived the converse of this question. It is true that he finds similar ideas in the declarations of the Second Vatican Council, but as long as he follows the Council's line 'which sees only Catholic Christians as fully incorporated in the Church', he is maintaining the principle 'ubi Petrus, ibi ecclesia', and is bound to gain the impression that 'thus Moltmann seems to incorporate non-Christians into the Church in a way that Vatican II chose not to do.'

100. A. Oepke, 'παρουσία', *TDNT* V, pp.858ff., 865.

101. K. Barth, *Dogmatics in Outline*, ET SCM Press and Philosophical Library 1949, pp.129ff.

102. J. Moltmann, *Theology of Hope*.

103. G. Scholem, *Die messianische Idee im Judentum*, pp.73f.: 'The greatness of the messianic idea corresponds to the tremendous weakness of Jewish history, which in exile was not prepared for intervention on the historical level. It has the weakness of the provisional, which does not expend itself. . . . Thus the messianic idea in Judaism enforced *life in deferment*, in which nothing can be done and completed in a final way.' The messianic idea in Christianity differs from this through the unique and final character of Christ's self-surrender on the cross. His resurrection from the dead brings the dynamism of the provisional into accord with the finality of the sacrifice, so that it would be possible to talk about a final interim period, but not about a holding back of life in the period of deferment.

IV The Church of the Kingdom of God

1. D. Bonhoeffer, *Ethics*, ed. E. Bethge, ET SCM Press and Macmillan 1955, p.181; rearranged edition, 1971, p.41.

2. K. Barth, 'The Christian Community and the Civil Community', in *Against the Stream: Shorter Post-War Writings*, SCM Press and Philosophical Library 1954, p.19: 'Furthermore, the object of the promise and the hope in which the Christian community has its eternal goal . . . consists not in an eternal Church, but in the *polis* built by God and coming down from heaven to earth.' D. Bonhoeffer, *Sanctorum Communio*, ET Collins and Harper & Row 1963, p.199: 'The concept of the kingdom of God does indeed embrace not only the consummation of the church but also the problems of the "new world", that is, the eschatology of civilisation and of nature.'

3. H. Küng has gathered together the considerable literature on this: cf. *The Church*, pp.132ff., and *Christsein*, Munich 1974, pp.618ff.

4. Cf. A. von Harnack, *Der Vorwurf des Atheismus in den drei ersten Jahrhunderten*. Texte und Untersuchungen zur Geschichte der altchristlichen Literatur 18.4, Berlin 1905.

5. At the peak of ecclesiastical power, the Fourth Lateran Council of 1215 (Innocent III) passed anti-Jewish measures which even exceeded the degrading laws of the Christian emperors Theodosius and Justinian. The results for the Jews of this absolutism are movingly described by A. Schwarz-Bart, *Der Letzte der Gerechten*, Frankfurt 1960.

6. F. Rosenzweig, *Der Stern der Erlösung*, III, Heidelberg 1954[3], p.197.

7. On this point see F.-W. Marquardt, *Die Entdeckung des Judentums für die christliche Theologie*, Munich 1967.

8. Küng, *Christsein*, p.159.

9. G. Schrenk, *Gottesreich und Bund im älteren Protestantismus vornehmlich bei Johannes Coccejus*, Gütersloh 1923; G. Weth, *Die Heilsgeschichte, ihr universeller und ihr individueller Sinn in der offenbarungsgeschichtlichen Theologie des 19. Jahrhunderts*, Gütersloh 1931.

10. Cf. the article 'Chiliasmus' in *RGG*[3] I, 1651f.; *LThK* II, 1058ff.; W. Nigg, *Das ewige Reich*, Zürich 1954[2]; P. Althaus, *Die letzten Dinge*, Gütersloh 1957[7].

11. Auberlen, quoted in Althaus, op. cit., p.306.

12. H. Berkhof, *Kirche und Kaiser. Eine Untersuchung der Entstehung der byzantinischen und der theokratischen Staatsauffassung im 4. Jahrhundert* (Göttingen 1947); A. Dempf, *Sacrum Imperium. Geschichts- und Staats-philosophie des Mittelalters und der politischen Renaissance*, Munich 1962[3].

13. F. D. E. Schleiermacher, *Briefe bei Gelegenheit der politisch-theologischen Aufgabe und des Sendschreibens jüdischer Hausväter* (1799), *Sämtliche Werke*, section 1, vol. 5, Berlin 1846, pp.1–39, 28f.: 'I demand further that they formally and publicly relinquish their hope of a Messiah; I believe that this is an important point which the state cannot yield them.'

14. Augsburg Confession, article XVII; Second Helvetic Confession, article XI. Nineteenth-century Lutherans of the 'salvation-history' school such as F. Delitzsch, J. C. K. von Hofmann and C. C. Luthardt declared that it was only *chiliasmus crassus* that was rejected, i.e., the expectation of a 'Mohammedan kingdom of hedonism and pleasure', not their own *chiliasmus subtilis*.

15. C. E. Luthardt, *Apologie des Christentums* II, Leipzig 1867, pp. 182ff., esp. p. 184. According to Auberlen Jerusalem will be the centre of the millennial kingdom and Israel will again rise to the summit of all mankind. It is only then that state, art and education will be truly Christian (Althaus, op. cit., p.306). On the whole subject now see also P. Beyerhaus, 'Evangelisation und Reich Gottes', *Internationaler Kongreß für Welt-Evangelisation*, 1974; this deduces from these ideas the rejection of the Christianization of the world in the period of the world's evangelization and draws the conclusion from the Yom Kippur war of 1973 that 'the era of the Gentiles' and with it the era of world mission is coming to an end. Neither conclusion will hold water, for liberating action is a part of the mission of Jesus and the church, not merely

evangelization. Neither of these is yet the messianic kingdom itself. Even the conversion of Israel is not yet the messianic kingdom itself.

16. Contrary to Ernst Bloch's statement: 'Ubi Lenin – ibi Jerusalem' (*Das Prinzip Hoffnung*, I, p.711). Cf. the whole section, 'Altneuland, Programm des Zionismus', I, pp.698–713. The Jewish philosopher E. Fackenheim also takes a critical view of Bloch: see 'The Commandment to Hope' in *The Future of Hope*, ed. W. Kapps, Philadelphia 1970, pp.81f.

17. Althaus, op. cit., p.309.

18. Ibid., p.313.

19. Ibid., p.309.

20. R. Bultmann, 'Prophecy and Fulfilment' in *Essays Philosophical and Theological*, ET SCM Press and Macmillan 1955, pp.182ff. Here (pp. 188ff.) Bultmann discusses critically the salvation-history theology of J. C. K. von Hofmann: 'How far, then, does Old Testament Jewish history represent prophecy fulfilled in the history of the New Testament community? It is fulfilled in its inner contradiction, its miscarriage' (p.205).

21. Ibid., p.208: 'Thus faith, to be a really justifying faith, must constantly contain within itself the way of the law as something which has been overcome; it must also, in order to be an eschatological attitude, constantly contain within itself the attempt to identify what happens in the secular sphere with what happens eschatologically, as something which has been overcome.'

22. G. Klein, 'Individualgeschichte und Weltgeschichte bei Paulus', *EvTh* 24, 1964, pp.126ff., talks about the removal of the special quality of Israel's history (p.155), about the 'indifference of all historical differences in pre-believing mankind' (p.159), and about the 'absolute indifference' to which pre-Christian humanity 'descends' theologically (p.160). The orthodox Lutheran Kliefoth expressed himself in similar terms; Althaus quotes him in passing (op. cit., p.313): 'The vocation which Israel really had was in the nature of things finished and at an end once it had reached its goal – when the Saviour had found his dwelling-place on earth, had completed the work of revelation, and had sent forth his gospel to all nations; and with this *Israel receded of its own accord into the ranks of the other nations.*'

23. See here the balanced interpretations of G. Eichholz, *Die Theologie des Paulus im Umriß*, Neukirchen 1972, and U. Wilckens, *Rechtfertigung als Freiheit. Paulusstudien*, Neukirchen 1974, pp.77–109.

24. E. Peterson, 'Die Kirche aus Juden und Heiden' in *Theologische Traktate*, Munich 1952, pp.239ff.

25. W. Schrage, 'Ecclesia und Synagoge', *ZThK* 60, 1963, pp.178–202; H. Kasting, *Die Anfänge der urchristlichen Mission*, Munich 1969, pp.127ff.; F. Hahn, *Das Verständnis der Mission im Neuen Testament*, Neukirchen 1963, pp.43ff.

26. E. Käsemann, 'Paul and Early Catholicism', in *New Testament Questions of Today*, p.241.

27. Rosenweig, op. cit. II, p.198.

28. *Fundamenten en Perspektieven van Belijden*, The Hague 1949.

29. *The Documents of Vatican II*, ed. W. M. Abbott, Geoffrey Chapman and Herder & Herder 1966, pp.663–6.

30. Compare the excellent *L'Attitude des Chrétiens à l'égard du judaïsme* published by the Comité épiscopal pour les relations avec le judaïsme, April 1973.

31. See here J. Moltmann, 'Messianic Hope in Christianity', *Concilium* vol. 7/8, no.10 (ET of Band 10 Heft 7/8), September/October 1974, pp. 155–61.

32. *L'Attitude*, loc. cit.: 'To see the commandments of Judaism as merely forced observances is greatly to undervalue them. The rites of Judaism are gestures which interrupt the everyday character of existence and remind those who observe them of the lordship of God.'

33. Rosenzweig, op. cit. III, p.197.

34. This seems to me the meaning of the final statement of *L'Attitude*: '. . . That they cast their old enmity away and turn to the Father with a fervency of hope which will be a promise for the whole world.' The Jewish reaction to the declaration through the Chief Rabbi of France, Jacob Kaplan, says in its final sentence: 'The chief rabbinate is happy to underline that the "orientations" of the French episcopate run parallel to the teaching of the great Jewish theologians, for whom the religions which have proceeded from Judaism have the task of preparing mankind for the dawn of the messianic era promised by the Bible.'

35. See here F. W. Marquardt, *Die Bedeutung der biblischen Landverheißungen für die Christen*, ThEx 116, 1964.

36. In this paragraph I have drawn particularly on *Dialog mit anderen Religionen. Material aus der ökumenischen Bewegung*, ed. H. J. Margull and S. J. Samartha, Frankfurt 1972.

37. Cf. the four volumes published in preparation for the Geneva Conference on Church and Society: *Christian Social Ethics in a Changing World*, ed. J. C. Bennett, *Responsible Government in a Revolutionary Age*, ed. Z. K. Matthews, *Economic Growth in World Perspective*, ed. D. Munby, and *Man in Community*, ed. E. de Vries, all SCM Press and Association Press 1966. See also J. Moltmann, 'Bringing Peace to a Divided World', *The Experiment Hope*, ET SCM Press and Fortress Press 1975, pp.72ff.

38. At the Bangkok Conference in 1973 this new situation was both demanded and evident. See *Bangkok Assembly 1973*, Minutes and Report of the Assembly . . . on World Mission and Evangelism, Geneva 1973.

39. Quoted from H. Küng, *Christsein*, p.89. I agree with his criticism of this theological formula.

40. K. Rahner expressly supported this ecclesiological expansion of the concept of the church: see 'Anonymous Christians', *Theological Investigations* VI, ET Darton, Longman & Todd and Seabury Press 1969, pp. 390ff. Here, unlike Rahner, we are adhering to the integration of the concept of the church in 'God's history' with the world, which we have already discussed in ch. II, § 4.

41. So H. Küng, *Christenheit als Minderheit*, Einsiedeln 1965, p.36: 'We can ask what is outside the church, but the question is difficult to

answer. But what is outside God and his plan of salvation is no question at all. If we look at God's plan of salvation, then there is no *extra*, only an *intra*, no outside, only an inside, since God "desires all men to be saved and to come to the knowledge of the truth. For there is one God, and there is one mediator between God and men, the man Christ Jesus, who gave himself as a ransom for *all*" [I Tim. 2.5f].'

42. H. Küng links his criticism of my book *The Crucified God* in his essay 'Die Religionen als Frage an die Theologie des Kreuzes' (*EvTh* 33, 1973, pp.401–23) with a recollection of early dialectical theology and its neglect of the question of the world religions. His essay is not designed 'to set up a counter-position to the theology of the cross but to give the necessary (Catholic) way of access to a theology which is rightly based on the gospel' (p.404). In *Christsein* Küng put the question 'Superior ignorance?' to the dialectical theologians. I hope I may be able to convince him that we are working together for an 'open theology of the cross' (p. 420). The more central the cross becomes, the more open the interest in other religions and the richer and broader the pneumatology. But this is really as much as to say: the more 'Evangelical' the more 'Catholic'!

43. Cf. here F. Heer, *Die dritte Kraft. Der europäische Humanismus zwischen den Fronten des konfessionellen Zeitalters*, Frankfurt 1959.

44. *De tribus impostoribus. Von den drei Betrügern (1958)*, ed. G. Bartsch, *Quellen und Texte zur Geschichte der Philosophie*, published by the Arbeitsgruppe für Philosophie an der Deutschen Akademie der Wissenschaften, Berlin 1960.

45. Cf. here A. Schilson, *Geschichte im Horizont der Vorsehung. G. E. Lessings Beitrag zu einer Theologie der Geschichte*, Mainz 1974.

46. This argument was put forward by W. Pannenberg, 'Towards a Theology of the History of Religions', *Basic Questions in Theology* II, ET SCM Press and Fortress Press 1971, pp.65ff. F. Wagner, *Über die Legitimät der Mission*, ThEx 154, Munich 1968, pp.45f., has taken these ideas further in his own way in order to prove Christianity's ancient 'claim to absoluteness' through its syncretistic openness for 'the elements of truth in other religions'.

47. Cf. H. Küng, *Christsein*, pp.102ff.: 'Christsein als kritischer Katalysator.'

48. *Dialog mit anderen Religionen*, p.20.

49. Compare here the values other religions can contribute to Christianity which are named in the *Dialog* (pp.20f., 26f. and passim) with Küng's list of the values Christianity can contribute to other religions (*Christsein*, pp.96ff.). Christians ought to begin with the values of the other religions. The representatives of other religions should talk about Christian values. Küng observes: 'For historical reasons, Western science and technology contain far too many elements stemming from the Jewish-Christian tradition for it to be easy to take over Western science and technology without calling one's own religious position in question' (p. 103). The observation can easily be misunderstood in an apologetic sense. Christianity itself is very much called in question by 'Western

science and technology', in spite of the allegedly 'far too many elements' in them deriving from Jewish-Christian tradition.

50. *Dialog mit anderen Religionen*, p.33.

51. I agree with and follow H. J. Margull here in his 'Verwundbarkeit. Bemerkungen zum Dialog', *EvTh* 34, 1974, pp.410–20.

52. *Dialog mit anderen Religionen*, p.87.

53. As already in Moltmann, *Theology of Hope*, pp.304f.

54. For a fuller exposition of this point see J. Moltmann, 'Die Wahrnehmung der Geschichte in der christlichen Sozialethik' in *Perspektiven der Theologie*, Munich 1968, pp.149–73.

55. R. Schneider, *Winter in Wien*, Munich 1959, p.197.

56. A. M. K. Müller, *Die präparierte Zeit*, Stuttgart 1972.

57. J. B. Metz and J. Moltmann, *Leidensgeschichte*, Freiburg 1974; D. Sölle, *Leiden*, Stuttgart 1973; A. M. K. Müller, 'Verwandelnde Kraft des Leidens' in *Lutherische Monatshefte* 13, 1974, pp.468–74.

58. Here I am following the ideas suggested by A. T. van Leeuwen, 'Op weg naar een economische theologie' in *Tijdschrift voor Theologie*, 1973, pp.391–406.

59. J. Schumpeter has described this process brilliantly in *History of Economic Analysis*, Allen & Unwin and Oxford University Press 1955.

60. There are very few philosophical and theological discussions about money but cf. G. Simmel, *Philosophie des Geldes*, Leipzig 1930[6]; F. Delekat, *Der Christ und das Geld*, ThEx 57, Munich 1957.

61. Hegel has described this very aptly in his analysis of the 'The System of Needs'. Cf. *Hegel's Philosophy of Right*, trans. T. M. Knox, Clarendon Press 1942, §§ 188ff., pp.126ff.

62. In connection with the following passage cf. G. Picht, 'Wir brauchen neue Uberzeugungen. Von der Wechselwirkung zwischen Wachstum und Werten', *EvKomm* 6, 1973, pp.329–32.

63. D. H. Meadows et al., *The Limits to Growth. A Report for the Club of Rome's Project on the Predicament of Mankind*, Potomac Books 1972. In *Grenzen der Zukunft*, Stuttgart 1973, K. Scholder has described the discussion that followed this study.

64. So M. Scheler, *Die Stellung des Menschen im Kosmos*, Munich 1949, p. 56.

65. *Humanökologie und Umweltschutz*, ed. E. von Weizäcker, Stuttgart 1972, pp.49ff.

66. H. Ozbekhan, 'The Triumph of Technology: "Can" Implies "Ought" ', a paper quoted by E. Fromm, *The Revolution of Hope*, Harper & Row 1968, pp.33ff.

67. A. T. van Leeuwen, op. cit., pp.396f.

68. The Bucharest Conference of the World Council of Churches on 'Science and Technology for Human Development', June 1974, *Anticipation* 19, Geneva November 1974.

69. M. Weber, *Basic Concepts in Sociology*, ET Philosophical Library, New York, and Peter Owen, London 1962, p.119.

70. *Zum politischen Auftrag der christlichen Gemeinde. Barmen II.*

Votum des theologischen Ausschusses der Evangelischen Kirche der Union, ed. A. Burgsmüller, Gütersloh 1974, p.253.

71. On the concept of democracy as the process of democratization cf. W.-D. Marsch, *Christlicher Glaube und demokratisches Ethos*, Hamburg 1958.

72. Contrary to the Augsburg Confession [cited from *The Creeds of the Evangelical Protestant Churches*, ed. P. Schaff, Hodder & Stoughton and Harper & Bros. 1877, pp.3ff.] article XVI: 'In the meantime it doth not disallow order and government of commonwealths or families, but requireth especially the preservation and maintenance thereof, as of God's own ordinances, and that in such ordinances we should exercise love.' The polemic against the 'Enthusiasts' in the Reformation period brought this conservative feature into Protestant orthodoxy. It was an element which overlooked Christian responsibility in forming the political orders themselves.

73. H. Berkhof, *Kirche und Kaiser*.

74. J. Bohatec, *England und die Geschichte der Menschen- und Bürgerrechte*, ed. O. Weber, Graz 1956.

75. G. Oestreich, 'Die Idee des religiösen Bundes und die Lehre von Staatsvertrag', in *Zur Geschichte und Problematik der Demokratie. Festgabe für H. Herzfeld*, Berlin 1957, pp.11–32. Oestreich sums up the earlier work of G. Jellinek, K. Wolzendorff and F. Hartung and takes it further by showing the inner connection between the right to resistance, federal theology and the doctrine of the political contract in early Reformed doctrines of the state.

76. See here the excellent volume of sources collected by F. Hartung, *Die Entwicklung der Menschen-und Bürgerrechte von 1776 bis zur Gegenwart. Quellensammlung zur Kulturgeschichte*, I.3, Göttingen 1964[3].

77. This is proved by the UNESCO collection: *Le Droit d'être un homme*, ed. J. Hersch, Geneva 1960.

78. That is why Articles 13 and 15 of the Universal Declaration of Human Rights of 1948 say: 'Everyone has the right to freedom of movement and residence within the borders of each State. Everyone has the right to leave any country, including his own, and to return to his country. Everyone has the right to a nationality. No one shall be arbitrarily deprived of his nationality nor denied the right to change his nationality.'

79. In 1966 the UN General Assembly passed two conventions on human rights, which were concerned with human rights in the economic and social sphere and which were intended to supplement the 1948 declaration. The United States and other countries, however, did not vote for the conventions because they allegedly gave priority to the interests of the state over individual rights. State interests must not be given priority when fundamental economic and social rights are formulated as human rights. This point is a matter of dispute between socialist and non-socialist countries. It is true that only basic economic rights make the exercise of political basic rights possible; but society (as represented by the state) cannot be conceded a priority which can no longer be

checked against human rights. The rights of the individual person cannot be viewed in isolation from society, but because of that the concession of human rights does not belong within the sovereignty of individual states.

80. Cf. E. Wolf, *Recht des Nächsten. Ein rechtstheologischer Entwurf*, Frankfurt 1958.

81. Article 14 of the Scottish Confession of 1560 therefore makes the right of resistance, as the duty of resistance, part of the fulfilment of the command to love our neighbour: '. . . to save the lives of innocents, to represse tyrannie, to defend the oppressed.' See K. Barth, *The Knowledge of God and the Service of God according to the Teaching of the Reformation*, Hodder & Stoughton 1938, Scribner 1939, pp.124ff., esp. p.131.

82. For more detail see Moltmann, 'Bringing Peace to a Divided World' in *The Experiment Hope*, pp.172ff.

83. For this very reason the hostility on the part of socialist states to Articles 18 and 19 of the Universal Declaration of Human Rights is incomprehensible. They begin: 'Everyone has the right to freedom of thought, conscience or religion.' Everyone has the right to a free expression of opinion; this right includes the freedom to express opinions without hindrance and to seek, to receive and to spread information and ideas with all means of communication without taking account of frontiers. It is precisely these free rights which encourage socialism in so far as it is directed towards a society of all mankind and an 'association' in which 'the free development of each is the condition for the free development of all' (Communist Manifesto). If the representatives of socialist states hold the rights to freedom of religion and information to be 'bourgeois', they forfeit their credibility and their legitimation on the grounds of their own manifesto; just as capitalist democracies forfeit their credibility and legitimation if they reject economic human rights to life, work, social security and a share in decision-making in their economic systems and call these things 'Communist'.

84. M. Landmann's view. Cf. his *Philosophische Anthropologie*, Berlin 1964², p.205: 'But the fact that man may and must keep on continually giving himself a face out of a final amorphism – this interweaving of lack of all-pervading form, capacity for being formed, and the task of achieving form proves itself a perennial *anthropinon* that endures through all transformations.' H. Plessner, *Conditio Humana*, Pfullingen 1964, p.49: 'I am, but I do not possess myself, characterizes the human situation in its physical existence.'

85. Cf. on the following passage, with evidence, Moltmann, 'Racism and the Right to Resist', *The Experiment Hope*, pp. 131ff. The quotation (p.132) comes from the Report of the Committee on Church and Society to the Fourth Assembly of the World Council of Churches at Uppsala in 1968 (see *The Uppsala Report*, ed. N. Goodall, Geneva 1968, p.241). The definition links up with a UNESCO definition. Cf. also 'Warum "schwarze Theologie"?', *EvTh* 34, 1974, pp.1–95, with contributions by J. Cone, E. Lincoln, H. Edwards, P. Lehmann, H. Gollwitzer, F. Herzog.

86. 'Programme to Combat Racism', *Central Committee of the WCC. Minutes . . . of the Twenty-fourth Meeting. Addis Ababa, January 1971*, Geneva 1971, p.238.

87. On this subject see E. Moltmann-Wendel, *Menschenrechte für die Frau*. Christliche Initiativen zur Frauenbefreiung, Munich, Mainz 1974; R. Ruether, *Liberation Theology. Human Hope Confronts Christian History and American Power*, Paulist/Newman Press 1972; L. Russell Hoekendijk, *Human Liberation in a Feminist Perspective – a Theology*, Philadelphia 1974.

88. Margaret Mead, *Male and Female*, Gollancz and William Morrow 1949; K. Millett, *Sexual Politics*, Rupert Hart-Davis 1971.

89. G. Jansen and M. Schmidt, *Empirische Korrelate zwischen Einstellung der Umwelt und dem Verhalten körperbehinderter Kinder*, Cologne 1968; A. Müller-Schön, 'Die Stigmatiserten der Gesellschaft' in *EvKomm* 4, 1971, pp.596ff.; U. Bach, 'Drängen wir die Behinderten geistig ins Getto?' in *Die Rehabilitation* 14, 1975, pp.18–28.

90. Jansen and Schmidt, op. cit.

91. Here I am following E. Fromm, *The Revolution of Hope*, pp.83ff.

92. Ibid., p.85

93. Ibid., pp.85f.

94. K. Stendahl, 'Die biblische Auffassung von Mann und Frau' in *Menschenrechte für die Frau*, pp.155ff. I am here following his exegesis of Gal. 3.28, adding the eschatological hope of Gal. 3.29.

95. On the following section see P. Tillich, *Systematic Theology* III, Pt. 5, 'History and the Kingdom of God', 1963, pp.297ff. = 1964, pp.317ff.; W. Pannenberg, *Theologie und Reich Gottes*, Gütersloh 1971; H. Gollwitzer, 'Die Revolution des Reiches Gottes und die Gesellschaft' in *Die Funktion der Theologie in Kirche und Gesellschaft*, ed. P. Neuenzeit, Munich 1969, pp.129–55.

96. In making this distinction I am following R. Schnackenburg, *Gottes Herrschaft und Reich*, Freiburg 1961[2].

97. Cf. article 'Antizipation', *Historisches Wörterbuch der Philosophie*, ed. J. Ritter, I, 1971, 419–25, and the comments by J. Moltmann, 'Extrapolation und Antizipation. Zur Methode in der Eschatologie' in *Weerwoord. Festschrift für H. Berkhof*, Nijkerk 1974, pp.201–8.

98. This is a critical comment on Tillich, op. cit., III, pp.339ff. = pp. 362ff.: 'The Ambiguities of Life under the Historical Dimension'.

V The Church in the Presence of the Holy Spirit

1. Cf. E. Jüngel and K. Rahner, *Was ist ein Sakrament? Vorstöße zur Verständigung*, Freiburg 1971; W. Pannenberg, *Thesen zur Theologie der Kirche*, Munich 1974; also: O. Weber, *Grundlagen der Dogmatik* II, Neukirchen 1962, pp.647ff.; H. Diem, *Die Kirche und ihre Praxis*, Munich 1963, pp.115ff. If one does not want to let the questionable concept of the sacrament drop altogether, as Schleiermacher suggested, and as Weber and Diem (and Pannenberg initially) do, in order to talk only about

baptism and the Lord's supper, then one can either subsequently extract the common substratum from the now detached description of baptism and Lord's supper, or else interpret the two events of baptism and Lord's supper, which are constitutive for the church, from what they have in common. Here we are attempting to do the latter, but shall not confine ourselves to the 'sacraments' of baptism and the Lord's supper. We shall place them in the wider context of the 'means of salvation' and 'ministries', in order to cover the reality and the efficacy of the church of Christ as comprehensively as possible.

2. P. Evdokimov, *L'Orthodoxie*, Paris 1960; N. Nissiotis, *Die Theologie der Ostkirche im ökumenischen Dialog*, Stuttgart 1968, especially pp.105f.

3. J. Dournes, 'Why are there Seven Sacraments?', *Concilium* vol. 1, no. 4 (ET of Band 4 Heft 1), January 1968, pp.35–44.

4. K. Rahner, op. cit., p.83.

5. H. Schmid, *Die Dogmatik der Evangelisch-Lutherischen Kirche*, Gütersloh 1893[7], pp.366ff.; H. Heppe and E. Bizer, *Die Dogmatik der Evangelische-Reformierten Kirche*, Neukirchen 1958, pp.468ff.

6. K. Rahner, op. cit., p.71.

7. K. Rahner, 'The Word and the Eucharist' in *Theological Investigations* IV, ET reissued Darton, Longman & Todd and Seabury Press 1974, ch. 10, pp.253ff.; H. Fries, *Wort und Sakrament*, Munich 1966, esp, pp.12f.

8. K. Rahner, *Was ist ein Sakrament?* p.69: 'A Catholic theology of the sacraments is least of all able to deny that the fundamental element of the sacrament is the Word, and that the 'matter', the element, is really only secondary compared with the Word, having a clarifying function in regard to it.'

9. K. Rahner, ibid., p.75.

10. E. Jüngel, op. cit., pp.33ff. I am drawing on his interpretation of Barth here. Cf. also A. V. Bauer, 'Inspiration als sakramentales Ereignis. Zum Verhältnis von Wort, Sakrament und Menschwerdung in der Theologie Karl Barths', *Trierer Theologische Zeitschrift* 72, 1963, pp.84–104.

11. K. Barth, 'Die Lehre von den Sakramenten' in *Zwischen den Zeiten* 7, 1929, p.439, quoted by Jüngel, op. cit., p.34.

12. *Church Dogmatics* II. 1, p.54.

13. Ibid., IV. 2, p.55. In this way Barth would like to distinguish the *unio personalis Christi* as clearly as possible from the *unio sacramentalis* of the church, in order to ward off the seductive notion of the church as *Christus prolongatus*.

14. Jüngel, op. cit., pp.32f. Cf. also Calvin, *Institutes* IV, 14. 2.

15. All the same, Bultmann (*Theology of the New Testament*, §34, Vol. I, pp.306ff.) is able to call baptism and the Lord's supper 'sacraments' on the basis of the analogies between them. But he understands both as particular modes of the proclamation of the word. Weber (op. cit., II, p.656) and Diem (op. cit., pp.129ff.) have suggested replacing the expression 'sacrament' by the concept of 'the rite of proclamation'.

16. E. Jüngel, op. cit., p.41.

17. N. Nissiotis, op. cit., p.68.

18. G. Bornkamm, 'μυστήριον', *TDNT* IV, pp.802ff., makes the derivation of the concept from apocalyptic clear and draws a dividing line between this and the mystery religions, in which Bultmann, Weber and others still mainly found the concept to be present.

19. Bornkamm, op. cit., pp.814f. We are reproducing this article here in some detail because the appeal made to it in systematic theology is often one-sided.

20. Ibid., p.822.

21. Pannenberg's view (op. cit., p.39) contrary to Barth. But his salvation-history eschatology of the world is not given an express pneumatological foundation in his thesis.

22. In the trinitarian understanding of God, the revealing and perfecting working of the Holy Spirit must be seen in conjunction with the working of the Spirit in the history of Christ himself. The work of the Holy Spirit is not an addition to the work of Christ. Christ was 'conceived' by the Holy Spirit, was baptized with the Holy Spirit, was given over to death and raised through the Holy Spirit. Just as an eschatological christology leads to a christological eschatology, so a pneumatic christology also leads to a christological pneumatology. The unity in the difference lies in the trinitarian history of God.

23. The early Protestant doctrine of the sacraments already stood under the sign of the *gratia Spiritus Sancti applicatrix*. For this one can adopt K. Niederwimmer's thesis: 'The experience of the Spirit is the constitutive elements of the first churches', *Unterscheidung des Geistes*, Kassel 1972, p.119.

24. For the homiletic aspect of the following discussion cf. R. Bohren, *Predigtlehre*, 1972², and also 'A Bolivian Manifesto on Evangelism in Latin America Today' (as issued by the Evangelical Methodist Church in Bolivia), reported in *Monthly Letter about Evangelism*, Geneva, February 1975. In using the phrase 'the proclamation of the gospel' we are distinguishing between proclamation and gospel. E. Käsemann, *An die Römer*, Göttingen 1973, p.19: 'The gospel is more than merely the message actualized in the church; it is God's proclamation of salvation to the world, a proclamation not at man's disposal and independent even of the church and its ministers. This divine proclamation continually realizes itself anew in the proclamation through the power of the Spirit.'

25. F. Nietzsche, *The Twilight of the Idols*, ET, *Complete Works* 16, Macmillan, New York 1910, T. N. Foulis 1911, p.24.

26. For a more detailed exposition see J. Moltmann, 'Wort Gottes und Sprache' and 'Verkündigung als Problem der Exegese' in *Perspektiven der Theologie*, Munich 1969, pp.93ff. and 113ff; also *Die Sprache der Befreiung*, Munich 1975², pp.139ff.

27. K. Barth, 'The Word of God and the Task of the Ministry' in *The Word of God and the Word of Man*, ET Hodder & Stoughton and Pilgrim Press 1928, pp.183–217; citation from p.186.

28. *Church Dogmatics* I. 1, p.159.
29. *Church Dogmatics* I. 1, pp.304f. So too Weber, *Grundlagen der Dogmatik*, II, p.646; Diem, *Die Kirche und Ihre Praxis*, pp.165ff.
30. W. Zimmerli, *Gottes Offenbarung, Gesammelte Aufsätze*, ThB 19, 1963, esp. pp.11ff.
31. E. Schweizer, *EGO EIMI*, FRLANT 56, 1939.
32. *Church Dogmatics* I. 1, p.307.
33. Ibid., I. 1, p.93.
34. Cf. O. Grether, 'Name und Wort Gottes im Alten Testament', BZAW, 64, 1934.
35. R. Bultmann, 'The Concept of the Word of God in the New Testament', *Faith and Understanding*, pp.286ff.
36. Ibid., p.301.
37. Ibid., p.311.
38. W. Pannenberg, 'Dogmatic Theses on the Doctrine of Revelation', in *Revelation as History*, ET Macmillan 1969, pp.152ff.
39. Ibid., p.155.
40. See especially Pannenberg, *Grundfragen systematischer Theologie*, Göttingen 1967, p.5 n. 2 (not in ET); *Thesen zur Theologie der Kirche*, Munich 1974, pp.32f.
41. The practical conclusions which are drawn from this are questionable. W. Pannenberg writes in *Thesen zur Theologie der Kirche* (pp.32f.): 'This authoritarian imparting of tradition must today be replaced by an informative mediation. Christian publicity especially will avail itself of this, but it also has its place in instruction. On the other hand, the sermon in church services will be able to uphold its special character through a more meditative, pastoral or, it may be, topical and ethical stress.' Does the sermon as a part of public worship not really become superfluous if we do not recognize that what it fundamentally has to proclaim is the forgiveness of sins and divine pardon? The service which the Reformation performed for the doctrine of the sacraments was not in reducing their number from seven to two, but in rediscovering the sacramental character of the sermon. Cf. Weber, *Grundlagen der Dogmatik*, II, p.646, n.1; and E. Bizer, *Fides ex auditu*, Neukirchen 1958, esp. pp.154ff.
42. Here I am following P. Stuhlmacher's account in *Das paulinische Evangelium I. Vorgeschichte*, Göttingen 1968. Cf. also Käsemann, *An die Römer*, pp.19ff.
43. G. Friedrich, 'εὐαγγέλιον', *TDNT* II, pp.714ff.
44. E. Sjöberg, *Der verborgene Menschensohn in den Evangelien*, Lund 1955, pp.2 and 13; Stuhlmacher, op.cit., p.47.
45. H. Schlier, *Wort Gottes. Eine neutestamentliche Besinnung*, Würzburg 1962[2], p.18.
46. Stuhlmacher, op. cit., pp.238ff.
47. O. Michel, 'Evangelium', *RAC* VI, 1112f.
48. Stuhlmacher, op. cit., p.287.
49. G. Bornkamm, 'Evangelien', *RGG*[3] II, 760.
50. Stuhlmacher, op. cit., p.287.

51. Cf. W. Marxsen, *Mark the Evangelist*, ET Abingdon Press 1969, pp.136f.
52. W. Marxsen, *Introduction to the New Testament*, ET Blackwell and Fortress Press 1968, pp.142, 144.
53. Käsemann, *New Testament Questions of Today*, p.66.
54. Ibid.
55. J. Petuchowski, 'Messianic Hope in Judaism', *Concilium* vol. 7/8, no. 10 (ET of Band 10 Heft 7/8), September/October 1974, pp.150–5; and J. Moltmann, 'Messianic Hope in Christianity', ibid., pp.155–61.
56. Schlier, op. cit., p.19: 'Through such an announcement and through the gift of the Holy Spirit, who makes present the crucified, risen and exalted Lord as the one who is to come, the days of the disciples' witness in the Holy Spirit already prove themselves to be the "last days", or the beginning of them. The fact of the Holy Spirit, who reveals Jesus Christ, and the fact of the witnesses' testimony, which the Spirit authorizes, is a proof that these "days" have dawned.'
57. H. Schmid, *Die Dogmatik der Evangelisch-Lutherischen Kirche*, pp. 394ff.; H. Heppe and E. Bizer, *Die Dogmatik der Evangelisch-Reformierten Kirche*, pp.486ff.; W. Jetter, *Die Taufe beim jungen Luther*, Tübingen 1954; E. Sommerlath and W. Kreck, article 'Taufe', *RGG*³ VI, 646–8; C. H. Ratschow, *Die eine christliche Taufe*, Gütersloh 1972.
58. Of the considerable literature cf. W. Bieder, *Die Verheißung der Taufe im Neuen Testament*, Zürich 1966; M. Barth, *Die Taufe – ein Sakrament?*, Zürich 1951; O. Cullmann, *Baptism in the New Testament*, ET SBT 1, 1950; K. Aland, *Did the Early Church Baptize Infants?*, ET SCM Press and Westminster Press 1963; J. Jeremias, *Infant Baptism in the First Four Centuries*, ET SCM Press and Westminster Press 1960; Ratschow, op. cit., pp.143ff.
59. Cf. Bieder, op. cit., pp.34ff.
60. P. Vielhauer, 'Johannes der Täufer', *RGG*³ III, 805.
61. Käsemann points this out emphatically, op. cit., pp.111ff.
62. Marxsen, *Mark the Evangelist*.
63. G. Bornkamm, G. Barth and H. J. Held, *Tradition and Interpretation in Matthew*, ET SCM Press and Westminster Press 1963.
64. H. Conzelmann, *The Theology of St Luke*, ET Faber & Faber 1960, Harper & Row 1961.
65. G. Bornkamm, 'Taufe und neues Leben bei Paulus' in *Das Ende des Gesetzes*, Munich 1952, pp.34ff.; H. Schlier, 'Die Taufe nach dem 6. Kapitel des Römerbriefs' in *Die Zeit der Kirche*, Freiburg 1966, pp.47–55, and cf. also pp.107–29; P. Stuhlmacher, 'Gerechtigkeit Gottes bei Paulus', op. cit., pp.220ff.; Käsemann, *An die Römer*, pp.150ff.; Eichholz, *Die Theologie des Paulus im Umriß*, pp.202ff.
66. K. Barth, *The Teaching of the Church regarding Baptism*, ET SCM Press and Allenson 1948. We shall not go expressly here into Barth's doctrine of baptism in *Church Dogmatics* IV. 4.
67. H. Schlier, 'Zur kirchlichen Lehre von der Taufe' (1943) in *Die Zeit der Kirche*, pp.107–28.

68. Barth stresses this viewpoint in his *Doctrine of Reconciliation*: as 'the revealer of his work' Christ has not yet reached his goal but is on the way to it. The knowledge of revelation therefore acquires the character of anticipation, and faith becomes in essentials hope.

69. P. Stuhlmacher rightly stresses this in 'Erwägungen zum ontologischen Charakter der καινὴ κτίσις bei Paulus' in *EvTh* 27, 1967, p.29.

70. Cf W. Jetter, *Was wird aus der Kirche?* Stuttgart 1968, pp.190ff.; M. Metzger, *Die Amtshandlungen der Kirche* I, Munich 1963, pp.149ff.

71. Cf. here the the reports on the Fourth World Conference on Faith and Order held at Montreal in 1963, and also the conferences held at Bristol in 1967 and Louvain in 1971, published by the World Council of Churches as Faith and Order Papers 38, 1963; 51, 1967; and 59, 1971; also E. Lange, *Die ökumenische Utopie oder: Was bewegt die ökumenische Bewegung?* Stuttgart 1972, pp.81ff.

72. These expressions are designed to bring out the connection between baptism and the Lord's supper. They show that the link is to be found in the people of God created by the gospel.

73. Thomas Aquinas, *Summa Theologica* III, qu. 60.3 (ET, Blackfriars ed., Eyre and Spottiswoode and McGraw-Hill, vol. 56, 1975, pp.10ff.): 'Hence as sign and sacrament it has a threefold function. It is at once commemorative (*signum rememorativum*) of that which has gone before, namely the Passion of Christ, and demonstrative of that which is brought about in us through the Passion of Christ, namely grace, and prognostic, i.e. a foretelling of future glory.'

74. Thomas related the sacraments to man's sanctification: the *causa sanctificationis* is the passion of Christ, the *forma nostrae sanctificationis* is grace, the *finis sanctificationis* is eternal life (loc. cit.). Kant transferred this terminology to the 'signs of history', seeing these as the real cyphers of God's providence or the intention of nature for the human race (cf. ch. II, § 3 above). Here we are relating the Lord's supper as an 'eschatological sign of history' to the history of God's promise. It answers the question: 'What can I hope for?'

75. Augustine's reflections on the experience of time may be drawn on here. 'It may be said rightly that there are three times: a time present of things past; a time present of things present; and a time present of things future. For these three do coexist somehow in the soul, for otherwise I could not see them. The time present of things past is memory; the time present of things present is direct experience; the time present of things future is expectation' (*Confessions* XI. 20.26). In this general experience time runs from the future through the present into the past (XI. 21. 27). Life is dispersed in the stream of transience. The specifically Christian experience of time, on the other hand, is different; this is the experience which faith has when it forgets what lies behind and strains forward to what lies ahead (Phil. 3.12ff.). In intense concentration it looks towards coming eternity (*Confessions* XI. 29. 39). It is this particular experience of the eschatological era which the soul has in the presence of the risen Christ in the Lord's supper.

76. In this section I am gratefully following the remarks of my teacher O. Weber, in *Grundlagen der Dogmatik* II, Neukirchen 1962, pp.678ff. His eschatological interpretation of the Lord's supper is one of the most fruitful points of departure for ecumenical discussion.

77. This is also Pannenberg's view in *Thesen zur Theologie der Kirche*, p.36, following E. Schlink.

78. Weber, op. cit., p.679.

79. On this question see: *Um Amt und Herrenmahl. Dokumente zum evangelisch/römisch-katholischen Gespräch*, ed. G. Assmann, M. Lienhard, H. Meyer and H.-V. Herntrich, Frankfurt 1974.

80. Cf. Pannenberg, op. cit., p.35.

81. Here I am expanding in a few ecumenical directions the reflections expressed by Weber under the title 'The Irrationality of the Feast' (op. cit., p.680).

82. Cf. H. Patsch, *Abendmahl und historischer Jesus*, Stuttgart 1972.

83. M.-L. Henry, *Glaubenskrise und Glaubensbewährung in den Dichtungen der Jesajaapokalypse*, BWANT 86, 1967.

84. Cf. here J. Jeremias, *The Eucharistic Words of Jesus*, ET, new ed., SCM Press and Westminster Press 1966; also A. C. Cochrane, *Eating and Drinking with Jesus. An Ethical and Biblical Inquiry*, Westminster Press 1974.

85. Weber, op. cit., p.682.

86. Here we are following H. Gese, 'Psalm 22 und das Neue Testament. Der älteste Bericht vom Tode Jesu und die Entstehung des Herrenmahles' in *Vom Sinai zum Zion. Alttestamentliche Beiträge zur biblischen Theologie*, Munich 1974, pp.180–201; cf. also Käsemann, 'The Pauline Doctrine of the Lord's Supper' in *Essays on New Testament Themes* ET, SBT 41, 1964, pp.108–35, esp. pp.127ff.

87. Weber gives a short summing up of the Reformation controversy on the Lord's supper (op. cit., pp.687ff.).

88. Weber, op. cit., p.708.

89. Weber, op. cit., p.708: 'Space can, as it were, be conceived of as "static". Time will not stand that. If the meal is assigned to time – the unique time of the saving event created for us and the coming time of its revelation and completion – the presence of Christ in it is to be understood temporally: he is "there" now, as the coming one, not graspable, but grasping us. In him the time is fulfilled, the past is present today and for us, in him the coming one is "there" today and for us.'

90. Weber, ibid., p.693: 'Hence the "est" is to be understood neither as significative nor as synekdochic, but in terms of salvation history – history in the sense of eschatological history.'

91. Cf. here the ecumenical declaration of the Dombes group in *Um Amt und Herrenmahl* (see n. 79 above), pp.105ff.

92. Ibid., p.106.

93. Weber, op. cit., p.683: 'The meal does not merely point backwards and 'upwards'. It is above all *open* in a forward direction.

94. This is expressed particularly well in the new forms and liturgies of

the *shalom* groups in Holland and the United States. Cf. H. Hoekendijk, *Die Zunkunft der Kirche und die Kirche der Zukunft*, Stuttgart 1964, pp. 58ff.; 'The Supper open to the World'; H. Weber, *Schalom – Schalom. Einführung Theorie und Praxis der Schalomarbeit*, Freiburg, 1972.

95. Of the considerable literature see here: O. Weber, *Versammelte Gemeinde. Beiträge zum Gespräch über Kirche und Gottesdienst*, Neukirchen 1949; J. Pieper, *Zustimmung zur welt. Eine Theorie des Festes*, Munich 1963; H. Hoekendijk, *Feier der Befreiung*, Kontexte 4, Stuttgart 1967, pp.124–31; Harvey Cox, *The Feast of Fools. A Theological Essay on Festivity and Fantasy*, Harvard University Press 1969; D. L. Miller, *Gods and Games. Toward a Theology of Play*, World Publishing Co., New York 1970; M. Bachtin, *Literatur und Karneval. Zur Roman-theorie und Lachkultur*, Munich 1969; J. Moltmann, *Theology of Joy*, and 'The Liberating Feast', *Concilium* vol. 2, no. 10 (ET of Band 10 Heft 2), February 1974, pp.74–84; G. M. Martin, *Fest und Alltag. Bausteine zu einer Theorie des Festes*, Stuttgart 1973; D. Trautwein, *Mut zum Fest*, Munich 1975.

96. These christological aspects are dominant in the Western church's theologies of worship. Cf. Martin, op. cit., p.81: 'The messianic church is a fellowship of remembrance and hope; its feasts activate remembrance and mobilize hope.'

97. The liturgy of the Eastern church sees itself in these contexts as the liturgy of the whole cosmos and its redemption. Cf. Nissiotis, op. cit., pp.105ff, esp. p.106: 'God's self-humiliation in Christ is reflected in the adoration of the redeemed cosmos.'

98. The typology of 'conventional theories of the feast' which Martin gives is too simplified, because Pieper's 'assent to the world' also contains critical elements, while my 'critical theory' of the feast also contains elements which are affirmative of existence. The 'expansion of consciousness' and 'heightening of life' which Martin looks for and advocates will have to bind together negation and affirmation dialectically.

99. This already emerges from the Lord's prayer, which does not say 'Let us come into thy kingdom' but 'Let thy kingdom come to us'. C. Blumhardt continually drew emphatic attention to this point.

100. D. Power, 'The Song of the Lord in an Alien Land', *Concilium* vol. 2, no. 10, February 1974, pp.85–106.

101. This is not a demand for a 'politicization' of worship, but a task for political theology, which enquires into the functions and the position of worship in the life of a society – its *Sitz im Leben*.

102. Cf. here E. Durkheim, *Grundformen des religiösen Lebens*, Neuwied 1969; C. Lévi-Strauss, *Structural Anthropology*, ET Basic Books, New York, 1963, Allen Lane, London 1968; A. Gehlen, *Urmensch und Spätkultur*, Bonn 1958; K. Lorenz, *Das sogenanate Böse. Zur Naturgeschichte der Aggression*, Vienna 1963.

103. H. Plessner has worked out the difference between production ('Herstellung') and presentation or portrayal ('Darstellung') phenomenologically in a very convincing way. See his *Zwischen Philosophie und Gesellschaft*, Berne 1953.

104. On this term see F. J. J. Buytendijk, *Das Menschliche. Wege zu seinem Verständnis*, Stuttgart 1958; A. Portmann, *Biologie und Geist*, Basle 1948.

105. W. F. Otto, *Die Gestalt und das Sein*, Düsseldorf 1955; K. Kérenyi, 'Vom Wesen des Festes' in *Antike Religion*, Munich 1971, pp.43–67; E. Hornung, *Geschichte als Fest*, Darmstadt 1966.

106. K. Marx, 'Towards a critique of Hegel's Philosophy of Right' in *Early Texts*, tr. D. McLellan, Blackwell and Barnes & Noble 1971, p.116.

107. F. Nietzsche, *The Will to Power*, § 916, ET Random House and Weidenfeld & Nicolson 1968, p.484.

108. M. Eliade, *The Myth of the Eternal Return*, ET Routledge & Kegan Paul and Pantheon Books 1955.

109. John Milton, *Hymn on the Morning of Christ's Nativity*.

110. For more detail see Martin, op. cit., pp.36ff.

111. On the following passage see Moltmann, *Theology of Hope*, pp.95ff., and the works by M. Buber, V. Maag, G. von Rad, W. Zimmerli and others there mentioned.

112. E. Fromm, *You shall be as Gods*, Holt, Rinehart & Winston 1966, Jonathan Cape 1967, p.194.

113. Ibid., p.199.

114. H. Braun's expression in *Jesus*, Stuttgart 1969, p.84.

115. R. Schutz, *Festival*, ET SPCK 1974.

116. Weber rightly makes this point in *Versammelte Gemeinde*, p.117.

117. Käsemann, 'Worship and Everyday Life: a Note on Romans 12–' in *New Testament Questions of Today*, p.191.

118. Quoted in Pieper, *Zustimmung zur Welt*, p.43.

119. Cf. Martin's thesis (p.49): 'The only theory of the feast which is messianically possible is: every day should be "Sunday", in the sense that Sunday will be "every day", the normal situation, the kingdom of God.'

120. On this distinction between celebration and feast, cf. Martin, op. cit., pp.74ff.; Trautwein, op. cit., pp.49ff.

121. I have taken over this expression from A. A. van Ruler, *Droom en Gestalte*, Amsterdam 1947.

122. R. Bohren recently took up this theme in *Fasten und Feiern*, Neukirchen 1973.

123. J. Moltmann, 'Zur Bedeutung des P. Ramus für Philosophie und Theologie im Calvinismus' in *ZKG* 68, 1957, pp.295ff; A. A. van Schelven, *Het Calvinisme gedurende zijn Bloeitijd*, 2 vols, Amsterdam 1951.

124. K. P. Fischer illustrates this very well from K. Rahner's work. Cf. *Der Mensch als Geheimnis. Die Anthropologie K. Rahners*, Freiburg 1974.

125. J. B. Metz, 'Karl Rahner – Ein theologisches Leben. Theologie als mystische Biographie eines Christenmenschen heute' in *Stimmen der Zeit*, 192, 1974, pp.305–16.

126. Here we are following suggestions made by Weber, *Grundlagen der Dogmatik* II, pp.399ff.; Bohren, op. cit., pp.19ff., and H. Burkhardt, *Das biblische Zeugnis von der Wiedergeburt*, Gießen and Basle 1974. Cf. also E. Cremer, *Rechtfertigung und Wiedergeburt*, Gütersloh 1907.

127. R. Bultmann, *The Gospel of John*, pp.135ff.

128. Weber, op. cit., p.401.

129. As we know, it was to preserve this spontaneity released by the Spirit that Luther rejected a *tertius usus legis* as a new form of legalism.

130. R. Bohren, op. cit., p.23.

131. I am here replacing the expression 'the work of grief' which S. Freud introduced. The work of memory can also be the work of grief, but not every memory is linked with grief.

132. W. Dilthey's view. Cf. *Gesammelte Schriften* V, p.253: 'One would have to wait for the end of life, and would only be able to survey the whole for the first time at the hour of death – the whole which would allow the relations of the parts to be determined.'

133. A. Dumas, 'God as Protest against the "Death of Man" ', *Concilium* 6.8 (ET of 8.6), June 1972, pp.75–89.

134. Weber, op. cit., p.772, with reference to D. Riesman, *The Lonely Crowd*, Yale University Press and Oxford University Press 1950.

135. E. Bethge, *Dietrich Bonhoeffer: Theologian, Christian, Contemporary* ET Collins (= *Dietrich Bonhoeffer: Man of Vision, Man of Courage*, Harper & Row) 1970.

136. Cf. especially C. Blumhardt, *Christus in der Welt. Briefe an Richard Wilhelm*, Zürich 1958; also the sermons and devotions ed. by R. Lejeune, I–IV, Leipzig and Zürich 1925–1937.

137. L. Ragaz, 'Der Kampf um das Reich Gottes' in *Blumhardt, Vater und Sohn – und weiter!* Leipzig and Zürich 1938.

138. D. Bonhoeffer, *Dein Reich komme*, Hamburg 1958, pp.6,11.

139. D. Bonhoeffer to Bethge, 21 July 1944, in *Letters and Papers from Prison*, ET, enlarged edition, 1971, p.370.

140. Schutz, *Festival*, pp.69ff.; cf. also his *Kampf und Kontemplation*, Freiburg 1974 (translation of *Lutte et Contemplation*).

VI The Church in the Power of the Spirit

1. Küng, *The Church*, p.363.

2. See K. Rahner, 'Das Charismatische in der Kirche' in *Das Dynamische in der Kirche*, Quaest. Disp. 5, 1958, pp.38–73. Rahner distinguishes between 'the charisma of the office' and 'non-institutional charismata'. The first are lawfully ordered, the second are not at our disposal and are merely bound to the person. Rahner is concerned to find a harmonious equilibrium between the two 'structures'. If the charisma were totally identical with the office, there would be a totalitarian church; if the office were to evaporate in the charisma, there would be enthusiasm. The dualism from which Rahner starts, however, is still the Sohm-Harnack dualism of Spirit and law.

3. The Calvinist church orders have always reflected their creed in their order and their order in their creed. Cf. J. V. Bredt, *Die Verfassung der reformierten Kirche in Cleve-Jülich-Berg-Mark*, Neukirche 1938; *Kerkorde van de Nederlandse Hervormde Kerk*, The Hague 1949.

4. R. Sohm, *Kirchenrecht* I, Leipzig 1892.

5. K. Barth's view in *Die Ordnung der Gemeinde. Zur dogmatischen Grundlegung des Kirchenrechts*, Munich 1955; E. Wolf, *Ordnung der Kirche* I–II, Frankfurt 1960–61; H. Dombois, *Das Recht der Gnade, Ökumenisches Kirchenrecht* I, Witten 1961. The expression 'confessing church law' comes from E. Wolf, *Rechtsgedanke und biblische Weisung*, Hamburg 1948. The Christian church is 'the church belonging to the Lord and his elect, who are therefore made brothers' (pp.89f.). This 'brotherly Christocracy' is a legally constituted community. Cf. here also E. Wolf, 'Das Problem der Rechtsgestalt der Kirche im Kirchenkampf', *Zeitschrift für evangelisches Kirchenrecht* 8, 1961–62, pp.1ff.

6. O. Weber, *Grundlagen der Dogmatik* II, pp.625ff.

7. Ibid., p.626.

8. Ibid., pp.626ff.

9. Küng, 'The Church as the Creation of the Spirit', *The Church*, pp.150ff.

10. Here I am following Käsemann's now classic essay, 'Ministry and Community in the New Testament', *Essays on New Testament Themes*, pp.63ff., laying stress on some particular points.

11. These terms, which are the ones used by Käsemann, do not suggest that the one *charis* is abstract and general.

12. W. Schrage, *Die konkreten Einzelgebote in der paulinischen Paränese*, Gütersloh 1961.

13. Käsemann, op. cit., p.75.

14. Ibid., pp.73f.

15. On the following passage cf. *Um Amt und Herrenmahl. Dokumente zum evangelisch/römisch-katholischen Gespräch*, ed. G. Gassmann, M. Lienhard, H. Meyer and H.-V. Herntrich, Frankfurt 1974. I am particularly concerned with the report of the Protestant-Catholic conversations in France through the Dombes group (pp.103–28) and the 'Memorandum deutscher ökumenischer Institute zur Amtsanerkennung' (pp.147–160).

16. This is also Küng's view in *The Church*, pp.363ff.; he begins his account of the church's ministries with the 'priesthood of all believers'.

17. E. Wolf, 'Zur Verwaltung der Sakramente nach Luther und lutherischer Lehre' in *Peregrinatio* I, 1954, pp.243ff., esp. p.255.

18. This is stressed by Weber, *Grundlagen der Dogmatik* II, pp.629ff.; Wolf, op. cit., pp.248ff. But Weber seems to me to go too far in relativizing the 'general priesthood' and to ascribe an authority to 'the office', even if it is 'divided', which takes too little account of the authority of the congregation as Christ's congregation. Cf. also J. Aarts, *Die Lehre Martin Luthers über das Amt in der Kirche*, Helsinki 1972.

19. See E. Lange's remarks on the ecumenical discussion today: *Die ökumenische Utopie oder was bewegt die ökumenische Bewegung?*, Stuttgart 1972, p.63.

20. E. Peterson has given an excellent critical account of political monotheism – 'one God, one emperor, one law, one kingdom'. See his 'Monotheismus als politisches Problem', *Theologische Traktate*, Munich

1951, pp.45–148. Unfortunately he has overlooked the simultaneous clerical monotheism of the Catholic church of the time. But his criticism of political monotheism (which he bases on trinitarian theology) must inevitably apply to clerical monotheism as well.

21. On this point see O. Weber, *Die Treue Gottes in der Geschichte der Kirche*, Neukirchen 1968, especially 'Calvins Lehre von der Kirche' (pp.19–104).

22. As early as the sixteenth century there was a dispute about the congregation's right to vote in the Calvinist church in France. Jean de Morely, *Traité de la discipline et police chrétienne*, Lyons 1562, and after him Petrus Ramus supported congregationalist and 'democratic' ideas, contrary to the order of the Genevan church and the oligarchy of the pastors supported by Theodore Beza. Their suggestions were rejected at the third national synod held at Orléans in 1562 and at the national synod held at La Rochelle in 1571, and were condemned as 'ochlocracy'. Beza's aristocratic ideas, however, were not in accord with the congregation's right to vote which Calvin envisaged, though under the supervision of the pastorate (Institutes IV. 3, 15). See here G. V. Lechler, *Geschichte der Presbyterial- und Synodalverfassung seit der Reformation*, 1854, pp.78ff.; K. Rieker, *Grundsätze reformierter Kirchenverfassung*, 1899, pp.143f.; J. Moltmann, 'Zur Bedeutung des Petrus Ramus für die Philosophie und Theologie im Calvinismus' in *ZKG* 68, 1957, pp.312ff.

23. The declaration of the Dombes group in *Um Amt und Herrenmahl*, pp.119ff., is one-sided. It talks on p.119 about 'the ministry of the whole church and the diversity of ministries in the church', in order after all on pp.120ff. to deduce the ministries from the one 'pastoral ministry'. That is why on p.127 the authority to preach and administer the Lord's supper by virtue of baptism is reduced through the calling in question of 'unordained believers'.

24. Here I am following the suggestions in the 'Memorandum deutscher ökumenischer Institute', *Um Amt und Herrenmahl*, pp.154ff.

25. M. Luther, WA 41, 209. Cf. G. Heintze, 'Allgemeines Priestertum und besonderes Amt', *EvTh* 23 1963, pp.617ff.

26. This links up with Weber's comment in *Grundlagen der Dogmatik* II, p.642: 'The *unity* of the ministry will then take the form of the common ground shared by *colleagues*: the ministries *together* form the "presbytery", but under the primacy of the ministry of the word.'

27. On the Catholic side this is often given as a reason for the priestly leadership of the congregation. This recognition should therefore also be the presupposition for the ecumenical fellowship in the Lord's supper. It seems to me, however, that the proclamation and the Eucharist, though they certainly stand in the centre of the assembled congregation, do not have to be linked charismatically with the leadership of the congregation. This centre can be preserved even if the congregation is led by someone who is neither pastor nor priest.

28. H. Küng, *Strukturen der Kirche*, Freiburg 1962, pp.19f., makes it clear that the council is not something particular in the church but is the

church in an essential sense. The church exists in council. Where there is no assembly there is no church.

29. *Um Amt und Herrenmahl*, p.153. Cf. also W. Pannenberg, 'Die Bedeutung der Eschatologie für das Verständnis der Apostolizität und Katholizität der Kirche' in *Katholizität und Apostolizität, Kerygma und Dogma*, Beiheft 2, 1971, pp.92–109.

30. Cf. Augsburg Confession, article VII: 'Item docent, quod una sancta ecclesia perpetuo mansura sit' ('is to continue for ever'). On the question of the 'perseverance of the saints' see J. Moltmann, *Prädestination und Perseveranz*, Neukirchen 1961.

31. Cf. P. Althaus, *Communio sanctorum* I, Gütersloh 1929.

32. Augsburg Confession VII: 'Est autem ecclesia congregatio sanctorum, in qua evangelium pure docetur et recte administrantur sacramenta.'

33. Ibid. 'Et ad veram unitatem ecclesiae satis est consentire de doctrina evangelii et de administratione sacramentorum.'

34. *Bekenntnisschriften und Kirchenordnungen der nach Gottes Wort reformierten Kirche*, pp.335f. 'The Christian church is the community of brethren in which Jesus Christ acts today, in Word and sacrament, through the Holy Spirit.'

35. Cf. ch. III, § 6.

36. This is how Barth defines the reality of God: 'The Being of God as the One who Loves in Freedom'. Cf. *Church Dogmatics* II. 1, § 28, pp. 257ff. By this he means God as man's friend.

37. Cf. here Küng, *The Church*, pp.241ff.

38. J. Moltmann, 'Theologische Kritik der politischen Religion' in J. B. Metz, J. Moltmann and W. Oelmüller, *Kirche im Prozeß der Aufklärung*, Munich and Mainz 1970, pp.11ff.

39. Cf. E. Troeltsch, *The Social Teaching of the Christian Churches*, 2 vols., ET Allen & Unwin and Macmillan, New York 1931. Here we are not following his sociological typology, however. Troeltsch distinguishes 'aggressive', 'tolerated' and 'assimilatory' groups, whereas we are following the theologically more appropriate typology of K. Schäferdiek, 'Sekten', *RGG*[3] V, 1658–61.

40. Cf. A. Adam, 'Christliches Mönchtum', *RGG*[3] IV, 1072–81.

41. In recent times Bonhoeffer drew the attention of Protestantism to this problem, suggesting a new kind of corporate practice. Cf. *Life Together*, ET Harper & Bros. and SCM Press 1954; *The Cost of Discipleship*, ET SCM Press 1948. See here G. W. Weber, *Gemeinde in East Harlem*, Munich 1963; *Treffpunkt Gemeinde. Jugend im Gemeindeaufbau*, Munich 1965; *The Church for Others. Two Reports on the Missionary Structure of the Congregation*, Geneva 1967; *The New Community in Christ. Essays on the Corporate Christian Life*, ed. J. Burtness, Minneapolis 1963.

42. Cf. *In Ängsten und siehe wir leben. Antworten und Angebote. Deutscher Evangelischer Kirchentag Frankfurt 1975*, Stuttgart 1975.

43. *Concilium* 11, 1975, No. 4 (no ET) gives excellent information about the 'grass-roots' community movement in Catholicism. For the German-

speaking area see especially F. Klostermann, *Prinzip Gemeinde*, Vienna 1965; H. Fischer, N. Greinacher, F. Klostermann, *Die Gemeinde*, Mainz 1970; F. Klostermann, *Gemeinde – Kirche der Zukunft, Thesen – Dienste – Modelle*, Freiburg 1974. On the growing cleft between clerics and laity in the Catholic church cf. J. K. Hadden, *The Gathering Storm in the Churches*, Anchor Books, New York, 1970.

44. Documento Pastoral de Conjunto, Nr. 10 CELAM, Conclusiones de Medillin.

45. J. B. Metz has once more brought the concept of 'the people' into the systematic discussion: 'Kurche und Volk oder der Preis der Orthodoxie', *Stimmen der Zeit* 192, 1974, 12, pp.797–811. It must be added that what is meant by people here is ὄχλος, the poor, repressed, despised and un-organized multitude on whom Jesus 'had compassion' (Matt. 9.36), not ἔθνος, which was what was meant in earlier theological discussions about church and people, mission and national characteristics. Whereas ἔθνη means in the Bible the collective identity of peoples and nations, and λαός the theological identity of the old and new people of God, ὄχλος means the poor who have simply no identity at all.

46. Quoted in A. J. Büntig, 'Die Basisgemeinden in der politischen Aktion' in *Concilium* 11, 1975, No. 4, p.273.

47. J. Caldentey, 'Die Bedeutung der christlichen Basisgemeinden für die Kirche' in *Concilium* 11. 4, p.273. But Luther had already taken a similar view. Cf. *Vorrede zur Deutschen Messe* (1526), *Werke*, ed. O. Clemen, III, Berlin 1929, pp.294ff.

48. Cf. J. Moltmann, 'The Church for the People', *Monthly Letter about Evangelism* 6/7, Geneva June/July 1975.

49. This view of the 'grass-roots' communities was stressed by the First World Congress 'Christians for Socialism' in Quebec, 1975: 'The en-deavours of "Christians for Socialism" in the people's struggle for libera-tion provides new impulses for entering actively into Christian groups (communautés) where a gospel of liberation is realized and a "people's church" is springing up. In this way a Christianity is developing which is bound up with the interests of the working classes and represents an alternative to the Christianity which is linked ideologically and struc-turally with the prevailing systems of exploitation' (*Evangelische Student-engemeinde-Nachrichten*, July 1975, 12).

50. Cf. S. D. Alinsky, *Leidenschaft für den Nächsten*, Gelnhausen and Berlin, 1973; H.-E. Bahr and R. Gronemeyer, *Konfliktorientierte Gemein-wesenarbeit*, Neuwied 1974, with the other literature cited there; W. Den-nig and H. Kramer, *Gemeinwesenarbeiter in christlichen Gemeinden*, Freiburg and Gelnhausen 1974.

51. Quoted by Bahr and Gronemeyer, p.84.

52. Ibid., p.106.

53. Cf. J.-L. Leuba, *Institution und Ereignis. Gemeinsamkeiten und Unterschiede der beiden Arten von Gottes Wirken nach dem Neuen Testament*, Stuttgart 1957 and the critical comments in Moltmann, *Perspektiven der Theologie*, pp.223f.

54. O. Weber, *Versammelte Gemeinde. Beiträge zum Gespräch über Kirche und Gottesdienst* (1949), Neukirchen 1975, p.32. For a similar stress on the rights and dignity of the individual congregation cf. H. Diem, *Restauration oder Neuanfang in der Evangelischen Kirche?*, Stuttgart 1974, pp.176ff. I should like to point expressly to these books, which are frequently overlooked.

VII The Marks of the Church

1. Cf. O. Weber, *Grundlagen der Dogmatik II*, Neukirchen 1962, pp. 609ff.; E. Schlink, *The Coming Christ and the Coming Church*, ET Oliver and Boyd 1967, Fortress Press 1968, pp.105ff.; H. Küng *The Church*, pp. 263ff.; *Katholizität und Apostolizität, Kerygma und Dogma*, Beiheft 2, 1971. Here the church's attributes are interpreted in an inward sense.

2. Cf. here H.-W. Gensichen, *Glaube für die Welt. Theologische Aspekte der Mission*, Gütersloh 1971, pp.129ff. He supplements the 'ecclesiocentric' interpretation of the church's attributes through the missionary one.

3. Schlink, op. cit., p.105; Küng, op. cit., p.273.

4. Schlink, op. cit., p.108.

5. Weber, op. cit., pp.609ff.

6. Schlink, op. cit., p.106; Weber, op. cit., p.611; Küng, op. cit., p.273.

7. M. Luther, *Von den Konziliis und Kirchen* (1539), WA 50, pp.628ff. See also the comments of Weber, op. cit., p.606, and Küng, op. cit., pp. 267ff.

8. The Commission on Faith and Order of the World Council of Churches took up this task at their meeting in Louvain in 1971. Cf. *Louvain 1971: Study Reports and Documents*, Faith and Order Paper 59, Geneva 1971.

9. Here we are first of all following Weber's ecclesiology, which is congregationally orientated (op. cit., pp.611ff.).

10. Cf. ch. III, § 7.

11. J. N. D. Kelly, 'Die Begriffe "katholisch" und "apostolisch" in den ersten Jahrhunderten' in *Kerygma und Dogma*, Beiheft 2, pp.9ff.

12. Cf. here W. Pannenberg, 'Die Bedeutung der Eschatologie für das Verständnis der und Katholizität Apostolizität der Kirche' in *Kerygma und Dogma*, Beiheft 2, pp.92ff.

13. Weber stresses this as well, op. cit., p.619.

14. Kelly, op. cit., pp.10f.

15. Pannenberg's view, op. cit., p.109.

16. Cf. ch. IV, § 2.

17. Cf. ch. IV, § 4.

18. Cf. J. Moltmann, 'Gott in der Revolution' in *EvKomm* 1, 1968, pp. 569ff., These 5; Gutiérrez, *A Theology of Liberation*, pp.213ff.

19. See Weber, op. cit., p.618; Küng, op. cit., pp.319ff.

20. Schlink, op. cit., p.107; Küng, op. cit., p.328.

21. Cf. A. Boyens, 'Das Stuttgarter Schuldbekenntnis vom 19 Oktober 1945 – Entstehung und Bedeutung' in *Vierteljahreshefte für Zeitgeschichte* 19, 1971, pp.374–97; H. Ludwig, 'Karl Barths Dienst der Versöhnung. Zur Geschichte des Stuttgarter Schuldbekenntnisses' in *Zur Geschichte des Kirchenkampfes, Gesammelte Aufsätze* II, Göttingen 1971, pp.265–310.

22. Cf. article 'Heilig' in *Theologisches Begriffslexikon zum Neuen Testament*, ed. L. Coenen, II. 1, Wuppertal 1967, pp.645–57.

23. The origin of this Reformed expression is still uninvestigated. It has been in common use since the middle of the nineteenth century.

24. 'The Decree on Ecumenism', 6 (*The Documents of Vatican II*, ed. W. M. Abbott, p.350): 'Christ summons the Church, as she goes her pilgrim way, to that continual reformation of which she always has need, insofar as she is an institution of man here on earth.' Quoted in Küng, op. cit., p.341.

25. Thomas Aquinas, *Summa Theologica* III, qu. 8. 3. 2.

26. Gutiérrez rightly criticizes these phrases in *A Theology of Liberation*, p.290.

27. Ibid., pp.300f.

28. Schlink (op. cit. p.108) has stressed this 'special place'.

29. Kelly, op. cit., pp.15ff.

30. Irenaeus, *Against Heresies* III, 3.1, quoted by Kelly, op. cit., pp. 18f.

31. Pannenberg, op. cit., p.95; cf. also Moltmann, *Theology of Hope*, pp.190ff.

32. J. Moltmann, op. cit., pp.283ff.: 'The Hermeneutics of the Apostolate'.

33. A. A. van Ruler, *Theologie van het Apostolaat*, Nijkerk 1954, p.20; cf. also H. J. Margull, *Theologie der missionarischen Verkündigung*, Stuttgart 1959.

34. Van Ruler, op. cit., p.26. Cf. also Gensichen, *Glaube für die Welt*, pp.179ff., on the problem of 'the young churches'.

INDEX OF NAMES